SOCIAL MARKETING

SECOND EDITION

This book is dedicated to the thousands of current and future practitioners on the front line, responsible for influencing behaviors that will improve our health and safety, protect the environment, and contribute to our communities.

Never doubt that a small group of thoughtful, committed citizens can change the world; indeed, it is the only thing that ever has.

—Margaret Mead

SOCIAL MARKETING
Improving the Quality of Life

Philip Kotler
Northwestern University

Ned Roberto
Asian Institute of Management

Nancy Lee
Social Marketing Services Inc.

SECOND EDITION

SAGE Publications
International Educational and Professional Publisher
Thousand Oaks ▪ London ▪ New Delhi

Blood donor photograph by Craig Harrold, courtesy of Puget Sound Blood Center.

For information:

Sage Publications, Inc.
2455 Teller Road
Thousand Oaks, California 91320
E-mail: order@sagepub.com

Sage Publications Ltd.
6 Bonhill Street
London EC2A 4PU
United Kingdom

Sage Publications India Pvt. Ltd.
M-32 Market
Greater Kailash I
New Delhi 110 048 India

Printed in the United States of America

Library of Congress Cataloging-in-Publication Data

Kotler, Philip.
   Social marketing: Improving the quality of life / by Philip
Kotler, Ned Roberto, Nancy Lee. — 2nd ed.
      p. cm.
   Includes bibliographical references and index.
   ISBN 0-7619-2434-5 (pbk.)
      1. Social marketing. 2. Behavior modification. I. Title:
Improving the quality of life. II. Roberto, Ned. III. Lee, Nancy, 1932- IV.
Title.
   HF5414 .K67 2002
   658.8—dc21

                                                    2001007178

This book is printed on acid-free paper.

06   7

Acquisitions Editor:	Marquita Flemming
Editorial Assistant:	MaryAnn Vail
Copy Editor:	Carla Freeman
Production Editor:	Diane S. Foster
Typesetter:	Tina Hill
Proofreader:	Scott Oney
Indexer:	Molly Hall
Cover Designer:	Ravi Balasuriya

Contents

Foreword   xi

Preface   xiii

Acknowledgments   xv

PART I   Understanding Social Marketing

CHAPTER 1   Defining Social Marketing   3

Marketing Highlight: The 21st Century   4

What Is Social Marketing?   5

Where Did the Concept Originate?   8

How Does Social Marketing Differ From Commercial
Sector Marketing?   10

When Is Social Marketing Used and for What Purpose?   12

What Social Issues Can Benefit From Social Marketing?   14

What Are Other Ways to Influence Public Behavior?   17

How Does Social Marketing Relate to Other Approaches?   19

Marketing Dialogue   21

CHAPTER 2   Outlining the Strategic Marketing Planning Process   29

Marketing Highlight: Lowering Blood Pressure   30

Chapter Overview   34

What Are the Steps in the Social Marketing Planning Process?   34

Why Is a Systematic Planning Process Important?   43

Where Does Marketing Research Fit Into the Planning Process?   44

CHAPTER 3   Discovering Keys to Success   **47**

Marketing Highlight: Tobacco Prevention   48
Chapter Overview   51
What Is a Successful Campaign?   51
What Are the Key Elements of Successful Campaigns?   51
Beyond Success   66

PART II   Analyzing the Social Marketing Environment

CHAPTER 4   Determining Research Needs
and Resources   **73**

Marketing Highlight: Blood Donation   74
Chapter Overview   77
When Is Research Used in the Planning Process?   77
What Major Types of Research Are Used?   77
What Steps Are Included in Designing a Research Project?   81
Research Highlight: Quantitative and Qualitative
Research for Breast Cancer Screening   85

CHAPTER 5   Mapping the Internal and
External Environments   **91**

Marketing Highlight: Tobacco Industry Response   92
Chapter Overview   94
Choose a Campaign Focus   95
Identify a Campaign Purpose   97
Conduct a SWOT Analysis   97
Research Highlight: Personal Interviews for Caring
Adult Relationships With Youth   105
Marketing Dialogue   107

PART III   Establishing Target Audiences, Objectives, and Goals

CHAPTER 6   Selecting Target Markets   **111**

Marketing Highlight: Physical Activity   112
Chapter Overview   116
What Steps Are Involved in Target Marketing?   116
What Variables Are Used to Segment Markets?   117

What Criteria Are Used for Evaluating Segments? 124
How Are Target Markets Selected? 128
What Approach Should Be Chosen? 129
Research Highlight: Self-Administered Survey
  for Psychographic Segmentation 132

CHAPTER 7   Setting Objectives and Goals   137

Marketing Highlight: Water Conservation 138
Chapter Overview 142
Behavior Objectives 143
Knowledge and Belief Objectives 146
The Nature of Social Marketing Goals 148
Objectives and Goals at the Draft Stage 154
The Role of Objectives and Goals in Campaign Evaluation 154
Research Highlight: Secondary Data for Program Goal Setting 156

CHAPTER 8   Deepening Our Understanding of the
              Target Audience and the Competition   161

Marketing Highlight: Drinking and Driving 162
Chapter Overview 166
What More Do We Need to Know About Our Target Audience? 167
What Models Might Be Used to Explore Our Audience
  Perspectives Further? 169
Who Is the Competition in a Social Marketing Environment? 174
What Are Four Key Tactics to Create Competitive Advantages? 175
Why Is It Necessary to Review and Potentially Revise Target Markets,
  Objectives, and Goals After This Step? 179
Research Highlight: Formative and Evaluation Research
  Using Qualitative and Quantitative Techniques 182

PART IV   Developing Social Marketing Strategies

CHAPTER 9   Product: Designing the Market Offering   189

Marketing Highlight: Women & Infant Children Programs (WIC) 190
Chapter Overview 194
What Is the Product in a Social Marketing Effort? 195
What Are Three Levels of the Product? 195
What Decisions Will Need to Be Made at Each Level 198

How Are These Decisions Made and How Do They
  Affect the Product's Positioning? — 203
Research Highlight: Focus Groups for Increased
  Contraceptive Use — 208

CHAPTER 10 Price: Managing Costs of Behavior Change — 213

Marketing Highlight: Litter Prevention — 214
Chapter Overview — 217
What Is the Price of a Social Marketing Product? — 217
What Are Major Categories and Types of Costs? — 217
What Are Major Strategies for Managing Costs? — 220
What Pricing-Related Tactics Are Used to Manage
  Costs and Balance the Scale? — 220
Considerations When Setting Prices for Tangible
  Objects and Services — 229
Research Highlight: Informal Interviews
  for Teen Sexual Abstinence — 231

CHAPTER 11 Place: Making Access Convenient — 237

Marketing Highlight: Safe Gun Storage — 238
Chapter Overview — 242
What Is *Place* in a Social Marketing Environment? — 243
What Is the Objective When Developing a
  Place Strategy? — 243
How Do We Make Access to the Social Marketing
  Product More Convenient? — 244
What Are Guidelines for Managing More Formal
  Distribution Channels? — 251
Research Highlight: Observation Research for
  Needle Exchange Programs — 254

CHAPTER 12 Promotion: Creating Messages — 259

Marketing Highlight: Sexual Assault Prevention — 260
Chapter Overview — 264
Message Strategy: What Do We Want to Say? — 264
Message Execution Strategy: How Do We Want to Say It? — 266

Principles and Theories for Decision Making:
    Designing Messages and Choosing an
    Executional Strategy   273
Pretesting   279
Research Highlight: Telephone Survey for Prevention of Sudden
    Infant Death Syndrome (SIDS)   283

CHAPTER 13   Promotion: Selecting Media Channels   287

Marketing Highlight: AIDS Prevention   288
Chapter Overview   292
What Are Major Media Channels to Consider?   292
Choosing Specific Media Vehicles   303
What Timing Decisions Need to Be Made?   303
What Factors Influence Media Strategies?   304
What Principles Can Guide Decision Making?   307
Research Highlight: Clinical Trial for Skin Cancer Detection   315

PART V   Managing Social Marketing Programs

CHAPTER 14   Developing a Plan for Evaluation and Monitoring   323

Marketing Highlight: Nutrition   324
Chapter Overview   327
What Will Be Measured?   327
How Will It Be Measured?   332
When Will It Be Measured?   333
Additional Considerations and Concerns   334
Research Highlight: Evaluation Planning for Team Nutrition Program   337

CHAPTER 15   Establishing Budgets and Finding Funding Sources   345

Marketing Highlight: Suicide Prevention   346
Chapter Overview   348
Determining Budgets   349
Finding Funding Sources   351
Appealing to Funders   360
Implications to the Draft Plan   362
Research Highlight: Baseline and Tracking Survey for
    Drowning Prevention   364

CHAPTER 16   Completing an Implementation
Plan and Sustaining Behavior   371

Marketing Highlight: Water Quality   372
Chapter Overview   376
Implementation Plans   376
Sustainability   383

CHAPTER 17   Making Ethical Decisions   391

Marketing Highlight: Animal Rights   392
Chapter Overview   394
Ethical Considerations: At Every Decision Point   395
American Marketing Association Code of Ethics   399

Appendix: Social Marketing Planning Worksheet   405

Credits   419

Name Index   421

Subject Index   423

About the Authors   435

Foreword

Social marketing is clearly in the growth phase of its practical and intellectual life cycle. On the practical side, from its early introduction in the field of family planning in the early 1970s, social marketing first slowly migrated into related fields of public health in international and national settings. Examples included the efforts of the Academy for Educational Development in promoting child survival in South America, Southeast Asia, and Africa and the work of Porter Novelli on the U.S. National High Blood Pressure Education Program.

By the late 1980s and early 1990s, there was a marked acceleration in the adoption of social marketing approaches by a growing array of international and domestic agencies and creation of organizations and institutions to support this growth. Work on family planning naturally led to work on the HIV/AIDS epidemic, and this helped propel the Centers for Disease Control and Prevention into the adoption of social marketing approaches to many of its other programs. The World Bank recognized the power of social marketing in international contexts and began a continuing series of strategic interventions and distance learning programs on social marketing. Health Canada developed a major social marketing capability and positioned itself to provide wide support for the field electronically.

Recognizing the growing importance and power of social marketing, a number of individuals with social marketing job titles began to appear. Consultancies acquired social marketing capabilities, and firms such as Fleischmann Hillard, Burson Marsteller, and Ogilvy and Mather hired social marketing specialists. At the turn of the century, UNAIDS sponsored a major conference to learn more about how it might incorporate social marketing frameworks for its important work. And social marketing increasingly moved into new subject areas, including the environment, traffic safety, and child abuse.

On the intellectual side, the field also saw accelerating growth. Following early publications by Manoff and Fine in the 1970s, books began to appear in the late 1980s and early 1990s by Kotler and Roberto and myself, and the *Social Marketing Quarterly* began publication. Regular conferences on social marketing were started by the University of South Florida and later, by an ad hoc group of academics and practitioners in Washington, D.C. The latter Innovations in Social Marketing Conference, in turn, led to an important collection of papers and then to an ad hoc meeting convened by Porter Novelli that proved a major stimulus for the creation of the Social Marketing Institute. The Social Marketing Institute has emerged to become a major clearinghouse for the field and will be an eventual major source of training, best practices, and conferences.

Social marketing institutions have also sprung up internationally. The principal social marketing listserver now has over 750 participants in over 40 countries. There is a Centre for Social Marketing at Strathclyde University in Scotland, and one has just been created in Warsaw, Poland. Interest in social marketing in Australia and New Zealand is on the rise, and a first workshop was just held in South Africa.

But there is still much to be accomplished. Although social marketing topics regularly appear in texts and readings books, there is no place where one can get a degree or even a "concentration" in social marketing. The mainstream marketing community and its principal institutions have yet to support in major ways the migration of its powerful concepts and tools to this burgeoning new domain.

Textbooks such as this one will serve a major purpose in continuing the acceleration of growth in the field. But still there needs to be much more education and research. Social marketing concepts need to appear routinely in degree programs in business, public health, public policy, environmental management, and the like, both in the United States and elsewhere. Foundations and organizations like the American Marketing Association need to step up their financial and personnel support.

As this book attests, social marketing is an extremely powerful set of concepts and tools that can accomplish much to relieve the pain and suffering of populations around the world and to address social problems that have their roots in undesirable behaviors. We are fortunate to have some of the best thinkers and writers in our field—such as represented in this volume—committed to making this happen.

—Alan R. Andreasen
Washington, D.C.

Preface

We envision a world where people are healthy and safe, protecting the environment, and contributing to their communities. This book for *students and professionals* has been designed to support organized efforts to improve our quality of life. It draws upon the philosophy, logic, concepts, and tools of social marketing presented in prior texts and journals. It includes the writings and great thinking of experts and veterans in the field. We think it is the most complete resource to date for understanding and practicing this discipline.

Our aim is to turn social marketing into a step-by-step process so that anyone working for a cause in the area of *health, safety, environment, or community involvement* can plan and execute more effective social marketing campaigns. Each of the eight steps in the process is richly supported by actual cases and research efforts. Included are more than *25 in-depth cases and close to 100 examples* of social marketing campaigns and efforts; *12 research highlights* represent the scope of research methodologies. The appendix for the text includes *worksheets for each step* that can be used by students and practitioners to complete a social marketing plan.

In this book we examine salient problems of advanced industrial countries, but acknowledge that other social problems are prominent elsewhere. We feel, however, that this methodology is sound for application in most situations.

We have used the social marketing process described in this book in our own social marketing consulting engagements, with great success. Our methodology has been classroom-tested and refined with students who prepared social marketing campaigns using the 8-step planning process. This verified for us that the presented materials transform into effective campaigns.

We know that most readers (faculty, students, and professionals) who have opened the pages of this book are currently involved, or will be involved, in planning, implementing, or supporting one or more social causes. We hope the book provides you and your associates with a new level of expertise and effectiveness.

—Philip Kotler

—Ned Roberto

—Nancy Lee

Acknowledgments

The authors thank the many contributors for cases and write-ups on social marketing campaigns and efforts, especially Alan Andreasen, Jennifer Archer, Nancy Ashley, Elizabeth Bennett, Carol Bryant, John Britt, Mike Broder, Sue Eastgard, Katharine Fitzgerald, Daniel Garzia, Gary Gorland, Jeff Hicks, Rhonda Hunter, Nicole Kerr, Heidi Keller, Craig Lefebvre, Jim Lindenberger, Jeff Linkenbach, Martin McCarthy, James Mintz, Michael Newton-Ward, Guy Seese, Hilary Seese, Preeti Shridhar, William Smith, Megan Warfield, and Keith Warnack.

In addition, the authors offer the following personal acknowledgments.

For Philip Kotler

My gratitude goes to Donald Jacobs, former dean of the Kellogg School, and Dipak Jain, current dean of the Kellogg School, for supporting the time involved in preparing this completely new book on social marketing.

For Ned Roberto

I would like to thank the former dean of the Asian Institute of Management, Jess Gallegos, and the current dean, Ed Morato, for allowing me the time needed to attend to this project.

For Nancy Lee

Thank you Phil and Ned for the opportunity to join you in this important effort, and thank you Sage Publications for your guidance and diligence. I thank my mother for her big dreams, my father for his big questions, my brother for his big shoulder, and my sister for her big heart. I also thank my wonderful colleagues, partners, friends, neighbors, family, and dog Happy, who helped me laugh and have fun in the hardest of times. Most of all, I would like to thank my dear husband, Terry, who provided an ever-ready abundance of encouragement, love, and support.

PART I

Understanding
Social Marketing

KEY CHAPTER QUESTIONS

1. What is social marketing?

2. Where did the concept originate?

3. How does social marketing differ from commercial sector marketing?

4. When is it used and for what purpose?

5. What social issues can benefit from social marketing?

6. What are other approaches to influencing public behavior?

CHAPTER 1
Defining
Social Marketing

*[An estimated] half of all deaths can be attributed to the
following root causes and thus could be considered
"premature": tobacco . . . diet & activity levels . . . alcohol . . .
infectious agents . . . toxic agents . . . firearms . . . sexual
behavior . . . motor vehicles . . . illicit drug use.*

—University of California at Berkeley Wellness Letter[1]

*NASA has found that the ozone hole was bigger than ever this
year, almost 13 times as large as it was in 1981. At its peak . . .
the hole . . . was larger than North America and extended
over the tip of South America at times.*

—U.S. News & World Report[2]

MARKETING HIGHLIGHT: THE 21ST CENTURY

As you read the following grim statistics based on estimates for the past year in the United States, you can be confident that this book will describe practical and successful marketing strategies to improve our future report cards.

Health

- Each day, more than 4,000 youths aged 11 to 17 tried their first cigarette.[3]
- More than 40,000 women died from breast cancer.[4]
- More than 30,000 men died from prostate cancer.[5]
- Close to 40% of adults aged 18 and over had no leisure-time physical activity.[6]
- More than 5,000 infants were born with fetal alcohol syndrome.[7]
- An estimated 1 million teens became pregnant.[8]
- More than 50,000 new cases of malignant melanoma were diagnosed.[9]
- 5 to 10 million adolescent girls and women struggled with an eating disorder and borderline conditions.[10]

Safety

- More than 3,000 children and teens died from gunshot wounds.[11]
- More than 16,000 people were killed in alcohol-related crashes.[12]
- An estimated 3,000 people died in home fires.[13]
- More than 8% of high school youth attempted suicide.[14]

Environment

- 4 million tons of paper were thrown away (in garbage) by American office workers.[15]
- 4.5 trillion nonbiodegradable cigarette butts were littered worldwide.[16]

Community

- More than 5,000 people on waiting lists for organ transplants died.[17]
- Only 51.2% of eligible voters voted in the U.S. presidential election.[18]

WHAT IS SOCIAL MARKETING?

Social marketing is one strategy for addressing these social issues as well as many others. We offer the following definition of social marketing:

> *Social marketing is the use of marketing principles and techniques to influence a target audience to voluntarily accept, reject, modify, or abandon a behavior for the benefit of individuals, groups, or society as a whole.*

Most often, social marketing is used to influence an audience to change their behavior for the sake of improving health, preventing injuries, protecting the environment, or contributing to the community. Table 1.1 cites examples, illustrating the basic elements of this definition and applying them to each of the four major social arenas referred to throughout this text.

Figure 1.1. Discouraging Alcohol Use During Pregnancy

We're Selling a Behavior

Similar to commercial sector marketers who sell goods and services, social marketers are selling behavior change. Change agents typically want target audiences to do one of four things: (a) accept a new behavior, (b) reject a potential behavior, (c) modify a current behavior, or (d) abandon an old behavior. (See Figure 1.1.) Benchmarks may also be established for knowledge (education or information) and belief (attitude or feelings) change. They are not ends in themselves but are the means of preparing the way for the behavior change.

The Behavioral Change Is Voluntary

Perhaps the most challenging aspect of social marketing is that it relies on voluntary compliance rather than legal, economic, or coercive forms of influence. In many cases, social marketers cannot promise a direct benefit or immediate payback in return for a proposed behavior change. (See Figure 1.2.)

Figure 1.2. RockTheVote.org Encourages Young Adults to Vote, Even Provides Application for Absentee Ballots Online

TABLE 1.1   Examples Illustrating Definition Elements

Social Arena: Social Issue	Health: Birth Defects	Safety: Drowning	Environment: Water Supply and Water Quality	Community Involvement: Voting
Influence a Target Audience	Pregnant women.	Parents of toddlers.	Male homeowners who live in the suburbs.	College students living out of state.
Potential Behaviors to Promote:				
Accept a New Behavior	Take a multivitamin that includes 400 micrograms of folic acid.	Put a life vest on your toddler at the beach.	Replace your lawn with native plants and ground covers.	Apply for an absentee ballot.
Reject a Potential Behavior	Do not drink alcohol.	Never leave your toddler alone in the bathtub.	Do not use fertilizers that contain toxic chemicals.	Do not submit an application if you have a permanent absentee ballot.
Modify a **Current Behavior**	Drink at least eight glasses of water a day.	To model the behavior, parents should also always wear life vests when boating.	Water deeply but slowly, so it penetrates and reaches roots.	Read details about candidates and issues.
Abandon an Old Behavior	If you smoke, quit.	Do not use "water wings" as a substitute for a life vest.	Do not water your lawn if it's going to rain.	Mail your ballot before the deadline.
Use Marketing Principles and Techniques ("4Ps")	Promotion: Messages on coasters at bars.	Product: Retail displays of coast-guard-approved life vests.	Price: $50 rebate on electric mulching mowers.	Place: Absentee ballots online.
Benefit	Healthier babies.	Safer toddlers.	Water availability for the community and lower rates.	Youths experience having a voice.

We Use Traditional Marketing Principles and Techniques

The most fundamental principle underlying marketing is to apply a *customer orientation* to understand what target audiences currently know, believe, and do. The process begins with *marketing research* to understand market segments and each segment's potential needs, wants, beliefs, problems, concerns, and behaviors. Marketers then select *target markets* they can best affect and satisfy. They establish *clear objectives and goals.* They then use four major tools in the marketer's toolbox, the "4Ps," to influence target markets: *product, price, place, and promotion,* also referred to as the *marketing mix.* They carefully select product benefits, features, prices, distribution channels, messages, and media channels. (See Figure 1.3.) The product is positioned to appeal to the desires of the target market to improve their health, prevent injuries, protect the environment, or contribute to their community more effectively than the competing behavior the target market is currently practicing or considering. Once a plan is implemented, results are monitored and evaluated, and strategies are altered as needed.

Figure 1.3. Using Traditional Pricing Techniques

We Select and Influence a Target Audience

Marketers know that the marketplace is a rich collage of diverse populations, each having a distinct set of wants and needs. They know that what appeals to one individual may not appeal to another. Marketers divide the market into similar groups (market segments), measure the relative potential of each segment to meet organizational and marketing objectives, and then choose one or more segments (target markets) for concentrating their efforts and resources. (See Figure 1.4.) For each target, a distinct mix of the 4Ps is developed, one chosen to appeal to the targeted market segment.

Figure 1.4. A Targeted Approach

Figure 1.5. Individuals Are Often the Beneficiaries

The Beneficiary Is the Individual, Group, or Society as a Whole

Unlike commercial sector marketing, in which a primary intended beneficiary is the corporate shareholder, the primary beneficiary of the social marketing program is the individual, a group, or society as a whole. (See Figure 1.5.)

WHERE DID THE CONCEPT ORIGINATE?

When we think of social marketing as "influencing public behavior," it is clear that campaigning for voluntary behavior change is not a new phenomenon. Consider efforts to free the slaves, abolish child labor, influence women's right to vote, and recruit women into the work force. (See Figure 1.6.)

Launching the discipline formally more than 25 years ago, the term *social marketing* was first introduced by Philip Kotler and Gerald Zaltman, in a pioneering article in the *Journal of Marketing,* to describe "the use of marketing principles and techniques to advance a social cause, idea or behavior."[19] In intervening decades, growing interest in and use of social marketing concepts, tools, and practices has spread from public health to use by environmental and community advocates, as is evident in the partial list of seminal events, texts, and journal articles in Box 1.1.

Figure 1.6. "Rosie the Riveter," Created by the War Ad Council to Help Recruit Women

BOX 1.1
Social Marketing: Seminal Events and Publications

1970s

1971: The term *social marketing* is coined in a pioneering article, "Social Marketing: An Approach to Planned Social Change," in the *Journal of Marketing*, by Philip Kotler and Gerald Zaltman.[20]

More distinguished researchers and practitioners join the voices for the potential of social marketing, including Alan Andreasen (Georgetown University), James Mintz (Federal Department of Health, Canada), William Novelli (cofounder of Porter Novelli Associates), and William Smith (Academy for Educational Development).

1980s

World Bank, World Health Organization, and Centers for Disease Control and Prevention start to use the term and promote interest in social marketing.

1981: An article in the *Journal of Marketing*, by Paul Bloom and William Novelli, reviews the first 10 years of social marketing.[21] It highlights the lack of rigor in the application of marketing principles and techniques in critical areas of the field, including research, segmentation, and distribution channels.

1985: A text, *Social Marketing: New Imperative for Public Health*, by Richard Manoff, focuses on the issue of message design in social marketing programs.[22]

1988: An article in the *Health Education Quarterly*, "Social Marketing and Public Health Intervention," by R. Craig Lefebvre and June Flora, gives social marketing widespread exposure in the field of public health.[23]

1989: A text, *Social Marketing: Strategies for Changing Public Behavior*, by Philip Kotler and Ned Roberto, lays out the application of marketing principles and techniques for influencing social change management.[24]

1990s

Academic programs are established, including the Center for Social Marketing at the University of Strathclyde, in Glasgow, Scotland, and the Department of Community and Family Health, at the University of South Florida, led by Associate Professor Carol Bryant.

1990: The first annual national conference, "Social Marketing and Public Health," is sponsored by the University of South Florida, College of Public Health.

1992: An article in the *American Psychologist*, by James Prochaska, Carlo DiClemente, and John Norcross, presents an organizing framework for achieving behavior change, considered by many as the most useful model developed to date.[25]

1994: A publication is launched: *Social Marketing Quarterly*, by Best Start, Inc., and the Department of Public Health, University of South Florida.

1994: The first annual "Innovations in Social Marketing Conference" was held.

1995: A text, *Marketing Social Change: Changing Behavior to Promote Health, Social Development, and the Environment*, by Alan Andreasen, makes a significant contribution to both the theory and practice of social marketing.[26]

1998: A text, *Marketing Public Health: Strategies to Promote Social Change*, by Michael Siegel and Lynne Donor, presents detailed principles, examples, and practical theory for public health practitioners.[27]

1999: The Social Marketing Institute is formed in Washington, D.C., with Alan Andreasen, from Georgetown University, as interim executive director.

HOW DOES SOCIAL MARKETING DIFFER FROM COMMERCIAL SECTOR MARKETING?

There are a few important differences between social marketing and commercial sector marketing:

• Most agree that a major distinguishing factor lies in the type of product sold. In the case of commercial sector marketing, the marketing process revolves primarily around the selling of *goods and services.* In the case of social marketing, the marketing process is used to sell *behavior change.* Yet the principles and techniques of influencing are the same in both arenas.

• In the commercial sector, the primary aim is *financial gain.* In social marketing, the primary aim is *individual or societal gain.* Given this focus on financial gain, commercial marketers often favor choosing primary target market segments that will provide the greatest volume of profitable sales. In social marketing, segments are selected on the basis of a different set of criteria, including prevalence of the social problem, ability to reach the audience, readiness for change, and others that are explored in depth in Chapter 6 of this text. In both cases, however, marketers seek to gain the greatest returns on their investment of resources.

• Although both social and commercial marketers recognize the need to identify and position their offerings relative to the competition, their competitors are very different in nature. Because, as stated earlier, the commercial marketer is most often focused on selling goods and services, the *competition is often identified as other organizations offering similar goods and services* or that satisfy similar needs. In social marketing, because the focus is on selling a behavior, the *competition is most often the current or preferred behavior of the target market* and the perceived benefits associated with that behavior. In social marketing, we identify and examine the behavior our target market would prefer over the one we are promoting, and why this is so.

• In many ways, social marketing is more difficult than commercial marketing. Consider trying to influence people to act as follows:

– Give up an addictive behavior.   (Stop smoking.)

– Change a comfortable lifestyle.   (Reduce thermostats.)

– Resist peer pressure.   (Be sexually abstinent.)

– Go out of their way.   (Pull over to talk on the cell phone.)

– Be uncomfortable.   (Get a mammogram.)

– Establish new habits.   (Exercise 5 days a week.)

– Spend more money.   (Buy recycled paper.)

– Be embarrassed.   (Go in for a colorectal exam.)

– Hear bad news.   (Have your cholesterol tested.)

– Risk relationships.   (Take the keys from a drunk driver.)

– Give up leisure time.   (Volunteer.)

– Reduce pleasure.   (Take shorter showers.)

– Give up looking good.   (Let lawns go brown in the summer.)

– Spend more time.   (Flatten cardboard boxes before putting them in recycling bins.)

Despite these differences, we also see many similarities between social and commercial sector marketing:

• *A customer orientation is applied.* The marketer knows that the offer (product, price, place, and promotion) will need to appeal to the target audience.

• *Exchange theory is fundamental.* The consumer must perceive benefits that equal or exceed the perceived costs.[28]

• *Marketing research is used throughout the process.* Only by researching and understanding the specific needs, desires, beliefs, and attitudes of target adopters can the marketer build effective strategies.

• *Audiences are segmented.* Strategies must be tailored to the unique wants, needs, resources, and current behaviors of differing market segments.

• *All 4Ps are considered.* A winning strategy requires integrating the 4Ps, not just relying on advertising.

• *Results are measured and used for improvement.* Feedback is valued and seen as "free advice" on how to do better next time.

WHEN IS SOCIAL MARKETING USED, AND FOR WHAT PURPOSE?

Who Does Social Marketing?

In most cases, social marketing principles and techniques are used by those on the front lines for improving public health, preventing injuries, protecting the environment, and engendering community involvement. They include the following:

Professionals working for governmental agencies and organizations to include:

Centers for Disease Control and Prevention

Departments of health

Departments of social and human services

Community health clinics

Departments of transportation

Departments of ecology

U.S. Environmental Protection Agency

U.S. Department of Agriculture

Public utilities

Departments of wildlife and fisheries

U.S. Department of the Interior

National Institute of Health

World Health Organization

U.S. Coast Guard

National Traffic Safety Administration

Professionals working for nonprofit organizations, associations, and foundations to include:

Green Peace

Nature Conservancy

World Wildlife Fund

Friends of the Earth

People for the Ethical Treatment of Animals

American Cancer Society

American Red Cross
American Heart Association
American Lung Association
American Diabetes Association
Organ donation centers
Blood donation centers
Eating disorders awareness and prevention programs
Planned Parenthood
Healthcare providers
American Dental Association
Healthy Mothers Healthy Babies
David and Lucile Packard Foundation
Robert Wood Johnson Foundation
Bill and Melinda Gates Foundation
Produce for Better Health Foundation

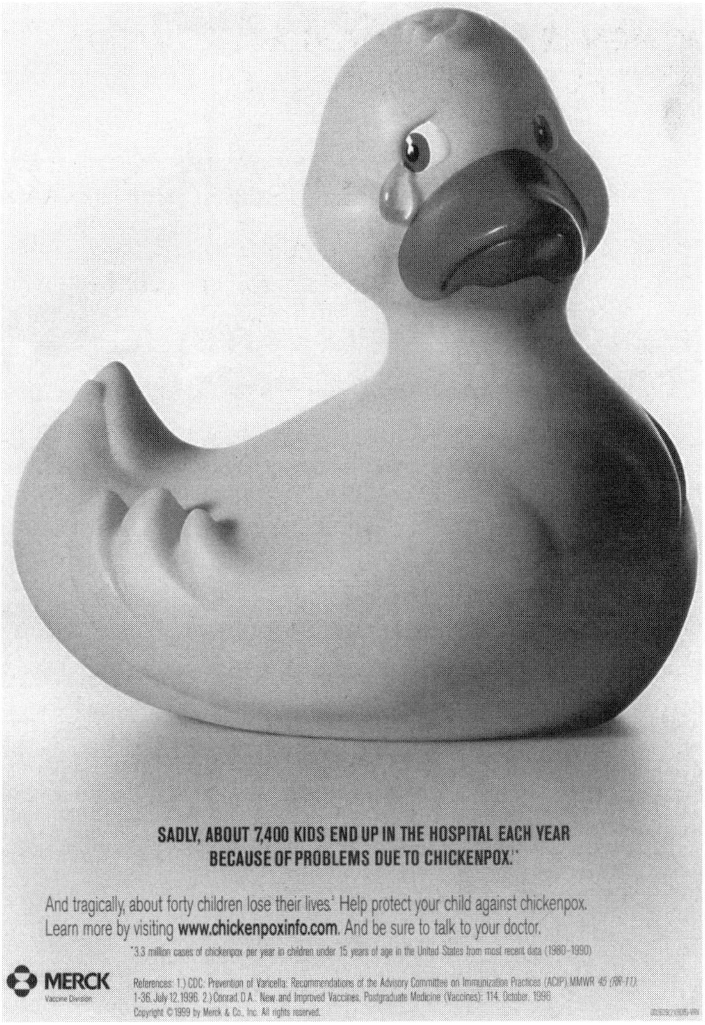
SADLY, ABOUT 7,400 KIDS END UP IN THE HOSPITAL EACH YEAR BECAUSE OF PROBLEMS DUE TO CHICKENPOX.*
And tragically, about forty children lose their lives.² Help protect your child against chickenpox.
Learn more by visiting www.chickenpoxinfo.com. And be sure to talk to your doctor.
*3.3 million cases of chickenpox per year in children under 15 years of age in the United States from most recent data (1980–1990)
MERCK
Vaccine Division
References: 1.) CDC: Prevention of Varicella: Recommendations of the Advisory Committee on Immunization Practices (ACIP). MMWR 45 (RR-11): 1-36. July 12, 1996. 2.) Conrad, D.A., New and Improved Vaccines. Postgraduate Medicine (Vaccines): 114. October, 1996.
Copyright © 1999 by Merck & Co., Inc. All rights reserved.

Figure 1.7. Pharmaceutical Company Promotion for Immunizations

Professionals working in a for-profit organization in positions responsible for corporate philanthropy, marketing, or community relations might develop and implement social marketing campaigns to benefit their customers and also contribute to organizational goals, such as brand identity or even increased sales. For example:

- An insurance company that promotes the use of bike helmets and reminds people to check their fire alarm batteries on a regular basis
- A pharmaceutical company that promotes immunizations in a magazine ad (See Figure 1.7.)
- A nursery that gives workshops on natural gardening

- An appliance manufacturer that promotes an energy-efficient line

- A sports team that volunteers team members' time to mentor youth at risk

Finally, there are marketing professionals who provide services to organizations engaged in social marketing campaigns, such as advertising agencies, public relations firms, and marketing research firms.

WHAT SOCIAL ISSUES CAN BENEFIT FROM SOCIAL MARKETING?

Table 1.2 presents 50 major social issues that could benefit from the application of social marketing principles and techniques. They include the four major arenas mentioned earlier: health promotion, injury prevention, environmental protection, and community involvement.

Relative to circumstances most eminent and real, social marketing principles and techniques were present in the aftermath of the terrorist attacks on September 11th, 2001. Messages and efforts included the following:

- People near the site of the wreckage in New York City were encouraged to *wear cloth facemasks.*

- Those who had walked in debris from the collapsed buildings were warned to *wash asbestos off their shoes.*

- Postal workers began *wearing protective gloves.*

- Some who used the stairs in the World Trade Center after the attacks reported the benefit of the practice of *putting an arm on the shoulder of the person in front of you to guide yourself through the rubble and barriers.*

- Airline pilots were reported to have encouraged brave passengers to *throw something (anything) at someone who stands up and threatens to hijack the plane.*

- An extra plea was made for volunteers to find and *donate extra-large sizes of clothing for firefighters.*

- People with rare and valuable blood types were encouraged to *gather together at the front of the line.*

- At airport security, officials pleaded with travelers to *have your computer out of your bag and your pocket change in your carry-on.*

TABLE 1.2 50 Major Issues Social Marketing Can Benefit

FOR IMPROVED HEALTH

Tobacco use	Almost one in four adults aged 18 and over smoke.[29]
Heavy/binge drinking	Nearly 20% of 18- to 24-year-olds binge drink four or more times a month.[30]
Alcohol use during pregnancy	An estimated 5,000 infants are born with fetal alcohol syndrome each year.[31]
Physical inactivity	40% of adults aged 18 and over have no leisure-time physical activity.[32]
Teen pregnancy	Nearly 1 million teen girls become pregnant each year.[33]
Sexually transmitted diseases	Among sexually active high school students, more than 40% report not using condoms during most recent sexual intercourse.[34]
Fat intake	67% of persons aged 2 years and older consumed more than the recommended 30% of calories from total fat (1994-96).[35]
Fruit and vegetable intake	Only 28% of persons aged 2 years and older met daily minimum recommendations of at least two daily servings of fruit; less than half of persons aged 2 years and older had at least three daily servings of vegetables (1994-96).[36]
High cholesterol	30% of adults aged 18 and over have been diagnosed with high cholesterol (1999).[37]
Obesity	More than a third of adults aged 18 and over are at risk for healthproblems related to being overweight.[38]
Breastfeeding	Only 29% of mothers meet recommendations to breastfeed infants until they reach at least 6 months of age.[39]
Breast cancer	More than 20% of females aged 50 and over have not had mammograms within the past 2 years.[40]
Prostate cancer	Only about half of all prostate cancers are found early.[41]
Colon cancer	Only about a third of colorectal cancers are found early.[42]
Osteoporosis	50% of women and 12% of men aged 50 and over will have an osteoporosis-related fracture in their lifetime.[43]
Folic acid to prevent birth defects	Only 21% of females (ages 15-44) began pregnancy with the recommended 400 mg of folic acid each day (1991-1994).[44]
Immunizations	Only 73% of young children aged 19 to 35 months were fully immunized in 1998.[45]
Skin cancer	Approximately 70% of American adults do not protect themselves from sun's dangerous rays.[46]
Oral health	By the age of 9, over half of schoolchildren in the United States have dental caries.[47]
Diabetes	About one third of the nearly 16 million people with diabetes are not aware that they have the disease.[48]
Blood pressure	Only about a fourth of those diagnosed with high blood pressure have it under control.[49]
Eating disorders	Half of 9- to 10-year-old girls feel better about themselves if they are on diets.[50]

FOR INJURY PREVENTION

Drinking and driving	16,068 deaths were due to alcohol-related traffic accidents in the year 2000.[51]
Other traffic accidents	An estimated 25% to 50% of crashes can be attributed to driver distraction.[52]
Seat belts	An estimated 30% of drivers and adult passengers do not always wear their seat belts.[53]
Booster seats	Only about 6% of the 20 million children who need booster seats are using them.[54]
Suicide	Almost 15% of high school students nationwide had made specific plans to attempt suicide in 1999.[55]
Sexual assault	8% of high school age girls said "yes" when asked whether "a boyfriend or date has ever forced sex against your will."[56]

(Continued)

TABLE 1.2   (Continued)

Drowning	Drowning is the second leading cause of injury-related death to children aged 14 and under.[57]
Domestic violence	31% of American women report having been physically or sexually abused by a husband or boyfriend at some point in their lives.[58]
Gun storage	More than 50% of firearm-owning parents with children aged 4 to 12 reported storing a firearm loaded or unlocked in their homes.[59]
Fires	Almost 50% of fires and 60% of fire deaths occur in the estimated 8% of homes with no smoke alarms.[60]
Falls	In the year 2000, more than 40,000 people were taken to hospital emergency rooms in the United States because of injuries from riding scooters.[61]
Household and other poisons	More than 1.1 million poisonings among children aged 5 and under were reported in 1998.[62]

TO PROTECT THE ENVIRONMENT

Waste reduction: reduce, reuse, recycle	Municipal waste generated in 1999 was 374,631,000 tons, with only 31% recycled.[63]
Wildlife habitat protection	Roughly 70% of the major marine fish stocks depleted from overfishing are being fished at their biological limit.[64]
Forest destruction	It is estimated that forest cover has been reduced by as much as 50% worldwide.[65]
Toxic fertilizers and pesticides	Of the 65% continental watersheds surveyed, 7% are sufficiently contaminated to pose potential risk to people who eat fish and to fish and wildlife.[66]
Water conservation	The United Nations projects a 50% to 100% increase in use of irrigation water by 2025, which is already in short supply in many countries.[67]
Air pollution from automobiles	Road vehicles account for 31.8% of nitrogen oxide emissions, representing the most pressing air quality issue facing the United States today.[68]
Air pollution from other sources	Using a push mower instead of a power mower will reduce carbon dioxide emissions by 80 pounds per year.[69]
Composting garbage and yard waste	An estimated 30% to 50% of all trash in landfills in the United States could have been composted.[70]
Unintentional fires	More than 7 million acres burned in the United States in the year 2000, an area equal in size to Massachusetts, Rhode Island, and Delaware combined.[71]
Conserving energy	Global energy use is projected to increase more than 2% annually for the next 15 years and will raise greenhouse gas emissions about 50% higher than current levels.[72]
Litter	One mile of highway contains approximately 16,000 pieces of litter, and the estimated cost of pickup is 30 cents per piece of litter.[73]
Watersheds	Almost a third of all watersheds have lost more than 75% of their original forest cover.[74]
Acid rain	In Asia, sulfur dioxide emissions are expected to triple by 2010 if current trends continue.[75]

FOR COMMUNITY INVOLVEMENT

Organ donation	In 2001, more than 75,000 patients were on waiting lists for transplants.[76]
Blood donation	Less than 5% of healthy Americans eligible to donate blood actually do each year.[77]
Voting	Only 51% of all eligible voters voted in the 2000 U.S. presidential election.[78]

NOTE: Estimated/approximate statistics. Data are for the United States unless otherwise noted.

A variety of news and special programs seized an opportunity to reinforce existing social marketing messages:

- If you really want to protect yourself from a premature death, you should stop smoking, buckle your seat belt, and exercise at least 3 times a week.

- Each year in the United States, more than 16,000 people are killed in traffic accidents involving drunk driving.

WHAT ARE OTHER WAYS TO INFLUENCE PUBLIC BEHAVIOR?

Marketing is not the only approach to influence or change public behavior. Here, we describe four other approaches.

Technology

Sometimes a technological innovation or enhancement supports behavior change or significantly contributes to the social issue:

- Some new gas pumps inhibit the ability to "top off" the tank, thus avoiding ozone-threatening spillage.

- Some cars have automatic seat belts that wrap around the passenger when the door is closed.

- In some states, ignition locks require Breathalyzers for serious offenders. (See Figure 1.8.)

Economics

Behavior can often be changed through economic pressures and incentives:

- Increasing taxes on cigarettes

- Increasing fines and enforcement for littering

Figure 1.8. Ignition Interlock Breathalyzer Device

◆ Offering lower electrical rates during nonpeak hours or providing incentives for conservation (See Figure 1.9.)

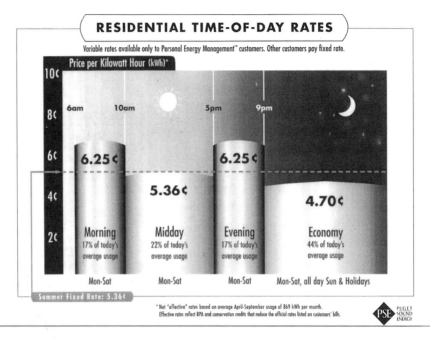

Figure 1.9. Using Price Incentives to Change Behavior

Figure 1.10. State Governor Announces New Tougher Laws for Drunk Driving

Legal/Political/ Policy Making

Sometimes when all else fails, the laws have to get tougher:

◆ In some states, booster seats are required for children until they are 8 years old or until the child weighs 80 pounds.

◆ Many states have passed a .08% blood alcohol level limit for drinking and driving. (See Figure 1.10.)

◆ Some states have considered laws requiring deposits on cigarettes similar to those requiring deposits on beverage containers (and rewarding their return).

Education

Although the line between social marketing and education is a fine one, most see education as a useful tool for the social marketer, but one that does not work alone. Most often, education is used to communicate information and/or build skills, but it does not give the same attention and focus to creating and sustaining behavior change. It primarily applies only one of the four marketing tools, promotion. For example:

- Information on how AIDS is spread
- Publications on child immunization schedules. (See Figure 1.11.)

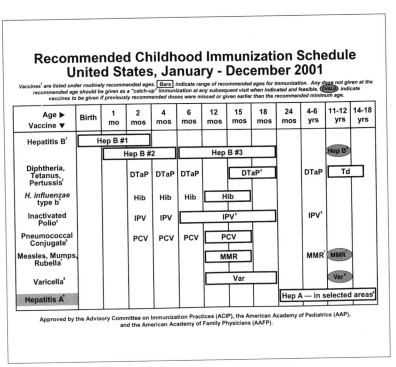

Figure 1.11. Child Immunization Schedule

HOW DOES SOCIAL MARKETING RELATE TO OTHER APPROACHES?

Social marketing is largely a mix of economic, communication, and educational strategies. The social marketer is similar to the engineer who draws from fundamental sciences to create a desired outcome. When the tools of economics, communication, and education fail to work, the social marketer then turns to technological solutions, if any can be found. As a last resort, the social marketer may turn to the law or courts to require a certain behavior.

CHAPTER SUMMARY

1. Social marketing is the use of marketing principles and techniques to influence a target audience to voluntarily accept, reject, modify, or abandon a behavior for the benefit of individuals, groups, or society as a whole.

2. There are a few important differences between social marketing and commercial sector marketing. Social marketers focus on selling behaviors, whereas commercial marketers are more focused on selling goods and services. Commercial sector marketers position their products against those of other companies, whereas the social marketer competes with the audience's current behavior and associated benefits. The primary benefit of a "sale" in social marketing is the welfare of an individual, a group, or society, whereas in commercial marketing, the primary benefit is shareholder wealth.

3. Social marketing principles and techniques are most often used to improve public health, prevent injuries, protect the environment, and increase involvement in the community.

4. Those engaged in social marketing activities include professionals in public sector agencies, nonprofit organizations, foundations, corporate marketing, community relations, advertising, public relations, and market research.

5. Other approaches to changing behavior and having an impact on social issues include technological innovations, economic pressures, laws, and education.

KEY TERMS AND CONCEPTS

Social marketing
Target audiences
Voluntary behavior change
Marketing principles and
   techniques
Beneficiaries
Commercial marketing
Technological strategies

Economic strategies
Legal strategies
Educational strategies
Health promotion
Injury prevention
Environmental protection
Community involvement

ISSUES FOR DISCUSSION

1. A few major differences between commercial marketing and social marketing were noted in this chapter. Do you see other important differences?

2. For what social issues other than the 50 presented in Table 1.2 might social marketing efforts be effective?

3. Relative to reducing tobacco use, what would be an example of a technological, economic, legal, and educational strategy?

MARKETING DIALOGUE

◊ *Are we really the same as commercial marketing?*

◊ *Do we want to be?*

◊ *Do we care?*

Some social marketing practitioners believe it is time for social marketing to declare its own identity, develop its own definition, and distinguish itself as a unique and separate discipline. They argue as follows:[79]

> We have been at this for three decades now, and it's about time to define our discipline uniquely, rather than as a subset of commercial marketing. Our missions and motives and means and markets have very little in common.

> We have a marketplace very different from that of commercial marketers, and we therefore need different tools. The 4P model at the cornerstone of commercial marketing is an exaggeration of our typical activities. Let's stop kidding others and ourselves. Most professionals in this field have very few opportunities for influencing product design, pricing, and distribution channels. We don't really do everything. In the end, isn't 90% of what we do persuasive communication (at best)?

> We resent the notion that social marketing has the same motivations and therefore the same processes as those found in organizations for profit. Commercial ven-

tures are "in it" for the shareholders. We're in it for the public good. We don't like the association.

Others think it is critical for social marketing to stay connected to the marketing discipline, in theory and in practice. Their counterpoints include the following:

We need to move closer to—not further from—the disciplines and practices of commercial marketers. Marketing has been a powerful addition to the set of tools used in influencing public health and safety, protecting the environment, and encouraging community participation. We need to be constantly reminded that we are not merely educators or social advertisers who "may be content to work at the information or attitudinal level. Social marketers aim to bring about purchase and use and to close the sale."[80] We must begin to look at participating in product development, suggesting pricing strategies, and understanding and recommending distribution channels.

What's wrong with making a profit? And what's wrong with using practices that have been around longer than many of us have, and have been tried and tested and enhanced? Commercial marketers have spent billions of dollars learning what works and what doesn't. We should be benefiting from this, not reinventing it.

We need to encourage (even challenge) expert marketers from the commercial sector to join us and to specialize in this exciting niche of the marketing discipline. We should be proud of the rigor our field requires and demonstrate that we understand the contribution marketing can make.

Notes

1. University of California at Berkeley, School of Public Health. (1997). "What's Really Killing Us," *University of California at Berkeley Wellness Letter, 13*(11), 7.
2. *U.S. News & World Report,* (2000, 30 October), p. 14.
3. Grace, C. O. (1999, October 12). "3,000 New Teen Smokers Per Day," *The Washington Post* (Excerpts). Retrieved 9/08/01 from http://no-smoking.org/oct99/10-12-99-6.html
4. American Cancer Society. (2001). Retrieved from http://www.cancer.org
5. Ibid.
6. National Health Interview Survey (NHIS), Centers for Disease Control and Prevention (CDC), National Center for Health Statistics (NCHS). (1997). As cited in Healthy People 2010 Web site, Sec. 22, "Physical Activity and Fitness." Retrieved 9/12/01 from http://www.health.gov/healthypeople/document/html/volume2/22physical.htm

7. *Journal of the American Medical Association.* (1991). As cited in National Organization on Fetal Alcohol Syndrome (NOFAS) Web site. Retrieved 9/09/01 from http://www.nofas.org/main/what_is_FAS.htm

8. Henshaw, S. K. (1996). *U.S. Teenage Pregnancy Statistics.* New York: Alan Guttmacher Institute; Forest, J. D. (1986). *Proportion of U.S. Women Ever Pregnant Before Age 20.* New York: Alan Guttmacher Institute. As cited in National Campaign to Prevent Teen Pregnancy Web site. Retrieved 9/09/01 from http://www.teenpregnancy.org/factstats.htm

9. American Cancer Society. (2001). As cited in CDC Web site, "Skin Cancer: A Largely Preventable Cancer." Retrieved 9/09/01 from http://www.cdc.gov/cancer/nscpep/skin.htm

10. Crowther et al. (1992); Fairburn et al. (1993); Gordon (1990); Hoek (1995); Shisslak et al. (1995). As cited in Eating Disorders Awareness and Prevention Web site, "Eating Disorders in the USA." Retrieved 10/11/01 from http://www.edap.org/edinfo/stats.html

11. CDC, NCHS. (1998). "Deaths: Final Data for 1998." As cited in press release, "Gun Deaths Among Children and Teens Drop Sharply" (July 24, 2000). Retrieved 10/11/01 from www.cdc.gov/nchs/releases/00news/finaldeath98.htm

12. National Highway Traffic Safety Administration (NHTSA). (2000). Retrieved 9/09/01 from http://www.nhtsa.dot.gov

13. National Fire Prevention Association (NFPA). (1998). Retrieved 9/12/01 from http://www.nfpa.org

14. CDC Youth Risk Behavior Surveillance. (1999). Table 13. Retrieved 9/12/01 from http://www.cdc.gov/mmwr/preview/mmwrhtml/ss4905a1.htm#tab12

15. *Time* Magazine. (2000, April/May). "Time for Kids," p. 2.

16. CigaretteLitter.Org. (2001). "Facts About Cigarette Butts and Litter." Retrieved 9/19/2001 from http://www.cigarettelitter.org

17. Bush, G. (2001, April 4). As cited in Transplant Recipients International Organization Web site. Retrieved 9/09/01 from www.trioweb.org/news/pr_4-15-01_c.html

18. Federal Election Commission. (2001). As cited in infoplease.com Web site, "National Voter Turnout in Federal Elections." Retrieved 10/11/01 from www.infoplease.com/ipa/A0781453.html

19. Kotler, P., & Zaltman, G. (1971, July). "Social Marketing: An Approach to Planned Change," *Journal of Marketing, 35,* 3-12.

20. Ibid.

21. Bloom, P., & Novelli, W. D. (1981). "Problems and Challenges in Social Marketing," *Journal of Marketing, 45*(2), 79-88.

22. Manoff, R. K. (1985). *Social Marketing.* New York: Praeger.

23. Lefebvre, R. C., & Flora, J. A. (1988). "Social Marketing and Public Health Intervention," *Health Education Quarterly, 15*(3), 299-315.

24. Kotler, P., & Roberto, E. L. (1989). *Social Marketing: Strategies for Changing Public Behavior.* New York: Free Press.

25. Prochaska, J. O., DiClemente, C. C., & Norcross, J. C. (1992). "In Search of How People Change: Applications to Addictive Behaviors," *American Psychologist, 47,* 1102-1114.

26. Andreasen, A. (1995). *Marketing Social Change: Changing Behavior to Promote Health, Social Development, and the Environment.* San Francisco: Jossey-Bass.

27. Siegel, M., & Doner, L. (1998). *Marketing Public Health: Strategies to Promote Social Change.* Maryland: Aspen.

28. Bagozzi, R. P. (1978, March-April). "Marketing as Exchange: A Theory of Transactions in the Marketplace," *American Behavioral Science*, 535-556.

29. CDC Behavioral Risk Factor Surveillance System (BRFSS). (2000). Prevalence Data Section. Retrieved 9/19/01 from http://www.cdc.gov/nccdphp/brfss

30. Ibid.

31. *Journal of the American Medical Association.* (1991). As cited in the National Organization of Fetal Alcohol Syndrome Web site. Retrieved 9/09/01 from http://www.nofas.org/main/what_is_FAS.htm

32. National Health Interview Survey, NHIS, CDC, NCHS. (1997). As cited in Healthy People 2010 Web site, Sec. 22. Retrieved 10/10/01 from http://www.health.gov/healthypeople/document/html/volume2/22physical.htm

33. Henshaw, S. K. (1996, May). *U.S. Teenage Pregnancy Statistics.* New York: Alan Guttmacher Institute; Forest, J. D. (1986). *Proportion of U.S. Women Ever Pregnant Before Age 20.* New York: Alan Guttmacher Institute. As cited in National Campaign to Prevent Teen Pregnancy Web site. Retrieved 9/09/01 from http://www.teenpregnancy.org/factstats.htm

34. CDC Youth Risk Behavior Surveillance. (1999). Table 32. Retrieved 9/12/01 from http://www.cdc.gov/mmwr/preview/mmwrhtml/ss4905a1.htm#tab32

35. Healthy People 2010 Continuing Survey of Food Intake by Individuals. (1994-1996). Healthy People 2010 Web site, Sec. 19, "Nutrition and Overweight." Retrieved 9/19/2001 from http://www.health.gov/healthypeople/document/html/volume2/19nutrition.htm

36. Ibid.

37. CDC, BRFSS. (1999). Retrieved 9/19/01 from http://www.cdc.gov/nccdphp/brfss

38. Ibid.

39. Mothers' Survey, Abbott Laboratories, Inc., Ross Products Division. (1998). As cited in Healthy People 2010 Web site, Sec. 16-19. Retrieved 10/11/01 from http://web.health.gov/healthypeople/document/html/objectives/16-19.htm

40. CDC, BRFSS. (2000). Retrieved 9/19/01 from http://www.cdc.gov/nccdphp/brfss

41. Health A to Z.Com. (1999). "Basic Facts About Prostate Cancer." Retrieved 10/11//01 from http://www.healthatoz.com/atoz/prostate/probasic.html

42. Colon Cancer Alliance. (1999-2000). "Colorectal Cancer: Facts and Figures." Retrieved 10/11/01 from http://www.ccalliance.org/cca/media/factsfigures.html

43. National Osteoporosis Foundation. (2001)."Disease Statistics." Retrieved 9/19/01 from http://www.nof.org/osteoporosis/stats.htm

44. National Health and Nutrition Examination Survey (NHANES), CDC, NCHS. (1991-1994). As cited in Healthy People 2010 Web site, Sec. 16-16. Retrieved 9/21/01 from http://www.health.gov/healthypeople/document/html/objectives/16-16.htm

45. National Immunization Survey (NIS), CDC, NCHS and NIP. (1998). Healthy People 2010 Web site, Sec. 4-24. Retrieved 9/18/01 from http://www.health.gov/healthypeople/document/html/objectives/14-24.htm

46. CDC 1992 National Health Interview Survey. (1992). As cited in "Skin Cancer: A Largely Preventable Cancer." Retrieved 10/11/01 from http://www.cdc.gov/cancer/nscpep/skin.htm

47. Brunelle, J. A. "Caries Attack in the Primary Dentition of U.S. Children" (Abstract). Proceedings of the 68th General Session, International Association for Dental Research. Cincinnati: 19th Annual Session, American Association for Dental Research, March 7-11, 1990. J Dent Res 1990; 9:180. As cited in American Academy of Family Physicians Web site (January, 2000). Retrieved 10/09/01 at http://www.aafp.org/afp/20000101/115.html

48. American Diabetes Association. (2001)."Facts and Figures." Retrieved 9/19/01 from http://www.diabetes.org/main/application/commercewf?origin=*.jsp&event=link(B1)

49. National Heart, Lung and Blood Institute, National High Blood Pressure Education Program Description, Table 1. (1976-1994). Retrieved 9/21/01 from http://www.nhlbi.nih.gov/about/nhbpep/nhbp_pd.htm

50. Mellin et al. (1991). As cited in Eating Disorders Awareness and Prevention Web site. Retrieved 6/18/01 from http://www.edap.org

51. NHTSA. (2001). Retrieved 10/09/01 from http://www.nhtsa.dot.gov/people/injury/alcohol/partnersprog/preface.html

52. AAA Washington. (2001). "The AAA Guide to Cell Phones and Driving." Retrieved 9/18/01 from http://www.aaawa.com/traffic_safety/cell_phones.html

53. CDC, BRFSS. (1997). Retrieved 12/04/01 from http://www.cdc.gov/nccdphp/brfss

54. NHTSA. (2001). As cited in Woman Motorist Web site, "Ford Taps Prominent Safety Advocate to Urge Booster Seat Use by Children in Automobiles." Retrieved 9/18/01 from http://www.womanmotorist.com/sfty/ford-booster-seats-2k-01.shtm

55. CDC Youth Risk Behavior Surveillance. (1999). Table 13. Retrieved 9/12/01 from http://www.cdc.gov/mmwr/preview/mmwrhtml/ss4905a1.htm#tab13

56. The Commonwealth Fund Survey of the Health of Adolescent Girls. (1997, November). As cited in Family Violence Prevention Fund Web site. Retrieved 9/19/2001 from http://endabuse.org/facts/

57. National Safe Kids Campaign. (2001). "Safety Tips and Resources: Water." Retrieved 9/18/01 from http://www.safekids.org/tier2_rl.cfm?folder_id=181

58. The Commonwealth Fund 1998 Survey of Women's Health. As cited in the Family Violence Prevention Fund Web site. Retrieved 9/19/01 from http://www.fvpf.org/facts/

59. National Safe Kids Campaign. "Safety Tips and Resources: Firearms." Retrieved 9/19/01 from http://www.safekids.org/tier3_cd.cfm?content_item_id=317&folder_id=172

60. NFPA. (2001). "NFPA Fact Sheets: Smoke Alarms." Retrieved 9/18/01 from http://www.nfpa.org/Education/Consumers_and_Families/Fire_Safety_Information/Home_Fire_Safety_Tips/Smoke_Alarms/smoke_alarms.html

61. Consumer Product Safety Commission. (2001). "Scooter Safety From CPSC." Retrieved 10/10/01 from http://www.cpsc.gov/kids/kidsafety/scoot.html

62. National Safe Kids Campaign. (2001). "Safety Tips and Resources: Poisons." Retrieved 10/10/01 from http://www.safekids.org/tier2_rl.cfm?folder_id=176

63. *Biocycle Magazine.* (1999). As cited in ZeroWaste America Web site. Retrieved 10/10/01 from http://www.zerowasteamerica.org/Statistics.htm

64. Public Broadcasting System (PBS): Bill Moyers Reports, "Earth on the Edge." (2001, June). *Discussion Guide,* p. 4. Retrieved 10/10/01 from http://www.pbs.org/earthonedge/

65. Ibid., p. 15. Retrieved 9/18/01 from http://www.pbs.org/earthonedge/

66. U.S. Environmental Protection Agency (EPA). Press release. (1998, January 7). Retrieved 9/23/01 from hhtp://yosemite.epa.gov/opa/admpress.nsf/b1ab9f485b098972852562e7004dc686/ff7dbb

67. United Nations Assessment. (1997). As cited in World Resources Institute Web site, "Water: Critical Shortages Ahead?" Retrieved 10/10/01 at http://www.wri.org/trends/index.html

68. EPA. (2000). *National Air Pollution Emissions Trends, 1900-1998.* As cited on About.com Web site, "Clean Air Act: Performance Statistics." Retrieved 10/10/01 from http://environment.about.com/newsissues/environment/cs/1airpollution/index.htm

69. EPA. (2001). "In the Yard." Retrieved 10/10/01 from http://www.epa.gov/oppeoee1/globalwarming/actions/individual/difference/yard.html

70. Van Cleef, L. (2001, April). Informationweek.com. Web site, "Breakaway." Retrieved 9/21/01 from http://www.informationweek.com/breakaway/835/landfill.htm

71. Wilkinson, T. (2001, May/June). "Prometheus Unbound," *Nature Conservancy,* p. 14

72. World Resources Institute. (2001).WRI Web site, "Global Trends." Retrieved 10/10/01 from http://www.wri.org/trends/index.html

73. Institute of Applied Research. As cited in Jefferson County Web site, "Landfill and Illegal Dumping." Retrieved 10/10/01 from http://www.jeffcointouch.com/news/dumpstatelaws.htm

74. Revenga et al. (1998). "Taking Stock of Ecosystems." World Resources Institute Web site. Retrieved 9/22/01 from http://www.wri.org/wr2000/forest_wrrboxes.html

75. World Resources Institute. (2001). WRI Web site, "Global Trends." Retrieved 10/10/01 from http://www.wri.org/trends/index.html

76. Bush, G. (2001, April 4). As cited in Transplant Recipients International Organization. Retrieved 9/09/01 from www.trioweb.org/news/pr_4-15-01.html

77. American Association of Blood Banks. (2001). "Facts About Blood and Blood Banking." Retrieved 10/11/01 from http://www.aabb.org/All_About_Blood/FAQs/aabb_faqs.htm#Facts

78. Federal Election Commission. (2001). As cited in infoplease.com Web site, "National Voter Turnout in Federal Elections." Retrieved 10/10/01 from at www.infoplease.com/ipa/A0781453.html

79. Synthesis of personal communications to authors, including comments in year 2000 from Social Marketing Listserve participants.

80. Kotler & Roberto, *Social Marketing*, p. 26.

KEY CHAPTER QUESTIONS

1. What are the eight major steps in developing a social marketing plan?

2. Why is this sequential, systematic process important?

3. Where does marketing research fit into the process?

CHAPTER 2
Outlining the Strategic Marketing Planning Process

The problem is how to make sure we are really using marketing to the fullest extent and not dropping into advertising alone, or product development alone, or ignoring the consumer because we think we know more than they do.

—William Smith, Executive Director,
Academy for Educational Development[1]

MARKETING HIGHLIGHT: LOWERING BLOOD PRESSURE

In this and subsequent chapters, we open with a case that highlights major principles presented in the chapter. The following case was chosen because it is one of the most long-standing behavior change programs and incorporates most elements of the planning model presented in this text.

The National High Blood Pressure Education Program

The National High Blood Pressure Education Program (NHBPEP), established in 1972, demonstrates success from using a strategic planning framework and a marketing mix that is more than social advertising.[2] The year the program began, less than one fourth of the American population knew of the relationship between hypertension, stroke, and heart disease. Today, more than three fourths of the population are aware of this connection. As a result, virtually all Americans have had their blood pressure measured at least once, and three fourths of the population have it measured every 6 months.[3]

Based on excerpts from the Web sites of the National Institutes of Health, National Heart, Lung, and Blood Institute, and the NHBPEP, details of this case illustrate basic components of social marketing planning. We have inserted theoretical notes in italics to highlight principles that are emphasized throughout this text.

Background and Situation

The NHBPEP is a cooperative effort among professional and voluntary health agencies, state health departments, and many community groups. It is coordinated by the National Heart, Lung, and Blood Institute of the National Institutes of Health. The ultimate program purpose is to reduce death and disability related to high blood pressure.

Several major hypertension control issues are part of this program:[4]

▶ Excessive stroke mortality in the southeastern United States

▶ Effective treatment practices

▶ Utility of lowering the systolic blood pressure in older Americans

▶ Role of lifestyle changes in preventing and treating hypertension

▶ Issues regarding special populations and their situations (e.g., African Americans, renal disease, women, children, and adolescents)

▶ Educational strategies directed at professional, patient, and public audiences and community organizations

Target Audiences

One in four American adults has high blood pressure. High blood pressure plays a role in about 700,000 deaths a year from stroke and heart and kidney diseases.[5] Several high-risk populations have been identified by the NHBPEP:[6]

▶ Women taking birth control pills

▶ Older persons

▶ African Americans

▶ People with diabetes

▶ People with high blood cholesterol

Following segmentation principles, the unique characteristics of each of these segments would be analyzed relative to a variety of factors: current knowledge, beliefs, and behaviors relative to desired behaviors; perceived benefits and costs of their current lifestyles; and perceived benefits, barriers, and costs to healthier lifestyles. On the basis of their differences, each segment will require a different supporting pricing, placement, and promotion program. (See Figure 2.1.)

Objectives and Goals

Behaviors promoted to diagnose and control high blood pressure include these six target behaviors, representing the organization's product line:[7]

1. Have your blood pressure checked. A desired level for most adults is around 120/80-mm Hg.

2. If you have high blood pressure, follow recommended lifestyle and medication plans, including the following:

   – Lose weight if you are overweight.

   – Be physically active.

   – Choose foods low in salt and sodium.

   – Limit your alcohol intake.

   – Take prescribed high blood pressure medication.

Again, following segmentation principles and strategies to influence each of the high-risk market segments will reflect the unique characteristics of the segment and will also position the desired behavior as being more appealing than the current behavior.

Figure 2.1. National High Blood Pressure Education Program (NHBPEP) Brochure Cover

Understanding Target Markets and the Competition

About 50 million Americans, one in four adults, have high blood pressure and less than 30% are controlling their condition.[8] Common perceived barriers and costs of desired behaviors to be addressed in strategy development include the following:

▶ It is hard for me to change my diet and to find the time to exercise.

▶ My blood pressure is difficult to control.

▶ My blood pressure varies so much, it's probably not accurate.

▶ Medications can have undesirable side effects.

▶ It's too expensive to go to the doctor just to get my blood pressure checked.

▶ It may be the result of living a full and active life. Not everybody dies from it.

An analysis of each high-risk segment would explore perceived benefits of current behaviors (e.g., real ice cream and a thick steak are some of life's great pleasures) and perceived benefits of desired behaviors (e.g., I can watch my grandchildren grow up).[9] By exploring these perceptions, the social marketer can formulate more effective communications to address the real values and concerns of the target audience.

Strategies

Products:

NHBPEP programs are designed to promote the six behaviors mentioned earlier in this case descrip-tion, along with others relevant to their program mission.

In the social marketing model, we have identified these behaviors as our products. Some social marketing pro-grams may include promoting services and tangible ob-jects, illustrated in this case by the promotion of home monitoring instruments. Program managers and plan-ners distinguish between the product (in this case, the six desired behaviors) and the product's positioning (the benefits satisfied if the target customer adopts the target behavior). Positioning strategies are developed to then persuade target segments that these benefits are equal to or greater than the benefits of their current behavior.

Price:

Program materials address common concerns with messages that reflect an understanding of the per-ceived costs of adopting the desired behavior (entry costs) and of abandoning the current one (exit costs).[10]

▶ "You don't have to make all of the changes immediately. The key is to focus on one or two at a time. Once they become part of your normal routine, you can go on to the next change. Sometimes, one change leads naturally to another. For example, increasing physical activity will help you lose weight."[11]

▶ "You can keep track of your blood pressure outside of your doctor's office by taking it at home."[12]

▶ "You don't have to run marathons to benefit from physical activity. Any activity, if done at least 30 minutes a day over the course of most days, can help."[13]

Place:

Places are chosen to make it easy for people to monitor their blood pressure, such as health clinics, community health centers, doctors' offices, malls, and even in homes.

Promotion:

Key messages focus on increasing awareness and understanding of the importance of knowing your blood pressure and the benefits of following recommended lifestyle changes. *Media channels* have included the following:

- ▶ Facts sheets, pamphlets, and brochures with recommendations for managing high blood pressure that are available from health care providers, by mail, and over the Internet

- ▶ Professional educational materials that provide guidelines for clinicians

- ▶ Web sites that include healthy diet and recipe information and tips on how to achieve a healthy weight

- ▶ A toll-free number that provides recorded information about high blood pressure prevention and control

- ▶ Special materials that are prepared for higher-risk populations:

  - – Women's informational guides on how to lower blood pressure

  - – Special booklets for Latinos and African Americans

- ▶ Mass media that include print advertisements, radio, and posters

- ▶ Special events that are organized, including the annual "May is High Blood Pressure Education Month"

Evaluation

"Mean blood pressures compared in four national health surveys conducted between 1960 and 1991 suggest a reduction of 10-mm Hg systolic pressure and 5-mm Hg diastolic pressure during this time period. These remarkable decreases indicate that the United States population has heard and acted on NHBPEP messages. More importantly, this significant reduction in mean blood pressures has led to a significant reduction of death rates from heart disease and stroke."[14]

"In January 2000, the Department of Health and Human Services launched Healthy People 2010, a national health promotion and disease prevention initiative that brings together national, state, and local government agencies; nonprofit, voluntary, and professional organizations; businesses; communities; and individuals to improve the health of all Americans, eliminate disparities in health, and improve in years and quality of healthy life. The NHBPEP has adopted the Healthy People 2010 goals that address reductions in hypertension-related mortality rates."[15]

CHAPTER OVERVIEW

Strategic planning involves answering four major questions:

- Where are we?

- Where do we want to go?

- How will we get there?

- How will we keep on track?

This chapter follows this broad planning perspective and presents eight steps in the marketing planning process. Each step is described briefly in this chapter, and Chapters 5 through16 provide more detailed explanations and examples. Worksheets following this outline are provided in the Appendix.

WHAT ARE THE STEPS IN THE SOCIAL MARKETING PLANNING PROCESS?

Table 2.1 presents a recommended outline for developing a social marketing plan. It groups each of the eight steps according to the broader strategic plan components.

Where Are We?

Step 1: Analyze the Social Marketing Environment

In this first step, relevant information is compiled to help determine target markets, objectives, goals, and strategies. (See Box 2.1.) The case illustrated in Boxes 2.1 to 2.5 reflects, in part, a program developed and implemented by Seattle Public Utilities. It illustrates each of the steps in the planning process.

TABLE 2.1 Social Marketing Plan Outline

WHERE ARE WE?

  The Social Marketing Environment

  Step 1:   Determine program focus

                Identify campaign purpose

                Conduct an analysis of Strengths, Weaknesses, Opportunities, and Threats (SWOT)

                Review past and similar efforts

WHERE DO WE WANT TO GO?

  Target Audiences, Objectives, and Goals

  Step 2:   Select target audiences

  Step 3:   Set objectives and goals

  Step 4:   Analyze target audiences and the competition

HOW WILL WE GET THERE?

  Social Marketing Strategies

  Step 5:   Product: Design the market offering

                Price: Manage costs of behavior change

                Place: Make the product available

                Promotion: Create messages
                               Choose media (communication) channels

HOW WILL WE STAY ON COURSE?

  Social Marketing Program Management

  Step 6:   Develop a plan for evaluation and monitoring

  Step 7:   Establish budgets and find funding sources

  Step 8:   Complete an implementation plan

BOX 2.1
Choosing a Focus and Analyzing the Environment

Identify potential approaches to address the issue at hand.

A variety of issues may be contributing to an area of social concern. The first phase of Step 1 is to identify and explore each of these.

The program manager of a local utility responsible for supporting community efforts for salmon recovery identifies, reviews, and considers numerous issues contributing to salmon decline in the region, including water supply, water quality, and habitat protection. It is noted that a variety of behaviors contribute to the decline in salmon, including commercial and sports fishing, land use, dams, urban landscaping, and residential gardening.

Develop program focus and campaign purpose for this plan.

An area of focus and a statement of purpose (impact) of a successful campaign are identified at this point. Campaign purpose reflects the benefit of a successful campaign. (Campaign objectives will focus on specific behaviors and will be developed in Step 4.)

Given the primary residential customer base of the utility, the focus of this campaign is narrowed to residential gardening practices that will help protect salmon habitats, now the campaign's focus and purpose. (See Figure 2.2.)

Figure 2.2. Salmon Friendly Gardening Logo

Conduct a SWOT analysis.

Internal strengths and weaknesses and external opportunities and threats relative to the chosen focus are explored and noted at this phase.

Marketing strategies will be developed to:

- Maximize several strengths (e.g., resources available for salmon recovery programs)

- Minimize known weaknesses (e.g., prior surveys indicating that gardeners not living on or near the water may have a hard time believing that their practices matter)

- Capture external opportunities (e.g., recent listing of Chinook salmon under the Endangered Species Act)

- Help prepare for potential threats (e.g., increased strong values and cultural norms for green lawns and traditional plants)

The SWOT analysis will include identifying major potential internal and external groups that can affect the success or failure of this effort.

The landscape industry has a key influence on residential garden designs, particularly those specializing in waterfront property and new housing developments. (See Figure 2.3.) Their support and opinions will need to be included in planning efforts and strategies.

(Continued)

BOX 2.1
(Continued)

A review of current and past efforts is included in the analysis of the environment.

We want to take advantage of lessons others have learned as well as consider using strategies and materials that have already been developed.

Prior campaigns used by this utility to promote safer gardening practices are reviewed. What worked? What didn't? What messages and materials, if any, can be "reused"? Several neighboring states have had similar issues with salmon recovery and will be contacted to learn from their successes and failures.

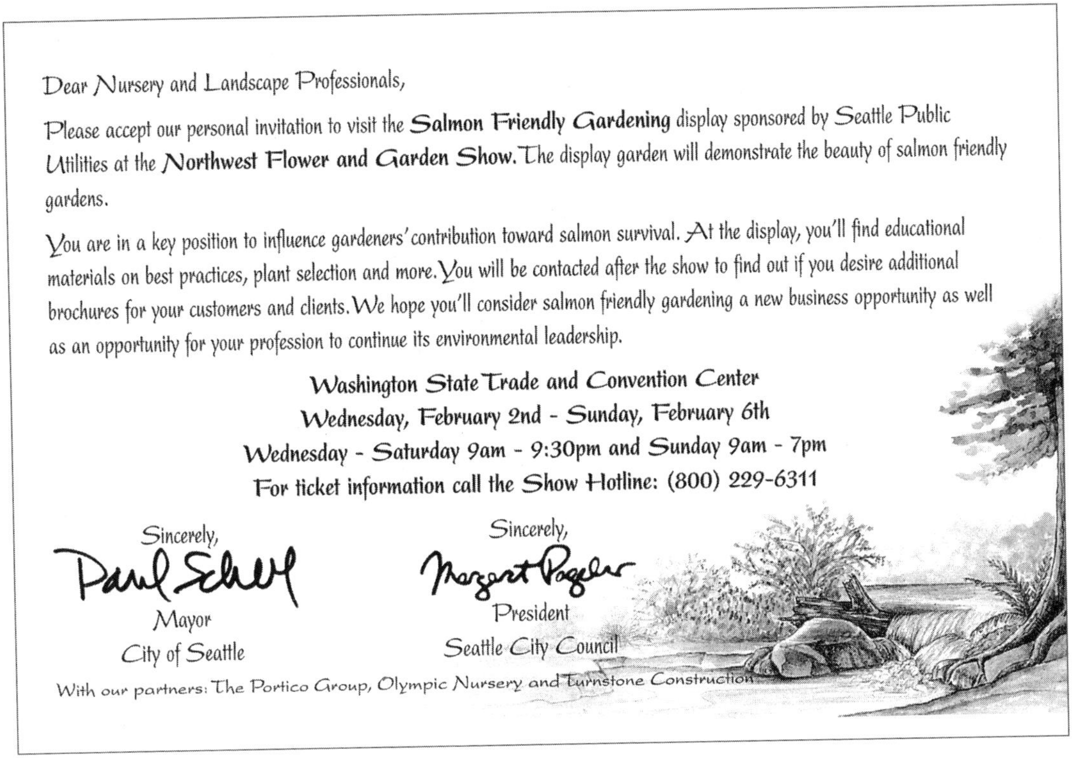

Dear Nursery and Landscape Professionals,

Please accept our personal invitation to visit the **Salmon Friendly Gardening** display sponsored by Seattle Public Utilities at the **Northwest Flower and Garden Show.** The display garden will demonstrate the beauty of salmon friendly gardens.

You are in a key position to influence gardeners' contribution toward salmon survival. At the display, you'll find educational materials on best practices, plant selection and more. You will be contacted after the show to find out if you desire additional brochures for your customers and clients. We hope you'll consider salmon friendly gardening a new business opportunity as well as an opportunity for your profession to continue its environmental leadership.

Washington State Trade and Convention Center
Wednesday, February 2nd - Sunday, February 6th
Wednesday - Saturday 9am - 9:30pm and Sunday 9am - 7pm
For ticket information call the Show Hotline: (800) 229-6311

Sincerely,

Paul Schell
Mayor
City of Seattle

Sincerely,

Margaret Pageler
President
Seattle City Council

With our partners: The Portico Group, Olympic Nursery and Turnstone Construction

Figure 2.3. Postcard to Landscape Architects

Where Do We Want to Go?

Step 2: Select Target Audiences

In this step, the "bull's-eye" for our marketing efforts is selected. (See Box 2.2.) It begins with segmenting the market and ends with choosing one or more targets.

BOX 2.2
Segmenting the Market and Selecting a Target

Segment the market into similar groups using one or more variables, such as demographics, geographics, psychographics, and behaviors.

Residential gardeners could be segmented on the basis of *demographics* (homeownership), *geographics* (proximity to water-fronts), *psychographics* (environmental ethics), and *behaviors* (membership in gardening clubs and readership of gardening periodicals).

Evaluate and choose one or more targets.

Further analysis may indicate that the market of greatest opportunity, based on *size, reachability, and readiness* for behavior change, are homeowners who are avid gardeners and care about the environment. In addition, master gardeners and professionals in landscape and nursery businesses are also selected as markets for focus and attention.

Step 3: Set Objectives and Goals

In this step, we decide what we want our target audience to do (objectives) and what they may need to know and believe to make the behavior change more likely. This is also the point in the planning process at which we establish quantifiable measures (goals), relative to our objective. (See Box 2.3.)

Step 4: Understanding the Target Audiences and the Competition

This important and often-skipped step explores *current knowledge, beliefs, and behaviors* of target audiences relative to objectives and goals established in Step 3. (See Box 2.4.) It is also the phase in which *competition, perceived benefits,* and *barriers to action* are identified and understood.[16]

How Will We Get There?

Step 5: Determine Strategies—The 4Ps

At this phase, the marketing mix is determined: a blend of strategies (4Ps) that will be integrated to appeal to the market. (See Box 2.5.)

BOX 2.3
Setting Objectives and Goals

Objectives are focused on what we want our target audience to do.	Strategies will be developed to influence residential gardeners to adopt six key behaviors:

1. Build healthy soil with compost.

2. Choose the right plant for the right place.

3. Use water wisely.

4. Use natural fertilizers and pest controls.

5. Direct rainwater appropriately.

6. Protect shoreline habitats.

We may also need to address what we want them to know and believe.	Campaign materials will emphasize these issues:

- The real threat to salmon extinction

- How gardening affects salmon

- How Salmon Friendly Gardens can be beautiful, healthy, and easy to maintain

Goals are specific and realistic. They will be used to evaluate campaign efforts and will therefore also need to be as measurable as possible.	Several quantifiable goals could be considered:

- Increase in sales of native plants in local nurseries

- Increase in sales of natural fertilizers and pesticides

- Reported increase of native plants in landscape designs developed by targeted professional groups

---

How Will We Stay on Course?

Step 6: Develop Evaluation and Monitoring Strategy

Two major components of evaluation are presented in Chapter 14: What will be measured, and how will it be measured? As noted earlier, objectives and goals established in Step 3 will be the foundation for this planning component.

Step 7: Establish Budgets and Find Funding Sources

On the basis of draft product benefits and features, price incentives, distribution channels, and proposed promotions, funding requirements will be summarized and compared with available and potential funding sources. Outcomes at this step may necessitate revisions of strategies, target audiences, and goals, or the need to secure additional funding sources.

BOX 2.4
Understanding the Target Audience

Relative to the objectives developed in Step 3, what does the target audience know?

Answers to several questions will help guide strategies by revealing current knowledge, beliefs, and behaviors of our target audience:

- Do gardeners know native plants?

- Do they know where to find them?

- Do they know where to plant them and how?

What do they believe?

- Do they believe their gardening habits can affect salmon habitats?

What is their current behavior?

- Do they currently buy native plants? Why? Why not?

- What are current levels of sales of natural fertilizers and pesticides relative to other forms?

What are we competing with?

- What types of plants do nurseries recommend and carry?

- What plants do our target markets currently like and buy the most? Why?

What barriers do they perceive?

- What concerns do gardeners have about planting native plants instead of what they normally put in that area of the garden? (See Figure 2.4.)

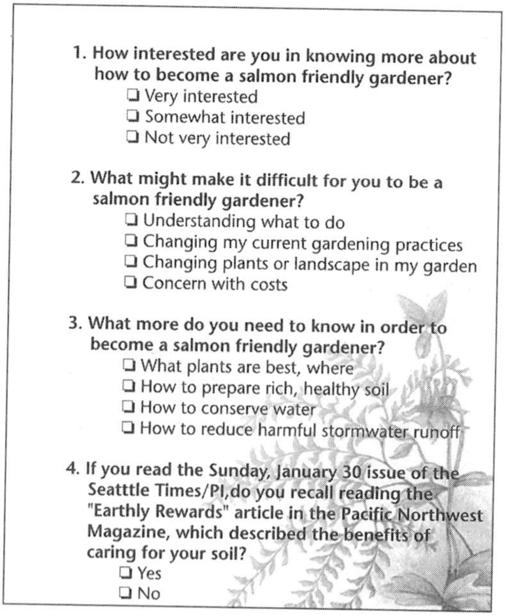

Figure 2.4. Survey Form Distributed at Garden Show

1. **How interested are you in knowing more about how to become a salmon friendly gardener?**
   - ❑ Very interested
   - ❑ Somewhat interested
   - ❑ Not very interested

2. **What might make it difficult for you to be a salmon friendly gardener?**
   - ❑ Understanding what to do
   - ❑ Changing my current gardening practices
   - ❑ Changing plants or landscape in my garden
   - ❑ Concern with costs

3. **What more do you need to know in order to become a salmon friendly gardener?**
   - ❑ What plants are best, where
   - ❑ How to prepare rich, healthy soil
   - ❑ How to conserve water
   - ❑ How to reduce harmful stormwater runoff

4. **If you read the Sunday, January 30 issue of the Seatttle Times/PI, do you recall reading the "Earthly Rewards" article in the Pacific Northwest Magazine, which described the benefits of caring for your soil?**
   - ❑ Yes
   - ❑ No

BOX 2.5
Developing the Marketing Mix

Product:

Our product is what we are selling. In social marketing, it is identified as a desired behavior and the associated benefits of that behavior. Many successful social marketing campaigns also include promoting tangible objects and services that support or facilitate behavior change.

This campaign effort is selling Salmon Friendly Gardening, as described by the six key behaviors noted earlier. In addition, several tangible objects and services will be highlighted and promoted:

- Native plants
- Natural fertilizers and pesticides
- Organic compost
- Kitchen garbage composters
- Workshops on Salmon Friendly Gardening

Price:

Our first step in pricing strategy is to identify what the target audience will have to "give up" when they adopt this behavior. These insights are then used to determine what could be offered or said that will (a) decrease actual or perceived costs of the desired behavior and/or (b) increase actual or perceived benefits of the desired behavior. Implications are also reflected in product, place, and promotional strategies.

Strategies will need to address common perceptions of increased costs:

Money (higher prices for some natural compost, fertilizers, and pesticides)

Convenience (finding a nursery that has a wide selection of native plants versus buying annuals at the grocery store)

Time (hand weeding versus spraying with chemicals)

Effort (creating and maintaining a compost pile)

Pleasures (giving up tea roses that are not native to this area)

Price strategies to minimize costs and increase benefits could include components such as these:

- Coupons for organic composts and natural fertilizers
- Discount prices on native plants at sponsoring retail partners
- Recognition yard signs saying "I'm a Salmon Friendly Gardener"

Place:

This is where the target audience will perform the behavior, acquire any tangible objects, receive any services associated with the campaign, and learn more about performing the behavior. This is distinct from media channels in which promotional messages are delivered (e.g., outreach workers, billboards, mailings, radio, events, signage, brochures, posters, Web sites, etc.).

- Local nurseries
- Retail outlets carrying fertilizers and pesticides
- Exhibits and workshops on planting native plants at the annual flower and garden show

(Continued)

BOX 2.5 (Continued)

Promotion:

There are two components of promotional strategies:

1. Message: What will you say to influence your target audience to know, believe, and do what you have established in your objectives?

2. Media Channels: Where will your messages appear?

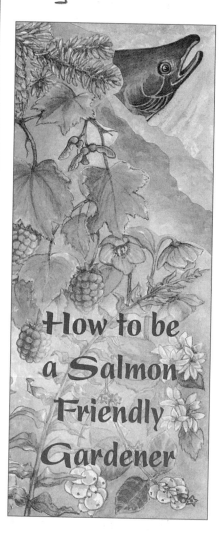

Key messages will address audience benefits and concerns, such as "Beautiful gardens can be salmon friendly and salmon friendly gardens can be beautiful."

Media channels consistent with identified target audiences and messages could include these:

- Brochures with detailed descriptions of key behaviors, listings of native plants, and directions for planting available at retail stores, community centers, and through gardening clubs (See Figure 2.5.)

- Exhibit at Annual Flower and Garden Show

- Newspaper story

- Articles in professional association newsletters

- Fact sheets for landscape industry professionals

- Postcard invitation to garden show sent to landscape architects and presidents of gardening clubs

- Documentary on public television

Figure 2.5. Brochure Cover

Step 8: Complete an Implementation Plan

The final step in the planning process is to develop an implementation plan that will provide detailed information on "who will do what, when, and for how much."

WHY IS A SYSTEMATIC PLANNING PROCESS IMPORTANT?

Only through the systematic process of *analyzing the marketplace* are we able to select an *appropriate target audience* for our efforts. Only through taking the time to *know our target audience* are we able to establish realistic *goals and objectives*. Only through developing an *integrated strategy* will we create real behavior change, a strategy that recognizes that our audience will be influenced by communications (promotion) as well as by perceived benefits (product), perceived costs (price), and perceived ease of access (place). Only by taking time up front to establish how we will *measure our performance* will we ensure that this critical step is taken to contribute to future successes.

The temptation, and often the practice, is to go straight to advertising or promotional ideas and strategies. We ask questions such as these:

- How can we know whether ads on the sides of buses (a media channel) are a good idea if we don't know how long the key message is?

- How can we know our slogan (message) if we don't know what we are selling (product)?

- How can we know how to position our product if we don't know what our audience perceives as the benefits and costs of their current behavior compared with the behavior we are promoting?

Although planning is sequential, the planner needs to be flexible, recognizing that there may be a good reason to go back and adjust a prior step before completing the plan. For example:

- Research at Step 4 may reveal that goals are too ambitious or that one of the target markets needs to be dropped.

- Ideal media determined in Step 5 might turn out to be cost prohibitive or not cost-effective when more carefully examined in Step 7 (Budgets).

The planning process is therefore more accurately described as spiral rather than linear.

WHERE DOES MARKETING RESEARCH
FIT INTO THE PLANNING PROCESS?

Properly focused marketing research can make the difference between a brilliant plan and a mediocre one and is at the core of success at every phase of this planning process. Each step has potential for the use of a variety of research methodologies and is discussed in Chapter 4. Chapters 4 through 15 also provide research cases illustrating these potential applications.

CHAPTER SUMMARY

1. There are eight steps included in developing a marketing plan that are emphasized throughout this text. They fit into these broader strategic planning phases: (a) Where are we? (b) Where do we want to go? (c) How will we get there? and (d) How will we keep on track?

2. A systematic planning process is recommended; we must resist the temptation to develop strategies and tactics prior to doing our homework.

3. At the same time, a spiral process is acknowledged, allowing for adjustments to the draft plan when investigations in subsequent steps reveal reasons to alter a prior step.

4. Finally, a strong case can be made for the use of marketing research throughout this planning process: analyzing the environment, selecting target markets, establishing goals and objectives, understanding audience perspectives, developing winning strategies, and measuring results.

KEY TERMS AND CONCEPTS

Strategic planning model
Eight planning steps
A systematic process
A spiral process
Use of marketing research

ISSUES FOR DISCUSSION

1. In the opening case on high blood pressure, what other additional promotional strategies would you consider?

2. In the Salmon Friendly Gardening example, what additional pricing incentives would you consider?

3. What is another example of an instance when you may need to go back and adjust a draft step in the planning process?

Notes

1. W. Smith, Social Marketing Listserve (personal communication, January 2001). Reprinted with permission.
2. Kotler, P., & Roberto, E. L. (1989). *Social Marketing: Strategies for Changing Public Behavior,* (p. 10). New York: Free Press.
3. National Heart, Lung, and Blood Institute. (2001). As cited in National High Blood Pressure Education Program (NHBPEP) Web site, Program Description. Retrieved 1/16/01 from http://whi.nih.gov/about/nhbpep/nhbp_pd.htm
4. Ibid.
5. National Institutes of Health (NIH). (2001). As cited in National Institutes of Health Web site. Retrieved 1/19/01 from http://www.nih.gov/health/hbp-tifl/2.htm
6. NIH. (2001). As cited in NIHBPEP Web site. Retrieved 1/19/01 from http://www.nih.gov/health/hbp-tifl/4.htm
7. National Institutes of Health. National Heart, Lung, and Blood Institute (2001). As cited in NIH Web site. Retrieved 1/19/01 from http://www.nih.gov/health/hbp-tifl/3.htm
8. NHBPEP. (2001). As cited in National Heart, Lung, and Blood Institutes. Web site. Retrieved 9/18/01 from http://hin.nhlbi.nih.gov/nhbpep_kit/about_m.htm
9. Andreasen, A. R. (1995). *Marketing Social Change: Changing Behavior to Promote Health, Social Development, and the Environment* (pp. 223-250). San Francisco: Jossey-Bass; McKenzie-Mohr, D., & Smith, W. (1999). *Fostering Sustainable Behavior* (pp. 1-45). Gabriola Island, British Columbia, Canada: New Society.
10. Michael E. Porter. (1998). *Competitive Advantage: Creating and Sustaining Superior Performance.* New York: Free Press.
11. National Institutes of Health. National Heart, Lung, and Blood Institute. (2001). Retrieved 1/19/01 from http://www.nih.gov/health/hbp-tifl/3.htm
12. Ibid.
13. Ibid.
14. National Heart, Lung, and Blood Institute. (2001). As cited in NHBPEP Web site. Program Description. Retrieved 1/16/01 from http://whi.nih.gov/about/nhbpep/nhbp_pd.htm
15. Ibid.
16. Andreasen, A. R. (1995). *Marketing Social Change: Changing Behavior to Promote Health, Social Development, and the Environment* (pp. 223-50). San Francisco: Jossey-Bass; McKenzie-Mohr, D., & Smith, W. (1999). *Fostering Sustainable Behavior* (p. 1-45). Gabriola Island, British Columbia, Canada: New Society.

KEY CHAPTER QUESTIONS

1. What is a successful campaign and what are criteria for determining success?

2. What are key elements of successful campaigns?

3. How can the campaign sustain behavior into the future?

4. How can the campaign leave a legacy?

CHAPTER 3
Discovering
Keys to Success

Many Americans know, all too well, what is wrong with health care. Ask the single mother who waits half a day in a crowded clinic for a 5-minute visit with a harried physician, or the unemployed worker who has been downsized out of his job and his health insurance. Their experience tells a devastating tale about our system's shortcomings.

But there is another, equally important story that concerns the problems we don't see anymore—at least not in the numbers of the past: young victims of polio, mumps, and measles; preschoolers with neurological problems caused by lead poisoning; people in the prime of life dying prematurely from tuberculosis and influenza; hordes of patients with rotting teeth. While we need to address persistent inequities, we also need to understand the basis of victories in public health—not just to keep up our hopes, but to learn how research, advocacy, public discussion, and policy fit together in successful campaigns for change.

—Stephen L. Isaacs and Steven A. Schroeder[1]

MARKETING HIGHLIGHT: TOBACCO PREVENTION

"Truth," an award-winning youth tobacco prevention campaign, was sponsored by the American Legacy Foundation, an independent organization created with tobacco settlement dollars. The following case includes excerpts from an article written by Jeffrey Hicks in early 2001 for *Tobacco Control* and tells the story of the campaign's regional launch in Florida prior to going national in January of 2000.

The Truth

Jeffrey J. Hicks, President
Crispin, Porter & Bogusky
Miami, Florida

This past summer Florida's Department of Health released the findings of its annual state-wide survey on youth tobacco use. The study found that since 1998 the percentage of youth using tobacco in the past 30 days had declined by 7.4 percentage points (from 18.5% to 11.1%) in middle school and by 4.8 percentage points (from 27.4% to 22.6%) in high school.[2]

Importantly,[3] the Florida declines occurred at a time when national levels of youth tobacco use remained mostly stable.[4] The Department of Health's recent study also found that across ages, demographics, and regions, youth who reported viewing six or more of the state's "truth" messages over the last 30 days were half as likely to have used tobacco as those who did not report seeing any "truth" ads.[5]

It is estimated[6] that the 30-month program has resulted in 49,000 fewer Florida smokers and the prevention of more than 16,000 tobacco related deaths in the future. The long-term health related savings are estimated to be in excess of a billion dollars.

"Truth," the unconventional counter-marketing effort which helped bring about these results, had its origin in the 1997 settlement between the tobacco industry and the State of Florida. Understanding the importance of prevention, the legislature and the late Governor, Lawton Chiles, earmarked a portion of the settlement for the creation of a dedicated anti-tobacco counter-marketing effort with the sole focus of reducing youth [smoking] prevalence. . . .

Real Money

Florida's settlement with big tobacco totaled $11.3 billion dollars and included provisions for the funding of a two year $200 million dollar youth anti-tobacco education and marketing effort. With the launch of "truth" in early 1998, Florida became the first state to use substantial settlement dollars in tobacco control. . . .

Unlike many anti-tobacco efforts of the past, due to its funding level, the Florida program had the benefit of all the tools of modern marketing. Advertisements were produced with some of the hottest commercial directors in the industry, Web sites were created using the newest types of animation, research was conducted by companies that had perfected their craft while working on some of the largest teen targeted private sector brands in the country. . . .

Rather than run for free at midnight or in programming with little teen viewership, "truth" aired on MTV, the Superbowl and in those programs that youth most wanted to see. . . . (See Figure 3.1.)

Figure 3.1. TV Spot

Youth Involvement

From the very beginning, youth have driven "truth." Two months after being hired, we convened a 500-person youth summit to gain insight into where youth felt the effort should head. Through annual summits and the creation of a youth review board, youth became our clients. They told us what they did and did not like and provided feedback to help guide the creative process.

Importantly, we looked to youth for inspiration and guidance, but

Figure 3.2. Truth Truck

did not rely on the youth to actually create the advertising. If Truth was to be inspirational, relevant and cool it had to be more than a poster contest. . . .

Youth Marketing vs. Program Marketing[7]

As we had done in other youth categories, our research was conducted qualitatively with young adult interviewers in places, such as malls and skate parks, where youth felt comfortable. Interviewers used bad language and without really trying, were seen as peers. Trust was built in the information gathering stage that went well beyond any interaction in a focus group. Trust led to real answers. . . .

With other youth brands as a starting point we assembled the media plan for "truth" that went beyond just television. The launch of the campaign included the publication of a proprietary "truth" tabloid style magazine which would be distributed in record stores and surf shops, a 10 city PR tour called the "truth train" and the production of a "truth truck" which became a fixture statewide at concerts, beaches and raves. (See Figure 3.2.)

Tone

Early on in our research we learned two important lessons about the overall tone that we needed to employ for "truth."

Despite the fact that 1,200 people die every day from tobacco related illnesses in the USA, youth did not see tobacco as a big deal. Their lives are filled with weighty decisions and influences—the implications of divorce, drugs, unwanted pregnancies and school shootings. . . .

While youth had varying points of view, there was incredible consensus around their distaste for social marketing and anti-tobacco efforts that pass judgment on tobacco users. Across the board, youth told us that they did not want to be told what to do. They wanted "the facts" and then to be left to make their own educated decisions. If we were to be successful, "truth" could not preach. "Truth" needed a message other than "don't."

The Anti-manipulation Strategy

After months of research and hundreds of interviews with youth we had a strategic breakthrough. We discovered some basic things about youth and tobacco that seem pretty obvious in hindsight.

First, we learned that there was 100% awareness that tobacco killed. Schools and health educators had done a great job of explaining the dangers of tobacco. Knowledge was not the problem. . . .

We learned that a youth's reason for using tobacco had everything to do with emotion and nothing to do with rational decision making. Tobacco was a significant, visible and readily available way for youth to signal that they were in control. Like piercing an ear or dying hair, using tobacco was a tool of rebellion and all about sending a signal to the world that the users made decisions for themselves. . . .

If we were to turn the tables on tobacco we surmised that we couldn't take away their tool of rebellion without giving them an alternative. Attacking the duplicity and manipulation of the profits before principles tobacco industry became "truth's" rebellion.

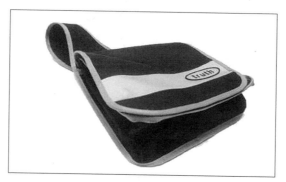

Figure 3.3. Tote Bag

the world. If we wanted youth to really embrace our anti-tobacco effort, it made sense that we should deliver it just like Adidas, Fubu or Abercrombie—in a branded form they understood. . . . (See Figure 3.3.)

Focus

The temptation when we started "truth" was to make the effort broad enough to encompass all ages and use the funding to tackle social issues beyond tobacco. As much as anything, "truth's" success in Florida has been defined by the ability of the Department of Health and all involved to focus on the one problem of youth tobacco use. Every initiative and line item of the budget has been scrutinized based solely on its impact on reducing youth tobacco prevalence.

These seven principles underpin the Florida "truth" anti-tobacco media campaign and, we believe, were critical to its success. Commencing 2001, the American Legacy Foundation has expanded and extended the "truth" campaign on a national basis, with funding from the Master Settlement Agreement.

Making *Truth* a Brand

Through our work in other youth categories we knew the important role brands played with youth. In a search to define one's identity, brands (like piercings, haircuts and even tobacco use) serve as a shorthand way for youth to identify themselves to

SOURCE: Hicks, Jeffrey J. (2001). "The Strategy Behind Florida's 'Truth' Campaign." *Tobacco Control, 10,* 1-2. Reprinted with permission.

CHAPTER OVERVIEW

Based on the decrease in numbers of youth smoking, many would declare the "Truth" campaign a huge success. But is this our only measure of success? What if the number had not gone down but analysis revealed that teens were smoking fewer cigarettes a day or that 90% of youth were able to identify the campaign message? What if subsequent research revealed that those who quit smoking had relapsed? Would it still be a success?

In this chapter, we examine how we define success. How do we know we've done a good job? Does the social problem need to be eradicated? Does everyone in the target audience need to "behave"? Is it enough for people to recall the campaign message? Do award-winning ads signal a victory?

WHAT IS A SUCCESSFUL CAMPAIGN?

The most credible and reliable *indicator of success* will be in our results. Did we meet or exceed campaign objectives and goals? Did the number of youth who started smoking each day decrease by our desired goal of 20% over a period of 2 years? Did we observe our goal of 50% of toddlers wearing life vests on the beach? Did we reach 25% of high school boys and girls with our intended assault prevention message that date rape is a felony? Can at least 40% of the target audience tell us the recommended level of moderate physical activity for adults, versus 25% prior to the campaign? Did litter on the roadways decrease by 2 million tons? Did 75% of registered voters vote?

Chapter 7 in this text presents options for establishing campaign objectives and goals that are specific, measurable, and realistic, as well as meaningful for the target audience, the sponsoring organization(s) and key constituent groups. Chapter 14 discusses evaluation measures and techniques and will restate the importance of establishing campaign objectives and goals, early in the planning process, which can be measured and will be agreed-upon signs of success.

WHAT ARE THE KEY ELEMENTS OF SUCCESSFUL CAMPAIGNS?

Campaigns presented in this chapter have been chosen to illustrate how each step in the planning process can contribute to the success of the campaign. They are presented in a sequence similar to our planning outline, illustrating the benefits of a thorough situation analysis, choosing the right target audiences, establishing realistic and meaningful goals and objectives, and using all elements of the marketing mix in an integrated fashion. The emphasis here is that each step in the planning process is important and can make or break success. However, this is not an analysis and presentation of the relative importance or cumulative effect of each step.

It should be noted that each of these campaigns used marketing research in the planning and evaluation process, reflecting a fundamental and steadfast dedication to understanding and satisfying the needs and perspectives of desired customers.

Each of the 12 elements and many of the examples presented in this chapter are expanded on in subsequent chapters. This will provide a consolidated overview of the range and nature of social marketing success.

■ Element #1: Take Advantage of What Is Known and Has Been Done Before

Reviewing past and similar campaign efforts is an important component of conducting a situation analysis and is one of the best investments of a planner's efforts. Benefits can be substantial, including learning from the successes and failures of others, having access to existing detailed information on market segmentation and ideal targets, finding innovative and cost-effective strategies, and discovering ideas and materials for creative executions.

The following example illustrates the financial benefits of spending time up front to see which existing research and campaigns might be helpful.

Sexual Assault Prevention

In the winter of 1998, the Washington State Office of Crime Victim Advocacy (OCVA) retained DeLaunay Phillips Communications to develop a statewide campaign to reduce the incidence of sexual assault among teenagers in the state. Campaign planning began with an audit of existing secondary research, a literature search, an inventory of existing materials being used in the state, and identification of similar campaigns in other states.

A nationwide literature search and review of state incidence reports provided useful data on the nature, incidence, causes, and trends in sexual assault. Existing national research studies revealed commonly held perceptions and misconceptions among teens regarding sexual assault. Reliable survey instruments were identified that could be used for measuring attitude and experiences relative to sexual assault and violence. Potential target markets and strategies began to emerge, and contacts with peers in other states located several campaign plans and media elements, including school curricula, posters, radio ads, and PSAs (public service announcements) worth considering.

Prior survey instruments were used to establish baseline measures, and several existing campaigns were then tested in focus groups with teens, assessing their potential for reaching campaign objectives and goals. One campaign from another state tested positively with all groups and was then revised to reflect local target audience perceptions and recommendations.

It is estimated that more than $30,000 was saved by using existing creative concepts. These budgeted dollars were then used to buy 2 additional weeks of radio spots on teen-oriented stations and 10,000 more posters to be distributed to classrooms around the state. In addition to this monetary impact, campaign planners cite significant savings in time and indirect costs that would have been incurred while conducting primary research and fully developing new creative concepts, slogans, and graphics.[8] (See Chapter 12 for more detail on this case.)

■ Element #2: Start With Target Markets That Are (Most) Ready for Action

Many causes and social change campaigns fail because the target market does not perceive problems, wants, or needs.[9] Campaigns increase chances of success (actual behavior change) when they start with market segments *most ready for action,* those which have one or more of the following ideal characteristics:

- A want or need the proposed behavior will satisfy or a problem it will solve (e.g., recent heart attack victims)

- The knowledge (information) regarding the benefits of the behavior and the costs of current or alternative behaviors (e.g., recent publicity on tougher drinking and driving laws)

- The belief that they can actually perform the behavior and that they will experience important benefits (e.g., exercising five times a week, 30 minutes at a time can improve sleep)

- Engagement in the desired behavior, but not on a regular basis, and the perception of some initial benefit (e.g., trying to quit smoking)

The following example illustrates the increased marketing and operational efficiencies this organization achieves by focusing on a very attractive segment.

Blood Donations_____

The Puget Sound Blood Center defines marketing as *relationship building* and places the highest value on the *repeat donor segment,* for good reasons. Their experience shows that it costs 10 times as much to acquire a new donor as it does to keep an established one. They know that if they can persuade just 10% of all donors to give blood just one more time each year, they will reach their annual donation goals, increase operational efficiencies, and reduce expenditures. They have identified clear benefits of targeting current donors: They are the most likely future donors, they have a lower reaction risk, they have a higher blood-usability rate, collection is more efficient, and they are the most credible recruiters of new donors.

Marketing tactics to increase repeat donations are aggressive and persuasive. Efforts are focused on making the first experience a pleasant one. Volunteers are the first and last persons a donor sees, and their sincerity is clear. After giving blood and sitting with a cup of juice and a cookie, donors are asked by volunteers whether they want to set up the next appointment, usually 2 months later. A reminder call or e-mail is placed the week prior to the next appointment.

First-time donors are mailed a donor card along with a message of thanks. (See Figure 3.4.). After 56 days, they are called by a telerecruiting team, who know from the information on computer screens that their previous donations were their first with the Blood Center and recognize the donors for that.

The only lifesaving technique that involves eating a cookie.

Figure 3.4. Postcard Used to Thank and Remind Donors

In the year 2000, this center attracted 206,000 people to give blood, and 88% of those were repeat donors. Over time, 50% of first-time donors, on average, have become repeat donors, implying a 50% customer retention rate.[10]

Element #3: Promote a Single, Doable Behavior, Explained in Simple, Clear Terms

In a world of information and advertising clutter, we often have only a few moments to speak with our audience. A simple, clear, action-oriented message is most likely to support our target market to adopt, reject, modify, or abandon a specific behavior. Our message should help the target audience know exactly what to do and whether they have done it. A simple slogan supports target audiences of the following well-known national campaign in knowing and remembering a strong recommendation for a longer and healthier life.

Nutrition

The National Cancer Institute (NCI) in cooperation with the Produce for Better Health Foundation have created "5 A Day for Better Health," a national program that approaches Americans with a simple, positive message: "Eat five or more servings of vegetables and fruit daily for better health."

This key message has been repeated using a well-integrated strategy and a multitude of venues over the years: plastic produce bags, grocery bags, in-store signage and displays, produce packaging labels, supermarket tours, recipe cards, brochures, grocery store newspaper ads, magazine articles, news stories, the Internet, radio news inserts, television news inserts (cooking/recipe spots), radio PSAs, television PSAs, billboards, CD-ROMS in elementary schools, nutrition newsletters, patient nutrition education materials, pay stubs, school curricula, preschool programs, food assistance program materials, church bulletins and newsletters, posters, restaurant menus, Girl/Boy Scout badges, 4-H materials, food bank program materials, health fairs, county fairs, cookbooks, children's coloring books, and videotapes.

Figure 3.5. The 5 A Day Message Is Used Consistently in the Media

Before the inception of the 5 A Day program in 1991, a small proportion (8%) of the American public understood at least part of the 5 A Day message. (See Figure 3.5.) By 1997, among American adults 18 years of age and over, there were increases in *knowledge* of the 5 A Day program itself (from 2% to 18%) and of its *messages* (from 8% to 19%).[11]

◼ Element #4: Consider Incorporating and Promoting a Tangible Object or Service to Support the Target Behavior

Many successful campaigns allocate resources for promoting tangible objects and services that will help sell and sustain behavior change (e.g., natural fertilizers, condoms, low-energy lightbulbs, litterbags, trigger locks for guns, smoking cessation classes). They represent enhanced opportunities for branding campaign messages and measuring impact. Wiebe concluded from an analysis of more than four social change campaigns that "the more a campaign resembles a commercial product campaign, the more successful it is likely to be."[12] As an additional benefit, incorporating a tangible product may also lead to natural corporate sponsors, as illustrated in the following example.

Drowning Prevention

"Stay on Top of It," a drowning prevention campaign in Washington State developed by Children's Hospital and Regional Medical Center, was designed to decrease the number of drownings among children in the state by increasing the use of life vests. A social marketing approach provided the overall structure for the campaign with a focus on a clear, desired behavior: Wear a Life Vest. The first year's campaign encouraged parents with toddlers to put life vests on their children when on beaches, docks, boats, and around swimming pools. Subsequent years focused on older children.

A life vest manufacturer (Mustang Survival) became a corporate sponsor, providing funds for promotion, life vests for loan programs, and discount coupons for children's life vests. (See Figure 3.6.) Retail displays in a variety of locations promoted campaign messages and offered information on choosing the right life vest for your child.

Figure 3.6. Coupon Used to Promote Life Vest Use

Campaign evaluation included baseline, tracking, and postcampaign telephone surveys. Elements of the Stay on Top of It campaign were recalled by 50% of families surveyed. Among parents aware of the campaign, reported life vest use by children on docks, beaches, or at pools increased from 20% to 34% (a 70% increase), and ownership of vests increased from 69% to 80% (a 16% increase). The life vest manufacturer reported an increase over the prior season of more than 25% in children's life vest sales. (See Chapter 15 for more detail on this case.)[13]

■ Element #5: Understand and Address Perceived Benefits and Costs

Based on a clear understanding of audience values, successful social marketing campaign strategies, such as the case presented next, are designed to *increase perceived or actual benefits of the desired behavior* and *reduce perceived or actual barriers and costs.* Parallel efforts strive to *decrease perceived benefits* and *increase perceived costs of competing, alternative behaviors.*[14]

Breastfeeding: Loving Support Makes Breastfeeding Work _____

Carol A. Bryant, Ph.D.

The Women and Infant Children Program (WIC) was established in 1972 to provide economically disadvantaged women, infants, and young children with nutrition education, supplementary nutritious foods, and referrals to appropriate health and social services.[15] Since 1989, Congress has designated a portion of the WIC allocation for each state to be used specifically for the support and encouragement of breastfeeding. Despite this, breastfeeding rates among WIC participants lag behind those in more affluent segments of the population. In 1995, 59.7% of infants in the United States were breastfed in the hospital, and 21.6% were breastfed at 6-months postpartum, in contrast to only 46.6% and 12.7%, respectively, of infants enrolled in WIC.[16]

In September 1995, Best Start Social Marketing and the U.S. Department of Agriculture, Food, and Nutrition Service (FNS) initiated a cooperative agreement to develop the WIC National Breastfeeding Promotion Project. This social marketing project is a comprehensive national effort to promote breastfeeding among families enrolled in WIC or those eligible to participate in the program.

Qualitative and quantitative methods were used to collect data from WIC participants, their family members, WIC employees, and other health care providers. Results showed that infant-feeding decisions reflected a careful assessment of breastfeeding's benefits and costs relative to its competition, bottle-feeding. Breastfeeding was viewed as a way to realize families' goals to have healthy babies and enjoy a special time with their newborns. Compared with infant formula, breast milk was considered by most to provide optimal health benefits and a closer maternal-infant bond. For many women, the enjoyment they expected to experience and the special time they associated with breastfeeding were the most important benefits.

However, although most women were attracted to these benefits, many were deterred by the sacrifices they would have to make. They worried that breastfeeding would create many embarrassing moments in public situations or open them to criticism from friends or relatives who viewed the behavior in a sexual light. Some women worried that breastfeeding would conflict with work, school, or social life; and some women worried that members of their close social network would feel "left out" of the feeding experience and fail to bond with their babies. Other "costs" associated with breastfeeding were pain, changes in dietary and health practices, and anxiety about their ability to produce the required quality and quantity of breast milk. In addition to the unfavorable ratio between benefits and costs, women's infant-feeding decisions reflected their lack of self-confidence as potential breastfeeders and a lack of support from relatives, friends, and some health care providers.

Building on this understanding of consumer values, the marketing plan for the WIC National Breastfeeding Promotion Project was designed to reposition the behavior so product benefits clearly outweighed costs and breastfeeding was clearly distinguished from its competition. The product strategy emphasized the close, loving bond and special joy that breastfeeding mothers share with their babies. The health advantages of breastfeeding were used in some materials, but the product strategy emphasized the emotional benefits because these most clearly distinguish the product from bottle-feeding. The behavior was positioned as a way families could realize their dreams of establishing special relationships with their children. The campaign brand symbol, "Loving Support Makes Breastfeeding Work," and program materials emphasized the role the support network of family members, friends, and the general public play in a mother's ability to breastfeed. This strategy is a significant departure from more traditional public health approaches in which breastfeeding has been positioned as a medical choice rooted in health benefits. (See Figure 3.7.)

Pricing strategy was another central component of the marketing plan. A key tactic for realizing the pricing strategy was the 3-Step Counseling Training Program designed to teach health care providers to identify clients' perceptions of the costs of breastfeeding and help mothers develop ways to lower them. Public information and consumer education materials were used to influence the public's attitudes about breastfeeding and correct common misperceptions about its "price."

The Loving Support Program was launched during World Breastfeeding Week (August 1-7, 1997), with a national press conference in Washington, D.C. Program materials or activities have been implemented in all 50 states and many U.S. territories. Evaluation in one state that implemented the program comprehensively demonstrated that it had affected WIC employees' knowledge about breastfeeding and their self-efficacy as counselors and WIC participants' perceptions of the benefits and costs. Most important, the programs also increased breastfeeding initiation and duration rates. After program implementation, rates at the intervention sites (44.8% at hospital discharge and 30.8% at

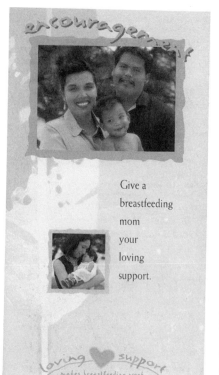

encouragement

Give a
breastfeeding
mom
your
loving
support.

loving ♥ support
makes breastfeeding work

Figure 3.7. Program Materials Emphasized the Role of the Support Network

4-months postpartum) were significantly higher than in control sites (30.9% at hospital discharge and 18.9% at 4-months postpartum).[17]

SOURCE: © 2001 by C. A. Bryant, University of South Florida. Reprinted by permission.

■ Element #6: Make Access Easy

In a society that places a premium on time, convenient access can be "a deal breaker." Successful campaigns provide target audiences *easy ways to sign up* (e.g., organ donation over the Internet), *convenient locations* to acquire tangible objects and perform the desired behavior (e.g., trigger locks available at major retail outlets and bloodmobiles at worksites), and *reasonable hours* for accessing services (e.g., recycling stations that are open evenings and weekends).

Efforts to make adoption easy were worth it to the utility featured in the following example.

Water Conservation

Seattle Public Utilities' Home Water Savers Program was designed to make things simple and extremely convenient for homeowners to conserve water.

During the summer of 1992, 300,000 showerheads were distributed door-to-door to about 90% of households in the utilities' service area. A package was left at each doorstep with a high-quality showerhead and easy-to-follow installation instructions.

Prior consumer research had tested several potential strategies to influence residents to do two things: (a) install this water-efficient model and (b) put their old showerheads in bags provided in the packages on their doorsteps, to be picked up within a few days. This was critical in order for program managers to know their installation rates. The messages from potential adopters were loud and clear: Make sure this showerhead is of high quality and make the process simple, easy, and convenient.

The simplicity and ease of participation of the program resulted in the highest rate of installation of water-efficient showerheads in the nation. The rate of installation was 65%, twice the expectation using national standards. And as an added benefit, approximately one third of residents who had installed their new showerheads reported in telephone surveys that they now took shorter showers and used less hot water for showering.[18] (See Figure 3.8.)

Figure 3.8. Promotional Materials Carried a Consistent Message.

■ Element #7: Develop Attention-Getting and Motivational Messages

Over the years, social researchers have concluded that a major success factor in mass communications to change public attitudes and behavior is the use of messages that are motivational, conveying benefits in an attention-getting and memorable way.[19]

An initial effort and message was so successful in the following campaign that other social issues in this state use a similar approach.

Seat Belt Usage

Those who live or travel in North Carolina have probably heard of the "Click It or Ticket" campaign in this state, which now has one of the highest percentages of seat belt use in the United States.

Governor Jim Hunt launched the program in 1993 to increase seat belt usage rates through persuasive campaign messages and stepped-up enforcement of this state's existing seat belt law. Public service ads were used to increase public awareness of the seriousness of the law and visibility of enforcement efforts. Nearly every law enforcement agency in the state participates in "Click It or Ticket," one of the most intensive law enforcement efforts of its kind. From 1993 to September 2001, more than 45,000 checkpoints and stepped-up patrols were held across the state. For those caught "with their belts down," a seat belt violation cost $25. Under North Carolina law, this fine goes to local schools.

Before "Click It or Ticket" began in 1993, only about 65% of North Carolinians buckled up. Those who didn't use seat belts cost North Carolina taxpayers millions of dollars in emergency services and health care. In 2000, seat belt use in North Carolina jumped as high as 84%, one of the highest rates in the nation. Fatal and serious highway injuries were cut by 14%. And as an added bonus, in 1994 and 1995, North Carolina auto insurers asked for a total of $33 million less than they would have had "Click It or Ticket" not been instituted, according to the North Carolina Department of Insurance.

North Carolina's "Click It or Ticket" was hailed as a "model for the nation" by the U.S. Transportation Secretary and, in fact, was the model for a southeast regional campaign conducted in May 2001. That eight-state effort was so successful that it was credited with increasing the national seat belt use rate to 73%, the highest rate ever.[20] (See Figure 3.9.)

In 1994, the year after "Click It or Ticket," North Carolina launched "Booze It & Lose It," which uses a similar approach to target impaired drivers. This campaign has been

Figure 3.9. North Carolina's Campaign Logo

replicated successfully by other states. Other North Carolina programs have adopted similar themes, such as the "Speed a Little, Lose a Lot" work zone safety campaign.[21]

■ Element #8: Use Appropriate Media and Watch for and Exploit Opportunities for Audience Participation

Successful campaigns use media vehicles and formats that effectively reach target adopters with spokespersons and sponsors to which adopters respond.[22]

The following example illustrates the impact that a small publicity stunt can have when a credible spokesperson is involved.

Energy Conservation

During an energy crisis on the United State's West Coast in the winter of 2001, a popular, well-respected radio talk show host was intrigued when he heard of a successful conservation effort in Israel in 1980. He then tried a similar strategy with his listening audience of several hundred thousand.

The campaign in Israel had taken place immediately after a popular television show dramatized Israel's overuse of electricity. The show's host asked the audience to leave the room and go around the house and turn off all extra lights. The viewers then saw the impact of their actions on their television screens, from a camera focused on the Israeli Electric Company's electricity consumption gauges. Within a few seconds, the gauges dropped sharply. The experiment that helped alter the belief that "my lights don't make a difference" saved an estimated 6% in aggregate electricity consumption during the 8 months of the campaign.[23]

Taking a similar approach, the American talk show host announced that he would try an experiment at 11:30 that morning and would be asking listeners to turn off and unplug anything electric that wasn't being used. He emphasized that he didn't want people to make any sacrifices. He just wanted them to turn off what they didn't need. At 11:28, the city's electric utility staff were standing by and read the current level of megawatts in use: "We're at 1,400 megawatts." At 11:30, the talk show host said "Go!" and for the next 5 minutes, he walked around the studios of the station with a handheld microphone and turned off conference room lights and unused computer monitors. He then called his daughter at home to make sure she was participating, all as an example for the listening audience.

At 11:35, the city utility public information officer came back on the air and reported impressive results. Usage had dropped by 40 megawatts, to 1,360. The decrease was enough to power 40,000 homes and represented $300,000 worth of electricity. The excitement over the success generated an hour-long program the next day on ways to conserve electricity (e.g., doing laundry in nonpeak hours and purchasing energy-saving appliances). The talk show host was presented a conservation award on air (an energy-saving lightbulb) by a member of the city council. For several weeks thereafter, local home and garden supply stores featured energy-saving appliances and lightbulbs.[24]

Element #9: Provide Response Mechanisms That Make It Easy and Convenient for Inspired Audiences to Act on Recommended Behaviors

The Pawtucket Heart Health Program (PHHP), in Rhode Island, has made extensive use of social marketing techniques to bring about significant reductions in cardiovascular disease risk factors, including blood pressure, cholesterol, smoking, obesity, and physical inactivity. Distinct strategies have been developed for key segments using a combination of marketing mix elements. Volunteers played an important role in the successful implementation of the project, and convenient response mechanisms have played an important role in volunteer recruitment.

Voluntary Involvement in Community Health Promotion

For the PHHP volunteer, involvement is key in meeting program goals, and several strategic elements are key in recruitment: (a) targeted strategies for specific types of volunteer positions designed to appeal to specific motives that are predictive of volunteering time, including desire for affiliation, power, and achievement; (b) detailed job descriptions that help match volunteers to ideal roles; and (c) systematic training, retention, and evaluation procedures.

In terms of tactical efforts to generate inquiry and response, PHHP uses a variety of vehicles to make response convenient. Volunteers In Action, the statewide voluntary action center, runs a column in Rhode Island's Sunday newspaper; this has been an effective way to reach interested citizens across the state. Stories in local newspapers and posters and signs at community events highlight ways for volunteers to help and provide information about getting involved. Brochures are also used to recruit volunteers. One of them, "Expand Your Horizons," includes descriptions of the program, the role of the volunteer in reaching the program's goals, and potential areas of involvement. A detachable response form is included, and when the volunteer team receives the form, an interview is scheduled. Brochures are handed out at public events and displayed in public areas.

Over the life of the program (1984-1991), efforts have yielded well over 1,000 volunteers, with documented donated service time totaling 125,000 hours.[25]

■ Element #10: Allocate Appropriate Resources for Media and Outreach

Many campaigns fail simply because adequate resources are not allocated for media *reach* (number of people in the target audience exposed to the message) or *frequency* (number of times the audience was exposed to the message). Prior steps in the planning process may have been completed successfully, with a market segment selected that was ready for action (e.g., environmentalists); a clear, action-oriented message (e.g., "Wash your plates after eight") and an incentive (e.g., lower utility rates during nonpeak hours). But if the word doesn't get out about these important behaviors and benefits, anticipated levels of participation may not be reached.

An integrated and extensive media campaign supported the following effort described in *The Nation's Health*.[26]

Reducing Tobacco Use Among Texas Youth

"In 1999, the Texas Legislature allocated $20 million for 2 years to the Texas Department of Health for tobacco reduction efforts. Realizing the money was not enough to institute an effective statewide program, the department implemented and evaluated pilot programs in 14 east Texas communities.

The results, released in January (2001), showed that areas that received high-level media campaigns combined with multiple school and community programs achieved the greatest success. . . .

High-level media campaigns included a Web site and television and radio ads geared toward 11- and 12-year-olds that featured a "cool, hip-talking animated duck." The "Tobacco is Foul" campaign was developed with teen input during each step of the process. . . .

School programs included training teachers in tobacco prevention education, laws restricting youth tobacco access and opportunities to involve schools in community-based tobacco control. Schools distributed tobacco prevention newsletters to students, conducted events for Kick Butts Day and World No Tobacco Day, created youth cessation support groups and formed youth tobacco coalitions. . . .

Tobacco use was measured in the areas before and after the pilot projects. . . .

In areas where school/community programs or multiple programs were combined with high-level media campaigns, tobacco use dropped, on average, 60% among sixth and seventh graders."[27]

SOURCE: "Comprehensive Programs Reduce Tobacco Use Among Texas Youth." *The Nation's Health* (March, 2001), p. 7. Reprinted by permission of the publisher.

■ Element #11: Allocate Adequate Resources for Research

Budget limitations are a reality for many, if not most, social marketing campaigns, and questions regarding the need for conducting marketing research are often raised. Successful campaign planners recognize unanswered questions critical to the success of the project. What concerns and barriers does the target audience have about adopting this new behavior? What would help them overcome these barriers? What more do they need to know in order to decide? What messages would motivate them most? The following example illustrates a creative way to conduct necessary research and at the same time meet campaign objectives.

Adult Physical Activity

The Washington Coalition for Promoting Physical Activity, with participants including the state's Department of Health, chose as its first project in 1998 a campaign to promote the U.S. Surgeon General's new guidelines on moderate physical activity and health. Data from existing surveys indicated that more than half the population was not physically active at a level that would improve their health. Studies also revealed that about 90% of those surveyed did not know the new, more moderate recommendations.

But the quantitative surveys didn't supply the reasons behind the numbers. Why weren't people more active? What was the competition? If people knew about the new, more moderate recommendations, would they become more physically active? There is a long list of health benefits associated with physical activity. Would it be that the health benefits motivated people or that the new guidelines made it easier to fit physical activities into their busy lives?

Faced with a limited budget, planners concluded that audience segmentation was critical if they were going to have a measurable impact. Who within the general population would be most likely to respond to the new recommendations? Planners predicted that middle-aged people would be most receptive and face fewer barriers to acting on the message. But coalition membership consisted of several organizations whose focus is families and children. If the campaign did not focus on young families, planners would need good research to back up their decisions.

The coalition was informed of the benefits of following a social marketing approach and what would be gained from conducting formative audience research. Members placed a high value on impact measurement and agreed to the strategy of selecting a smaller audience segment. Focus groups were planned with (a) adults aged 45 to 60 in a variety of family situations and (b) adults aged 25 to 40 with children living in the home. A coalition member, impressed with the evidence-based strategy, stepped forth with funding to add more groups with older adults aged 60 to 70. The entire first year's funding, which amounted to about 15% of the eventual budget (an unusually high allocation for many social marketing campaigns), was devoted to researching and selecting a target audience and conducting a baseline survey.

Eight focus groups led to the selection of a target audience (adults aged 50-70). Their advice was to be specific ("Be Healthy. Be Active. 30 minutes a day, 10 minutes at a time, 5 days a week.") and encouraging ("Feel Better. Look Better. Live Longer."). A combination of paid advertising and community-level events and activities were conducted in two pilot communities, followed by a benchmark survey at the 12-month point.

According to the survey, the campaign significantly increased awareness and understanding of the new guidelines. There was a 40% increase in unaided awareness of the new guidelines (from 19.3% to 27.3%). Those claiming awareness were more knowledgeable about specific recommendations than they had been prior to the campaign. There was a 72% increase in the numbers of respondents mentioning the message "5 days a week," and a 115% increase in the mentioning of "30 to 44 minutes a day." And those aware of the campaign (unaided) were more likely to say that they intended to increase their physical activity in the future, from 54% to 66%.

The coalition had proof that their campaign was effective and that it could now be confidently shared with additional communities and partners for rollout to other markets.[28] (See Chapter 6 for more details on this case.)

■ Element #12: Track Results and Make Adjustments

Successful campaigns establish ways to monitor progress and make important adjustments so that current or planned strategies support objectives and goals. This effort is obviously most important when there is still time to alter the plan.

In the following example, campaign target audiences and objectives were altered when research on audience perspectives raised insurmountable barriers to desired behaviors.

Eating Disorder Awareness and Prevention _____

GO GIRLS!™ (Giving Our Girls Inspiration & Resources for Lasting Self-Esteem) is an advocacy project launched in 1998 by the national nonprofit organization, National Eating Disorders Association. The initial purpose of the effort was to encourage and support teens in influencing positive images of youth in advertising, television programs, fashion shows, and retail displays. Research by this organization and others has indicated that teenagers' self-esteem is significantly influenced by their images of their bodies compared with those portrayed in these industries.

An initial project began with a group of marketing students from three high schools who developed a plan to influence modeling agencies, advertising firms, and retail stores to use a diversity of body sizes and shapes in ads, fashion shows, and displays. Initial objectives were ambitious: to (a) persuade modeling agencies to use teen models of various weights and sizes, (b) persuade advertising agencies to request a diversity of models for ads, and (c) persuade retail department stores to use a variety of mannequins in teen displays. Planned efforts included interviews of executives in these industries at the beginning, to understand any perceived barriers to using diverse images.

Initial interviews and presentations dampened the student marketers' enthusiasm as they listened to their target audience's problems: Modeling agencies provided models requested by advertisers; advertisers used models who fit into (small-sized) sample outfits from brand manufacturers; and retail executives indicated they had few, if any, options from mannequin manufacturers for teen displays.

The students adjusted their plan. They narrowed their audience to the merchandise managers of the retail stores, a segment with real decision-making authority and a problem they thought they could solve. Armed with media support from a local television station and a major newspaper reporter "at their side," they presented retail executives with a new idea, one they thought would help teens and would also work for the retailers. Given that factory-ordered mannequins would take several years to alter, they suggested stuffing existing soft-cloth mannequins so that they had larger-sized torsos.

The teens were jubilant when one of the department stores agreed to display mannequins with larger-sized torsos in their popular teen department. Local television and newspapers covered their successful efforts, spreading goodwill for one retail giant and casting a negative light over the other.[29]

BEYOND SUCCESS

Although meeting or exceeding relevant and meaningful campaign goals and objectives is reason for celebration, we would be remiss if we did not offer a stretch goal, an inspiring challenge for overachievers.

How Can the Campaign
Sustain Behavior Into the Future?

Through careful, customer-driven planning, ways can be found to accomplish the following ways to sustain behavior, a topic covered in more depth in Chapter 16.[28]

- Integrate messages and mechanisms into *existing infrastructures* (e.g., litter receptacles with automated recordings saying "Mmm . . . Got litter?" that are activated by passing pedestrians).
- Gain *commitments* from target adopters (e.g., certificates for "Backyard Wildlife Sanctuaries" issued when homeowners sign applications stating they will use only natural fertilizers and pesticides).
- Develop ongoing *prompts* in the environment (e.g., car bells that remind you to fasten your seat belt).
- Create *norms* and then make offenders more visible (e.g., a telephone number for reporting a single-occupant vehicle [SOV] in a high-occupancy vehicle [HOV] lane).
- Remove major *barriers* (e.g., provide do-it-yourself home blood pressure monitoring equipment).
- *Reward* our audiences for achieving 100% in the maintenance of the desired behavior (e.g., providing a day off for employees who used alternate transportation every day of the week for a year).
- *Support* our audiences in resisting "temptations" to return to old habits (e.g., an electronic messaging service providing encouragement at "weak moments in the day").

How Can the Campaign Leave a Legacy?

Can information and resources be provided by the following practices for those involved in future similar efforts?

- Documenting research and evaluation findings
- Writing and providing summaries of lessons learned
- Sharing materials for others to reproduce
- Making yourself available for consultation with colleagues and peers

Some say that most social issues have been dealt with successfully somewhere. We should be sharing and learning from these past efforts, willing to not reinvent the wheel, and eager to pass it on to those engaged in similar or future efforts.

CHAPTER SUMMARY

- The most credible and reliable indicator of success is the extent to which meaningful and relevant campaign objectives and goals were met.
- Twelve elements of successful campaigns were illustrated in this chapter and are expanded on in subsequent chapters. Campaigns presented in this chapter were chosen to illustrate how each step in the planning process can contribute to the success of the campaign. Here are the 12 elements we discussed:

1. Take advantage of what is known and has been done before.
2. Start with target markets that are (most) ready for action.
3. Promote a single, doable behavior, explained in simple, clear terms.
4. Consider incorporating and promoting a tangible object with the target behavior.
5. Understand and address perceived benefits and costs.
6. Make access easy.
7. Develop attention-getting and motivational messages.
8. Choose appropriate media channels and watch for opportunities for audience participation in traditional media vehicles.
9. Provide response mechanisms that make it easy and convenient for inspired audiences to act on recommended behaviors.
10. Allocate appropriate resources for media and outreach.
11. Allocate adequate resources for research.
12. Track results and make adjustments.

KEY TERMS AND CONCEPTS

Measures of success
Leveraging prior efforts
Markets ready for action
Single, doable behaviors
Tangible objects and services
Easy access
Motivational and attention-getting messages
Audience participation

Convenient response mechanisms
Allocation of appropriate resources for media and outreach
Allocation of appropriate resources for research
Track results and make adjustments
Sustain behavior
Leave a legacy

ISSUES FOR DISCUSSION

1. Relative to the "Truth" campaign, do you think the core strategy (rebellion against the tobacco industry and exposure of key facts) is most appropriate for middle school youth, high school youth, college youth, or all groups? Why?

2. What additional measures of success do you consider worthy of consideration?

3. In the case of blood donation, how do you address concerns that you are not focusing on increasing the percentage of the population who donates, merely the frequency?

4. In the showerhead installation case, how would you as program manager justify the additional proposed cost to retrieve old showerheads that households had replaced and left on their doorsteps?

Notes

1. "Where the Public Good Prevailed," by Stephen L. Isaacs and Steven A. Schroeder, *The American Prospect*, Volume 12, Issue 10: June 4, 2001. Reprinted with permission.
2. Bauer, U. E., Johnson, T. M., Hopkins, R. S., et al. (2000). "Changes in Youth Cigarette Use and Intentions Following Implementation of a Tobacco Control Program," *Florida Youth Tobacco Survey, 1998-2000, JAMA, 284*, 723-8.
3. J. Hicks, personal communication of information in this paragraph, February 2000. Not included in previously published text.
4. Centers for Disease Control and Prevention. (2000). "Trends in Cigarette Smoking Among High School Students in the U.S., 1991-1999."
5. Florida Department of Health. (2000, June). *Florida Youth Tobacco Study, 1998-2000.*
6. J. Hicks, personal communication of information in this paragraph, February 2000. Not included in previously published text.
7. The heading "Youth Marketing vs. Social Marketing" appeared in the previously published version.
8. Case Source: Katharine Fitzgerald, DeLaunay/Phillips Communications.
9. Kotler, P., & Roberto, E. L. (1989). *Social Marketing: Strategies for Changing Public Behavior* (p. 30). New York: Free Press.
10. Case Source: Keith Warnack, Puget Sound Blood Center.
11. Case source: Potter, J. D., Finnegan, J. R., Guinard, J. X., et al. (2000, November). *5 A Day for Better Health Program Evaluation Report* (NIH Publication No. 01-4904). Bethesda, MD: National Institutes of Health, National Cancer Institute. Retrieved 9/24/01 from http://dccps.nci.nih.gov/12-4-00.pdf
12. Wiebe, G. D. (1951-52, Winter). "Merchandising Commodities and Citizenship on Television," *Public Opinion Quarterly, 15*, 579-690.
13. Case Source: Elizabeth Bennett, Children's Hospital and Regional Medical Center.

14. Andreasen, A. R. (1995). *Marketing Social Change: Changing Behavior to Promote Health, Social Development, and the Environment* (pp. 223-250). San Francisco: Jossey-Bass; McKenzie-Mohr, D., & Smith, W. (1999). *Fostering Sustainable Behavior* (pp. 1-45). Gabriola Island, British Columbia, Canada: New Society.

15. Avruch, S., & Cackley, A. P. (1995.) "Savings Achieved by Giving WIC Benefits to Women Prenatally," *Public Health Reps, 110,* 27-34.

Ryan, A. (1997). "The Resurgence of Breastfeeding in the United States," *Pediatrics, 99*(4), 1-5.

Khoury, A. J., Hinton, A., Mitra, A., Sheil, H., & Moazeem, W. (2001). *Evaluation of Mississippi's Breastfeeding Promotion Program.* Final Report to the U.S. Department of Agriculture, Food, and Nutrition Service and Mississippi's Women, Infants, and Children (WIC) Program. Hattiesburg, MS: Center for Community Health, University of Southern Mississippi; Lindenberger, H., & Bryant, C. A. (2000). "Promoting Breastfeeding in the WIC Program: A Social Marketing Case Study," *American Journal of Health Behavior, 24*(1), 53-60.

16. Case Source: Preeti Shridhar, Seattle Public Utilities.

17. Kotler & Roberto, *Social Marketing,* p. 8.

18. National Highway Traffic Safety Administration (NHTSA) Press Release. (2001). Retrieved 10/01/01 at http://www.nhtsa.dot.gov/nhtsa/announce/press/pressdisplay.cfm?year=2001&filename=pr47-01.html

19. North Carolina Department of Transportation. (2000). North Carolina Governor's Highway Safety Program. Information retrieved 2/2/01 from www.dot.state.nc.us

20. Deutsch, J., & Liebermann, Y. (1985). "Effects of a Public Advertising Campaign on Consumer Behavior in a Demarketing Situation," *International Journal of Research in Marketing, 2,* 287-290, as cited in Kotler & Roberto, *Social Marketing,* p. 8.

21. Kotler & Roberto, *Social Marketing,* p. 102.

22. Case Source: Nancy Lee, Social Marketing Services, Inc.

23. Case source: Excerpts from Roncarati, D., Lefebvre, R. C., & Carleton, R. A. (1989). "Voluntary Involvement in Community Health Promotion: The Pawtucket Heart Health Program," *Health Promotion* (1), 11-18.

24. Case source: excerpts from *The Nation's Health* (March, 2001), p. 7. (The Official Newspaper of the American Public Health Association.)

25. For more information on the Texas initiative see: www.tdh.state.tx.us/otpc

26. Case Source: Heidi Keller, Office of Health Promotion, Washington State Department of Health.

27. Case Source: National Eating Disorders Association.

28. Andreasen, A. R. (1995). *Marketing Social Change: Changing Behavior to Promote Health, Social Development, and the Environment* (pp. 223-250). San Francisco: Jossey-Bass; McKenzie-Mohr, D., & Smith, W. (1999). *Fostering Sustainable Behavior* (pp. 46-81). Gabriola Island, British Columbia, Canada: New Society.

PART II

Analyzing the Social Marketing Environment

KEY CHAPTER QUESTIONS

1. When is marketing research used in the planning process?

2. What are the unique benefits of exploring past and similar social marketing efforts before undertaking new or additional research?

3. What are the major types of research used in developing social marketing plans?

4. What are key steps in designing marketing research projects?

CHAPTER 4

Determining Research Needs and Resources

If you want to know what consumers want, ask. That's the foundation of consumer research, and that's where true wisdom lies. The trick, of course, is knowing what questions to ask. And knowing how to listen to the answers.

—Faith Popcorn[1]

MARKETING HIGHLIGHT: BLOOD DONATION

The following case illustrates the use of research to develop social marketing strategies. In this research study conducted for America's Blood Centers, Brightline Media of Arlington, Virginia, describes the formative research used to determine key messages for communications to influence people to donate blood.

America's Blood Centers Nationwide Survey on Blood Donation

Mike Broder, President
Eric Wilk, Research Manager
Brightline Media
Arlington, Virginia

Introduction

Founded in 1962, America's Blood Centers (ABC) is the national network of nonprofit, independent community blood centers. ABC members serve more than 125 million people at 450 blood donation sites and more than 3,100 hospitals nationwide.[2] In May of 2001, America's Blood Centers conducted a survey to determine nationwide attitudes toward blood donation. The objective of the survey was to determine effective public messages and program changes that would increase blood donations.

Telephone interviews were conducted with 600 adults. Responses to the survey were gathered May 7 through May 9, 2001. The 95% confidence interval that is associated with a sample of this type produces a margin of error of plus or minus 4.1%.

Reasons for Giving Blood

As seen in Table 4.1, donors cite humanitarian reasons as their primary reason for giving blood. Four

of the top six responses are altruistic motives, such as helping the community or responding to a blood shortage.

Reasons for Not Donating Blood

When nondonors cite their reasons for not giving blood, there is an interesting split. About half the respondents (44%) cite health issues as their reason for not giving blood. This group is likely to be difficult to

TABLE 4.1   Reasons for Donating Blood

Reason For Donating	
Wanting to help others	34%
Responding to a blood drive	25%
Helping the community	13%
Hearing about a shortage	7%
Because I might need it someday	4%
Helping a local child	2%

recruit into donating. Few people are likely to risk their health to donate blood.

However, as seen in Table 4.2, more than half of nondonors (52%) cite other reasons for not giving blood, such as being scared of the process or not having thought about donating.

TABLE 4.2 Reason for Not Donating Blood

Reason for Not Donating Blood	
Never thought about it	17%
Too busy	15%
Scared of process	10%
Afraid of infection	4%
Don't know where/how to give	4%
Don't know anyone in need	2%

Many of these reasons could be eliminated through education and outreach programs that make people aware of the need for blood donations and the ease, speed, and safety of the process of donating blood.

Effective Messages to Encourage Blood Donation

As seen in Table 4.3, some of the messages test significantly better than others on the 1-7 compelling scale. (A response of "7" represents an "extremely compelling" argument, and a response of either "5" or "6" represents a "compelling" argument.")

The message: "A family member, friend, or child is in need" tests much more effectively than any of the other messages. It is rated "extremely compelling" by an impressive 86% of respondents and 92% of respondents find this message either "compelling" or "extremely compelling."

However, the multiple regression analysis yielded different results regarding the effectiveness of messages. The question of whether someone is likely to donate blood in the next 12 months is asked twice in the questionnaire. The first time the question is asked, it provides a clean read of the likelihood of the respondent to give blood. The question is repeated

TABLE 4.3 Messages to Encourage Blood Donation

Message	Extremely Compelling	Extremely Compelling and Compelling Combined
A family member, friend, or child is in need.	86%	92%
Lifesaving open-heart surgeries, cancer treatments, and emergency operations would be postponed due to blood shortages.	61%	86%
Precautions are taken so that there is no risk of contracting AIDS or hepatitis by donating blood.	61%	81%
Four million Americans would die every year without lifesaving blood transfusions.	55%	84%
Because you might need it someday.	54%	77%
America's blood supply is critically low.	51%	83%
An organized blood drive is taking place in your community.	32%	65%
The blood you donate stays in your community.	27%	50%

after the message series, to gauge the net impact of the messages in moving public opinion. This methodology allowed us to perform a multiple regression analysis measuring the impact of these specific messages on the movement between the two questions.

Multiple regression was performed on the message series to determine which variables would be most predictive of changes in attitude toward donating blood in the next 12 months. This technique identified the following statements in Table 4.4 as being the most predictive of change in opinion.

TABLE 4.4 Statements Most Predictive of Change

Statement	Beta Score
Four million Americans would die every year without lifesaving blood transfusions.	.148
An organized blood drive is taking place in your community	.147
The blood you donate stays in your community	.082

Characteristics of People Most Likely to Become Blood Donors

When respondents are asked a second time if they are likely to give blood in the next 12 months, the yes answer grows from 34% to 41%. This is obviously good news as the messages were able to have a positive net impact of 7%.

It should be noted that respondents who switched to yes regarding blood donation were far more numerous than respondents who switched to no. Roughly 8% of respondents switched to yes while only 2% switched to no.

The group of citizens most likely to change their opinion favorably regarding blood donation included a higher than average percentage of people who had donated 1-2 times, 18-34 year olds, and nondonors who cited "never thought about it" as their reason for not giving.

The group of citizens who remained *favorably* inclined toward blood donation included a higher than average percentage of people who had donated blood within the last 3 years, 18-44 year olds, and people who had given blood 3 to 10 times.

The group of citizens most likely to remain *unfavorably* inclined toward blood donation included a higher than average percentage of seniors, people who had never donated blood, and donors who had given 5 or more years ago.

Summary of Key Findings

▶ Humanitarian reasons, led by "wanting to help others," were the most frequently cited reasons for giving blood.

▶ Health reasons was the most commonly given reason for not donating blood.

▶ Initially, 34% of respondents planned to give blood in the next 12 months. After hearing the message series, this increased to 41%.

▶ In the message series, humanitarian reasons test well both in terms of intensity and in the multiple regression analysis.

▶ The most effective message was "A family member, friend, or child is in need," which 86% say is a very compelling reason.

▶ The most effective message in the multiple regression analysis was "Four million Americans would die every year without lifesaving blood transfusions."

SOURCE: Key Findings From America's Blood Centers' Nationwide Survey on Blood Donation. Summary information provided by Brightline Media of Arlington, Virginia. Mike Broder, President, and Eric Wilk, Research Manager.

CHAPTER OVERVIEW

Only by researching and understanding the specific needs, desires, beliefs, attitudes, and behaviors of target adopters can social marketers make decisions for program plans that will indeed influence change.[3]

In the process of developing a social marketing program, the planner will be faced with important decisions at almost every turn. As the ABC case illustrated, research was instrumental in selecting well-defined target markets, identifying perceived barriers and benefits of desired behaviors, and developing program strategies most likely to increase blood donations among targeted populations.

This chapter provides an overview of *when research is used* in the marketing planning process and major *types of research* commonly used. Suggested *steps for designing research projects* are also included.

Finally, a *research case* is included at the end of this and each of the next 11 chapters. Cases have been chosen to provide a range of research methodologies and to highlight the major topic for that chapter.

WHEN IS RESEARCH USED IN THE PLANNING PROCESS?

Research is used to help make decisions and is therefore applicable in *each of the planning steps.* In fact, as illustrated in Table 4.5, multiple decisions will need to be made with each step, and some form of research activity is likely to address the planner's questions and provide input for decision making. Table 4.5. lists the main research questions that might be studied in each of the eight steps in the planning process. Answers to questions identified in each step may be found in prior research or experience from prior similar campaigns. New, additional research is undertaken after existing sources are explored.

WHAT MAJOR TYPES OF RESEARCH ARE USED?

The social marketer can draw on a varied set of research techniques that are appropriate for decisions that need to be made.[4] Three useful ways to conceptualize research activities are described as follows. The first approach groups research activities according to *where they fit* in the planning process, the second *by whether desired research information already exists,* and the third by *technique* used to gather information or conduct research.

TABLE 4.5 Typical Decisions and Questions Addressed by Research

Step in the Planning Process	Typical Decisions and Questions
1. Analyze the environment	What approach to the social issue at hand should we focus on for this campaign? What issues do we need to resolve and promote to gain the support of internal and external groups? Should we use materials (e.g., slogans, ads) from similar campaigns elsewhere? Which ones? Do they need to be altered for our market?
2. Select target audiences	What segmentation variables should we use to create the most meaningful segments for targeting? Which segments should we focus the majority of our resources on?
3. Set objectives and goals	What specific behavior should we promote? What level of change is realistic to create with this campaign?

4. Deepen understanding of target audiences and the competition	Relative to the desired behavior:
	    What are perceived benefits?
	    What are perceived costs?
	    What are barriers?
	
	What major competing behaviors do we position against? With regard to the competing behavior:
	    What are perceived benefits?
	    What are perceived costs?

5. Develop strategies	What product enhancements will support behavior change? What should we do to make access more convenient? What incentives will be the most appealing? What messages will be the most motivating? Clear? Memorable? What media (communication) channels will be most cost-effective?
6. Develop a plan for evaluation and monitoring	What are the benchmarks that will tell us how we are doing and whether we need to make any changes? How will we know if we reached our goal and what we should do differently next time?
7. Establish budget and find funding sources	How much needs to be spent to reach our goal and have the desired impact? What potential corporate sponsors are the best matches for this effort?
8. Complete an implementation plan and sustain behavior	What prompts in the environment can be built in to sustain campaign messages and desired behaviors?

Research Characterized by Stage in the Process

Social marketers often label their research activities according to the stage in the strategic planning process that the research is addressing. Andreasen identifies three types that are described below:[5]

- *Formative research* is conducted to help analyze the marketing environment, select target markets, and develop preliminary strategies to address chosen markets.

- *Pretest research* is to evaluate a short list of alternative strategies and tactics, assure that chosen strategies and tactics have no major deficiencies, and "fine-tune possible approaches so that they speak to target audiences in the most effective way."[6]

- *Monitoring and evaluation research* is used to "find out how projects are doing so they can be fine-tuned to improve efficiency and effectiveness."[7] Monitoring includes ongoing measurement of program outcomes, often establishing baselines and subsequent benchmarks relative to goals. "Evaluation typically refers to a single final assessment of a project or program."[8]

Nowak and Siska define research activities according to discrete campaign phases in Table 4.6.

Research Characterized by Source

The term *primary research* is used to describe research that has not been conducted before and is tailored to the specific questions and decisions facing the campaign planner. *Secondary research* refers to information and research data that already exist somewhere, having been collected for another purpose.

To save time and money, social marketers are strongly encouraged to first explore sources of *secondary research*. Some of the best resources are peers and colleagues in similar organizations and agencies around the world, who often have information on prior similar efforts they are willing to share. Unlike those in commercial sector marketing competing fiercely for market shares and profits, social marketers are known to rally around social issues and to treat each other as partners and team players. Typical questions to ask peers responsible for similar issues and efforts include the following:

- What target audiences did you choose? Why? Do you have data and research findings that profile these audiences?

TABLE 4.6   Research Characterized by Campaign Phase

Campaign Phase	Research Undertaken	Definition
Precampaign	STRATEGIC PLANNING RESEARCH	Research that informs campaign or message design by identifying potential problems, target audiences, campaign concept or themes, and useful media channels or message vehicles.
	NEEDS ASSESSMENTS	Research that collects information to estimate what is "needed" (e.g., money, information, skills, social support) to solve defined problems of a target audience
Campaign/ Message development	TARGET AUDIENCE ANALYSIS	Research that selects, segments, and/or describes the target population(s) that the campaign is intended to address.
	FORMATIVE EVALUATION	Research undertaken to compare alternative campaign strategies or alternative campaign messages and/or improve the implementation operation, effects, or efficiency of a chosen strategy. Includes idea generation, concept testing, positioning statement, copy or message testing, and test market research.
	MESSAGE EFFICACY/ RESPONSE RESEARCH	Research designed to determine if under optimal conditions a campaign, messages, and/or produced materials will have the desired effect(s).
Postcampaign	PROCESS EVALUATION	Research that attempts to determine when, where, how often, and to whom campaign materials are being disseminated, shown, or aired.
	OUTCOME/ EFFECTIVENESS EVALUATION	Research designed to answer questions about the effects of a campaign or campaign materials and that compares this information with previously stated communication and/or behavioral objectives to determine the extent of discrepancy or congruence that exists.
Ongoing/Ad hoc	EXPLORATORY RESEARCH	Investigations designed to address communication issues as they arise including (a) recurring communication issues that have relevance beyond a single campaign or PSA, (b) assessing or developing research methods, or (c) evaluating the need for a mass media-based intervention.

SOURCE: From "Using Research to Inform Campaign Development and Message Design," by G. J. Nowak and M. J. Siska, in *Designing Health Messages* (p. 172), edited by E. Maibach & R. L. Parrott, Copyright © 1995, by Sage Publications. Reprinted by permission of Sage Publications, Inc.

- ◆ What behaviors did you promote? Do you have information on what benefits, costs, and barriers your target audience perceived? Did you explore their perceptions regarding competing alternative behaviors?

- ◆ What strategies (4Ps) did you use?

- ◆ What were the results?

- ◆ What strategies worked well?

- What would you do differently?

- Are there elements of your campaign that we could consider using for our program? Are there any restrictions and limitations?

This secondary research information may also be available within the social marketer's own organization. Searching through files for information on prior campaigns and asking around about what has been done before and what the results were is time well spent. If the data and circumstances of past similar campaigns are still true today for the current campaign being planned, our research efforts, at least at this point in the planning process, may be complete.

Research Characterized by Technique

A more generic approach is to classify research according to the technique or instrument used to gather the information or conduct the research. These are described in Table 4.7 and are grouped by those most commonly used for secondary research and those most commonly used for primary research. Primary research techniques are further categorized by whether they are qualitative or quantitative in nature.

- *Qualitative research* refers to research that is primarily exploratory in nature, seeking to identify and clarify issues. Sample sizes are usually small, and findings are not appropriate for measurement or projections to larger populations.

- *Quantitative research* refers to research that is conducted in order to reliably profile markets, predict cause and effect, and project findings. Sample sizes are usually large, and surveys are conducted in a controlled and organized environment.

WHAT STEPS ARE INCLUDED IN DESIGNING A RESEARCH PROJECT?

Andreasen recommends that we begin with the end in mind and calls this "backward research." He states, "The secret here is to start with the decisions to be made and to make certain that the research helps management reach those decisions."[9] Traditional steps involved in a research project would include the following:

1. *Purpose:* What decisions will this help us make? What questions will this help us answer?

TABLE 4.7 Research Characterized by Source and Technique

Source	Technique	Description/Examples
SECONDARY		
	Analysis of existing data and statistics	Local, state, national, and international data in publications, such as from the Census Bureau and reports on health and environmental indicators
	Literature search and review	Relevant articles in journals, periodicals, newspapers, and books
	Review of prior surveys and public opinion polls	Custom surveys conducted by others in the past and syndicated studies, such as the Gallup Poll
	Databases and information systems	Commercial and online services, such as A. C. Nielsen, Gallup, Arbitron, and Medline, as well as internal databases
PRIMARY	**Qualitative in nature**	
	Personal interviews	Primarily face-to-face or telephone, sometimes referred to as "expert" or "key informant" interviews
	Focus groups	Moderator facilitates a focused discussion with 8 to 10 participants, typically for about 2 hours
	Casual observation	Data are gathered by observing relevant audiences in real situations (e.g., trying on life vests)
	Group meetings	Discussions with internal and external groups to identify issues, explore strategies, and build support
	Quantitative in nature	
	Telephone surveys	Data are often gathered by research firms, most commonly using computer-assisted telephone interviewing
	Mail surveys	Often used when surveys are lengthy, detailed, require visual components, or need to be anonymous
	Intercept interviews	Respondents are approached for survey in locations such as malls, agency or business facilities, or at relevant sites (e.g., walking trails for physical activity surveys)
	Theater/exposure testing	Respondents observe ads or other campaign components in a theaterlike setting in which they "turn dials" to register responses, complete written surveys, or participate in follow-up interviews and discussions
	Controlled observations	Observation research is conducted on a large-scale basis, using controlled procedures (e.g., recording use of bike helmets)
	Control group experiments	Program elements are implemented with one market, and key indicators are compared with similar markets without the exposure
	Internal records and tracking mechanisms	Using existing records to profile and measure relevant issues and monitor efforts (e.g., composition of litter on freeways)
	Knowledge, Attitudes, Practices, Behavior (KAPB) Study	A name given to quantitative surveys of the target population to assess levels of awareness/knowledge, attitudes, and behaviors related to the program focus
	Online surveys	Collecting data through electronic surveys

2. *Informational objectives:* What specific information do we need to make this decision or answer the question?

3. *Audience:* Who do we need the information from?

4. *Technique:* What is the most efficient and effective way to gather this information?

5. *Sample size, source, and selection:* How many respondents should we survey, given our desired statistical confidence levels? Where do we get names? How do we select (draw) our sample so that our data are representative of our target market?

6. *Pretest and fielding:* Who will conduct the research and when?

7. *Analysis:* How will data be analyzed and by whom, to meet the planners' needs?

8. *Report:* What information should be included in the report, and what format should be used for reporting?

Table 4.8 illustrates several causes and the chosen information and objective, audience, and technique.

CHAPTER SUMMARY

1. Research is used to help make decisions and is therefore applicable in *each of the planning steps.*

2. Research is often characterized in one of three ways:

   - By *where it fits* in the planning process
   - By *whether desired research information already exits*
   - By *technique* used to conduct the research

3. Research characterized by where it fits in the planning process is often referred to as either *formative* (used for developing strategies), *pretest* (used to test preliminary strategies), *or monitor/evaluation research* (to see how we are doing).

4. Research that is being conducted for the first time is called *primary research,* and if it already exists, it is called *secondary research.*

5. Research techniques are varied and include both qualitative and quantitative approaches. *Qualitative* research is exploratory in nature, seeking to identify and clarify issues. *Quantitative* refers to research that is conducted to reliably profile markets, predict cause and effect, and project findings.

TABLE 4.8   Major Steps in Designing Research Projects

Step 1: Decision to Support	Step 2: Informational Objective	Step 3: Audience	Step 4: Technique
What approach to increased mentoring in the community should be the focus of our campaign?	How do our potential funders rate each of the potential campaign approaches in terms of interest in funding?	Foundations and corporations who have given to the organization in the past or have an interest in this social issue	In-person interviews conducted by the executive director of the agency
What market segments should be selected as targets for promoting annual breast cancer screening?	How large are the segments that are not currently having annual screening, recognize the importance, and have not had negative experiences in the past?	Women aged 50 and over in the state who are underinsured	Face-to-face interviews, mail surveys, and telephone surveys
Which of several creative concepts would work best for promoting physical activity and healthy eating?	What do members of the target audience say works well and doesn't work for each concept? What suggestions do they have for improvement?	Working adults aged 29 to 54	Intercept interviews in shopping malls
What service and communication enhancements should be employed at clinics to encourage male support of their partners' contraceptive use?	What are the major benefits and concerns that male partners have with encouraging their partners' contraceptive use?	Sexually active males aged 15 to 25	Focus groups
What key messages, slogans, and images should be used on campaign posters promoting abstinence among teens?	What do teens say are the worst consequences for having sex before they are ready?	Eighth-grade females	Informal interviews
What changes and increased efforts should be made in future campaigns promoting placing infants on their backs to protect them from SIDS?	What do parents currently know about the recommended positioning for sleeping?	Parents of infants under 1 year old and those planning to become parents within the next year	Telephone surveys

KEY TERMS AND CONCEPTS

Applicable to each planning step
Formative research
Pretest research
Monitoring research
Evaluation research
Primary research
Secondary research
Qualitative research
Quantitative research
Literature search and review
Personal interviews
Focus groups
Casual observation
Group meetings
Telephone surveys

Mail surveys
Intercept interviews
Theatre/exposure testing
Controlled observation
Control group experiments
Internal records and tracking
Knowledge, Attitudes, Practices, and Behavior (KAPB) Studies
Online surveys
Survey purpose
Sample size, source selection
Survey pretest
Survey fielding
Survey analysis

ISSUES FOR DISCUSSION

1. For a campaign to increase safe gun storage, what are potential research needs? Identify potential research purposes, informational objectives, audiences, and techniques.

2. Assume you are at the beginning stages of developing a plan to influence residents in the county to reduce water consumption by 10%. You have heard that similar water conservation campaigns have been conducted in a neighboring state. What questions would you have of a peer in this state?

3. Explain, in your own words, the basic differences between qualitative and quantitative research.

RESEARCH HIGHLIGHT: QUANTITATIVE AND QUALITATIVE RESEARCH FOR BREAST CANCER SCREENING

The *Florida Cares for Women Program* illustrates how the use of qualitative and quantitative research guides social marketers in program planning. In this project, research results enabled program planners to select the target audience; identify the motivators and barriers to breast cancer screening they should address; and select from the many potential information channels, spokesperson(s), and strategies to use for promoting breast cancer screening services to eligible women in Florida.

Florida Cares for Women Program

Carol A. Bryant, Ph.D.

Kelli McCormack Brown, Ph.D.

Melinda S. Forthofer, Ph.D.

James H. Lindenberger, Ph.D.

Breast cancer is the second leading cause of cancer deaths among women in the United States (American Cancer Society, 2000). Breast cancer mortality can be reduced by as much as 30% through clinical breast examinations and screening mammograms for women aged 49 years and older (U.S. Preventive Services Task Force, 1996). Despite the benefits of routine breast cancer screening and numerous efforts to increase screening rates, many women are not screened annually.

In 1996, the Florida Department of Health contracted with the University of South Florida College of Public Health and Best Start Social Marketing to design a comprehensive approach to increase utilization of free and low-cost mammograms among uninsured women over 50 years of age.

Research Methods

The social marketing team used a mix of qualitative and quantitative research methods. A literature review, focus groups, and in-depth interviews were used to identify factors associated with breast cancer screening. These qualitative findings were then used to develop a questionnaire for assessing women's knowledge, identifying predictors of screening behavior, self-reported screening behavior, and screening intentions regarding mammography. Initial drafts of the questionnaire were pilot tested among approximately 150 women in the selected audience population and reviewed by a panel of experts who recommended additional modifications. The final version consisted of 52 closed-ended items.

Telephone surveys were conducted with a random sample of Medicare recipients with Hispanic surnames living in five counties with large numbers of Hispanic residents. Door-to-door surveys were conducted in eight randomly selected counties from the 20 Florida counties funded to provide free and low-cost breast cancer screening services. Quota sampling was used in order to ensure a high probability of contacting the desired number of Anglo American, African American, and Hispanic women who represented both urban and rural populations. Within selected block groups, every other street was selected, with every house on the street canvassed. Door-to-door trained surveyors made two attempts to interview women living in the homes selected for the study. If the prospective participant was still not available after the second attempt, a survey was left for her to complete and return in a self-addressed stamped envelope. All interviews were conducted in English or Spanish, depending on respondent preference. Interviews lasted approximately 20 minutes.

The survey sample included 2,373 women out of approximately 4,090 women who were approached to participate in this study, for a response rate of approximately 58%.

After a specific segment of the population was selected as the focus for the project, in-depth interviews were conducted with members of this subgroup to gain a more vivid picture of their lifestyles, core values, and service needs. A secondary goal was to gather information needed for effective message design.

Application of Research Findings

Research results were first used to segment the population of underserved women into four distinct subgroups based on previous screening behavior and future intentions. The four segments included women who: 1) were screened annually; 2) had been screened in the past but did not plan to be screened

again in the future; 3) had never been screened and had no plans to have a mammogram; and 4) had been screened and planned to return but at intervals longer than recommended. Profiles were created of each group to help program planners decide which segment(s) to target. The first group was already complying with recommended standards and represented an unnecessary target for the marketing plan. Most women in the second group had painful and embarrassing experiences with previous mammograms and therefore were reluctant to repeat the experience. Program planners were unable to refer these women to special mammography facilities that can successfully lower these "costs" and therefore did not select this group. Women in the third and fourth groups were possible to reach with program resources, but the latter group represented the best "target of opportunity" for a program with limited resources because these women had already accepted the importance of screening and only had to be convinced to go annually (Bryant et al., 2001; McCormack Brown et al., 2000; Forthofer & Bryant, 2000).

Research results were then used to develop a multifaceted social marketing plan for the following:

▶ Enhance perceived benefits—promise peace of mind

▶ Lower costs and overcome barriers—offer discount coupons and use mass media to inform eligible women about the availability of free or low-cost mammograms, emphasize the importance of being screened annually

▶ Place services conveniently—extend service hours, provide direct telephone access to program staff for appointments, offer free transportation

▶ Select the right mix of promotional tactics—combine public information with consumer education, professional training, community outreach, policy development, and local service delivery improvements

▶ Select the most effective information channels, spokespersons, and message design elements

For example, research findings suggested that a variety of informational channels—physician referral, mass media, and community organizations—were needed to reach the target population. The social marketing plan recommended the development of materials for encouraging and supporting physician referrals and a community organizer's kit containing a fact sheet of local statistics, sample press release/newspaper articles, and resource list. Female physicians and cancer survivors were identified as the most effective spokespersons for promising peace of mind. Message design guidelines for developing electronic and print materials recommended the use of logical appeals to save money on an important preventive health measure and a factual, upbeat, and respectful tone. In keeping with these guidelines, television spots featured a female African American physician recommending that women over the age of 50 take the time "once a year" for screening, with the promise that regular screening offers "peace of mind." The announcement ended with a cancer survivor saying that screening had saved her life. Print materials included pictures of women from different ethnic backgrounds and provided information about service locations, hours, and fees, responses to common questions about mammograms, and ways to minimize discomfort during a mammogram. All campaign materials emphasized peace of mind as the benefit to be gained from regular screening and reinforced the importance of being screened annually. (See Figure 4.1.)

© 2002 by C. A. Bryant, K. McCormack Brown, M. S. Forthofer, and J. H. Lindenberger.

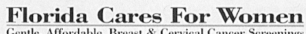

A Special Gift For Women 50 And Over.
Once A Year, Peace Of Mind.

From The Florida Cares For Women Program.
The new Florida Cares For Women Program makes it easy to get the yearly breast and cervical cancer screenings doctors recommend. The screenings are free or low cost if you do not have insurance or enough money. You may qualify for this special gift if you:

- Are 50 years of age or older   • Have little or no insurance
- Meet income guidelines (see chart on the back of this coupon).
- Have *not* been screened in the past year

Your Gift Is Waiting. Call Now.
To schedule a gentle, private exam at an office near you, call now. Because there is no greater gift than peace of mind.

Florida Cares For Women
Gentle, Affordable, Breast & Cervical Cancer Screenings

Figure 4.1. An Emphasis on the Major Benefits

References

American Cancer Society. (2000). *Cancer facts and figures.* Atlanta, GA: American Cancer Society. Retrieved April 24, 2000, from: www.cancer.org.statistics

Bryant, C. A., Forthofer, M. S., McCormack Brown, K., Alfonso, M. L., & Quinn, G. (2000). Social marketing approach to increasing breast cancer screening rates. *Journal of Health Education, 31*(6), 320-328.

Forthofer, M. S., & Bryant, C. A. (2000). Using audience-segmentation techniques to tailor health behavior change strategies. *American Journal of Health Behavior, 24*(1), 36-43.

McCormack Brown, K., Bryant, C. A., Forthofer, M. S., Perrin, K. M., Quinn, G. P., Wolper, B. S., & Lindenberger, J. H. (2000). Florida Cares for Women. *American Journal of Health Behavior, 24*(1), 44-52.

U.S. Preventive Services Task Force. (1996). Screening for breast cancer. In *U.S. Preventive Services Task Force Guide to Clinical Preventive Services* (2nd ed., pp. 73-87). Baltimore, MD: Williams & Wilkins.

Notes

1. Popcorn, F. (1992). *The Popcorn Report* (p. 148). New York: HarperCollins.
2. America's Blood Centers (ABC). (2001). "About ABC." Retrieved 7/31/01 from http://4.21.230.152/aboutabc/default.htm
3. Kotler, P., & Roberto, E. L. (1989). *Social Marketing: Strategies for Changing Public Behavior* (p. 62). New York: Free Press.
4. Kotler & Roberto, *Social Marketing,* p. 62.
5. Andreasen, A. R. (1995). *Marketing Social Change: Changing Behavior to Promote Health, Social Development, and the Environment* (p. 98). San Francisco: Jossey-Bass.
6. Ibid., p. 120.
7. Ibid., p. 98.
8. Ibid., p. 127.
9. Ibid., p. 101.

KEY CHAPTER QUESTIONS

1. How do you determine a campaign focus and purpose?

2. What is involved in conducting a situation analysis?

CHAPTER 5

Mapping the Internal and External Environments

Funny to hear that type of criticism, calling our ads over the top or morbid or some of the other things that have been mentioned in the press, because if killing over three million people every year around the world is not over the top and morbid, I don't know what is.

—Jared Perez, Spokesman,
"The Truth" Anti-Tobacco Campaign[1]

MARKETING HIGHLIGHT: TOBACCO INDUSTRY RESPONSE

A successful effort to reduce youth smoking in Florida is highlighted in Chapter 3. The following is one of several articles and features that appeared within weeks of the national campaign's launch; it highlights well this chapter's focus on environmental factors that can influence the success or failure of social marketing campaign efforts.

Keep the following questions in mind while reading this article:

1. Was this response from the tobacco industry predictable? Could anything have been done prior to the launch to minimize the impact of this response?
2. Was there a better response to the tobacco industry's moves to block the campaign?
3. Why did original allies take differing positions and advocate varying responses to the tobacco industry? Could this have been avoided?

"Fuming Over Smoking Ads,"
From the *Washington Post*, February 20, 2000

Marc Kaufman
Washington Post Staff Writer

When cigarette makers agreed to pay almost $250 billion in a landmark settlement with the states 18 months ago, anti-tobacco advocates hoped the national anti-smoking foundation that the deal created would become a formidable counterbalance to the tobacco industry's powerful marketing efforts.

Instead, the American Legacy Foundation (ALF) has been vociferously criticized by the very advocates who lobbied to create it. The foundation's decision last week to pull two controversial television ads under pressure from the tobacco industry has caused public health and anti-smoking advocates to charge that the group's independence and integrity have been seriously compromised.

Foundation officials said last week they pulled the ads to avoid a draining fight with the industry and its supporters as the first major anti-smoking campaign was being rolled out. They said they might try to use the ads in the future.

But reflecting the growing concern of anti-smoking advocates, Sen. Frank R. Lautenberg (D-NJ) said Friday he would lead other senators in calling for hearings if "the censorship" continues. Pulling the ads, he wrote in a letter to the foundation, "creates the unfortunate appearance that the foundation will back down when tobacco interests object, and undermines public confidence in the foundation's independence and ability to run an effective campaign."

The controversy—over two ads shot in and around Philip Morris headquarters in New York—has also exposed a largely unknown compromise written into the 1998 master settlement agreement between the tobacco industry and 46 state attorneys general. That agreement was signed after the Senate had killed a comprehensive tobacco bill, reducing the leverage of the attorneys general.

In exchange for $1.5 billion from the tobacco industry to fund the foundation's five-year national teen anti-smoking campaign, the attorneys general agreed in the settlement that the effort would not "vilify" the industry or its officers. The two ads were pulled last week after Philip Morris and several attorneys general complained that they were "inconsistent with the objectives of the settlement agreement" and that they vilified the industry.

But public health and anti-tobacco advocates say that attacking the industry for what they see as its duplicity—by producing a deadly product that it advertises as appealing and sophisticated—is essential for any successful anti-tobacco campaign.

"How can you run an anti-smoking campaign and not vilify the industry?" said former FDA commissioner David Kessler, an active anti-tobacco advocate. "It would be better to not take the money if the industry is able to pull the strings and take control."

"I'm very uncomfortable with the tobacco companies being the censors of what kind of anti-tobacco message can be used to reduce teenage smoking," said Mississippi Attorney General Mike Moore, who led the state's legal fight against the tobacco industry. His state was one of four that settled early with the industry, and he said there is no "anti-vilification" clause in his agreement.

"I think the Legacy Foundation has basically destroyed itself," said Stanton Glantz, a longtime anti-tobacco advocate at the University of California at San Francisco. "The tobacco companies always threaten aggressive ads, and you have to stand up to them. You just cannot turn over control of your ads to Philip Morris."

But officials of the foundation defend their decision as necessary to keep their anti-smoking campaign from being derailed by tobacco politics. State legislatures stand to receive more than $250 billion from the national tobacco settlement, and that money has created a powerful lobby eager to keep the agreement from being jeopardized in any way. . . .

The two ads that were "rotated out" by the foundation are part of a consciously "edgy" campaign called "the truth," inspired and often managed by teens. One of the ads, shot in grainy black-and-white, shows hundreds of body bags laid around the Philip Morris headquarters as a way to dramatize the death toll from cigarette smoking.

The second ad features an actress entering the Philip Morris building with a suitcase labeled "lie detector." She asks to speak with a marketing director about whether nicotine is addictive, and is escorted out by security. Both ads scramble the faces of Philip Morris employees and neither identifies the company. Nonetheless, Philip Morris threatened legal and other action after viewing the ads.

Jared Perez of Tallahassee, one of the young activists of "the truth" campaign, said he's "disappointed" that the ads were pulled.

"I definitely wish those ads were on the air," Perez said. "But I don't want to jeopardize the funding of the entire 'truth' campaign. Would that have really happened? That's a matter of speculation for us all."

That the foundation is looking over its shoulder so early in its life is what has anti-tobacco advocates so worried and mad. The agreement that created the organization describes it as independent of the tobacco companies that fund it, and its board includes governors, attorneys general, doctors and prominent public health leaders.

Foundation officials say inclusion of the anti-vilification clause was an important goal for the tobacco industry. One likely reason for their insistence on the clause, officials said, is that in recent months the companies have mounted major advertising campaigns to present themselves as "responsible corporate citizens."

Complicating the foundation's efforts to air the two controversial ads was the reluctance of major networks to show them. While the networks accepted two ads in "the truth" campaign, they resisted or rejected the ones shot at Philip Morris headquarters.

As seen by one top federal public health official, the foundation was in an enviable position several weeks ago—with the tobacco companies attacking it and the networks undermining its efforts.

"That opposition could have been used to their benefit if they had chosen to fight," the official said. "Instead, they gave in and put themselves in a stupid,

ridiculous position. . . . If it had been me, I would have tested the waters and let them sue."

Despite the setbacks, foundation president Healton is optimistic that "the truth" campaign will ultimately help inspire a decline in teen smoking. Three dozen more ads are scheduled to be released this year, in what is believed to be the largest public health campaign in the nation's history.

And by the end of last week, Healton said, the networks had agreed to run some of them.

SOURCE: Kaufman, M. (2000, February 20). "Fuming Over Smoking Ads." *The Washington Post.* Reprinted with permission.

CHAPTER OVERVIEW

The reaction of the tobacco industry, the media, and others to "The Truth" campaign television spots is a vivid demonstration that programs, efforts, and target audiences will be subject to forces in the environment that the social marketer will need to consider (ahead of time) and manage.

Mapping the social marketing environment early in the planning process makes it possible for social marketers to anticipate these forces and to develop strategies that minimize their impact and enable timely and orderly adaptations in the life cycle of a social marketing program.

This chapter describes Step 1 of the planning process, *analyzing the social marketing environment.* It discusses one of the first, and sometimes most difficult, decisions, that of choosing one approach from all the potential (or desirable) ways to address the *social issue.* The process involves identifying potential approaches, analyzing each one relative to relevant criteria, and choosing a *focus* for plan development. Next, the broad *purpose of the plan* is articulated, identifying the impact of a successful campaign. Consider the case of "The Truth" campaign, for example:

+ The *social issue* is tobacco use.

+ The *focus* is youth empowerment.

+ The *purpose* is reducing youth tobacco use.

Establishing a focus and purpose provides a framework for *mapping the current environment and likely future environment.* This involves a SWOT analysis, which explores the internal (micro) and external (macro) environments to identify factors that represent Strengths to maximize, Weaknesses to minimize, Opportunities to capture, and Threats to prepare for in our plan. This SWOT analysis is conducted relative to the chosen focus of the plan: in this case, youth empowerment.

Other activities include *reviewing past and similar efforts* and an analysis of the *competition.* We are including a *review of past and similar efforts* as a part of the situation analysis. In this model, we identify the competing behaviors after establishing desired behaviors in Step 4.

CHOOSE A CAMPAIGN FOCUS

Each campaign requires choosing a focus and involves several steps.

Identify Potential Approaches for Campaign Focus

Decision making begins with identifying the major potential approaches that might contribute to solving or supporting the social issue, as illustrated in Table 5.1. These may be approaches that the sponsoring organization has discussed or undertaken in the past; they may be new for the organization, recently identified as areas of greatest opportunity or emerging need; or they may be ones that other organizations have focused on and should be considered for this organization.

Evaluate Each Potential Approach and Choose a Focus

The following criteria can be used for choosing the most appropriate focus:

Behavior Change Potential
Is there a clear behavior that can be promoted to address the issue? Offering enhanced counseling services for pregnant teens does not have the same potential that a "safe sex" or "abstinence" focus would have.

Market Demand
How many people would benefit from a behavior change campaign with this focus? The number of youth that would potentially benefit from a mentoring campaign that focuses on volunteers for youth at risk is not as great as one focusing on

TABLE 5.1 Identifying Potential Approaches for Campaign Focus

Social Issue and Hypothetical Sponsoring Organization	Potential Approaches for Focus
Unintended pregnancies (nonprofit organization)	• Birth control • Abstinence • Sexual assault prevention • Talking to your child about sex • Adoption opportunities • Abortion counseling
Drinking and driving (state traffic safety commission)	• Designated drivers • Underage drinking and driving • Promoting new tougher laws (.08% vs. .10% alcohol limit) • Military personnel • Repeat offenders • Not letting a friend drive drunk
Air pollution (regional air quality control council)	• Carpooling • Mass transit • Walking to work • Telecommuting • Not topping off gas tanks • Gas lawn mowers
Mentoring youth (nonprofit organization)	• Parents identifying and supporting mentors for their children • Recruiting volunteer mentors • Potential interested mentors "letting themselves be known" to parents and children • Programs focusing on youth at risk • Programs focusing on reaching "mainstream" youth through paid mentors

encouraging all parents to identify and support other caring adult relationships in their children's lives.

Market Supply

Is this issue already being addressed by other organizations and campaigns? A quick audit may reveal that millions of dollars have been spent in recent years promoting and supporting alternative transportation modes, such as mass transit and carpooling, and that several campaigns are planned in the near future. It might be further revealed, however, that little effort has been dedicated to influencing drivers not to top off their gas tanks, one of the potential behaviors for ozone protection.

Organizational Match

Is this a good match for the sponsoring organization? Is it consistent with its mission and culture? Can its infrastructure support promoting and accommodating the behavior change? Does it have staff expertise to develop and manage the effort? If, for example, it focused on recruiting volunteers for mentoring youth, would it be likely to have more phone calls, referrals, and follow-up requirements than if it simply encouraged parents to find mentors?

Funding Sources and Appeal

Which approach has the greatest funding potential? A campaign for underage drinking and driving may have the greatest potential for partnerships with non-profit organizations such as Mothers Against Drunk Drivers (MADD) and corporate sponsorships from the beer industry.

The best focus would then have a high potential for behavior change, fill a significant need and void in the marketplace, match the organization's capabilities, and have a high funding potential. (See Table 5.2.)

IDENTIFY A CAMPAIGN PURPOSE

Next, we articulate the broad purpose of the campaign. It answers the questions "What is the potential impact of a successful campaign?" and "What difference will it make?"

How does purpose differ from our objective, identified as Step 3 in our planning process? An *objective* in a social marketing campaign is what we want our target audience "to do." Our campaign *purpose* is the ultimate impact (benefit) of adopting the behavior to the target audiences, groups, and/or society.

Table 5.3 illustrates the increased potential for motivation and response when speaking of the campaign's purpose versus objective.

CONDUCT A SWOT ANALYSIS

The environment of the chosen campaign focus consists of *internal factors and external forces* that can affect the social marketer's ability to develop and maintain

TABLE 5.2   Potential Rationale for Choosing Campaign Focus

Social Issue and Hypothetical Sponsoring Organization	Campaign Focus	Potential Rationale
Unintended pregnancies (nonprofit organization)	Teen abstinence	Recent governmental funding for campaigns promoting abstinence in middle schools and high schools Controversial nature of "safe sex" campaigns in school environment Statistics revealing that a majority of middle school youth are abstinent, creating opportunities for promoting social norms
Drinking and driving (state traffic safety commission)	Underage drinking and driving	Recent mass media campaign announcing lower alcohol limits for adults is raising questions among youth regarding laws for underage drinking Incidence data indicates that teens represent a significant number of fatal drinking and driving accidents State traffic safety commission needs to meet goals to reduce drinking and driving accidents and recognize lack of recent efforts with this market
Air pollution (regional air quality control council)	Not topping off gas tanks	Consumer research in other regions revealed a high level of willingness to stop topping off gas tanks after hearing the (low) costs and benefits Ease of getting the message out by developing stickers for gas pumps Other local campaigns currently existing targeting other behaviors, especially carpooling and mass transit
Mentoring (nonprofit organization)	Encouraging parents to identify and support other nonparent adult relationships for their children	Most consistent with organization mission and constituent groups Concern with safety issues when parent not involved Other campaigns and programs focusing on mentoring youth at risk Lack of infrastructure to promote and manage volunteer mentors

TABLE 5.3 Distinguishing Between Campaign Purpose and Objective

Social Issue and Hypothetical Sponsoring Organization	Campaign Purpose (Potential Impact)	Campaign Objective (Desired Behavior)
Unintended pregnancy (nonprofit organization)	Reduced teen pregnancies	Choose abstinence
Drinking and driving (state traffic safety commission)	Reduced injuries from underage drinking and driving	Teens: Don't have even one drink and drive
Air pollution (regional air quality control council)	Reduced volatile organic compounds in the atmosphere caused by gas spillage	Don't top off the gas tank
Mentoring (nonprofit organization)	Increased number of caring adult relationships in the lives of all children	Parents: Identify and support caring, nonparent adult relationships for your children

successful influence on target audiences. By identifying these forces, strategies can be developed that will withstand and even leverage their impact.

The Microenvironment: Internal Factors

The microenvironment consists of factors close to the social marketing program that can affect campaign resources, service quality, and our ability to influence and respond to target audiences. We need to know what resources are currently available, where this project currently falls on internal political agendas and priorities, the reputation and image of the program, and our current internal allies as well as potential opponents.

The process begins with an audit of several factors, typically including those illustrated in Figure 5.1.

Resources: Levels of funding, staffing, and expertise

Past Performance: Prior successes and failures, issue and program image and reputation

Service Delivery: Ability to deliver any programs or services that will be offered to target audiences

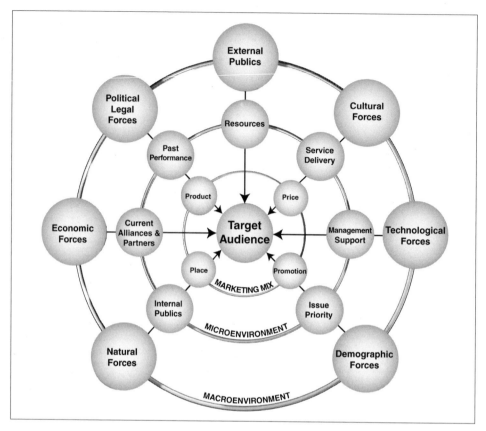

Figure 5.1. Factors Influencing Our Target Audience and Our Efforts

Management Support: Extent to which this effort will have management attention and support

Issue Priority: Extent to which the focus for the campaign is considered a top priority by key publics

Internal Publics: Peers and colleagues within the agency, organization, or corporation who have interest and influence relative to program efforts

Current Alliances and Partners: Coalitions, corporate partners, and task forces addressing the social issue at hand with which there are existing relationships

On the basis of this information, a list is made of major strengths to be maximized and weaknesses to be minimized relative to the chosen campaign focus. Examples of different campaigns are shown in Table 5.4.

TABLE 5.4 Examples of Strengths and Weaknesses Relative to Chosen Focus

Campaign Focus and Hypothetical Sponsoring Organization	*Internal Strengths*	*Internal Weaknesses*
Abstinence (nonprofit organization)	State school superintendent office funding for abstinence campaigns will provide financial and expert resources for producing campaign materials. A strong existing network of schools and home and family life teachers are interested in conducting campaigns in their schools.	School curricula are under pressure to focus on essential learning academic requirements. Program coordinator for the project has several other projects underway, placing time available for managing this project in jeopardy.
Underage drinking and driving (state traffic safety commission)	Recent statewide campaign announcing newer, tougher drinking and driving laws could be adapted to the teen population, using some existing campaign themes and elements. Staff have experience with developing prior campaigns.	Based on an effort with this age-group several years ago, some commission members are skeptical that an advertising campaign will work, and they will want additional options. Court and corrections facilities are already "bogged down," and any effort to increase citations may not be supported.
Not topping off the gas tank (regional air quality control council)	Several industry representatives on the council have expressed interest in supporting the effort with retail displays and signage. Little effort has been made in the past on this topic and may be "news" to target audiences.	There are no current funding sources for campaign elements. There may be conflicting desired approaches, given the diverse nature of council members.
Encouraging parents to identify and support other nonparent adult relationships for their children (nonprofit organization)	Five years of expertise training local youth organizations in the importance and nature of youth developmental assets. Organization staff are well respected and connected with community youth leaders and foundations.	Several key board members and current funders are concerned with narrowing the scope of the organization's effort. There is no existing infrastructure to support a "volunteer" mentor program.

The Macroenvironment: External Forces

The macroenvironment is the set of forces typically outside the influence of the social marketer, but they must be taken into account. (See Figure 5.1.) Major categories to explore include the following:[2]

> *Cultural Forces:* Trends and events affecting society's basic values, perceptions, preferences, and behaviors (norms)
>
> *Technological Forces:* Potential for new technologies, products, and market opportunities
>
> *Demographic Forces:* Trends in population size, age, gender, race, occupation, location, and other similar statistics
>
> *Natural Forces:* Current and emerging environmental issues and concerns
>
> *Economic Forces:* Trends affecting buying power and spending
>
> *Political/Legal Forces:* Laws and actions of governmental agencies that could affect campaign efforts and/or target audiences
>
> *External Publics:* Groups outside the organization with actual or potential impact on target audiences

This review culminates with the identification of major opportunities and threats relative to the campaign focus. Examples are shown in Table 5.5.

CHAPTER SUMMARY

1. The first step in developing a marketing plan is to analyze the social marketing environment, and it includes several phases:

   - Choosing a campaign focus
   - Clarifying the purpose (broad impact) of the campaign
   - Conducting a SWOT analysis
   - Reviewing past and similar efforts

2. Choosing a campaign focus involves identifying potential approaches that can contribute to resolving or supporting the social issue, analyzing these relative to relevant criteria, and choosing one that becomes the foundation for plan development.

TABLE 5.5   Examples of Opportunities and Threats Relative to Campaign Focus

Campaign Focus Hypothetical Sponsoring Organization	*External Opportunities*	*External Threats*
Teen abstinence (nonprofit organization)	There is continued increased concern on a national level about the economic and social impact of teen pregnancies, which are now being quantified more reliably. The threat of AIDS is more real now to youth.	Several large and increasingly vocal parent groups are likely to oppose an additional program. State grants stipulate that campaigns must have an abstinence focus and must be developed by young people. It may be difficult to find youth who want to participate with this focus.
Underage drinking and driving (state traffic safety commission)	MADD organizations may have an interest in partnering in a campaign. The state legislature is considering amending laws to allow for pulling over vehicles for more minor offenses.	Recent report on results from DARE (Drug Abuse Resistance Education) programs are raising questions regarding the effectiveness of similar approaches. Teens have been exposed to and may be tired of the "Don't drink and drive" and "Choose a designated driver" messages.
Not topping off the gas tank (regional air quality control council)	Consumer surveys indicate that drivers find "not topping off the gas tank" an easy behavior to adopt. Concern for the environment is among the top five in the region.	Some technical experts indicate that refraining from topping off the tank does not have the impact some believe and may provide negative publicity and feedback. Topping off the tank is a cultural norm.
Encouraging parents to identify and support other nonparent adult relationships for their children (nonprofit organization)	Existing mentoring programs have already raised awareness of the benefits for youth at risk. Parents, especially those in dual-income households, report that they are finding it more and more difficult to set aside quality time with their children.	Parents may see the suggestion that their children need other adults in their lives as a negative comment that they are not doing enough. Child development experts may respond that it is more important to be promoting that parents spend more time with their children.

3. Clarifying the purpose of the campaign is important for motivating project participants, as well as appealing to potential funders. The purpose of the campaign is a broad statement describing the ultimate impact of a successful campaign—not to be confused with campaign objectives, which focus on behaviors or on what we want target audiences "to do."

4. Conducting a SWOT analysis involves an audit of the internal (micro) environment, as well as the external (macro) environment to identify Strengths to maximize, Weaknesses to minimize, Opportunities to capture, and Threats to prepare for in the remaining planning process.

5. A key aspect of this environmental analysis is identification of internal and external publics that can influence the success or failure of campaign efforts.

KEY TERMS AND CONCEPTS

Behavior change potential
Resources
Past performance
Service delivery
Management support
Issue priority
Internal publics
Current alliances and partners
Cultural forces
Technological forces
Demographic forces
Natural forces
Economic forces
Political/legal forces
External publics

Campaign focus
Campaign purpose
Mapping environment
SWOT
Microenvironment
Internal factors
Strengths and weaknesses
Macroenvironment
External factors
Opportunities and threats
Past efforts
Market demand
Market supply
Organizational match

ISSUES FOR DISCUSSION

1. What are several potential areas of campaign focus for the issue of air pollution?

2. Assume that a focus of reduced auto trips has been selected for a campaign to help decrease pollution from automobiles. What is a potential campaign objective?

3. Relative to an objective to get workers to telecommute one day a month, what are some examples of potential strengths and weaknesses, opportunities, and threats that a public agency sponsoring this campaign might face?

RESEARCH HIGHLIGHT: PERSONAL INTERVIEWS FOR CARING ADULT RELATIONSHIPS WITH YOUTH

This research highlight illustrates the difficulties many organizations face in making decisions to choose an area of focus for a social marketing campaign. As noted earlier in this chapter, a systematic research approach can facilitate a rational, successful outcome, as it did in this case.

It's About Time for Kids

Nancy Ashley
Principal, Heliotrope

Background

Seattle's *It's About Time for Kids* is a collaborative effort of nonprofit youth-serving agencies, leaders from the corporate and foundation sectors, Children's Hospital, the local school board, United Way, and others.

It's About Time for Kids aims to ensure that youth possess the specific skills, attributes, and values ("developmental assets") shown by research both to increase prosocial behaviors and to decrease at-risk behaviors. This organization began when a small group of community leaders began looking for more effective approaches to address the complex needs of the city's young people. They found the asset-building approach of Search Institute,[3] headquartered in Minneapolis, to offer the most promising route.

In 1995, *It's About Time for Kids* conducted the Search Institute's student survey to measure the existing asset levels of local youth. It has offered work-shops on how different organizations can integrate asset-building principles into their work and successfully advocated for policy and funding changes in the community.

By 2000, it became obvious *It's About Time for Kids* needed to directly reach parents and other adults to fully capitalize on the successful organizational and policy shifts it had created. Shifting the community's social norms to have everyone participating in building assets for young people meant that it was time to reach out to individuals. *It's About Time for Kids* chose a social marketing approach to ensure the highest likelihood of success in moving people to action, not just giving them information.

Its executive committee struggled long and hard with the concept of choosing only one asset for the focus of its social marketing campaign. The assets model is cumulative—the more assets a young person has, the more likely he or she is to become caring, responsible, and capable. Therefore, picking one asset out of the list of 40 was contrary to the organization's approach up until this time. To make this choice, the group embarked on an intense, research-based decision process.

Purpose of Research

With the guidance of a social marketing expert, *It's About Time for Kids* staff devised a set of questions to guide its board in selecting one asset to be the focus of its social marketing campaign: What assets . . .

1. Are the most needed (i.e., fewest kids have them)?
2. Are the most critical (i.e., correlate with youth at risk behaviors)?
3. Would serve the broadest base of youth in the community?
4. Are the best match for our organization to promote and support?
5. Are not already being handled by others?
6. Would have the most appeal to potential funders?

Secondary Research and Literature Review

It's About Time for Kids had an important resource in the Search Institute student survey it had conducted. That survey showed how Seattle youth rated on each of the 40 assets, which provided guidance for the first research question. In addition, Search Institute has published survey results from 100,000 youth around the country that provided further context.

To determine which assets were most critical to a young person's choices of risky or prosocial behavior, the group turned to the extensive synthesis of research on each asset compiled by Search Institute. In addition, it relied on additional child and adolescent development research in the fields of resiliency, mentoring, and positive youth development and considered the results of local focus groups with youth. Collectively, these sources provided strong guidance on Question 2.

An Internet search and contacts with other organizations with similar efforts were initiated to provide some assistance on Question 5. Questions 3, 4, and 6 involved opinions and judgments of the board.

Internal Group Discussions

Armed with the research described above, the consultant and *It's About Time for Kids* staff selected four assets they believed best fit the answers to the research questions. Their results were presented to the executive committee, which extensively debated the pros and cons of each one, as well as agonized once more over the need to choose only one asset in order to have an effective social marketing campaign. The executive committee at last agreed that the four assets selected were the strongest and most compelling choices, and arranged for the full board to engage in the selection.

At the board meeting, board members did a rating exercise for the four proposed assets, based on the research questions. Responses were calculated on the spot, so they could see the "score" for each option (some questions were weighted more heavily than others). The board selected one asset as its top choice, and directed the staff to gather further information before making a final decision.

External Interviews

The board wanted to consider the opinions of potential funders, partners, organizations with similar efforts, and child development experts in the final decision. The *It's About Time for Kids* director contacted more than 20 people to discuss their potential interest in and support for the top two choices and to help identify any potential duplication of existing efforts.

The results of the interviews were conveyed to the executive committee, which then made the final decision to focus on Asset #3, called "Other caring adults." This asset reflects the importance of non-parent supportive adults in the lives of young people. Research indicates these caring adults can make a big difference for kids in many areas of their lives. In addition, once that relationship is formed, the adult has the ability to influence a large number of other assets. That factor was critical to the executive committee, which wanted to retain the cumulative power of assets.

Result

It's About Time for Kids will hold eight focus groups with parents of children in kindergarten through high school to test the appeal and viability of this top choice. In addition, the group decided to test a second option that was also highly rated in the external interviews. The focus groups are designed to determine which of the two options has the greatest perceived benefits and which has the fewest barriers and concerns.

© 2002 by Nancy Ashley, Heliotrope, Seattle, Washington.

MARKETING DIALOGUE

Two well-publicized programs targeting social issues among teens were in the news within months of each other early in 2001. Both emphasized a classroom-based approach with an emphasis on abstinence. Both were criticized for lackluster results. They provide an excellent example of the intense dialogues surrounding choosing approaches to solving social issues. Some maintained that past results provided direction for improved program strategies. Others editorialized that school-based programs would never work and that resources to address teen drug, alcohol, and tobacco use should be redirected to more productive programs.

What's Needed? Just a Twist or a Complete Turn?

Programs in the Spotlight

DARE, launched in 1983, promotes a drug and alcohol abstinence message, with police officers stressing that all drugs are "equally dangerous," T-shirts, bumper stickers, and the message "Just say no." According to a *Newsweek* article from February 2001,

> Over the last decade, studies have repeatedly shown that the simplistic message of the $226 million program has little effect on keeping kids from abusing drugs. . . . Kids who go though the program in elementary school are just as likely to use drugs later as kids who don't.[4]

Similarly, findings were released in December of 2000 from a 15-year, $15 million study in Washington State; the study followed 8,400 students, from third grade into high school, who took part in special classes focused on tobacco prevention education. Course content included a focus on increasing awareness of the influences encouraging tobacco use, teaching students skills to resist these forces, and making certain that students understood that most students (the norm) were not using tobacco. The study found "almost no difference in the smoking rates between youths who took part in special classes and those who didn't."[5]

Some Say, "Just Enhance Strategies"

According to the same *Newsweek* article mentioned above,

DARE officials announced plans to improve the program and have funding of $13.7 million from the Robert Wood Johnson Foundation. The new DARE, to be launched in seventh and ninth grades in six cities this fall, will reduce the lecturing role of local cops and involve the kids in a more active way.[6]

Optimists in Washington State look at these findings as input for future programs. "We're going to use this good science to make sure we don't repeat what didn't work" (State Health Secretary).[7] Dr. Robert Jaffe of the Washington State Medical Association said, "This reinforces that it takes a comprehensive, sustainable program."[8] Future efforts will likely combine school-based programs with additional strategies that have been shown to be successful in other states, such as "high-profile, creative media campaigns in nonschool environments, increased taxes on tobacco products and stricter enforcement of youth access laws."[9]

Others Say, "Redirect Resources"

A very different view held by some is that these programs are a waste of taxpayer dollars, foundation grants, and school classroom time that could be better spent on the 3Rs. They believe that resources should be directed to programs that have been proven to make a difference, such as access to health care and improvements in basic education. Such opponents have little faith in enhancing and revamping approaches they believe are fundamentally flawed, a view they feel has been finally confirmed.

Notes

1. Perez, J., National Public Radio (NPR). (2000, February 2). *All Things Considered.*
2. Kotler, P., & Armstrong, G. (2001). *Principles of Marketing.* Upper Saddle River, NJ: Prentice Hall.
3. Search Institute is an independent, nonprofit, nonsectarian organization whose mission is to advance the well-being of adolescents and children by generating knowledge and promoting its application. It generates, synthesizes, and communicates new knowledge.
4. Kalb, C. (2001, February 26). "DARE Checks Into Rehab." *Newsweek*, 56.
5. Grygiel, C. (2000, December 21). "Officials to Push New Anti-Tobacco Program." *Seattle Post-Intelligencer*, pp. A1, A16.
6. Kalb, C. (2001, February 26). "DARE Checks Into Rehab." *Newsweek*, 56.
7. Grygiel, C., "Officials to Push New Anti-Tobacco Program." *Seattle Post-Intelligencer.*
8. Ibid.
9. *Seattle Post-Intelligencer.* (2000, December 23). "We've Many Ways to Convince Kids About Smoking." Op-Ed.

PART III

Establishing Target Audiences, Objectives, and Goals

KEY CHAPTER QUESTIONS

1. What are the three steps involved in target marketing?

2. What variables are commonly used to segment markets?

3. What criteria are used for evaluating segments?

4. How are target markets selected?

5. What approach should be chosen?

CHAPTER 6

Selecting
Target Markets

What we plant in the soil of contemplation, we shall reap in the harvest of action.

—Meister Eckhart[1]

MARKETING HIGHLIGHT: PHYSICAL ACTIVITY

The following case, from the Washington State Department of Health, illustrates how existing data, formative research, and experience and were used to segment, evaluate, and choose target markets.

Feel Better. Look Better. Live Longer.
A Campaign Promoting Moderate Physical Activity

Heidi Keller
Director of the Office of Health Promotion
Washington State Department of Health

People know that exercise is good for them. In fact, most people questioned in focus groups in Washington State could tell you precisely how much exercise is recommended, but they weren't doing it.

A 1998 statewide survey revealed that 85% of the adult population were not exercising at the vigorous level that would lead to "fitness" and less than half were active at the moderate level that would improve health. They said they didn't have time, didn't feel athletic, and didn't want to "work out" or "sweat." This led health promotion activists to wonder: Could people be convinced to be more active if they knew that significant health benefits accrue from much less effort than previously thought?

A coalition of health, fitness, and educational organizations in Washington State decided to try.

Background

According to Washington's Physical Activity, Nutrition, and Tobacco Survey, 94% of those surveyed believed that exercise was good for their health, but only about 15% were exercising vigorously, and only about 45% were moderately active on a regular basis. About 60% said they were aware that new guidelines had been issued but only 9% knew what they were.

With this in mind, the diverse organizations that formed the Washington Coalition for Promoting Physical Activity (WCPPA) decided to increase public awareness of new guidelines on physical activity and health. The social marketing approach was selected on the basis of its reliance on data for decision making and adherence to an evaluation component. The coalition was committed to choosing one project that was measurable, and doing it well.

Identifying the Audience Most Likely to Change

Given a small budget, project planners relied on audience segmentation to successfully motivate the most people with the least effort. They decided to test messages to learn which audience segment was most motivated to change. Would people be more likely to change physical activity behavior if they knew the following?

▶ It would result in measurable long-term health benefits.

▶ Many everyday activities count.

▶ They would feel better immediately.

Start With Existing Data

Narrowing the target audience involved using existing quantitative data (the Behavioral Risk Factor Surveillance System) and consideration of the behavioral determinants that would either support or detract from a person's decision to become more active.

Quantitative data indicated that women were less active than men, the youngest adults (aged 18-24) were more active than older adults, and physical activity levels dropped most dramatically in the age group 25 to 34 years. This data painted a vivid picture of the population's current level of physical activity but didn't explain why.

Subjective assessments of potential targets were made to select the group with the highest probability of success. Young adults (18-24 years)—the most active category—were not considered a good target segment because they were already quite active. The dramatic decrease in physical activity in the group 25 to 34 years old made them a needy segment to pursue. Middle-aged adults would have more time and more motivation to adopt health improvement behavior. Older adults were similarly appealing; however, they were less active and less healthy and might require more effort to influence.

Other questions arose:

▶ Could motivating messages be equally effective for both women and men?

▶ What were the unique barriers between age groups that the coalition could address?

Formative Research

Eight focus groups were held in three sites: four age 45 to 60 groups, two age 25 to 34 groups, and two age 60 to 70 groups.

Participants were recruited on the basis of age, gender, and activity level (engaged in physical activity less than 5 days a week, 30 minutes a day).

Focus Group Agenda and Findings

Participants were told about the new recommendations for moderate physical activity and health (5 days a week, 30 minutes a day, at least 10 minutes at a time). Long-term health benefits—decreased risk of several diseases and disabling conditions—were presented. Immediate benefits—improved mood, living longer independently—were also discussed.

Most participants were surprised and encouraged. They found the health benefits compelling and that activities (such as yard work or brisk walking) were within their grasp and close to what they were already doing. "For these benefits," they said, "it's worth it to just increase what I've been doing." Still, many were also skeptical. They found the benefits hard to believe and wanted proof from a credible source.

The majority said they could meet the guidelines with a little more time and effort. They also said that "just knowing and believing this is true" was motivating, which indicated to the coalition that their knowledge objective had merit.

From a *price* perspective, participants found the new guidelines worth the effort. They were delighted that they could achieve the "benefits at such a reasonable cost," even squeezed into 10-minute segments. From a *place* perspective, the everyday activities had great appeal: "I don't have to join a club." The *product* being offered (30 minutes a day, at least 10 minutes at a time, 5 days a week) fit their self-image: "I don't have to be a jock. I don't have to sweat."

From a target market perspective, responses indicated that the campaign should be designed to influence people not currently exercising regularly or vigorously, who don't want to "work out," but want the benefits and like the idea of "squeezing" it into everyday life. Although people in this profile were found across age groups, the highest incidence appeared to be in the group aged 50 to 70. This group was selected as the target for the campaign. It was also concluded that the campaign didn't need to be gender specific to be effective.

Planners used additional advice from focus groups to develop a campaign that promoted community activities (classes and events), facilities (walking trails and mall walking programs), and the fact that everyday activities such as yard work and vacuuming can improve your health.

Be healthy. Be active.

Feel better, look better, live longer

The benefits of physical activity are remarkable. It can lower your risk of diabetes, heart disease, high blood pressure and cholesterol. It can boost your energy, lower your stress and improve your balance. And you can get these benefits through everyday activities. Physical activity fits with life.

For more information, visit our Web site at www.BeActive.org
Washington Coalition for Promoting Physical Activity and the Washington Department of Health

Figure 6.1. Campaign Poster Incorporated Benefits Perceived by Target Audience

Objectives

Based on the feedback, the coalition set these campaign objectives:

▶ To raise awareness of the new guidelines and the remarkable health benefits

▶ To dispel the belief that fitness means you have to change your clothes, go to a gym, and sweat

Strategy

Planners concentrated efforts in communities that already had physical activity programs under way. Physicians and researchers active in the coalition and community leaders served as spokespersons.

The campaign made one key promise: People who are physically active feel better, look better, and live longer.

The campaign was disseminated through a combination of carefully targeted paid (newspaper inserts and radio advertisements) and unpaid (news media coverage, posters, newsletters, worksites, and private sector partners) distribution channels. (See Figures 6.1 and 6.2.)

Be healthy. Be active.

From the Washington Coalition for Promoting Physical Activity and the Washington Department of Health—Summer 1999

To Spokane's Shirley and Greg Thompson, physical activity is key to maintaining strength and flexibility.

"Just keep moving"

So much for so little

Physical activity provides a long list of health benefits

By now most Americans know the recommendations for exercise and fitness, and they have decided that they just can't do it. Only 15 percent of Washington residents are regularly active at a vigorous, aerobic level. But there's great news for the rest of us.

Physical activity need not be vigorous to improve health, according to the Surgeon General's Report on Physical Activity and Health. In fact scientists have found that people who are active at a more moderate level experience a long list of measurable benefits. Prevention of heart disease, high blood pressure and high cholesterol are obvious. But there are more that might surprise you.

People who are regularly physically active decrease their risk of diabetes and its complications, as well as the risk of

Figure 6.2. Local Newspaper Inserts Provided Real Testimonials

A baseline telephone survey with 400 adults aged 50 to 70 was conducted in April 1998 and again 1 year later.

Evaluation

The benchmark survey among 50- to 70-year-olds revealed a 40% increase in unaided awareness of the new guidelines. The increase in knowledge of activities that count was similarly dramatic: a 230% increase in the mention of yard work and a 116% increase in the mention of vacuuming.

People held greater belief in the benefits of moderate physical activity: a 55% increase in the mention of feeling better and a 245% increase in the mention of living longer.

People familiar with the campaign were more than 20% more likely to increase their physical activity in the next 6 months than people who were not (66.1% vs. 54%).

Galvanizing Effect

Founders of the Washington Coalition for Promoting Physical Activity believed the best way to mobilize volunteers—and keep them—was to achieve an early success. Social marketing was instrumental in several ways. It provided a logical, step-by-step process that made sense to members. Inviting members to observe formative research helped them buy into letting the audience drive decisions. And the benchmark evaluation provided proof that their efforts made a measurable difference.

CHAPTER OVERVIEW

At this point in the planning process, we have completed a situation analysis that has provided the following:

- A *focus for our plan* (e.g., use of cell phones while driving)

- A *clear purpose* (e.g., reduced injuries from accidents caused by cell phone use)

- *Strengths to maximize* (e.g., impressive statistics on accidents involving cell phone use)

- *Weaknesses to minimize* (e.g., those who argue that the cell phone wasn't "at fault")

- *Opportunities to capture* (e.g., new hands-free models on the market)

- *Threats to prepare for* (e.g., telecommunication lobbyists)

- Possible discovery of *existing campaigns* that will be useful for our efforts

WHAT STEPS ARE INVOLVED IN TARGET MARKETING?

Our task now is to select target markets for the campaign, defined as "a set of buyers sharing common needs or characteristics that the company decides to serve."[2] Identifying them is a 3-step process:

1. *Segment the market.*

First, the market (audience) for the campaign is divided into smaller groups who might require unique and similar strategies in order to change behavior. Those grouped together have something in common (needs, wants, motivations, values, behavior, lifestyles, etc.) that makes them likely to respond similarly to program efforts. (Cell phone users might be grouped according to whether they never pull over to talk on the phone, try to pull over, or always pull over.)

2. *Evaluate segments.*

Each segment is then evaluated on a variety of factors to assist with prioritizing segments using a rational process. (Cell phone user segments, for example, might be rated in terms of incidence of accidents, attitudes toward change, ability to identify, and reach with targeted media.)

3. *Choose one or more segments for targeting.*

Ideally, a few segments are selected as targets for the campaign, and strategies will then be developed to appeal uniquely to this market. (In our cell phone usage example, a campaign with scarce resources might first focus on those who try to pull over, recognizing that they already have some recognition of the behavior's costs and benefits and may be easier to influence.)

Segmentation and targeting provides numerous benefits, long familiar to corporate sector marketers who "know that they cannot appeal to all buyers in their markets, or at least not all buyers in the same way."[3] This process provides the following benefits:

- *Increased effectiveness:* Programs are designed to address a market's unique needs, wants, and behaviors.

- *Increased efficiencies:* Resources strategically directed at a unique market are likely to produce greater results for every dollar spent.

- *Input for resource allocation:* Evaluation of segments provides objective measures for distribution of resources.

- *Input for developing strategies:* Detailed profiles of a segment provide rich insights into what will influence an audience to change a behavior.

Even if, for a variety of purposes, programs are developed for all markets, segmentation at least organizes and provides a framework for developing strategies that are more likely to be successful with each of the markets.

WHAT VARIABLES ARE USED TO SEGMENT MARKETS?

Options for segmenting a market are vast, and still expanding. Traditional approaches used by commercial sector marketers for decades are described in this section, as well as unique models successfully applied by social marketing theorists and practitioners.

Traditional Variables

Segmentation variables typically used to describe consumer markets are outlined in Table 6.1. Each is applicable to a social marketing environment, as follows.[4]

TABLE 6.1   Major Segmentation Variables for Consumer Markets

Variable	Sample Classifications
Geographic	
World, region, or country	North America, Western Europe, Middle East, Pacific Rim, China, India, Canada, Mexico
Country region	Pacific, Mountain, West North Central, West South Central, East North Central, East South Central, South Atlantic, Middle Atlantic, New England
City or metro size	Under 5,000; 5,000-20,000; 20,000-50,000; 50,000-100,000; 100,000-250,000; 250,000-500,000; 500,000-1,000,000; 1,000,000-4,000,000; 4,000,000 or over
Density	Urban, suburban, rural
Climate	Northern, southern
Demographic	
Age	Under 6, 6-11, 12-19, 20-34, 35-49, 50-64, 65+
Gender	Male, female
Family size	1-2, 3-4, 5+
Income	Under $10,000; $10,000-$20,000; $20,000-$30,000; $30,000-$50,000; $50,000-$100,000; $100,000 and over
Occupation	Professional and technical; managers, officials, and proprietors; clerical, sales; craftspeople; supervisors; operatives; farmers; retired; students; homemakers; unemployed
Education	Grade school or less; some high school; high school graduate; some college; college graduate
Religion	Catholic, Protestant, Jewish, Muslim, Hindu, other
Race	Asian, Hispanic, Black, White
Generation	Baby boomer, Generation X, echo boomer
Nationality	North American, South American, British, French, German, Italian, Japanese
Psychographic	
Social class	Lower lowers, upper lowers, working class, middle class, upper middles, lower uppers, upper uppers
Lifestyle	Achievers, strivers, strugglers
Personality	Compulsive, gregarious, authoritarian, ambitious
Behavioral	
Occasions	Regular occasion, special occasion
Benefits	Quality, service, economy, convenience, speed
User status	Nonuser, ex-user, potential user, first-time user, regular user
Usage rate	Light user, medium user, heavy user
Loyalty status	None, medium, strong, absolute
Readiness stage	Unaware, aware, informed, interested, desirous, intending to buy
Attitude toward product	Enthusiastic, positive, indifferent, negative, hostile

SOURCE: From *Principles of Marketing*, 9th ed. (p. 252), by P. Kotler and G. Armstrong. Copyright © 2001. Reprinted by permission of Pearson Education, Inc., Upper Saddle River, NJ.

Demographic segmentation divides the market into groups on the basis of variables common to census forms: age, gender, marital status, family size, income, occupation, education, religion, race, and nationality. These are the most popular bases for grouping markets, for several reasons. First, these are some of the *best predictors* of needs, wants, barriers, and behaviors. Second, this type of information about a market is *more readily available* than it is for other variables, such as personality characteristics or attitudes. Finally, these are often the *easiest ways to describe and find a targeted segment* and to share with others working to develop and implement program strategies.

Example: A demographic basis for segmentation could be quite appropriate in planning an immunization campaign because immunization schedules vary considerably according to age. Planners might understandably create unique strategies for each of the following population segments in their local community:

- Birth to 2 years (3%)

- 3 to 6 years (5%)

- 7 to 17 years (20%)

- Adults, 18 to 64 years (52%)

- Seniors, 65 years and over (20%)

Geographic segmentation divides a market according to geographical areas, such as continents, countries, states, regions, counties, cities, and neighborhoods, as well as related elements, such as commute patterns, places of work, and proximity to relevant landmarks.

Example: An organization focused on reducing the number of employees driving to work in single-occupant vehicles might find it most useful to develop strategies based on *where employees live* relative to the worksite, current vanpools, current car pools, and each other. The planner might then decide that the first four groups below represent the greatest opportunity for "hooking up" employees with attractive alternative and/or existing forms of transportation:

- Employees living on current vanpool routes (10%)

- Employees living within 5 miles of current car pools (5%)

- Employees living within 5 miles of each other (15%)

- Employees living within walking or biking distance of the workplace (2%)
- All others employees (68%)

Psychographic segmentation divides the market into different groups on the basis of social class, lifestyle, values, or personality characteristics. (See the research highlight at the end of this chapter on the VALS segmentation.) Planners may find that their market varies more by a personal value, such as concern for the environment, than by some demographic characteristic, such as age.

Example: A campaign to reduce domestic violence might find it most important to develop campaign programs based on levels of self-esteem among potential victims:

- High self-esteem (20%)
- Moderate self-esteem (50%)
- Low self-esteem (30%)

Behavior segmentation divides the market on the basis of knowledge, attitudes, and behaviors relative to the product being sold. Several variables can be considered within this approach: segmenting according to *occasion* (when the product is used or decided on), *benefit sought* (what the segment wants from using the product), *usage levels* (frequency of usage), *readiness stage* (relative to buying), and *attitude* (toward the product/offering).

Example: A blood donation center may increase efficiencies by prioritizing resource allocation according to donation history, allocating the most resources to loyal donors, those who have given in the past:

- Gave more than 10 times in past 5 years (10%)
- Gave 2 to 10 times in past 5 years (10%)
- Gave only once, less than 5 years ago (5%)
- Gave only once, more than 5 years ago (5%)
- Never given at this blood center (70%)

In reality, marketers rarely limit their segmentation to the use of only one variable, as we did to illustrate each variable above. More often, they use a combination of variables that provide a rich profile of a segment or help to create smaller, better-defined target groups.[5]

Social Marketing Models for Segmentation

Two models used by social marketing practitioners illustrate the use of a combination of variables to define a segment for strategy development. In both cases, the market is segmented primarily *relative to behavior variables:* knowledge, beliefs, and current behaviors. Because we are "selling" a behavior, segmenting our market relative to the behavior we are selling proves to be one of the most relevant and powerful strategies. Then, each segment can be profiled and further defined using other important variables, such as age, income, family size, personality type, and so on.

Stages of Change

The *stages of change model,* also referred to as the *transtheoretical model,* was originally developed by Prochaska and DiClemente in the early 1980s[6] and has been tested and refined over the past two decades. In a 1994 publication, *Changing for Good,* Prochaska, Norcross, and DiClemente describe six stages that people go through to change behavior.[7] Examples to illustrate each are included below:

Precontemplation:
"People at this stage usually have no intention of changing their behavior, and typically deny having a problem."[8]

In the case of an effort to convince people to quit smoking, this segment is not thinking about quitting, and they probably don't even consider their tobacco use a problem.

Contemplation:
"People acknowledge that they have a problem and begin to think seriously about solving it."[9]

This segment of smokers is considering quitting for any number of reasons but haven't definitely decided they will and haven't taken any steps.

Preparation:
"Most people in the Preparation Stage are planning to take action within the very next month, and are making the final adjustments before they begin to change their behavior."[10]

In this segment, smokers have decided to quit and may have told others about their intentions. They probably have decided how they will quit and by when.

Action:
"The Action Stage is one in which people most overtly modify their behavior and their surroundings. They stop smoking cigarettes, remove all desserts from the house, pour the last beer down the drain, or confront their fears. In short, they make the move for which they have been preparing."[11]

This segment has recently stopped smoking cigarettes. It may not be, however, a new "habit" yet.

Maintenance:
"During Maintenance (individuals) work to consolidate the gains attained during the action and other stages and struggle to prevent lapses and relapse."[12]

This segment has not had a cigarette for perhaps 6 months or a year and remains committed to not smoking. They work to remind themselves of the benefits they are experiencing and distract themselves when "tempted" to relapse.

Termination:
"The termination stage is the ultimate goal for all changers. Here, [a] former addiction or problem will no longer present any temptation or threat."[13]

This segment is not tempted to return to smoking. They are now "nonsmokers" for life.

One of the attractive features of this model is that the authors have identified a relatively simple way to assess a market's stage. They suggest four questions to ask, and, on the basis of responses (decisions), respondents are categorized in one of the four stages.[14] Table 6.2 summarizes the groupings by stage of change, on the basis of the four responses.

In the model shown in Box 6.1, the "name of the marketer's game" is to *move segments to the next stage.*

TABLE 6.2 Determining Stage of Change

Decision/ Response Taken	Decision/Response Taken By:				
	Precontemplation Segment	Contemplation Segment	Preparation Segment	Action Segment	Maintenance Segment
I solved this problem more than 6 months ago	No	No	No	No	Yes
I have taken action within the past 6 months	No	No	No	Yes	Yes
I intend to take action in the next month	No	No	Yes	Yes	Yes
I intend to take action in the next 6 months	No	Yes	Yes	Yes	Yes

---

BOX 6.1
Stages of Change Progression

Precontemplation ⇒ Contemplation ⇒ Preparation ⇒

Action ⇒ Maintenance ⇒ Termination[15]

The authors (Prochaska, Norcross, and DiClemente) caution, however:

> Linear progression is a possible but relatively rare phenomenon. In fact, people who initiate change begin by proceeding from contemplation to preparation to action to maintenance. Most, however, slip up at some point, returning to the contemplation, or sometimes even the precontemplation stage, before renewing their efforts.[16]

Figure 6.3 is the authors' graphic representation of the more likely patterns of change, a spiral one.

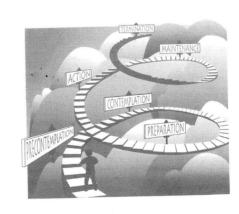

Figure 6.3. The Spiral of Change

Healthstyles Segmentation System

Another segmentation model used for health-related program planning appears in Table 6.3. This system incorporates several segmentation variables, including demographics, pyschographics, and behaviors (knowledge, attitudes, and behaviors related to personal health). Resulting segments provide planners with a rich and memorable picture of each potential target audience, aiding in the development of winning strategies for that market. For example, a physical activity campaign wanting to influence "Decent Dolittles," who may not have confidence in their ability to exercise, might emphasize the benefits of moderate physical activity, how it can fit into everyday life and activities, and the opportunities to "hang out with their friends" while doing it. By contrast, a strategy to influence the "Tense but Trying" segment would switch the emphasis to the health benefits of exercise, especially for stress-related illnesses.

Ideal Segmentation Strategies

As noted earlier, it is rare that a market will be segmented using only one variable. However, one base is often used as a primary way to group a market (e.g., age for immunization); then, each segment is further profiled, and perhaps narrowed, by using additional important and relevant variables that predict response to strategies (e.g., education and income levels within each of the age segments for immunization).

"The most appropriate segmentation variables are those that best capture differences in the behavior of target adopters."[17] For social marketing planning, we encourage planners to consider using behavior-related segmentation variables as the primary base for profiling the market, similar to the ones in the stages of change model described earlier. Segments are then profiled using other meaningful variables. Table 6.4 illustrates a hypothetical profile of market segments that a planner might compile at this stage in the planning process. It uses Andreasen's version of the stages of change model, which collapses the six stages to four, a model more manageable for some programs. (In the table, the issue is litter on roadways. The market is people who smoke in cars.)[18]

WHAT CRITERIA ARE USED FOR EVALUATING SEGMENTS?

Once the marketplace has been grouped into meaningful population segments, the next task is to evaluate each segment in preparation for decisions regarding selecting target markets.

TABLE 6.3   Healthstyles Segmentation System, American Healthstyles Audience
Segmentation Project

Decent Dolittles (24%)

They are one of the less health-oriented groups. Although less likely to smoke or drink, they also are less likely to exercise, eat nutritiously, and work to stay at their ideal weights. Decent Dolittles know that they should be performing these behaviors to improve their health, but they do not feel that they have the ability. Their friends and family tend to avoid these behaviors as well. They describe themselves as "religious," "conservative," and "clean."

Active Attractives (13%)

They place a high emphasis on looking good and partying. Active Attractives are relatively youthful and moderately health oriented. They tend not to smoke and limit their fat intake more than do other groups. They are highly motivated, intending to exercise and keep their weight down, but they do not always succeed at this. Alcohol consumption is an important part of their lifestyle, and Active Attractives often are sensation seekers, constantly looking for adventure. They describe themselves as "romantic," "dynamic," "youthful," and "vain."

Hard-Living Hedonists (6%)

They are not very interested in health and tend to smoke and drink alcohol more heavily and frequently than do other groups. They also enjoy eating high-fat foods and do not care about limiting their fat intake. Despite this, they tend not to be overweight and are moderately physically active. Although they are the group least satisfied with their lives, they have no desire to make any health-related changes. Hard-Living Hedonists also are more likely to use stimulants and illicit drugs than are other segments. They describe themselves as "daring," "moody," "rugged," "independent," and "exciting."

Tense but Trying (10%)

They are similar to the more health-oriented segments except that they tend to smoke cigarettes. They are average in the amount of exercise they get and in their efforts to control their fat intake and weight. They have a moderate desire to exercise more, eat better, and control their weight more effectively as well. The Tense but Trying tend to be more anxious than other groups, with the highest rate of ulcers and use of sedatives and a higher number of visits to mental health counselors. They describe themselves as "tense," "high-strung," "sensitive," and "serious."

Noninterested Nihilists (7%)

They are the least health oriented and do not feel that people should take steps to improve their health. Accordingly, they smoke heavily, actively dislike exercise, eat high-fat diets, and make no effort to control their weight. Despite this, they tend to drink alcohol only moderately. Of all the groups, Noninterested Nihilists have the highest level of physical impairment, the most sick days in bed, and the most medical care visits related to an illness. They describe themselves as being "depressed," "moody," and "homebodies."

Physical Fantastics (24%)

They are the most health-oriented group, leading a consistently health-promoting lifestyle. They are above average in not smoking or drinking, exercising routinely, eating nutritiously, and making efforts to control their weight. They tend to be in their middle or latter adult years and have a relatively large number of chronic health conditions. Physical Fantastics follow their physicians' advice to modify their diets and routinely discuss health-related topics with others.

Passively Healthy (15%)

They are in excellent health, although they are somewhat indifferent to living healthfully. They do not smoke or drink heavily and are one of the most active segments. Although they eat a high amount of dietary fat, they are the trimmest of all the groups. The Passively Healthy do not place much value on good health and physical fitness and are not motivated to make any changes in their behaviors.

SOURCE: Reprinted by permission of Sage Publications Ltd. from Maibach, E. A., Maxfield, A., Ladin, E. A. K., Slater, M., "Translating Health Psychology Into Effective Health Communication: The American Healthstyles Audience Segmentation Project," in *Journal of Health Psychology, 1*, pp. 261-277. As appeared in Weinreich, N., *Hands on social marketing: A step-by-step guide*, (p. 55).

TABLE 6.4 Hypothetical Segmentation Using Stages of Change as Primary Bases

Stage of Change	Precontemplation	Contemplation	Preparation for or in Action	Maintenance
Behavior and intent	Throw cigarette butts out the window and aren't concerned about it.	Throw cigarette butts out the window, feel bad about it, and have been thinking about not doing it.	Sometimes throw cigarette butts out the window and sometimes use ashtray. Trying to increase use of ashtray.	Never throw cigarette butts out the window; use ashtray instead.
Size	20%	30%	30%	20%
Geographics (residence)	Rural (10%) Suburban (40%) Urban (50%)	Rural (8%) Suburban (55%) Urban (37%)	Rural (6%) Suburban (65%) Urban (29%)	Rural (5%) Suburban (70%) Urban (25%)
Demographics (age)	16-21 (60%) 21-34 (25%) 35-50 (10%) 50+ (5%)	16-21 (53%) 21-34 (22%) 35-50 (15%) 50+ (10%)	16-21 (45%) 21-34 (20%) 35-50 (20%) 50+ (15%)	16-21 (30%) 21-34 (18%) 35-50 (27%) 50+ (25%)
Psychographics (environmental ethic)	Environmentally: Concerned (10%) Neutral (30%) Not concerned (60%)	Environmentally: Concerned (15%) Neutral (45%) Not concerned (40%)	Environmentally: Concerned (30%) Neutral (40%) Not concerned (30%)	Environmentally: Concerned (60%) Neutral (30%) Not concerned (10%)

For social marketers, Andreasen cites several factors for evaluating segments relative to each other.[19] Factors included follow, with typical questions that might be asked to establish each measure. To further illustrate each factor, a situation is described in which a state health agency is deciding whether middle school age students would be the most attractive segment for promoting abstinence and safe sex.

1. Segment Size

How many people are in this segment? What percentage of the population do they represent? (How many middle school youth are in the state?)

2. Problem Incidence

How many people in this segment are either engaged in the "problem-related behavior" or not engaged in the "desired behavior"? (What percentage of middle school youth are sexually active?)

3. Problem Severity

What are levels of consequences of the problem behavior in this segment? (What is the incidence of sexually transmitted diseases and pregnancy among middle school youth?)

4. Defenselessness

To what extent can this segment take care of themselves versus needing help from others? (What percentage of middle school youth have access to condoms and report they are using them?)

5. Reachability

Is this an audience that can be easily identified and reached? (Are there media channels and other venues that we can use for abstinence and safe sex messages specifically targeting middle school youth?)

6. General Responsiveness

How "ready, willing, and able" to respond are those in this segment? (How concerned are middle school youth with sexually transmitted diseases and pregnancy? How does this compare with high school students or college students? Which group has been most responsive to similar campaign messages in the past?)

7. Incremental Costs

How do estimated costs to reach and influence this segment compare with those for other segments? (Are there free or inexpensive distribution channels for condoms for middle school youth? How does this compare with those for high school and college students? Are there campaigns from other states that have been proven to work well with middle school youth, or will we need to start from scratch?)

8. Responsiveness to Marketing Mix

How responsive is this market likely to be to social marketing strategies (product, price, place, and promotion)? (What are the greatest influences on middle school youth's decisions relative to their sexual activity? Will the parents of middle school youth, more so than high school or college parents, be concerned with potential programs and messages?)

9. Organizational Capabilities

How extensive is our staff expertise or availability of outside resources to assist in the development and implementation of activities for this market? (Is our experience and expertise with middle school youth as strong as it is with high school and college students?)

One potential evaluation methodology would use these nine factors to quantitatively score each segment, creating a rational way to rank and prioritize them. Two major steps are involved, the first calculating a *potential for effectiveness* score and the second, a *potential for efficiency* score.

1. *Effectiveness scores* are determined from statistics and incidence data on four of the factors: segment size, problem incidence, problem severity, and defenselessness. The segment's population size is multiplied by percentages for incidence, severity, and defenselessness (i.e., size × incidence × severity × defenselessness). The resulting number becomes the segment's "true" market size relative to potential effectiveness.

2. *Efficiency scores* are determined from assessments of segments on the next five factors: reachability, responsiveness, incremental costs, responsiveness to marketing mix elements, and organizational capabilities. This process would require assigning some quantitative value or score for each segment relative to each factor.

HOW ARE TARGET MARKETS SELECTED?

Market segmentation has identified and described relevant market segments. *Evaluation activities* provided information on each segment that will help the planner take the next step, deciding which and how many segments will be *target markets* for the campaign or program being planned.

Three approaches are typical for commercial sector marketers and are useful concepts for the social marketer to consider:[20]

Undifferentiated Marketing: The organization decides to use the same strategy for all segments, focusing on what is "common in the needs of consumers rather than on what is different."[21] This approach is also sometimes referred to as *mass marketing* and is trying to reach and influence the most people at one time.

Example: Undifferentiated campaigns include those promoting issues of concern to a large cross section of the population: drinking eight glasses of water a day, wearing seat belts, not drinking and driving, flossing teeth, sun protection, water conservation, learning CPR, voting, organ donation.

Differentiated Marketing: The organization develops different strategies for different audiences. This approach often includes allocating more resources to priority segments.

Example: Campaigns that would benefit from a differentiated strategy are those in which segments have clear and distinguishable wants and needs, as well as recommended behaviors. This approach might be used for campaigns promoting water safety, physical activity, breast cancer screening, and commute trip reduction.

Concentrated Marketing: In this approach, sometimes referred to as niche marketing, some segments are eliminated altogether, and resources and efforts often concentrate on developing the ideal strategy for one or only a few key segments.

Example: Campaigns with narrow and concentrated focuses might include promoting folic acid to women in childbearing years, encouraging horse farmers to cover manure piles to avoid contamination of streams, AIDS prevention outreach programs to drug abusers, or recruiting young single men as volunteers for mentoring youth at risk.

As introduced in the prior section, segments could be prioritized and ranked at this point using effectiveness and efficiency scores. This would be especially useful for campaigns using a differentiated or concentrated approach in which the most efficient and effective segments will be targeted.

WHAT APPROACH SHOULD BE CHOSEN?

Most organizations involved in social marketing (public sector agencies and nonprofit organizations) are faced with limited budgets. Segments will need to be prioritized, with a disproportionate amount of resources allocated to the most effective and efficient segments. Some segments will need to be eliminated from the plan.

Target markets (markets of greatest opportunity) emerge as those with the greatest need and are the most ready for action, easiest to reach, and best match for the organization. Measures used to assess each of these are as follows:

- *The greatest need:* size, incidence, severity, and defenselessness
- *Most ready for action:* ready, willing, and able to respond

- *Easiest to reach:* identifiable venues for distribution channels and communication

- *Best match:* organizational mission, expertise, and resources

Targeting markets of *greatest opportunity* may run counter to a social marketer's natural desire and inclination (or mandate) either (a) to ensure that all constituent groups are reached and served (markets are treated equally) or (b) to focus resources on segments in which the incidence and severity of the problem is the gravest, (markets of greatest need). Concerns can be addressed by emphasizing that this is the most effective and efficient use of scarce resources, reassuring others that segmentation enables plans to be developed that are likely to succeed with individual segments, and explaining that additional segments can be addressed over time. We are simply prioritizing resources and efforts in an objective, systematic, and cost-effective way.

CHAPTER SUMMARY

1. Selecting target markets is a 3-step process: (a) segment the market, (b) evaluate segments, and (c) choose one or more segments for targeting.

2. Traditional variables used to describe consumer markets include demographics, geographics, psychographics, and behavior variables.

3. Two additional models frequently used by social marketing practitioners include the *stages of change model,* originally developed by Prochaska and DiClemente in 1983, and the *healthstyles segmentation system.*

4. Target markets are evaluated on the basis of efficiency and effectiveness measures, using variables outlined by Andreasen and presented in this text: segment size, problem incidence, problem severity, defenselessness, reachability, general responsiveness, incremental costs, responsiveness to marketing mix, and organizational capabilities.

5. Three common targeting approaches include undifferentiated marketing (same strategy for all segments), differentiated marketing (different strategies for different audiences), and concentrated marketing (a few key segments are targeted with unique strategies).

6. It was recommended that the markets of "greatest opportunity" are those with the greatest need, most ready for action, easiest to reach, and the best match for the organization.

KEY TERMS AND CONCEPTS

Target markets
Segment markets
Evaluate segments
Choose targets
Traditional segmentation variables
Demographic variables
Geographic variables
Psychographic variables
Behavior variables
Stages of change
Precontemplation
Contemplation
Preparation
Concentrated marketing
Action

Maintenance
Termination
Healthstyles segmentation
Segment size
Problem incidence
Problem severity
Defenselessness
Reachability
General responsiveness
Incremental costs
Undifferentiated
   marketing
Differentiated marketing
Markets of greatest
   opportunity

ISSUES FOR DISCUSSION

1. Thinking back to the marketing highlight on physical activity, how might strategies (product, price, place, and promotion) differ for a campaign targeting 25- to 34-year-olds?

2. For a campaign targeting HIV/AIDS prevention, describe three potential target market segments using at least three variables.

3. Why do you think many program planners have concerns with a concentrated (niche) marketing approach? What advice do you have?

RESEARCH HIGHLIGHT: SELF-ADMINISTERED SURVEY FOR PSYCHOGRAPHIC SEGMENTATION

The following text is a description of the well-known VALS™ Segmentation. The VALS system uses a self-administered questionnaire to categorize U.S. adult consumers into groups with distinctive mindsets. Readers may access the VALS Web site and take the VALS questionnaire online to determine their psychographic profiles.[22]

The VALS™ Segment Profiles

Psychographic Segmentation System

The primary VALS consumer types are shown graphically in the VALS Network. (See Figure 6.4.) The main dimensions of the VALS Network are self-orientation (the horizontal dimension in the figure) and resources (the vertical dimension in the figure).

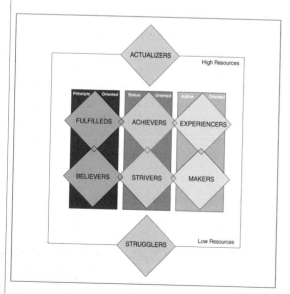

Figure 6.4. The VALS™ Segmentation System

Network of Distinctive, Interconnected Segments

Using the self-orientation and resources dimensions, VALS defines eight primary types of adult consumers who have different attitudes and exhibit distinctive behavior and decision-making patterns. Neighboring types can be combined for analysis. For example, a company might decide to develop advertising to appeal to a combined group of Experiencers and Makers. Primary types can also be analyzed by splitting them into smaller groups by their secondary types. The primary VALS type is the type the consumer is most like, and the secondary type is the type the consumer is second most like.

Self-Orientation

People pursue and acquire products, services, and experiences that provide satisfaction and give shape, substance, and character to their identities. They are motivated by one of three powerful self-orientations: principle, status, and action. Principle-oriented consumers are guided in their choices by abstract, idealized criteria, rather than by feelings, events, or desire for approval and opinions of others.

Status-oriented consumers look for products and services that demonstrate the consumers' success to their peers. Action-oriented consumers are guided by a desire for social or physical activity, variety, and risk taking.

Resources

Resources refer to the full range of psychological, physical, demographic, and material means and capacities people have to draw upon. It encompasses education, income, self-confidence, health, eagerness to buy things, intelligence, and energy level. It is a continuum from minimal to abundant. Resources generally increase from adolescence through middle age but decrease with extreme age, depression, financial reversal, and physical or psychological impairment.

Actualizers

Actualizers are successful, sophisticated, active, "take-charge" people with high self-esteem and abundant resources. They are interested in growth and seek to develop, explore, and express themselves in a variety of ways—sometimes guided by principle and sometimes by a desire to have an effect, to make a change.

Image is important to Actualizers, not as evidence of status or power but as an expression of their taste, independence, and character. Actualizers are among the established and emerging leaders in business and government, yet they continue to seek challenges. They have a wide range of interests, are concerned with social issues, and are open to change. Their lives are characterized by richness and diversity. Their possessions and recreation reflect a cultivated taste for the finer things in life.

Fulfilleds

Fulfilleds are mature, satisfied, comfortable, reflective people who value order, knowledge, and responsibility. Most are well educated and in (or recently retired from) professional occupations. They are well-informed about world and national events and are alert to opportunities to broaden their knowledge. Content with their career, families, and station in life, their leisure activities tend to center around the home.

Fulfilleds have a moderate respect for the status quo institutions of authority and social decorum, but are open-minded to new ideas and social change. Fulfilleds tend to base their decisions on firmly held principles and consequently appear calm and self-assured. While their incomes allow them many choices, Fulfilleds are conservative, practical consumers; they look for durability, functionality, and value in the products they buy.

Achievers

Achievers are successful career and work-oriented people who like to, and generally do, feel in control of their lives. They value consensus, predictability, and stability over risk, intimacy, and self-discovery. They are deeply committed to work and family. Work provides them with a sense of duty, material rewards, and prestige. Their social lives reflect this focus and are structured around family, church, and career.

Achievers live conventional lives, are politically conservative, and respect authority and the status quo. Image is important to them; they favor established, prestige products and services that demonstrate success to their peers.

Experiencers

Experiencers are young, vital, enthusiastic, impulsive, and rebellious. They seek variety and excitement, savoring the new, the offbeat, and the risky. Still in the process of formulating life values and patterns of behavior, they quickly become enthusiastic about new possibilities but are equally quick to cool.

At this stage in their lives, they are politically uncommitted, uninformed, and highly ambivalent about what they believe.

Experiencers combine an abstract disdain for conformity with an outsider's awe of others' wealth, prestige, and power. Their energy finds an outlet in exercise, sports, outdoor recreation and social activities. Experiencers are avid consumers and spend much of their income on clothing, fast food, music, movies, and video.

Believers

Believers are conservative, conventional people with concrete beliefs based on traditional, established codes: family, church, community, and the nation. Many Believers express moral codes that are deeply rooted and literally interpreted. They follow established routines, organized in large part around home, family, and social or religious organizations to which they belong.

As consumers, Believers are conservative and predictable, favoring American products and established brands. Their income, education, and energy are modest but sufficient to meet their needs.

Strivers

Strivers seek motivation, self-definition, and approval from the world around them. They are striving to find a secure place in life. Unsure of themselves and low on economic, social, and psychological resources, Strivers are concerned about the opinions and approval of others.

Money defines success for Strivers, who don't have enough of it, and often feel that life has given them a raw deal. Strivers are impulsive and easily bored. Many of them seek to be stylish. They emulate those who own more impressive possessions, but what they wish to obtain is often beyond their reach.

Makers

Makers are practical people who have constructive skills and value self-sufficiency. They live within a traditional context of family, practical work, and physical recreation and have little interest in what lies outside that context. Makers experience the world by working on it—building a house, raising children, fixing a car, or canning vegetables—and have enough skill, income, and energy to carry out their projects successfully.

Makers are politically conservative, suspicious of new ideas, respectful of government authority and organized labor, but resentful of government intrusion on individual rights. They are unimpressed by material possessions other than those with a practical or functional purpose (such as tools, utility vehicles, and fishing equipment).

Strugglers

Struggler lives are constricted. Chronically poor, ill-educated, low-skilled, without strong social bonds, elderly, and concerned about their health, they are often resigned and passive. Because they are limited by the need to meet the urgent needs of the present moment, they do not show a strong self-orientation. Their chief concerns are for security and safety.

Strugglers are cautious consumers. They represent a very modest market for most products and services, but are loyal to favorite brands.

SOURCE: SRI Consulting Business Intelligence "VALS™ Psychographic Segmentation. Retrieved 3/16/01 from SRI Consulting Business Intelligence Center at http://future. sri.com/VALS/VALS.segs.shtml. Reprinted by permission.

Notes

1. From Franklin Covey Weekly Quotes. (2001, June 3). Available on the World Wide Web at http//www.franklincovey.com
2. Kotler, P., & Armstrong, G. (2001). *Principles of Marketing* (p. 265). Upper Saddle River, NJ: Prentice Hall.
3. Ibid., p. 244.
4. Ibid., pp. 253-259.
5. Ibid., p. 259.
6. Prochaska, J., & DiClemente, C. (1983). "Stages and Processes of Self-Change of Smoking: Toward an Integrative Model of Change." *Journal of Consulting and Clinical Psychology, 51,* 390-395.
7. Prochaska, J., Norcross, J., & DiClemente, C. (1994). *Changing for Good* (pp. 40-46.) New York: Avon Books.
8. Ibid., pp.40-41.
9. Ibid., pp. 41-43.
10. Ibid., p. 43.
11. Ibid., p. 44.
12. Ibid., p. 45.
13. Ibid., p. 46.
14. Ibid., p. 68.
15. Ibid., p. 47.
16. Ibid., p. 47.
17. Kotler, P., & Roberto, E. L. (1989). *Social Marketing: Strategies for Changing Public Behavior* (p. 149). New York: Free Press.
18. Andreasen, A. R. (1995). *Marketing Social Change: Changing Behavior to Promote Health, Social Development, and the Environment* (p. 148). San Francisco: Jossey-Bass.
19. Ibid., pp. 177-179.
20. Kotler, P., & Armstrong, G., *Principles of Marketing,* pp. 265-268.
21. Ibid., p. 266.
22. SRI Consulting Business Intelligence Center. (2001)."VALS™ Psychographic Segmentation." Available on the World Wide Web at http://future.sri.com/VALS/VALS.segs.shtml

KEY CHAPTER QUESTIONS

1. What is the primary objective of a social marketing campaign?

2. What other objectives may be included?

3. What are campaign goals, and how do they differ from objectives?

4. What role do objectives and goals play in campaign evaluation?

CHAPTER 7

Setting Objectives and Goals

In the 48 hours after Charles Andrew Williams shot up his high school in Santee, California, 16 more kids in California were arrested or detained for making threats or taking guns to school. . . . The culture cracked down on itself: on Friday night KGTV, an ABC affiliate in San Diego, televised the memorial service for Williams' victims; then for roughly 35 minutes, it dropped its regular programming and showed only a text message urging parents to turn off the TV and spend time talking to their kids.

—Nancy Gibbs[1]

MARKETING HIGHLIGHT: WATER CONSERVATION

This case, which concerns water conservation in Seattle, highlights specific behavior, knowledge, and belief objectives, as well as a measurable, realistic goal.

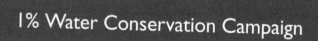

1% Water Conservation Campaign

Preeti Shridhar
Strategic Advisor, Marketing
Seattle Public Utilities

Background

Seattle, an area known for its many rainy days, in reality has significant water supply/demand challenges. Several water supply factors contribute to an urgent need to balance water availability.

Seattle Public Utilities (SPU) provides water to 26 suburban cities and water districts. SPU serves more than 1.3 million residential and business customers and is responsible for managing water resources for the region, while acting as an environmental steward. The following factors have a direct affect on water supply and demand in the greater Seattle area:

▶ Population: A 10% growth in population is expected over the next 10 years.

▶ Endangered Species Act: The federal government listed the Chinook salmon under the Endangered Species Act (ESA). This limits the amount of water SPU can use from rivers to meet its supply obligations.

▶ Summer peak: Summer is a very dry season in Seattle. This is also the time that the demand for water is at its peak, resulting from outdoor watering.

▶ Variations in snowfall: The Seattle area watershed is the main source of water to the Seattle region. Seasonal variations in snowfall affect the available water supply, and drought years can create extreme water shortages.

Establishing and marketing an aggressive conservation program has been selected as the best option to meet these challenges. It is the least expensive and most environmentally friendly option.

Program Objective and Goal

Campaign Objectives:

Behavior objectives:

Through the use of pricing, tangible products, and communications, influence residents and businesses to act as follows:

▶ Purchase high-efficiency appliances.

▶ Implement natural landscape and gardening practices.

▶ Practice water conservation actions, such as taking shorter showers.

Knowledge objectives:

▶ Know that 1% reduction every year for 10 years is the goal for all residents.

▶ Know about the different products and programs available to residents that can help achieve the 1% reduction.

Belief objectives:

▶ Water is precious and should never be wasted.

▶ Everyday actions have an impact on water supply, environment, and salmon.

▶ Water-efficient technologies and products consume less water while having little or no impact on lifestyles.

Campaign Goal

Reduce personal and business water consumption by 1% every year for 10 years.

Target Audiences

Almost 65% of the customers served by SPU are urban residential. The other 35% are businesses, commercial/industrial, and large organizations. Because this campaign crosses virtually all audiences, 1% Water Conservation should reinforce the ethic message with all audiences and target specific efforts to unique audiences.

Primary Audiences

Money is not available to simultaneously reach all audiences effectively, and given that some audiences will be more responsive than others, strategies will be tailored to appeal especially to these groups:

▶ Females

▶ Single-family homeowners

▶ 35- to 64-year-olds

▶ Household income above $50,000

Secondary Audiences

▶ Commercial sector

Strategies

A multidimensional strategy was developed to market 1% Water Conservation. The components of this strategy included the following elements.

Product

1% Water Conservation products include conservation tips and education, as well as professional services (landscape audits) and specific water-efficient appliances and technologies (tangible objects):

▶ Toilet rebates—A rebate program is targeted at homeowners and commercial customers to replace their existing toilets with low-flow models.

▶ WashWise—A point of purchase promotion and rebate is offered for high-efficiency clothes washers.

▶ Landscape—Audits, financial incentives, and "natural landscaping education" is offered to residents and commercial customers.

▶ Schools program—An education effort that focuses on elementary schools.

▶ Water Smart technology—Products and services are provided for commercial air-conditioning and laundry. Industries include hospitality, health care, school districts, and research organizations.

Price

Discount incentives and rebates were used to promote several appliances. Many jurisdictions imposed higher rates for excessive usage and seasonal surcharges during peak demand months to significantly lower demand.

Promotion/ Communications Strategies

Because the program is a 10-year effort, the campaign to lay the foundation for the ethic and build support for the 1% Water Conservation program will be a multiyear effort.

Focus during the first 2 years will concentrate on communicating about the ethic. Later years will focus more on the "how" message and delivering 1% programs. With the ethic established, the audience will be primed for long-term behavior changes to be suggested through the various 1% products and offerings.

Branding 1% Water Conservation

One of the most ambitious strategies is to *brand* the conservation ethic. Creating a brand identity for the program and creating brand awareness so that a range of options, from simple behavior changes, such as taking shorter showers, to purchasing water-efficient toilets, could ride on the strength and recognition of the brand.

The 1% logo and graphic were created with the tag line: "What will you save today?" (See Figure 7.1.) The question in the tag line speaks to the individual and addresses both altruistic and economic connotations and responsibilities. The visual depiction shows that all things in nature are connected: the individual's role, the water supply, the environment, and the region's salmon. This brand appears in everything from television ads and brochures to rebate offerings for businesses.

Public Relations

Several press and public events throughout the campaign are the key strategic emphasis of the marketing plan. This campaign is kept fresh through a variety of media events that focus on various aspects of the 1% Water Conservation program. Here are some examples of the public relations campaign:

▶ A kick-off event at the start of the campaign in which the Mayors of Seattle and Bellevue change out existing appliances to water-efficient ones in a family's home and demonstrate water conservation tips. Mayors watering lawns and changing toilets! It was in the news in all the regional TV stations, newspapers, and other press.

▶ A recognition ceremony at the Pike Place Market, a Seattle icon, where the businesses in the market were showcased for their commitment to reducing water use.

▶ A public offering of low-flow toilet rebates is anticipated to attract many homeowners turning in old toilets for new ones.

Figure 7.1. Campaign Logo for Water Conservation

Advertising

Paid advertising is being used as a major vehicle to build the 1% Water Conservation brand, to establish the "why" in the minds of residents. It reinforces the ethic and establishes the value of water so that residents are motivated to participate in the programs. A media mix of print and television comprise the paid media portion of the campaign. The television ad appeared on network television through the months of peak water consumption in the summer; a newspaper insert emphasized why 1% was important to the region and gave program details and choices to consumers; and a print ad offered a rebate for efficient appliances and hastened consumers to "Act Now." An insert in major newspapers went to more than 600,000 households. (See Figure 7.2.) Direct mail was used to provide program details and local information from participating utilities and was also planned for businesses and commercial customers to provide rebate offers and financial incentives. A Web site (savingwater.org)

Figure 7.2. Newspaper Insert Used to Reach 600,000 Residents

and a dedicated information telephone number were set up as integral tools to support the campaign. And tent cards were used in restaurants during drought periods. (See Figure 7.3.)

Evaluation Strategy

In order to track the success of efforts and to respond to the needs of the consumers in future campaigns, a comprehensive evaluation strategy is in place. This includes regular surveys, focus groups, and analysis of water consumption data.

Figure 7.3. Tent Card Used in Restaurants During Drought Periods

CHAPTER OVERVIEW

Once target markets for a campaign have been selected, we have the foundation for building our campaign strategy. Our next step is to establish *campaign objectives, the primary objective always being the very specific behaviors we want to influence our audience to accept, modify, abandon, or reject.* As illustrated in our case on water conservation, several doable behaviors explained in simple, clear terms were promoted to achieve a decrease in residential water consumption.

This chapter presents examples of *behavior objectives* (something we want our audience to do), as well as two additional types of objectives: *knowledge objectives* (something we want them to know) and *belief objectives* (something we want them to believe). As will become clear, campaign objectives are different from campaign purpose, defined earlier as the ultimate impact of a successful campaign.

After determining campaign objectives, campaign *goals* that are specific, measurable, and realistic are established that will be *used to evaluate campaign efforts.* Ideally, they specify

TABLE 7.1 Cell Phone Usage: Potential Campaign Objectives and Goals

Issue	*Traffic accidents and injuries*
Focus	Cell phone usage in cars
Purpose	Reduced traffic accidents associated with using cell phones while driving
Campaign objectives: Behavior objective	To pull over to use a cell phone (see Figure 7.4)
Knowledge objective	To know the percentage of traffic accidents involving someone talking on a cell phone
Belief objective	To believe that talking on a cell phone, even a "hands-free" model, can be a distraction
Campaign goal	Increase the number of people who pull over to use their cell phones by 25%

rates of change in behavior, such as the increase in numbers of those in the target audience performing the desired behavior after the campaign.

Objectives and goals established at this point should be considered *draft objectives and goals*. We may learn in Step 4, when we deepen our understanding of target audiences, that our objectives and goals are not realistic, clear, and/or appropriate for our audience and that they must be revised. And we may find when developing preliminary budgets that we will need to reduce our goals due to funding considerations.

Finally, objectives and goals will affect campaign evaluation. Given the fact that campaign goals represent the foundation for campaign evaluation, it is critical that goals are relevant to campaign efforts and are feasible to measure.

Referring back to our cell phone example from Chapter 6, Table 7.1 illustrates key concepts presented in this chapter.

BEHAVIOR OBJECTIVES

All social marketing campaigns should be designed and planned with a specific behavior objective in mind. Even if the planner discovers that the campaign needs to include additional knowledge and belief components, a behavior objective will need to be identified that these elements will support. Behavior objectives in social marketing campaigns have several important characteristics:

◆ Ideally, they are simple, clear, doable acts, even though they may not be perceived as easy (e.g., quitting smoking).

Figure 7.4. Campaign Messages Encourage Drivers to Pull Over If They Need to Talk on the Phone

- We should be able to picture our target audience performing the behavior (e.g., removing the plastic insert from the cereal box before sorting for recycling).

- Our target audience should be able to determine that they have performed the behavior (e.g., placing infants in cribs on their backs to reduce the risk of infant death).

- Although a campaign may promote more than one behavior, it should be recognized that different tactics or strategies might be necessary to promote each one (e.g., using a litterbag will be a different behavior than covering loads in pickup trucks).

- The campaign objective is not the ultimate slogan or campaign message, although it is used to develop both (e.g., "Eat five fruits and vegetables a day" became "5 A Day").

- The objective is not quantifiable as we are defining it. The goal is the quantifiable, measurable component that provides the ability to measure and track the impact of efforts (e.g., a blood bank's goal may be to increase the number of donors by 10% in the next fiscal year).

Table 7.2 presents examples of potential behavior objectives for many of the social issues identified in Chapter 1. Examples presented are singular and hypothetical.

TABLE 7.2 Examples of Potential Behavior Objectives

Health Promotion	Examples of Potential Behavior Objectives for Specific Audiences
Tobacco use	Don't start smoking.
Heavy/binge drinking	Drink less than five drinks at one sitting.
Alcohol and drug use during pregnancy	Don't drink alcoholic beverages if you are pregnant.
Physical inactivity	Exercise moderately 30 minutes a day, 5 days a week, at least 10 minutes at a time.
Teen pregnancy	Choose abstinence.
Sexually transmitted diseases	Use a condom.
Fat gram intake	Make sure total fat grams consumed are below 30% of total daily calories.
Fruit and vegetable intake	Eat five servings of fruits and vegetables a day.
Water intake	Drink eight glasses of water a day.
Obesity	Have your body mass index measured by a health care professional.
Breast cancer	Learn the proper procedure for examining your breasts.
Prostate cancer	Talk with your health care provider about an annual prostate exam if you are 50 years of age or older.
Oral health	Use a cup to give an infant juice instead of a bottle.
Osteoporosis	Get 1000 to 1200 milligrams a day of calcium.
Injury Prevention	
Drinking and driving	Keep your blood alcohol level below .08% if you are drinking and driving.
Seat belts	Buckle your seat belt before you put your vehicle in gear.
Domestic violence	Have a plan that includes a packed bag and a safe place to go.
Gun storage	Store handguns in a lockbox or safe or use a reliable trigger lock.
Fires	Check smoke alarm batteries every month.
Falls	Include some form of strength building in your exercise routine.
Household poisons	Place recognizable stickers on all poisonous products in the kitchen, bathroom, bedroom, basement, and garage.

(Continued)

TABLE 7.2 (Continued)

Protecting the Environment	Examples of Potential Behavior Objectives for Specific Audiences
Waste reduction	Buy bulk and unpackaged goods rather than packaged items.
Wildlife habitat protection	Stay on established paths when walking through forests.
Forest destruction	Use materials made from recycled tires and glass for garden steps and paths.
Toxic fertilizers and pesticides	Follow instructions on labels and measure precisely.
Water conservation	Replace old toilets with new low-flow models.
Air pollution from automobiles	Don't top off the gas tank when refueling your car.
Air pollution from other sources	Use an electric or push mower instead of a gas-powered model.
Forest fires	Chip wood debris that can be used for composting instead of burning it.
Conserving electricity	Turn off computer monitors when leaving work at the end of the day.
Litter	Clean out litter that might blow out of the back of your open pickup truck.
Community Involvement	
Volunteering	Give 5 hours a week to a volunteer effort.
Mentoring	Encourage and support caring relationships between your child and a nonparent adult.

In reality, several audiences and objectives would be developed to address each of these complex and far-reaching concerns.

KNOWLEDGE AND BELIEF OBJECTIVES

When conducting the situation analysis (Step 1), the planner may have learned from prior similar campaigns or from existing secondary research on the topic that typical audiences need a little help before they act. They may need to have some *knowledge* (information or facts) and/or *belief* (values, opinions, or attitudes) before they are convinced that the action is worth the effort. Those in the precontemplation stage, for example, typically don't believe they have a problem. Those in the contemplation stage may not have made up their mind that the effort (cost) is worth the gain (benefit). Even those in the action stage may not be aware of their accomplishments and are therefore vulnerable to relapses.

This need for increased knowledge and/or beliefs might also be revealed in Step 4, in which research is conducted to deepen our understanding of our target audience and the competition relative to our behavior objective. In this case, we return to Step 3 in our plan and add knowledge and/or belief components to our campaign objectives.

Knowledge objectives are those relating to statistics, facts, and other information and skills your target audience would find motivating or important. Typically, the information has simply been unavailable to the audience or unnoticed. Here are some examples:

- Statistics on *risks* associated with current behavior (e.g., percentage of obese women who have heart attacks versus those not medically obese)

- Statistics on *benefits* of the proposed behavior (e.g., percentage of men over the age of 50 with prostate cancer and the survival rates associated with early detection through annual exams)

- Facts on *attractive alternatives* (e.g., lists of flowering native plants that are drought and disease resistant)

- Facts that *correct misconceptions* (e.g., cigarette butts are not biodegradable and can take more than 10 years to disintegrate completely)

- Facts that might be *motivating* (e.g., learning that moderate physical activity has been proven to have some of the same important medical benefits as vigorous physical activity)

- Information on *how to perform* the behavior (e.g., prepare a home for an earthquake)

- *Resources* available for assistance (e.g., phone numbers battered women can call to find temporary shelter)

- *Locations* for purchase of goods or services (e.g., locations where handgun lockboxes can be purchased)

- Current *laws and fines* that may not be known or understood (e.g., a fine of $950 can be imposed for tossing a lit cigarette)

Belief objectives are those relating to attitudes, opinions, feelings, or values held by the target audience. The target audience may have current beliefs that the marketer may need to alter in order for them to act, or we may find that an important belief is missing. For example, the audience may need to formulate the following notions:

- They will personally *experience the benefits* from adopting the desired behavior (e.g., increased physical activity will help them sleep better).

- They are *at risk* (i.e., they currently believe they are capable of driving safely with a blood alcohol level of over .08%).

- They will be *able to successfully perform* the desired behavior (e.g., talk to their teenager about thoughts of suicide).

- Their individual behavior *can make a difference* (e.g., taking mass transit to work).

- They *will not be viewed negatively* by others if they adopt the behavior (e.g., not accepting another drink).

- The costs of the behavior will be *worth it* (e.g., having an annual mammogram).

- There will *be minimal negative consequences* (e.g., worrying that organ donation information might be shared with third parties).

These knowledge and belief objectives provide direction for developing strategies (the marketing mix) in Step 5. They have important implications *especially for developing key messages and communication strategies* that provide the information and arguments that will be most motivating. Advertising copywriters, for example, will reference these objectives when developing communication slogans, script, and copy. There are also opportunities for other elements of the marketing mix to support these additional objectives: an immunization product strategy that incorporates a wallet-sized card to ensure that parents know the recommended schedule; an incentive offered by a utility for trading in gas mowers for mulch mowers as a way to "convince" homeowners of their harm to the environment; or a special Web site dedicated to purchasing booster seats, sponsored by a children's hospital, as a testimonial to the safety concern.

Table 7.3 provides examples of each of the objectives described. It should be noted that even though each campaign illustrated has a knowledge and belief objective, this is neither typical nor required. As stated earlier, the behavior objective is the primary focus.

THE NATURE OF SOCIAL MARKETING GOALS

Ideally, social marketing goals establish a desired level of behavior change as a result of program and campaign efforts. In this ideal scenario, current levels of behavior are known for the target markets, and the planner establishes a future level that the plan will be developed to achieve. This is similar to commercial sector marketers, who establish sales goals for their products when developing annual marketing plans and then develop strategies and resource allocations consistent with these goals.

As illustrated below, ideal goals are quantifiable, measurable, and relate to the specific campaign focus, target audience, and time frame:

TABLE 7.3 Purpose, Audience, and Objectives

Campaign Purpose	Target Audience	Behavior Objective	Knowledge Objective	Belief Objective
Reduced birth defects	Women in child-bearing years	Get 400 micrograms of folic acid every day.	For it to help, you must take it before you become pregnant and during the early weeks of pregnancy.	Without enough folic acid, the baby is at risk for serious birth defects.
Reduced child injuries from auto-mobile accidents	Parents with children aged 4 to 8	Put children who are aged 4 to 8 and weigh less than 80 pounds in booster seats.	Traffic accidents are the leading cause of death for children aged 4 to 8.	Children aged 4 to 8 weighing less than 80 pounds are not ade-quately protected by adult seat belts.
Improved water quality	Small horse farmers within 5 miles of streams, lakes, or rivers	Cover and protect manure piles from rain.	Storm water runoff from piles can pol-lute water resources.	Even though your manure pile is small, it does contribute to the problem.
Increased number of registered organ donors	People renewing driver's licenses.	Register to be an organ donor when you renew your driver's license. (See Figure 7.5.)	Your family may still be asked to sign a consent form for your donation to occur.	Information will be kept private and can only be accessed by authorized officials.

◆ Increase by 25% in a 24-month period the per-centage of women over the age of 50 who get an-nual mammograms.

◆ Increase the percentage of people wearing seat belts at checkpoints from 60% in 2001 to 75% in 2003.

◆ Decrease the amount of glass, paper, aluminum, and plastic litter on roadways by 4 million pounds in 2 years.

◆ Increase the average number of caring adults in the lives of middle school youth from 1.5 to 3.0 over a period of 3 years.

Figure 7.5. Indiana Organ Procurement Organization Encourages Residents to Register When Renewing Driver's Licenses

TABLE 7.4 Hypothetical Objectives and Goals

Purpose	Behavior	Knowledge	Belief
Reduce birth defects	What we want them to do	What they may need to know before they will act	What they may need to believe before they will act
Objective	Get 400 micrograms of folic acid every day.	For it to help, you need to take it before you become pregnant, during the early weeks of pregnancy. (See Figure 7.6.)	Without enough folic acid, the baby is at risk for serious birth defects.
Goal[a]	Increase the percentage of women aged 18 to 45 who take a daily vitamin containing folic acid from 25% in 1995 to 40% in 2001.	Increase the percentage of women aged 18 to 45 who know folic acid should be taken before pregnancy from 2% in 1995 to 20% in 2001.	Increase the percentage of women aged 18 to 45 who believe folic acid prevents birth defects from 4% in 1995 to 30% in 2001.

a. Survey data is from folic acid telephone survey conducted by the Gallup Organization in 1995, 1997, 1998, and 2000, commissioned by the March of Dimes and supported by the Centers for Disease Control and Prevention. Goal is for nonpregnant women.

Get the **"B"** Attitude

That's "B" for the B vitamin folic acid.
Get the attitude by taking it every day. Folic acid may help save your baby from birth defects of the brain and spinal cord. But you have to take it every day before you get pregnant and in the first few weeks of your pregnancy for it to help.

B vitamin folic acid — Why you need it
A baby needs folic acid right after it's conceived, before you even know you're pregnant. Folic acid helps the baby's brain and spinal cord develop properly. Without enough, the baby could have serious birth defects called neural tube defects.

March of Dimes

In the example presented earlier on folic acid for women in their child-bearing years, behavior, knowledge, and belief goals might be developed as illustrated in Table 7.4.

In reality, this process is difficult or impractical for many social marketing programs. Baseline data on current levels of behavior for a target market may not be known or may not be available in a timely or economically feasible way. Projecting future desired levels (goal setting) often depends on data and experience from years of tracking and analyzing the impact of prior efforts. Many social marketing efforts are conducted for the first time, and historic data may not have been recorded or retained. Social marketing planners in these situations can explore several excellent resources that may provide data that will guide efforts to establish baselines as well as goals:

• *Behavior Risk Factor Surveillance System (BRFSS)* was developed by the Centers for Disease Control (CDC), headquartered in Atlanta, Georgia. It is

Figure 7.6. Promoting Daily Use of a Vitamin Before Pregnancy

BOX 7.1
Healthy People 2010: Leading Health Indicators

What are the Leading Health Indicators?

The Leading Health Indicators will be used to measure the health of the Nation over the next 10 years. Each of the 10 Leading Health Indicators has one or more objectives from Healthy People 2010 associated with it. As a group, the Leading Health Indicators reflect the major health concerns in the United States at the beginning of the 21st century. The Leading Health Indicators were selected on the basis of their ability to motivate action, the availability of data to measure progress, and their importance as public health issues.

The Leading Health Indicators are—

> Physical Activity
> Overweight and Obesity
> Tobacco Use
> Substance Abuse
> Responsible Sexual Behavior
> Mental Health
> Injury and Violence
> Environmental Quality
> Immunization
> Access to Health Care

SOURCE: Department of Health and Human Services. Healthy People 2010: Understanding and Improving Health. 2nd ed. Washington, DC: U.S. Government Printing Office, November 2000.

used by states throughout the country to measure and track the prevalence of major risk behaviors among Americans, including tobacco use, sexual behavior, injury prevention, physical activity, nutrition, and prevention behaviors, such as breast, cervical, and colorectal cancer screening. Details on this system are included in the research highlight at the end of this chapter. Data are available over the Internet and, for many of the behaviors, provide statistics by state.

• *Healthy People 2010* is managed by the Office of Disease Prevention and Health Promotion and the U.S. Department of Health and Human Services. It is a set of health objectives for our nation to achieve by the year 2010 and is used by states, communities, professional organizations, and others to develop programs to improve health. Nearly all states have developed their own "Healthy People" plans, building on national objectives and tailoring them to their specific needs. Box 7.1 presents information from the Healthy People 2010 Web site on leading health indicators, the 10 high-priority areas for the nation's health.[2] Each indicator has specific targets, as illustrated in Box 7.2.[3]

BOX 7.2
Healthy People 2010:
Details on Specific Targets for Substance Abuse

Alcohol and illicit drug use are associated with many of this country's most serious problems, including violence, injury, and HIV infection. The annual economic costs to the United States from alcohol abuse were estimated to be $167 billion in 1995, and the costs from drug abuse were estimated to be $110 billion.

In 1998, 79% of adolescents aged 12 to 17 years reported that they did not use alcohol or illicit drugs in the past month. In the same year, 6% of adults aged 18 years and older reported using illicit drugs in the past month; 17% reported binge drinking in the past month, which is defined as consuming five or more drinks on one occasion..

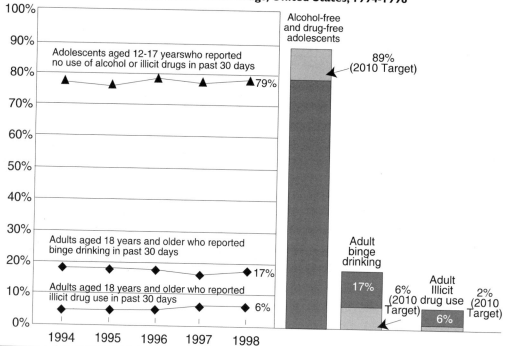

Use of Alcohol and/or Illicit Drugs, United States, 1994-1998

SOURCE: Department of Health and Human Services. Healthy People 2010: Understanding and Improving Health. 2nd ed. Washington, DC: U.S. Government Printing Office, November 2000.

The objectives selected to measure progress among adolescents and adults for this Leading Health Indicator are presented below. These are only indicators and do not represent all the substance abuse objectives in Healthy People 2010.

- Increase the proportion of adolescents not using alcohol or any illicit drugs during the past 30 days.
- Reduce the proportion of adults using any illicit drug during the past 30 days.
- Reduce the proportion of adults engaging in binge drinking of alcoholic beverages during the past month.

• Explore the availability of data from *peers in other agencies* who may have conducted similar campaigns.

• Often, *nonprofit organizations and foundations* with a related mission (e.g., the American Cancer Society) may have excellent data helpful to establishing meaningful campaign goals.

Alternatives for Goal Setting

If baseline data are not available and setting goals relative to behavior change is not practical or feasible at the time, the following alternatives might be considered for goal setting:

Establish goals for campaign awareness and recall

Example: A statewide tobacco prevention program establishes a goal for the first 3 months of an advertising campaign for 75% of the target audience (adults who smoke) to correctly recall the campaign slogan and two of the four television ads, on an unaided basis. Results will then be presented to the state legislature to support continued funding of the campaign.

Establish goals for levels of knowledge

Example: A program for improved nutrition among low-income families sets a goal that 50% of women participating in a pilot project correctly identify and describe the recommended daily servings of fruits and vegetables.

Establish goals for acceptance of a belief

Example: A chain of gas stations is conducting a pilot project to influence customers not to top off their gas tanks; they establish a goal that 80% of customers report they believe topping off a gas tank can be harmful to the environment, versus 25% prior to the campaign launch.

Establish goals for a response to a campaign component

Example: A water utility will consider a campaign a success if 25% of residential customers call a well-publicized toll-free number or visit a Web site for a listing of drought-resistant plants.

Establish goals for intent to change behavior

Example: A state coalition promoting moderate physical activity is eager to know whether a brief 6-week pilot program increased interest in physical activity. They establish a goal that states their "reported intention to increase physical activity in the next 6 months from 20% to 30%, a 50% increase in behavior intent."

Establish goals for the campaign process

Example: A school-based program promoting abstinence has a goal that 40 abstinence campaigns are developed and implemented by youth in middle schools and high schools around the state during the upcoming school calendar year.

In situations such as these, in which campaign goals are not specifically related to behavior change, it should be reemphasized that campaign objectives should still include a behavior objective. Alternative goals will relate to some activity that supports and promotes the desired behavior.

OBJECTIVES AND GOALS AT THE DRAFT STAGE

In Step 4 of our planning process, we will deepen our understanding of our target audience. We will learn more about their knowledge, beliefs, and current behavior related to objectives and goals established at this point. It is often necessary to then revise and finalize objectives and goals that are more realistic, clear, and appropriate.

THE ROLE OF OBJECTIVES
AND GOALS IN CAMPAIGN EVALUATION

One of the last steps (Step 6) in developing a social marketing plan will be to develop an evaluation plan, a process covered in Chapter 14. It is important to emphasize at this point, however, that the planner will return to Step 3 of the plan, campaign objectives and goals, and will need to select methodologies and develop plans to measure these stated goals. For some of the examples presented in this chapter, the following items would need to be measured:

- ◆ Number of mammograms among low-income women in the pilot
- ◆ Number of people wearing seat belts stopped at checkpoints
- ◆ Pounds of specific types of litter on roadways
- ◆ Number of middle school youth with caring adult relationships

◆ Number of women in childbearing years taking folic acid

◆ Number of children aged 4 to 8 using booster seats

◆ Number of small horse farmers who covered their manure piles

◆ Number of new organ donors registering with the department of licensing

◆ Percentage of airline travelers who have their computers out of their bags when they arrive at checkpoints

The message is simple. Establish a goal that is meaningful to campaign efforts and that will be feasible to measure.

CHAPTER SUMMARY

1. The primary objective of a social marketing campaign is behavior change. All social marketing campaigns should be designed and planned with a specific behavior objective in mind, something we want our target audience to do. Behavior objectives should be clear, simple, doable acts, which the target audience will know they have completed.

2. Occasionally, the social marketer will also need to establish one or two additional objectives. *Knowledge objectives* (something we want our target audience to know) are those relating to statistics, facts, and other information your target audience would find motivating or important. *Belief objectives* (something we want our target audience to believe) are those relating to attitudes, opinions, or values held by the target audience. The target audience may have current beliefs that the marketer may need to alter in order for them to act, or we may find that an important belief is missing.

3. *Goals* are quantifiable, measurable, and relate to the specific campaign focus, target audience, and time frame. Ideally, they establish a desired level of behavior change as a result of program and campaign efforts. When establishing and measuring behavior change is not practical or economically feasible, alternatives can be considered, including ones that measure campaign awareness, response, process, and/or increase in knowledge, beliefs, and intention.

4. Given the fact that campaign goals represent the foundation for campaign evaluation, it is critical that goals are relevant to campaign efforts and feasible to be measured.

KEY TERMS AND CONCEPTS

Campaign objectives
Behavior objectives
Knowledge objectives
Belief objectives
Behavior Risk Factor
   Surveillance System (BRFSS)
Healthy People 2010

Behavior change goals
Knowledge goals
Belief goals
Response goals
Intent-to-change goals
Campaign process goals

ISSUES FOR DISCUSSION

1. Relative to a campaign with a focus on pregnant women and the health of their babies, what are four potential behavior objectives?

2. For one of these behavior objectives identified in Issue #1, what are some potential knowledge and belief objectives?

3. For an objective of influencing employees to turn off computer monitors when leaving work at the end of the day, what is a potential behavior change goal? Knowledge goal? Belief goal?

RESEARCH HIGHLIGHT:
SECONDARY DATA FOR PROGRAM GOAL SETTING

Since the early 1980s, the Centers for Disease Control and Prevention (CDC) has tracked major health risk behaviors, using standardized telephone surveys with citizens around the country conducted in conjunction with state health departments. Included in this overview are (a) a summary of the system and (b) a list of topics covered in the telephone survey.[4]

Surveillance of Health Risks: Foundation for Public Health Action

Surveillance is the essential underpinning for all efforts by CDC and the states to promote health and prevent disease. Surveillance is the tool that provides the necessary data to define the disease burden, identify populations at highest risk, determine the prevalence of health risks, and guide and evaluate disease prevention efforts at the national, state, and local levels.

Unlike at the beginning of this century, chronic diseases are now our nation's leading killers. Two chronic diseases, cardiovascular disease and cancer, account for almost two-thirds of all deaths among Americans. In many cases, the roots of chronic diseases are grounded in a limited number of health-damaging behaviors practiced by people every day for much of their lives. These behaviors include

▶ Lack of physical activity.

▶ Poor nutrition (e.g., high-fat, low-fiber diets).

▶ Tobacco use.

▶ Underuse of known prevention strategies, such as breast, cervical, and colorectal cancer screening.

Reducing the prevalence of these and other behaviors that endanger the health of Americans demands strategies such as public and provider education, prevention research, and policy and environmental changes that facilitate healthy living. To be effective, however, these strategies must be supported by ongoing surveillance of health risks.

CDC's Unique State-Based Surveillance

In the early 1980s, CDC worked with the states to develop the Behavioral Risk Factor Surveillance System (BRFSS). This state-based system, the first of its kind, made available information on the prevalence of risk behaviors among Americans and their perceptions of a variety of health issues.

Now active in all 50 states, the BRFSS continues to be the primary source of information on major health risk behaviors among Americans. State and local health departments rely heavily on BRFSS data to

▶ Determine priority health issues and identify populations at highest risk.

▶ Develop strategic plans and target prevention programs.

▶ Monitor the effectiveness of intervention strategies and progress toward achieving prevention goals.

▶ Educate the public, the health community, and policymakers about disease prevention.

▶ Support community policies that promote health and prevent disease.

In addition, BRFSS data enable public health professionals to monitor progress toward achieving the nation's health objectives outlined in Healthy People 2000: National Health Promotion and Disease Prevention Objectives. BRFSS information is also used by researchers, voluntary and professional organizations, and managed care organizations to target prevention efforts. Recognizing the value of such a system in addressing priority health issues in the coming century, China, Canada, and other countries have looked to CDC for assistance in establishing BRFSS-like systems for their own populations.

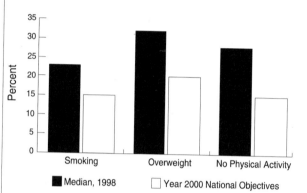

Prevalence of Behavioral Risk Factor Among Adults for Cardiovascular Disease

Versatility of the BRFSS Benefits States

Unlike many surveillance systems, the BRFSS is flexible enough to satisfy individual state needs while also meeting information needs at the national level.

The benefits of the BRFSS for states include the following:

▶ **Data can be analyzed in a variety of ways.** BRFSS data can be analyzed by a variety of demographic variables, including age, education, income, and racial and ethnic background. The ability to determine populations at highest risk is essential in effectively targeting scarce prevention resources.

▶ **The BRFSS is designed to identify trends over time.** For example, state-based data from the BRFSS have revealed a national epidemic of obesity.

▶ **States can add questions of special local interest.** For example, following the bomb explosion at the Alfred P. Murrah Federal Building in Oklahoma City, the Oklahoma BRFSS included questions on such issues as stress, nightmares, and feelings of hopelessness so that health department personnel could better address the psychological impact of the disaster.

▶ **States can readily address urgent and emerging health issues.** Questions may be added for a wide range of important health issues, including diabetes, oral health, arthritis, tobacco use, folic acid consumption, use of preventive services, and health care coverage. In 1993, when flooding ravaged states along the Mississippi River, Missouri added questions to assess the impact of the flooding on people's health and to evaluate the capability of communities to respond to the disaster.

Although the BRFSS is flexible and allows for timely additions, standard core questions enable health professionals to make comparisons between states and derive national-level conclusions. BRFSS data have highlighted wide disparities between states on key health issues. In 1998, for example, the prevalence of current smoking among U.S. adults ranged from a low of 14% in Utah to a high of 31% in Kentucky. These data have also been useful for assessing tobacco control efforts. For instance, BRFSS data revealed that the annual prevalence of cigarette smoking among adults in Massachusetts declined after an excise tax increase and antismoking campaign were implemented.

The BRFSS is the perfect instrument for adding state-specific questions. What else do we have for surveying the behavior of the general adult population?

—Epidemiologist, Connecticut Department of Public Health

Notes

1. Gibbs, N. (2001, March 19). "It's Only Me." *Time,* p. 22.
2. Office of Disease Prevention and Health Promotion (ODPHP). U.S. Department of Health and Human Services is the coordinator of the Healthy People 2010 Initiative. Information retrieved 10/1/01 from http://www.health.gov/healthypeople/LHI/lhiwhat.htm
3. Ibid.
4. Behavioral Risk Factor Surveillance System (BRFSS), 2000. Survey data, National Center for Chronic Disease Prevention and Health Promotion, Centers for Disease Control and Prevention, U.S. Department of Health and Human Services. Retrieved 3/23/01 from Centers for Disease Control Web site at http://www.cdc.gov/nccdphp/brfss/at-a-gl.htm

KEY CHAPTER QUESTIONS

1. What more do we need to understand about our target audience relative to our draft objectives and goals?

2. What are potential models and theories that might be used to explore our audience perspectives further?

3. Who is the competition in a social marketing environment?

4. What are four key potential tactics to create advantages over the competition?

5. Why is it necessary to review and potentially revise target markets, objectives, and goals after this step in the planning process?

CHAPTER 8

Deepening Our Understanding of the Target Audience and the Competition

The more deeply you understand people, the more you will appreciate them, the more reverent you will feel about them. To touch the soul of another human being is to walk on holy ground.

—Stephen R. Covey[1]

MARKETING HIGHLIGHT: DRINKING AND DRIVING

This case highlights development of campaign strategies based on achieving a clearer understanding of audience perspectives. The MOST of Us™ Campaign, at Montana State University, in Bozeman, was originally funded by the Montana Department of Transportation, Traffic Safety Bureau. In the following section, written in early 2001, Dr. Jeff Linkenbach, director of the Montana Social Norms Project, explains the process of using data to analyze the needs of the statewide population of young adults. This pioneering effort and its initial positive results represent the first statewide social norms campaign effort. The Montana Social Norms Project has also conducted campaigns targeting parent-teen communication, adult seat belt use, and teen tobacco use.

MOST of Us™

Jeff Linkenbach, Ed.D.
Director of the Montana Social Norms Project

People live with a lot of wrong perceptions, ideas, and notions,
and when they invest their lives in them it is dangerous.

—Ticht Nhat Hanh

Background and Situation Analysis

During the 1990s, I directed health promotion efforts for college students at Montana State University. Throughout this time, college health professionals were seeking solutions beyond merely educating individual students to make healthier choices—especially around the issue of alcohol misuse. The entire field of college health promotion was turning attention toward reshaping the campus environment by addressing the larger social context in which students drink. Accordingly, any successful program to reduce harm from alcohol abuse would have to focus on community alcohol use norms.

In 1997, the Bureau Chief of the Traffic Safety Bureau in the Montana Department of Transportation had entered a quandary regarding the best use of state resources for reducing alcohol-related crashes among Montana's young adults. While Montana's approximate number of 90,000 young adults comprised only 12% of all licensed drivers, they accounted for over 26% of all alcohol-related crashes (ref. 1). [See reference notes after case text.]

College prevention programs recorded that the social norms approach to prevention was reporting 18-21% reductions in heavy drinking and associated consequences (such as impaired driving) amongst undergraduate college students in as little as two years (refs. 2, 3, 4). Research demonstrates the existence of a significant gap between the actual and perceived norms for alcohol use amongst college students and their peers (refs. 5, 6, 7). These findings have led to successful campaigns utilizing marketing techniques to promote greater awareness of the actual moderate alcohol use norms practiced by the majority of students on campus.

Target Audiences, Objectives, and Goal

Since frequent heavy episodic drinking (i.e., males drinking 5 or more drinks consecutively or females drinking 4 or more drinks consecutively and doing this 3 or more times weekly) among college students has been found to increase the probability of driving while impaired, or riding with an impaired driver (ref. 8) by 10 to 16 times, we sought to reduce heavy drinking as a way to decrease the number of alcohol-related crashes among young adults. The social norms model would be tried, but only if data could be obtained to show that the same disparity existed between perceptions and actual alcohol use norms for Montana's young adult target population as was seen among college students. Since the majority (66%) of young adults were not enrolled in Montana's colleges, a survey method broader than traditional campus surveys was needed. Furthermore, this question about whether the misperceptions of alcohol use norms existed for noncollege young adults had never been explored.

In order to provide initial baseline data for a social norms campaign, the Montana Young Adult Alcohol Use Phone Survey was developed. Analysis of the statewide phone survey data revealed four key findings. First, most young adults in Montana were relatively moderate and safe drinkers or abstained from alcohol use. This finding accurately frames the context of the young adult drinking culture. Second, the patterns of misperceptions found in this research coincide in two directions: (a) young adults tend to exaggerate the amount of heavy episodic drinking

among peers, and (b) they tend to underestimate the prevalence of risk-reducing behaviors of their peers. Third, the general pattern of misperceptions remains for both men and women amidst these gender differences. Finally, this pattern of misperceptions was found to be virtually the same whether looking at college students or young adults not in college.

Social Marketing Strategies

These findings provided key implications for possible campaign direction. The application of social norms theory through marketing techniques, which had been successful among college students, might also have similar effects across a statewide population of young adults. Moreover, a statewide marketing campaign could increase or reinforce the effectiveness of campus-specific campaigns.

Social Marketing Program Management

The statewide campaign targeting a reduction in heavy episodic drinking and impaired driving had only acquired a minimal budget and resources for campaign materials development. The campaign would have to rely on donated television and radio airtime. Leveraging resources and support of local efforts would be critically needed.

In order to meet this challenge of program implementation, the Montana Model of Social Norms Marketing was created (ref. 9). This seven-step process would give key stakeholders a common process for implementing and evaluating local campaign efforts. [See Figures 8.1. and 8.2.] A core model requirement was to provide dedicated, rigorous data gathering and transform it into social norms messages. That is, a process for capturing and mirroring actual norms as a way of counteracting the widespread misperception.

This model provided a blueprint process for creating campaigns that mirrored successful campaigns

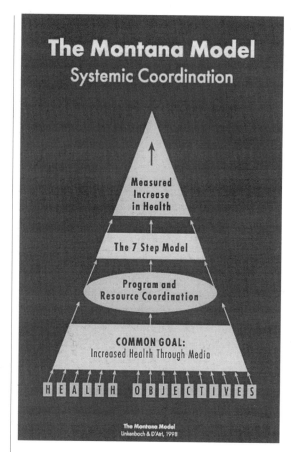

Figure 8.1. The Montana Model, Illustrating the Context for the 7 Steps Social Norms Marketing Model

on individual college campus settings. Since most health campaigns had operated from a fear-based or health terrorism approach (ref. 10) without much attention to outcome data, the bulk of this work would center on strategic planning and media advocacy (Step 1 in this model). Campus and community partnerships were established through regional and national conferences. Press opportunities and campaign efforts were legitimized through key stakeholder events that involved the governor and public support from college presidents. MOST of Us™ was established as a brand to unify efforts. Branding was used in developing statewide television and radio

public service announcements and print materials to support local efforts. [See Figure 8.3.] Through ongoing feedback, from an initial two-month campaign, the focus of our message was refined from targeting a reduction in heavy episodic or "binge" drinking, to one which directly addressed our primary objective of reducing impaired driving.

Evaluation

Ongoing surveys and data analysis confirmed the campaign's effectiveness. Analysis showed that strategic use of low budget print and free television

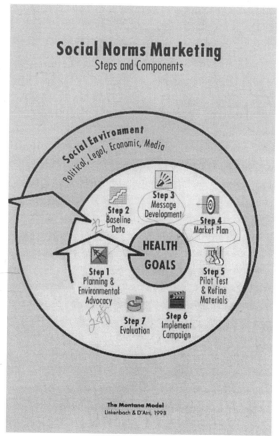

Figure 8.2. Seven Steps for Social Norms Marketing, From the Montana Model

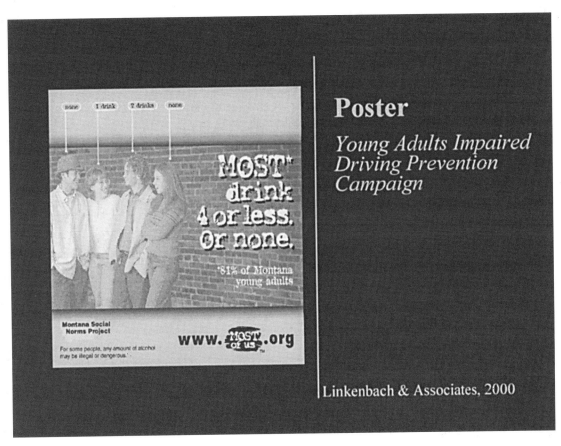

Figure 8.3. Poster to Alter Current Perceptions

and radio airtime would have to be exponentially expanded in order to measure impact on reducing alcohol-related crashes among 18- to 24-year-olds. Achieving only an approximate 1.5% decrease (after controlling for population differences) in alcohol-related crashes in the target group over a two-year period of time was far below campaign objectives. Different surveys revealed that only about 40% of the target group was being exposed to the campaign message—an amount far below the critical mass needed to significantly shift behaviors.

On a very promising note however, the data revealed that the social norms approach to preventing impaired driving in a statewide population of young adults was working. That is, there was a significant behavioral difference for those young adults that could recall a "MOST of Us™ Prevent Drinking & Driving" message. It was as though a "MOST of Us™ protective factor" was operating in those young adults who could recall our campaign message. Specifically, data on reported impaired driving in the previous 30 days was much lower for those that remembered our campaign message (15.5%) as compared to those young adults (25.2%) who could not recall any impaired driving message. Even more pronounced was the difference from those young adults (28.8%) that reported driving while impaired who only recalled hearing some other (i.e., fear-based) anti-impaired driving message (ref. 11).

References

1. Montana Department of Transportation (1991-1997). *Traffic Safety Bureau Problem Identification Statistics.*

2. Haines, M. P. (1998, Winter). Social norms: A wellness model for health promotion in higher education. *Wellness Management (14)*, 4.

3. Johannessen, K. (1998). *Results from the University of Arizona Social Norms Project.* Unpublished research results submitted for publication.

4. Perkins, H. W. (1998.) *An Overview of the Social Norms Approach to Prevention.* Presentation at the 1st Annual Prevention & Safety Conference on the Social Norms Approach, Big Sky, MT.

5. Perkins, H. W., & Berkowitz, A. D. (1986). Perceiving the community norms of alcohol use among students: Some research implications for campus alcohol education programming. *International Journal of the Addictions (21)*, 961-976.

6. Perkins, H. W. (1991). Confronting misperceptions of peer drug use norms among college students: An alternative approach for alcohol and drug education programs. *Peer Prevention Program Implementation Manual.* Fort Worth, TX: Higher Education Leaders/Peers Network, Texas Christian University.

7. Perkins, H. W., & Wechsler, H. (1996). Variation in perceived college drinking norms and its impact on alcohol abuse: A nationwide study. *Journal of Drug Issues, 26*(4), 961-974.

8. Wechsler, H., Davenport, A., Dowdall, G., Moeykens, B., & Castillo, S. (1994). Health and behavioral consequences of binge drinking in college: A national survey of students at 140 campuses. *Journal of the American Medical Association 272*, 1672-1677.

9. Linkenbach, J., & D'Atri, G. (1998). *The Montana Model.* An unpublished training manual developed for the Montana Social Norms Project.

10. Linkenbach, J. (1998). *Beyond Health Terrorism.* An unpublished paper presented at the Western Regional Environmental Prevention Summit, Center for Substance Abuse Prevention. Great Falls, MT.

11. Linkenbach, J., & Perkins, W. (2000). Misperceptions of alcohol norms in a statewide population of young adults: Implications for the application of a social norms campaign. Manuscript accepted for publication in *The Social Norms Monograph.*

CHAPTER OVERVIEW

At this point in the planning process, we have selected target markets and we know what we want them to do. We may also have identified something we need them to know and/or believe, having determined that this may be necessary before they will act. As the MOST of Us™ case demonstrates, altering an existing belief can be key to behavior change.

Before proceeding to developing strategies, we will take some time to deepen our understanding of our audience relative to the specific behaviors we identified in Step 3. When we selected target audiences, we had a focus for our campaign (e.g., intentional littering on roadways). We then determined our objectives (e.g., desired behaviors, such as using a litterbag) and goals (e.g., increase the number of litter bags in cars at annual checkpoints). We now need to return to our target audiences and explore their current behavior, knowledge, and beliefs relative to this specific objective.

This exploration will assist us in choosing customer-oriented product, price, place, and promotional strategies. Several social marketing theories, models, and instruments exist for exploring our audience and will be described in this chapter.

We also discuss the nature of competition in the social marketing environment and outline four potential positioning tactics for consideration in developing our marketing mix.

Finally, we stress the importance of returning to our selection of target markets (Step 2) and objectives and goals (Step 3) and making any changes that might be warranted given what we learn from listening to our customers.

WHAT MORE DO WE NEED TO KNOW ABOUT OUR TARGET AUDIENCE?

Assume that you are responsible for developing a plan to help reduce the amount of litter on roadways. You have developed behavior objectives: Use a litterbag and cover loads in the back of open pickup trucks. You have a geographic, demographic, and psychographic profile of people who litter; but this doesn't tell you what your target audience knows and believes about littering. It doesn't tell you what (preferred) behaviors and associated benefits you are competing with. Imagine how important (and helpful) it would be for you to know the answers to the following questions before developing strategies in Step 5:

What would they rather do than the behavior we are promoting and why?

- What *benefits* do they see to their current behavior?

  They might tell us they throw the pop can out the window because the remaining liquid might spill on the floor of the car and that a leak-proof litterbag that sealed would be ideal, a *product* implication.

- What *costs* do they see to their current behavior?

  We might discover that they currently don't think they'll be seen littering and therefore don't worry about it. If they thought they could get caught, however, and that the penalties were severe, they say they would think twice. This might lead us to establishing an 800 number for citizens to report littering, a *promotion* and *place* implication.

What do they know about the desired behaviors?

- Do they know there is a law that you are supposed to have a litterbag in the car and that fines for littering can be as much as $500? If not, increased awareness might be important, a *price* and *promotion* implication.

- Do they know where to get free litterbags? If not, making locations visible and accessible might be important, a *place* implication.

- Do they know how to properly secure loads? If not, a demonstration booth at county fairs and annual new car and truck shows might be effective, a *promotion* implication.

- Do they know how much litter is dumped on freeways every year and how much it costs the state to pick it up? If not, perhaps during an annual litter awareness week, bags full of litter collected on the roads could be piled in a visible section along the road, a *promotion implication.*

What do they believe?
What are their values and attitudes relative to the desired behaviors?

- What *benefits* do they see to using litterbags and securing their loads? "What's in it for them" to do this?

  If we find out that being a good role model for their children matters more than being a good environmental steward, messages about saving the earth should be secondary, a *promotional* implication.

- What do they perceive it will *cost* them to adopt this behavior?

  We may learn that they toss beer bottles out the window so they won't be caught with open containers in their cars. Our challenge will then be to understand which penalties for littering might be perceived to be as great or greater than the one for the current behavior, a *pricing* implication. Some states have found that community service penalties in which the litterer is required to spend time picking up litter is perceived as a severe cost.

- What *barriers* do they have to performing the behavior?

  We may find out that most of our target audience (single males 18-24 years old) "wouldn't be seen" with one of the state's white plastic litterbags with cartoon graphics in their black leather interior car. This may lead us to the need for developing a new "cool" litterbag, a *product* implication.

In Chapter 7, objectives for four hypothetical campaigns were developed and presented. In Table 8.1, we expand on these examples, presenting potential scenarios that further research might reveal regarding our audience. Relative to our objective (desired behavior), what do they currently (prefer to) do, what do they know, and what do they believe?

TABLE 8.1   Finding Out What Our Target Audience Currently Knows, Believes, and Does Relative to Our Behavior Objective

Objective	Do	Know	Believe
Folic acid: Get 400 micrograms of folic acid every day.	Some are taking a multi-vitamin but not on a regular basis.	May not know that about half of pregnancies are unplanned.	May believe they get enough folic acid in their daily diet.
Booster seats: Put children in booster seats aged 4 to 8 years weighing under 80 pounds.	Most use a seat belt and put the child in the back seat.	May not know where to find or how to choose booster seats.	May believe seat belts are "good enough" for children in school.
Water quality: Cover and protect manure piles from rain.	Most leave them uncovered.	May have seen a few articles in the community paper on the water quality problems in the area.	May not believe their manure piles are contributing much to the problem.
Organ donation: Register to be an organ donor when you renew your driver's license.	Most are not registering.	May not know that their family members will be asked to give final consent.	May believe that this might affect the quality of their medical care and decisions related to life support.

WHAT MODELS MIGHT BE USED TO EXPLORE OUR AUDIENCE PERSPECTIVES FURTHER?

Deepening our understanding of target audiences can be accomplished in a variety of ways, always beginning with a review of existing literature and research and discussions with peers and colleagues. If, after this review, informational gaps still exist, it may be important to conduct original research using qualitative methods, such as focus groups and personal interviews, and/or quantitative instruments, such as telephone and self-administered surveys.

As discussed in Chapter 4 (Research), one of the first steps in planning research projects is to identify our informational objectives. Several models are available for organizing and prioritizing question areas and are described by several social marketing theorists and practitioners.

Knowledge, Attitude, Practice, and Beliefs (KAPB)

Andreasen describes this survey model:

These are comprehensive surveys of a representative sample of the target population designed to secure information about the social behavior in question and on the current status of the target audience's: Knowledge, Attitudes, Practices, Beliefs.

KAPB studies are relatively common in social marketing environments, especially in the area of health. They are very often carried out routinely by local governments, the World Bank, or the United Nations. For this reason, they are sometimes available to social marketers as part of a secondary database.[2]

As an example, a KAPB-type study was conducted by the Gallup Organization for the March of Dimes in 1995, 1997, 1998, and 2000 and was supported by the Centers for Disease Control and Prevention.[3] Telephone surveys conducted nationwide were designed to track knowledge and behavior related to folic acid among women aged 18 to 45. Consider how these summary findings in the year 2000 would shape campaign strategies and priorities:

- 9 out of 10 women did not know that folic acid should be taken prior to pregnancy.

- More than 8 out of 10 women did not know that folic acid could help prevent birth defects.

- Only 1 in 3 women not pregnant at the time of the survey reported consuming a multivitamin containing folic acid daily.

The Health Belief Model (HBM)

Brown describes this model originally developed by social psychologists Hochbaum, Kegels, and Rosenstock, who were greatly influenced by the theories of Kurt Lewin.

The HBM states that the perception of a personal health behavior threat is itself influenced by at least three factors: general health values, which include interest and concern about health; specific health beliefs about vulnerability to a particular health threat; and beliefs about the consequences of the health problem. Once an individual perceives a threat to his/her health and is simultaneously cued to action, and his/her perceived benefits outweighs his/her perceived costs, then that individual is most likely to undertake the recommended preventive health action. Key descriptors include:

- Perceived Susceptibility: Perception of the likelihood of experiencing a condition that would adversely affect one's health

- Perceived Seriousness: Beliefs a person holds concerning the effects a given disease or condition would have on one's state of affairs: physical, emotional, financial, and psychological

- Perceived Benefits of Taking Action: The extent to which a person believes there will be benefits to recommended actions

- Perceived Barriers to Taking Action: The extent to which the treatment or preventive measure may be perceived as inconvenient, expensive, unpleasant, painful, or upsetting

- Cues to Action: Types of internal and external strategies/events that might be needed for the desired behavior to occur[4]

This model suggests that the social marketing planner would benefit from reviewing or conducting research to determine audience perceptions of susceptibility, seriousness, benefits, barriers, and perceptions of effective "cues to action" *before* developing campaign strategies.

Innovation Diffusion Model

Kotler and Roberto describe the concept of diffusion (or spread) of the adoption of new behaviors through a population and its applicability to social marketing referencing original work by Rogers and Shoemaker:

The ability of social marketers to plan and manage the diffusion or spread of adoptions to the largest possible target-adopter population requires an understanding of both individual behavior and the mechanisms by which new ideas and practices spread to the larger group or population of target adopters. . . .

Innovation diffusion research suggests that different types of adopters accept an innovation at different points in time. Table 8.2 summarizes the size, timing of adoption, and motivations for adoption of each target-adopter segment. The diffusion process begins with a small (2.5 percent) segment of innovative-minded adopters. These adopters are drawn to novelty and have a need to be different. They are followed by an early segment of target adopters (13.5 percent), who are drawn by the social product's intrinsic value. A third early majority segment (34 percent) perceive the spread of a product and decide to go along with it, out of their need to match and imitate. The late majority (34 percent) jump on the bandwagon, and the remaining segment, the laggards (16 percent), follow suit as the product attains popularity and broad acceptance.[5]

TABLE 8.2 Elements of the Diffusion Innovation Model That Are Useful for Diffusion Planning

Target-Adopter Segments	Hypothetical Size (%)	Timing Sequence of Adoption	Motivation for Adoption
Innovator segment	2.5	First	Need for novelty and need to be different
Early adopter segment	13.5	Second	Recognition of adoption object's intrinsic/convenience value from contact with innovators
Early majority segment	34.0	Third	Need to imitate/match and deliberateness trait
Late majority segment	34.0	Fourth	Need to join the bandwagon triggered by the majority opinion legitimating the adoption object
Laggard segment	16.0	Last	Need to respect tradition

SOURCE: Adapted with permission of The Free Press, a division of Simon & Schuster, Inc., from *Communications of Innovations: A Cross-Cultural Approach* (2nd ed.), by Everett M. Rogers, with F. Floyd Shoemaker. Copyright ©1962, 1971 by The Free Press.

The usefulness of this model at this stage in the planning process would be in providing additional information regarding (a) what might motivate our target audience to adopt the new behavior given where they are in the adoption sequence and (b) how to "speed the diffusion along" to remaining segments.

The Social Cognitive Theory/ Social Learning Theory

Fishbein summarized Bandura's description of the social cognitive theory, also referred to as the social learning theory:

The Social Cognitive Theory states that two major factors influence the likelihood that one will take preventive action:

First, like the Health Belief Model, a person believes that the **benefits of performing the behavior outweigh the costs** (i.e., a person should have more positive than negative outcome expectancies).

Second, and perhaps most important, the person must have a sense of personal agency or **self-efficacy** with respect to performing the preventive behavior . . . must believe that he or she has the skills and abilities necessary for performing the behavior under a variety of circumstances.[6]

Social Norms

Linkenbach describes the social norms approach to prevention, with clear potential implications to strategy development:

The social norms approach to prevention emerged from college health settings in the mid-1980s in response to the seemingly intractable issue of high-risk drinking by college students.[7] Wesley Perkins and Alan Berkowitz,[8] social scientists at Hobart, Williams, and Smith Colleges discovered that a significant disparity existed between actual alcohol use by college students and their perceptions of other students' drinking. Simply put, most college students reported that they believed drinking norms were higher and riskier than they really were.

The major implication of these findings is that if a student believes that heavy alcohol use is the norm and expected by most students, then regardless of the accuracy of the perception, he or she is more likely to become involved in alcohol abuse—despite his or her own personal feelings. Perkins came to call this pattern of misperception the "reign of error" and suggested that it could have detrimental effects on actual student drinking.[9] According to Berkowitz,[10] if college students think, "everyone is doing it," then heavy drinking rates rise due to the influence from "imaginary peers." Simply stated, whether and how much students drink partly depend on their perceptions of campus drinking norms. Students take in a variety of information about what they see as typical or normative among their peers. When they see several students using alcohol, they may feel more pressure to fit in by drinking more. When they see fewer students drinking they feel less pressure and may drink less.[11] Perkins identifies this pattern as a self-fulfilling prophecy.[12] The more students who overestimate the drinking behavior of their peers and tend to believe that high-risk drinking is common (i.e., normative), the more high-risk drinking will actually occur.

This model highlights the potential benefit of understanding perceived versus actual behaviors among target audiences. Results may signal an opportunity to correct the perception.

Themes From All Models

Fishbein's summary of behavior change interventions covers themes from most of the models presented in this chapter:

Generally speaking, it appears that in order for a person to perform a given behavior one or more of the following must be true:

1. The person must have formed a strong **positive intention (or made a commitment)** to perform the behavior;

2. There are **no environmental constraints** that make it impossible to perform the behavior;

3. The person has the **skills** necessary to perform that behavior;

4. The person believes that the **advantages** (benefits, anticipated positive outcomes) **of performing the behavior outweigh the disadvantages** (costs, anticipated negative outcomes);

5. The person perceives more **social (normative) pressure** to perform the behavior than not perform the behavior;

6. The person perceives that performance of the behavior is **more consistent than inconsistent with his or her self-image,** or that its performance does not violate personal standards that activate negative self-actions;

7. The person's **emotional reaction to performing the behavior is more positive than negative;** and

8. The person perceives that he/she has the **capabilities** to perform the behavior under a number of different circumstances.[13]

WHO IS THE COMPETITION IN A SOCIAL MARKETING ENVIRONMENT?

Social marketers have tough competitors, for we define *the competition* as follows:

◆ Behaviors and associated benefits our target audience would prefer over the ones we are promoting (e.g., taking long showers)

◆ Behaviors they have been doing "forever" that they would have to give up (e.g., driving alone to work)

◆ Organizations and individuals who send messages that counter or oppose the desired behavior (e.g., the "Marlboro Man")

Table 8.3 illustrates the challenges facing social marketers. Consider the pleasures and benefits we are asking them to give up. Consider the economic power of organizations and sponsors that are sending messages countering those we are sending. Consider the persuasiveness and influence of typical key messengers.

TABLE 8.3   Examples of Competing Behaviors and Messages

Behavior Objective	Competing Behaviors	Competing Messages and Messengers
Drink less than five drinks at one sitting.	Getting really "buzzed"	Budweiser
Exercise moderately 30 minutes a day, 5 days a week, 10 minutes at a time.	Sleeping in	Roommate
Drink eight glasses of water a day.	Drinking lattés	Starbucks
Don't smoke or chew tobacco.	"Chilling out" with friends	Camel cigarettes
Store handguns in a lockbox or safe or use a reliable trigger lock.	Having a handgun ready to go if needed	National Rifle Association
Keep your blood alcohol level below .08% if you are drinking and driving.	Picking up dates at a party	Friends
Wear a life vest.	Tanning	Fashion ads showing tan shoulders and arms
Clean out litter that might blow out of the back of your open pickup truck.	Getting to the job site on time	Boss
Use an electric or push mower instead of a gas-powered model.	Using the existing lawn mower	Spouse
Give 5 hours a week to a volunteer effort.	Spending time with family	Your kids

WHAT ARE FOUR KEY TACTICS TO CREATE COMPETITIVE ADVANTAGES?

How do we compete? We use the same principles and techniques used in the commercial sector. We *position* our product relative to the competition so that our audience perceives the following:

- *Greater benefits* in the behavior we are promoting than in their current or preferred behaviors

◆ *Lower costs and fewer barriers* to adapting the desired behavior than their current or preferred behavior

◆ *Social pressures or norms* that signal this as an acceptable cultural value

Our challenge is to develop product positioning, price, place, and promotional strategies that will do a better job of attracting and satisfying our target audience than the competition does. We want to create a competitive advantage,

an advantage over competitors gained by offering consumers greater value, either through lower prices or by providing more benefits that justify the higher prices. The key to winning and keeping customers is to understand their needs and buying processes better than competitors do and to deliver more value.[14]

As will be described later in this section, social marketers are encouraged to take this one step further and promise not just more, but "higher values" than those offered by competing behaviors.

McKenzie-Mohr and Smith confirm the task:

The function of a social marketing program, then, is to change the ratio of benefits and barriers so that the target behavior becomes more attractive. There are four non-mutually exclusive ways (tactics) that this can be done.

1. Increase benefits of the target behavior.
2. Decrease the barriers (and/or costs) to the target behavior.
3. Decrease the benefits of the competing behavior(s).
4. Increase the barriers (and/or costs) of the competing behaviors.[15]

Table 8.4 is a simple illustration of what would be in reality a more exhaustive list of benefits and costs that would be created (ideally) from audience research. There may also be more than one preferred or alternative behavior identified as the competition.

An important component of this research process will include exploring the priority of benefits and barriers/costs within each of the quadrants. We are searching for the "higher value," the key benefits to be gained or costs that will be avoided by adopting the desired behavior. As illustrated in Table 8.5, interviews with people who throw litter on roadways might reveal hot buttons that will guide positioning, as well as other elements of the strategic marketing mix.

An additional model for developing competitive advantages is focused on creating *competitive superiority,* a more rigorous objective. The same four tactics mentioned earlier are used in tandem, as illustrated in Table 8.6. A *benefit-to-benefit*

TABLE 8.4 Finding Out What Our Target Audience Perceives About the Competition

	Desired Behavior	*Competing Behavior*
	Take 400 micrograms of folic acid.	**Just "wing it" and assume I'll get it in my regular diet.**
Perceived benefits	I'll have a healthier baby.	I don't have to remember.
Perceived barriers/costs	I don't know cost of tablets and which ones to buy.	If I'm not careful, my child could have birth defects.

	Desired Behavior	*Competing Behavior*
	Use a booster seat.	**Using a regular adult seat belt.**
Perceived benefits	It is safer.	My child feels grown-up.
Perceived barriers/costs	It's a hassle to switch seats between cars.	My child could be injured.

	Desired Behavior	*Competing Behavior*
	Cover the manure piles.	**Leave the manure piles uncovered.**
Perceived benefits	I can be a good citizen.	My farm looks better; plastic tarps don't look good.
Perceived barriers/costs	I will need to go find/purchase a tarp.	We may be fined if we don't act voluntarily now.

	Desired Behavior	*Competing Behavior*
	Register to be an organ donor.	**Don't register.**
Perceived benefits	I could save someone's life.	I don't need to talk with family.
Perceived barriers/costs	My family may be upset if my body is disfigured.	People needing organs may die because of a lack of donors.

TABLE 8.5 Competitive Analysis for Positioning and Other Strategic Decisions

	Desired Behavior	Competing Behaviors	
	Use a Litterbag	Tossing Beer Cans Out the Window	Tossing Fast-Food Bags Out the Window
#1 Perceived benefit:	It's a good role model for my children.	I won't get caught with an open container of alcohol in my car.	It's easier.
Other perceived benefits:	I do my part for the environment. Save tax dollars. Reduce guilt.	It won't rattle around on the floor. I don't have to pick it out of my car later and put it in the trash.	I avoid the smell of old food in my car. I avoid the trash all over my car. I don't have to pick it up out of my car later and put it in the trash.
#1 Perceived barrier/cost: Other perceived barriers/costs:	Having to find one and remember to put it in the car. Having to remove it from my car and put it in a receptacle. Having it under my feet or on the floor. Having liquid spill out of it. Looking like "a nerd" with a white plastic bag in my black leather interior car.	I might have to do community service and pick up 197 litter. I could get caught and fined. I could hurt someone.	I might have to do community service and pick up litter. I could get caught and fined. I'm contributing to litter on the roadways that looks bad and will have to be picked up.

superiority tactic appeals to "higher values" than those perceived for the competition (e.g., a child who wants and needs a parent is compared to the short-term pleasures from smoking). A *cost-to-benefit superiority* tactic places an emphasis on decreasing costs/barriers to adopting the desired behavior and at the same time, decreasing perceived benefits of the competition (e.g., success stories from cessation classes include testimonials from a spouse talking about how nice it is to have clean air in the house). A *benefit-to-cost superiority* tactic places an emphasis on the benefits of the desired behavior and the costs of the competing behavior(s) (e.g., abilities

TABLE 8.6 Creating Competitive Superiority

Competing Behavior	Desired Behavior	
	Increase Benefits	*Decrease Costs/Barriers*
Decrease benefits:	Tactic A: Benefit-to-benefit superiority tactic	Tactic B: Cost-to-benefit superiority tactic
Increase costs/barriers:	Tactic C: Benefit-to-cost superiority tactic	Tactic D: Cost-to-cost superiority tactic

of teen athletes who don't smoke are compared with those who do). A *cost-to-cost superiority* tactic relies on a favorable comparison of costs of the desired behavior relative to the competition (e.g., short-term nicotine withdrawal symptoms are compared with living with emphysema).

WHY IS IT NECESSARY TO REVIEW AND POTENTIALLY REVISE TARGET MARKETS, OBJECTIVES, AND GOALS AFTER THIS STEP?

This new in-depth understanding of target audiences may signal a need to revise target markets (Step 2) and/or objectives and goals (Step 3) because it may reveal one or more of the following situations:

One of the target markets has beliefs that we would have a difficult time changing or may not want to:

> "Moderate physical activity like that is 'wimpy,' and I'd rather increase vigorous activity from 2 to 3 days a week if I do anything more."

The desired behavior has too many insurmountable barriers for one or more target markets:

> "I can't get to the Farmers Market to use my coupons because they close before I get off work."

The audience tells us the behavior objective isn't clear:

> "I don't understand what reducing my BMI means."

Perceived costs are too high:

> "Quitting smoking while I'm pregnant looks impossible, but I might be able to cut down to a half a pack a day."

The behavior objective has already been met:

> "My child already has a couple of caring adult relationships outside the home, so for you to suggest I go find one says you're not talking to people like me."

We learn that a major knowledge objective isn't needed but a belief objective is:

> "I already know that tobacco kills one out of three users. I just don't believe I'll get addicted."

The original behavior objective isn't the solution to the problem:

> "I always cover the load in the back of my pickup truck with a tarp. The problem is, it still doesn't keep stuff from flying out. What we need is a net or cable that holds the tarp down."

The goal is too high:

> "This latest survey says that 75% of high school seniors are sexually active so a goal of 50% choosing abstinence looks impossible with this group!"

CHAPTER SUMMARY

1. After establishing our objectives (desired behaviors) and goals in Step 3, we need to return to our target audiences and explore their current behavior, knowledge, and beliefs relative to this specific objective and goal level. This insight is critical to developing customer-oriented strategies.

2. Research is important at this phase of our planning process, but this may not mean that it needs to be new research. Relevant information about our target audiences may already exist and should be explored before undertaking new efforts.

3. Several social marketing theories and models regarding behavior change are helpful in identifying and organizing questions to explore with our audiences: Knowledge, Attitude, Practices, and Beliefs (KAPB) studies; the health belief model; innovations diffusion model; social cognitive theory/social learning theory; and the social norms approach.

4. The competition in social marketing environments is tough, for it includes these challenges: behaviors our target audience would prefer to do and the pleasures and benefits associated with them, behaviors our target audience is currently doing that may be lifelong habits, and strong messages and "messengers" that are counter to the behaviors we are promoting. An in-depth analysis of perceived benefits, barriers, and costs of the desired and competing behaviors is key to developing positioning strategies and identifying competitive advantages.

5. Four potential tactics for positioning our desired behavior were presented: (a) increase benefits of the target behavior, (b) decrease the barriers and/or costs to the target behavior, (c) decrease the benefits of the competing behavior, and (d) increase the barriers and/or costs of the competing behavior. Although decisions regarding these tactics will actually be made in Step 5 (Strategy), this homework becomes a valuable planning resource.

6. We may learn the following from listening to our customers: (a) One or more of the target markets we selected should be eliminated or placed as a low priority, (b) our objective needs to be clarified or changed, and/or (c) our goal needs to be redefined and/or increased or decreased. In this case, we return to our draft plan and revise these components.

KEY TERMS AND CONCEPTS

Perceived benefits
Perceived costs
Perceived barriers
KAPB studies
Innovation diffusion model
Health belief model

Social cognitive/social
  learning theory
Social norms
Competition
Competitive superiority

ISSUES FOR DISCUSSION

1. For a desired behavior (objective) of using an electric instead of a gas mower, what are potential perceived benefits? Costs?

2. What would be potential tactics to (a) increase perceived benefits and (b) decrease perceived costs of using an electric versus a gas mower?

3. For a desired behavior of volunteering 5 hours a week, what are potential competing behaviors? What are potential perceived costs and benefits of volunteering? What are potential perceived benefits and costs of one of the competing behaviors identified?

RESEARCH HIGHLIGHT: FORMATIVE AND EVALUATION RESEARCH USING QUALITATIVE AND QUANTITATIVE TECHNIQUES

This research case highlights the extensive use of a variety of research techniques at several stages in the planning and evaluation process.

PEP: The Personal Energy Plan

Nicole Angelique Kerr, RD, MPH
Health Communications Specialist
Division of Nutrition and Physical Activity
Centers for Disease Control and Prevention

Background

In June 1997, the Centers for Disease Control and Prevention, Division of Nutrition and Physical Activity (NuPAC), implemented the Personal Energy Plan (PEP)[16]—a 12-week worksite demonstration project—through managed care organizations at five distinct worksites throughout the U.S. PEP was developed as the next phase in an iterative, consumer-based, formative research process designed to encourage individual behavior change to improve health.

The PEP program set out to persuade worksite personnel to increase their daily physical activity levels and healthy eating behaviors by focusing on **benefits of these behaviors** as well as ways to **decrease barriers to them**. The scientific basis for the consumer-oriented program was based on:

1. Choosing a diet low in fat (U.S. Department of Agriculture, 1990);
2. Choosing a diet with plenty of vegetables and fruits (U.S. Department of Agriculture, 1990); and
3. Accumulating 30 minutes or more of moderate-intensity physical activity over the course of most days of the week (Pate et al., 1995; U.S. Department of Health and Human Services (USDHHS), 1996).

Methods

The initial phase of this worksite intervention was to identify, segment, and select primary target audiences. This was accomplished by incorporating an iterative approach and integrating a comprehensive review of the social, behavioral, and epidemiological research on nutrition and physical activity, as well as a market analysis and an environmental scan of national organizations working in the areas of physical activity and nutrition.

Behavior change is much more likely to be successful when the target audience is ready to make changes, as is the case with individuals in the contemplation or preparation stages for exercise (Marcus & Simkin, 1993). Thus, we confined our target group to those people in contemplation and preparation stages for moderate physical activity and healthy eating.

Various target audiences were identified by the literature review, market analysis, and environmental scan. Each target audience was assessed according to various criteria, which resulted in a target audience initially segmented on age (middle-aged adults ages 29-54), ethnicity (African American/Caucasian), educational level (range from high school graduate/equivalent to some graduate school), gender, and stages of behavior change (contemplation and preparation stages tend to engage in more physical activity and/or eat more fruits and vegetables and less fat). The influence of children present in the home (18 years old or younger) on parent diet and physical activity patterns also was examined.

Over one-quarter of the sample identified was in the contemplation or preparation stages for healthy eating and/or moderate physical activity. All exercise and nutrition groups were then profiled according to responses to survey measures assessing demographics, daily average nutrient intake, attitudes toward exercise, types of physical activity behaviors, general health attitudes, and self-reported chronic disease status. Also assessed were attitudes toward health/nutrition media, and media use.

During March and April 1995, an initial round of focus groups were conducted with the above segmented audience to assess participants' perceptions of healthy eating and physical activity as they related to the following:

- ▶ Their relative importance
- ▶ Important determinants of (and barriers to) eating healthy and getting more activity
- ▶ Knowledge of the impact of poor nutrition and sedentary lifestyles on health
- ▶ Knowledge related to recommendations for physical activity and a healthy diet
- ▶ Reactions to the idea of messages that combine healthy eating and physical activity information
- ▶ The credibility of sources (both organizational and personal) for healthy eating and physical activity messages

A second round of focus groups were conducted with the target audience that included testing nutrition and physical activity message concepts. The choice of which concept to incorporate into an eventual campaign was based on what appealed to participants in terms of making the behaviors appear achievable, worthwhile, and sustainable. To this end, the idea of "creating more energy" in one's life was chosen. To further refine the execution of this concept, 312 central location intercept interviews were conducted with the target audience in December 1995, at eight shopping malls across the country.

Project staff decided to implement the campaign through the worksite setting based on further consumer research, which showed that 62% of the target audience is employed and—in most instances—spends at least two-thirds of their time at work. In addition, many worksites have resources for promotional and media activities.

A worksite packet of materials was developed from the previously tested concepts and was tested with the target audience through further focus group research. (See Figures 8.4 and 8.5.) The kit materials included:

- ▶ An overview of the stages of change including the pros/cons of modifying behavior

Figure 8.4. Worksite Packet Materials

Figure 8.5. Worksite Packet Materials

▶ Tip sheets offering ideas on how to become more active or eat healthier to help participants reach their goals

Participant input on the materials was sought with regard to suitability for the workplace, design, motivation to change value, readability, credible sponsorship, and suggestions for improvement. Project staff then incorporated the focus group participants' comments into a revision of the materials.

In June 1997, The Personal Energy Plan (PEP) was implemented through managed care organizations at five distinct worksites throughout the United States.

Findings

A total of 1,932 contemplators and preparers participated in PEP across all five worksites. Of those, 839 (43.4%) completed the 12-week program and the pretest and posttest surveys, which included a stage of change assessment tool. Significant forward movement among contemplators and preparers occurred during the 12-week program, with as many as 20% moving into the action stage for both healthy eating and physical activity behaviors.

Of those who identified themselves as contemplators for healthy eating at the pretest, 95% moved forward into another stage of change. Of those who identified themselves as pretest preparers or late preparers for healthy eating, almost 46% moved forward into the action stage.

▶ A quiz so that participants would be able to prioritize areas where they could make changes

▶ "Steps to success" to motivate the individual to move to the next stage of behavior change

▶ A monthly calendar for recording accomplishments and goals

Eighty nine percent of self-identified contemplators for physical activity at pretest moved forward into preparation, late preparation, or action at posttest. Of those who self-identified as pretest preparers or late preparers for physical activity, approximately 22% moved forward into the action stage of change.

Although some participants did not move forward along the continuum of stages of change, they did exhibit behavior changes when responding to individual questions about eating and activity behaviors.

In addition, when asked what the top three benefits were that they achieved in the PEP program, participants most often responded with both positive behavior changes and increased awareness levels. The top two benefits listed by participants were increased/continued physical activity and improved/maintained healthy eating habits. A third benefit was increased awareness of areas for improvement.

Conclusions

The ultimate goal of a social marketing program is to change behavior, with a secondary outcome of increased awareness, through intervention strategies tailored to target audiences. Both process and outcome evaluation data for the PEP program show that self-directed intervention materials targeted specifically to selected segments of the population can be effective in producing healthy eating and moderate physical activity behavior change in contemplators and preparers in a worksite setting.

References

Marcus, B. H., & Simkin, L. R. (1993). The stages of exercise behavior. *Journal of Sports Medicine and Physical Fitness, 33*, 83-88.

Pate, R. R., Pratt, M., Blair, et al. (1995). Physical activity and public health: A recommendation from the Centers for Disease Control and Prevention and the American College of Sports Medicine. *Jama, 273*(5), 402-407.

Prochaska, J. O., & DiClemente, C. C. (1983). Stages and processes of self-change in smoking: Toward an integrative model of change. *Journal of Consulting and Clinical Psychology, 51*, 390-395.

U.S. Department of Agriculture. (1990). *Nutrition and your health: Dietary guidelines for Americans* (USDA Publication No. 273-930). Washington, DC: U.S. Government Printing Office.

U.S. Department of Health and Human Services (USDHHS). (1996). *Physical activity and health: A report of the Surgeon General.* Atlanta, GA: U.S. Department of Health and Human Services, Centers for Disease Control and Prevention, National Center for Chronic Disease Prevention and Health Promotion.

Fred Fridinger, Ph.D., contributing author Michele Volansky, MPH, contributing author

Notes

1. Covey, Steven R. (2001, May 20). Weekly quotes. http//www.franklincovey.com
2. Andreasen, A. R. (1995). *Marketing Social Change: Changing Behavior to Promote Health, Social Development, and the Environment* (pp. 108-109). San Francisco: Jossey-Bass.
3. March of Dimes. Folic Acid and the Prevention of Birth Defects: A National Survey of Prepregnancy Awareness and Behavior Among Women of Childbearing Age, 1995-2001. Executive Summary. Conducted by The Gallup Organization. Retrieved 10/2/01 from http://www.modimes.org/Programs2/FolicAcid/Health_Professionals.htm
4. McCormack Brown, K. R. (1999). Health Belief Model. Retrieved 4/2/01 from http://www.hsc.usf.edu/~kmbrown/Health_Belief_Model_Overview.htm

5. Kotler, P., & Roberto, E. L. (1989). *Social Marketing: Strategies for Changing Public Behavior* (pp. 119, 126-127). New York: Free Press.

6. Fishbein, M., summarizing Bandura (1986, 1989, 1999) in *Developing Effective Behavior Change Intervention,* p. 3. The Communication Initiative. Summary of Change Theories and Models. Slide 5. Retrieved 4/2/01 from http://www.comminit.com/power_point/change_theories/sldoo5.htm

7. Dejong, W., & Linkenbach, J. (1999). "Telling It Like It Is: Using Social Norms Marketing Campaigns to Reduce Student Drinking." *American Association of Higher Education Bulletin, 52,* 11-13, 16.

8. Perkins, H. W., & Berkowitz, A. D. (1986). "Perceiving the Community Norms of Alcohol Use Among Students: Some Research Implications for Campus Alcohol Education Programming." *International Journal of the Addictions, 21,* 961-976.

9. Perkins, H. W. (1991). "Confronting Misperceptions of Peer Drug Use Norms Among College Students: An Alternative Approach for Alcohol and Drug Education Programs." *Peer Prevention Program Implementation Manual.* Fort Worth, TX: Higher Education Leaders/ Peers Network, Texas Christian University.

10. Berkowitz, A. D. "Following Imaginary Peers: How Norm Misperceptions Influence Student Substance Abuse." In G. Lindsay and G. Ralf (Eds.), *Project Direction* (Module No. 2). Muncie, IN: Ball State University.

11. Dejong & Linkenbach, "Telling It Like It Is," *American Association of Higher Education Bulletin, 52,* 11-13, 16.

12. Perkins, H. W., & Wechsler, H. (1996). "Variation in Perceived College Drinking Norms and Its Impact on Alcohol Abuse: A Nationwide Study." *Journal of Drug Issues, 26*(4), 961-974.

13. Fishbein, M., in *Developing Effective Behavior Change Intervention,* pp. 5-6. The Communication Initiative. Summary of Change Theories and Models. Slide 6. Retrieved 4/2/01 from www.comminit.com/power_point/change_theories/sld006.htm

14. Kotler, P., & Armstrong, G. (2001). *Principles of Marketing* (p. 270). Upper Saddle River, NJ: Prentice Hall.

15. McKenzie-Mohr, D., & Smith, W. (1999). *Fostering Sustainable Behavior* (p. 5). Gabriola Island, British Columbia, Canada: New Society.

16. This is an edited version of a previously published article: "PEP: The Personal Energy Plan— A Worksite Approach to Improving Health Through Increased Physical Activity and Healthy Eating," by Nicole A. Kerr, with Fred Fridinger and Michele Volansky, *Social Marketing Quarterly, 5*(3), September 1999, pp. 113-116.

PART IV

Developing
Social Marketing
Strategies

1. What is the product in a social marketing effort?

2. What are three levels of the product?

3. What decisions will need to be made at each level?

4. How are these decisions made, and how do they affect the product's positioning?

CHAPTER 9

Product: Designing the Market Offering

Some of the most successful adaptations to climate change probably won't involve high-tech gizmos or global taxes. They'll be as simple as the strips of cloth distributed to women in Bangladesh, which they use to screen cholera-causing microbes from water. Villages where women strained water have reduced cholera cases by 50 percent.

—Nancy Shute[1]

MARKETING HIGHLIGHT:
WOMEN & INFANT CHILDREN PROGRAMS (WIC)

This case highlights a service quality improvement strategy to positively influence target markets.

Increasing Utilization in the Texas WIC Program

Carol A. Bryant, Ph.D. and
James H. Lindenberger, Ph.D.

Background

The Special Supplemental Nutrition Program for Women, Infants & Children (WIC) is one of the most successful social service and public health initiatives in the nation. The program offers pregnant women, infants, and children living in households that fall below 250% of the poverty guidelines with nutrition information, supplemental food packages, health screenings and referrals, and immunizations.

During the early 1990s, many families who could have benefited from WIC were not participating in the program. The Texas Department of Health contracted with Best Start Social Marketing to develop a marketing program and outreach strategies for attracting new customers and retaining those already enrolled.

Target Audience

Extensive formative research was conducted with the three primary target populations: eligible families who were not currently participating in the WIC program (eligible); families currently enrolled in the program (participant); and employees working in 88 local WIC clinics and state administrative offices (staff). (Employee satisfaction and client responsive service delivery are also essential prerequisites for encouraging participation.)

Research

For each study component, a mix of qualitative and quantitative research methods were used to segment audiences and identify the factors that influence satisfaction with and participation in the WIC program (Bryant et al., 1998; Bryant et al., 2001; Coreil et al., 2000).

The study of *eligible* families was conducted using focus groups, telephone interviews, and a mail survey of a random sample of pregnant Medicaid recipients to identify perceived benefits, costs, and other factors that influenced families' decisions to enroll in WIC.

The *participant* study relied on qualitative data from focus groups and telephone interviews, and a survey of participants in rural, mid-sized city and metropolitan locales in areas throughout Texas.

The *staff* component of the project included in-depth interviews and focus groups with WIC administrators, agency directors, clinical and clerical staff members, and a survey distributed to employees.

tional videotapes; rude treatment by WIC staff; lack of Spanish-speaking staff; and rude treatment while redeeming WIC food vouchers at the grocery store).

Results

Eligible Study

Research results identified several important attitudes and perceptions that influenced enrollment decisions. Most families were familiar with portions of WIC's food package, but few were aware of additional services that greatly enhanced the program's attractiveness. Barriers to participation in WIC included families who:

▶ Were unaware that WIC also offers other nutritious foods, individualized nutritional risk assessment and counseling, education classes, immunizations, and referrals to other health and social service programs/services.

▶ Would suffer embarrassment if identified as a recipient of a free food program.

▶ Felt that it would "rob" them of their sense of self-sufficiency.

▶ Believed WIC benefits were in short supply and should only be accepted by those with the greatest need.

▶ Did not recognize that they were automatically income-eligible for WIC.

▶ Believed their income was too high to qualify.

▶ Did not think women would qualify if they or their husbands worked, if they lived with relatives whose incomes were too high, or if they had been denied Food Stamps.

▶ Were apprehensive about participating in a program their friends and relatives had complained about (e.g., long waits at WIC clinics to obtain food cards and listen to educa-

Research was used to segment the eligible population into subgroups of women who could benefit from WIC and to identify specific issues to recruit them. For example, women who were employed, completed high school, and earned incomes 135-185 percent of the Federal poverty level were the least likely to know they were income-eligible for WIC. This segment was selected as a target for clarifying eligibility requirements.

Research found audience segments with the highest proportions of women who had never enrolled in the WIC program. From the research results, a plan was created that addressed women's misperceptions of the program's benefits. Outreach materials were designed to emphasize the nutrition education, health checkups, immunizations, and referrals WIC provided. These materials attempt to reframe WIC as a program parents can be proud to use for raising healthy children.

Participant Study

Program participants had positive perceptions of Texas WIC, with 64% rating the program "very good," 30% "good," and 6% "fair." Program benefits rated most highly were: health and nutrition information (57%); money saved on grocery bills (51%); nutritious foods (39%); and having their children's blood, height, and weight checked (23%). While families valued WIC's many services, they also encountered difficulties that made participation costly. These included the following:

▶ Long waiting times for initial certification, nutrition education, and receiving food cards

▶ Difficulty securing and paying for supervised child care when visiting WIC clinics

▶ Disrespectful or rude treatment by clinic staff

▶ Rude or inconsiderate treatment by grocery cashiers

▶ Problems redeeming food cards

▶ Displeasure with specific types or brands of food offered by the WIC program

▶ Embarrassment to participate in a government assistance program

Staff Study

Staff reported that the primary benefits of working for WIC were satisfying their desire to help others and professional gratification of doing a good job. WIC employees enjoyed serving as WIC team members, saying that this sense of "camaraderie" was key to feeling good about their jobs.

The most significant costs of working in the WIC program were pressure to expand enrollment, poor supervision, racial tension with participants, disrespectful participants, staff shortages, and cramped, noisy work areas that impeded client flow and efficient service.

Conclusions

WIC program utilization was closely tied to customer and employee satisfaction. WIC participants felt they should receive high quality nutrition education, pleasant encounters with staff, ease in obtaining food supplements, and respect for their struggles to provide for their children. Staff thought they deserved good clinic facilities to help them serve their participants, opportunities for professional advancement, appreciation from participants, and recognition from administrators for their hard work.

Marketing Plan

A comprehensive social marketing plan was developed to provide a customer-centered approach to program structure and service delivery. It specified policy change recommendations, service delivery improvements, staff and vendor training, internal promotion, public information and communications, client education, and community-based interventions. (See Figure 9.1 and Table 9.1.)

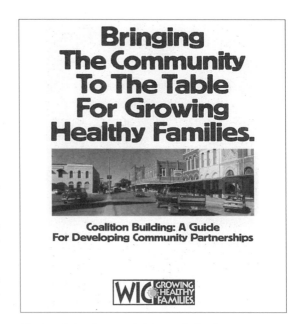

Figure 9.1. Outreach Materials for Increasing Participant Enrollment

Program Implementation

Using the social marketing plan as a guide, messages, outreach materials, training programs, data collection instruments and other resources needed to implement and evaluate the program were developed. Each component was made consistent with the overall marketing strategy. Marketing messages and mass media materials were rigorously pretested and redesigned until they proved to be effective.

TABLE 9.1   The Texas WIC Social Marketing Plan

Major Components[a]	Examples of Specific Strategies[b]
Policy recommendations	1. Recognition for staff performance, including customer service awards. 2. Career growth opportunities for staff, with a clear career path. 3. Use of computers to communicate policy changes more effectively between state and local staff. 4. Revised appointment scheduing policies to improve clinic efficiency and create more "user friendly" certification and food card issuance procedures (e.g., online, computerized policy manuals for staff).
Service delivery	1. Increased accessibility by offering WIC services at day care centers, employers, grocery stores, migrant camps, and more flexible clinic hours (night, lunch time, and one Sat./month). 2. Child-friendly clinics where children can play, eat nutritious snacks, and learn about nutrition in childproofed areas supervised by staff, paraprofessionals, and volunteers. 3. Peer buddy system—paraprofessionals act as advocates/guides for participants waiting for clinic services, ensure that participants have required documentation, answer questions about certification and food cards, and give "smart shopping" tips. 4. Improvements in grocery store experiences with a new food card redemption system (fewer cards to be signed at register) and a "products brochure" to depict allowable WIC foods for participants and serve as a reference for cashiers.
Training	1. Staff training and continuing education. 2. Grocery store cashier training program, videotape about customer service and the WIC transaction.
Nutrition education	1. Nutrition education facilitator training in interactive teaching skills to discuss nutrition and new, nontraditional WIC subjects (e.g., parenting, child development) issues with participants. 2. "Food and Family" educational magazine for WIC participants.
Tracking system	1. Monitoring system to track participant satisfaction with the food package, nutrition education, food redemption, clinic service, and clinic environment. 2. Track staff satisfaction with supervision, clinic environment, ability to provide WIC services, and participant contact. 3. Training for local agency directors in interpreting results, identifying and overcoming service delivery problems.
Health communication plan	1. Messages to reposition WIC's image—to a comprehensive health and education program offering nutritious foods, screening, social support, and referral to other services (e.g., through 30 sec. "Nutrition Tips" radio spots). 2. Messages to increase awareness of income eligibility criteria.
Community outreach	1. Community organizers' kit to assist local agency directors in working with program partners in increasing referrals of eligible families to WIC. 2. Kit includes outreach materials targeted to health professionals and eligible families.

a. This chart includes examples of strategies developed for each component of the social marketing plan.

b. The first five components are designed to increase participant and staff satisfaction; the last two are intended to increase participant enrollment (Bryant et al., 1998).

The program's caseload grew from 582,819 in October 1993 to 778,558 in October 1998—an increase of almost 200,000 participants.

References

Bryant, C. A., Lindenberger, J. H., Brown, C., Kent, E., Schreiber, J. M., Bustillo, M., & Canright, M. W. (2001). A social marketing approach to increasing enrollment in a public health program. (Case study of the Texas WIC program). *Human Organization, 60*(3), 234-246.

Bryant, C. A., Kent, E., Brown, C., Bustillo, M., Blair, C., Lindenberger, J., & Walker, M. (1998, Winter). A social marketing approach to increase customer satisfaction with the Texas WIC program. *Marketing Health Care Services,* 5-17.

Coreil, J., Bryant, C. A., & Henderson, N. (2000). *Social and behavioral foundations of public health.* Thousand Oaks, CA: Sage.

Rush, D., Sloan, N. L., Leighton, J., Alvir, J. M., Horwitz, D. G., Seaver, W. B., Garbowski, G. C., Johnson, S. S., Kulka, R. A., Holt, M., Devore, J. W., Lynch, J. T., Virag, T. G., Woodside, M. B., & Shanklin, D. S. (1988a). Longitudinal study of pregnant women. *American Journal of Clinical Nutrition, 48,* 439-483.

Rush, D., Leighton, J., Sloan, N. L., Alvir, J. M., Horwitz, D. G., Seaver, W. B., Garbowski, G. C., Johnson, S. S., Kulka, R. A., Holt, M., Devore, J. W., Lynch, J. T., Virag, T. G., Woodside, M. B., & Shanklin, D. S. (1988b). Study of infants and children. *American Journal of Clinical Nutrition, 48,* 484-511.

Rush, D., Alvir, J. M., Kenney, D. A., Johnson, S. S., & Horwitz, D. G. (1988c). Historical study of pregnancy outcomes. *American Journal of Clinical Nutrition, 48,* 412-428.

CHAPTER OVERVIEW

At this point in our planning process, our preliminary homework and decision making is complete:

- We have selected our target markets and developed rich descriptions using relevant demographic, geographic, psychographic, and behavior variables.

- We know what we want our audience to do and what they may need to know and/or believe in order to act.

- We know what benefits, barriers, and costs they perceive relative to the desired behavior we are promoting.

- We know how this stacks up against the competition, their current or preferred behavior.

Now, it is time to decide how we are going to influence our target audience to accept the desired behavior, using all elements of the marketing mix. This chapter will focus on developing our product strategy, determining how to present the desired behavior so that it is most motivating to our target audience, and exploring opportunities for tangible objects and services that will support behavior change.

We begin by designing our product platform, the foundation on which all other elements of the marketing mix will be built. As is discussed in this chapter, there are three levels of that platform, each involving several decisions about our market offering.

These decisions will be based on what we've learned to date about our target audience, their wants, needs, and perceptions. They will also be based on how we want our product to be "positioned" in their minds, what we want our audience to think, and how we want them to feel about the proposed desired behavior. As illustrated in the highlight on WIC programs, this customer orientation proved critical to reaching program objectives and goals.

WHAT IS THE PRODUCT IN A SOCIAL MARKETING EFFORT?

In social marketing, our product is what we are selling, the desired behavior and the associated benefits of that behavior. It also includes any *tangible objects* and *services* developed to support and facilitate the target audience's behavior change. It is, therefore, as described by commercial sector marketers, a "complex bundle of benefits" that we offer to the market to satisfy some need.[2] Using a drinking and driving campaign as an example:

Desired behavior:	Keep blood alcohol content (BAC) below .08% if you are going to drive.
Associated benefits:	Avoid a citation for driving under the influence (a DUI), serious accidents, impounded car, and increased car insurance.
Tangible object:	A Breathalyzer sold over the Internet.
Service:	Free taxi service on New Year's Eve.

WHAT ARE THREE LEVELS OF THE PRODUCT?

Traditional marketing theory identifies three levels of a product: *core product, actual product,* and *augmented product.*[3] (See Figure 9.2.) This platform is helpful to the social marketing planner in conceptualizing and designing the product strategy.

Core Product: The core product, the center of the product platform, answers the questions: "What's in it for the customer to buy our product?" "What benefits will they receive?" "What needs will the desired behavior satisfy?" "What problems will it solve?" The core product is not the behaviors or accompanying tangible objects and

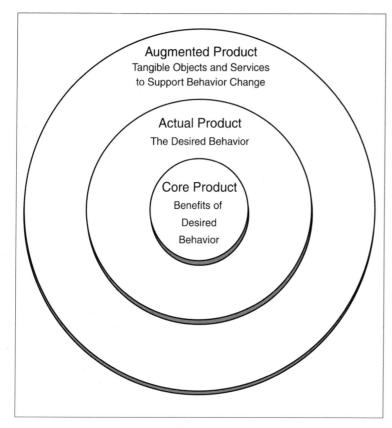

Augmented Product
Tangible Objects and Services
to Support Behavior Change

Actual Product
The Desired Behavior

Core Product
Benefits of
Desired
Behavior

Figure 9.2. Three Levels of the Social Marketing Product

services we will be promoting. It is the benefits our audience will experience when they perform the behavior, benefits they say are the most valuable to them (e.g., moderate physical activity will make me feel better, look better, and live longer). Charles Revson, of Revlon, provided a memorable quote illustrating the difference between product features (our actual product) and product benefits (our core product): "In the factory we make cosmetics; in the store, we sell hope."[4]

Actual Product: Surrounding the core product is the specific *behavior* we are promoting (e.g., exercise 5 days a week, 30 minutes a day, at least 10 minutes at a time). It is what is required in order to achieve the benefits identified as the core product. Additional components at this level may include any *brand names* developed for the behavior (e.g., Washington State's campaign slogan "Be Healthy. Be Active. 30/10/5"); the *campaign's sponsoring organization* (e.g., state department of health); and any *endorsements* (e.g., Surgeon General).

Augmented Product: This level includes any *tangible objects and services* the social marketer promotes along with the desired behavior. Although they may be considered optional, they are sometimes exactly what was needed to provide encouragement (e.g., a walking buddy), remove barriers (e.g., a detailed resource guide and map of local walking trails and organized walking programs), or sustain behavior (e.g., a journal for tracking exercise levels). They may also provide opportunities to brand and to "tangibilize" the campaign, creating more attention, appeal, and memorability for target audiences.[5]

Table 9.2 provides examples of these three product levels for many of the social issues identified initially in this text. For each issue, only one benefit, behavior, and

TABLE 9.2 Examples of Three Product Levels

Core Product (Benefits)	Actual Product (Behavior)	Augmented Product (Tangible Objects and Services)
For Health Promotion		
Longer and healthier life	Quit smoking.	1-800# Quit Line
Prevention of alcohol poisoning	Drink in moderation.	Breathalyzers in bars
Reduction of stress, cholesterol, and chances for heart disease and colon cancer	Engage in moderate physical activity 30 minutes a day, 5 days a week, at least 10 minutes at a time.	Community walking clubs
Prevention of unintended pregnancies and STDs (sexually transmitted diseases)	Use a condom.	Condoms with different colors and patterns
Improved general health	Drink eight glasses of water a day.	64-ounce durable plastic bottle
Natural immunities for infants and mother-child bonding	Breastfeed for at least 6 months.	In-home nurse consultation
Early detection and treatment of breast cancer	Conduct a monthly self-breast exam.	Laminated instruction card for placement on shower nozzle
Protection from preventable diseases	Immunize children on time.	Wallet-size immunization card
Prevention of decay, gum disease, and associated systemic blood diseases	Floss your teeth daily.	Dental floss attached to television remote control
Reduced risk of heart attack	Monitor your blood pressure regularly.	Home blood pressure monitoring equipment
Reduce risk of salmonella poisoning	Wash hands and work surfaces thoroughly after handling raw poultry.	Colored chopping blocks: yellow for poultry, red for meat, and green for vegetables
For Injury Prevention		
Prevention of injury for self and others	Don't drink and drive.	Free taxi rides on New Year's Eve
Suicide prevention	Know when to intervene and what to say.	Gatekeeper training for teachers, counselors, and youth group leaders
Sexual assault prevention	Walk with a friend after class at night.	University escort service if you don't have someone to walk with
Drowning prevention	Wear a life vest.	Slender, suspender-like vests with inflatable pull tab

(Continued)

TABLE 9.2 (Continued)

Core Product (Benefits)	Actual Product (Behavior)	Augmented Product (Tangible Objects and Services)
Protection from physical abuse	Call for help if you are being abused.	Help Line for domestic abuse
Assistance and medical help for someone who has fallen	Get help if you fall.	Alert buttons in case of a fall
To Protect the Environment		
Improved water quality	Plant native plants.	Natural gardening workshops
Preservation of old growth forests	Buy recycled materials.	Decking made from recycled plastic milk and water cartons
Protection of children, pets, and wildlife from toxic chemicals	Read instructions and measure pesticides properly.	Magnifying glass attached to pesticide container
Adequate water supply	Reduce water consumption by 10%.	Shower pressure reduction device
Reduced landfills	Compost garbage and yard waste.	Garbage compost tumbler
Prevention of forest fires	Dispose of cigarettes properly.	Disposable cigarette pouches
Avoidance of electric power blackouts	Conserve electricity.	New energy-saving lightbulbs
Avoidance of costly fines and penalties	Use a litterbag.	Litterbags that are leak-proof and that seal
For Community Involvement		
Saving someone's life	Become a donor.	National Organ Donor Card
Helping members of your community	Volunteer 5 hours a week.	Training for crisis line

service/tangible object are presented. In reality, there might be several included in one campaign or program effort.

WHAT DECISIONS WILL NEED TO BE MADE AT EACH LEVEL

Level One: Decisions about the *core product* focus primarily on *what potential benefits should be stressed.* This process will include reviewing (from Step 4) audience perceptions of (a) benefits from the desired behavior and (b) perceived costs of the competing behaviors that the desired behavior can help the target audience avoid. Decisions are then made on which of these should be emphasized in a campaign.

Example: Interviews with teens often reveal several perceived benefits that youth associate with not smoking: doing better in school, doing better in sports, being seen as smart, and looking and feeling good. They may also have revealed the following perceived costs: You could get addicted and not be able to quit, you might die, you'll stink, and you won't be as good in sports. Further discussions may indicate that a couple of these (e.g., fear of addiction and dying young) are the most concerning and should be highlighted in the campaign. (See Figure 9.3.) In this case, the core product for the campaign becomes, "By not smoking, you don't risk addiction and dying young."

Figure 9.3. A Testimonial Used to Persuade Youth That Tobacco Is Addictive

Level Two: Decisions regarding the *actual product* (the desired behaviors) to be promoted were made in Step 3 when behavior objectives were established (e.g., eat five fruits and vegetables a day). Additional decisions now may include a name that will be associated with the behavior (e.g., 5 A Day) and identification of sponsors and endorsements to include in campaign communications (e.g., Centers for Disease Control and Prevention, Produce for Better Health Foundation). Sponsor and endorsement decisions are important because they can significantly affect the credibility as well as the appeal of a campaign. Research indicates that credibility is a function of expertise, trustworthiness, and likability, so perceptions of target audiences may need to be explored.[6]

Example: Telephone surveys could ask litterers to rank the impact on their littering of a variety of potential endorsements of an anti-litter campaign: department of ecology, state patrol, department of transportation, department of licensing, department of fish and wildlife, department of natural resources, and the state traffic safety commission. It might not be surprising to find that responses indicate that the best (visible) sponsoring organizations for a campaign would be the department of licensing and/or the state patrol, because these organizations are perceived as having the most impact on potential penalties and driving privileges, important personal benefits to these drivers.

Level Three: Many more decisions will need to be made relative to the *augmented product.* As noted earlier, there are two major potential elements of an augmented product: (a) accompanying services and (b) tangible products that might support the behavior change.

Services are often distinguished as offerings that are intangible and do not result in the ownership of anything.[7] In the social marketing environment, examples of services that support the desired behavior change might include *education-related services* (e.g., parenting workshops on how to talk to your kids about sex); *personal services* (e.g., escorts for students back to their dorms at night); *counseling services* (e.g., a crisis line for people considering suicide); *clinical services* (e.g., community clinics for free immunizations); and *community services* (e.g., hazardous waste mobiles for disposal of toxic waste products). It should be noted that services that are more sales oriented in nature (e.g., demonstrations on the efficiency of low-flow toilets) fall into the promotional category and will be discussed in Chapter 13.

Some decisions regarding service elements are described as follows.

Should a new service be developed and offered? For example, given the apparent success and popularity of toll-free tobacco "Quit Lines" to support smoking cessation in other states, a community without one might want to develop and launch a line to accompany mass media campaigns encouraging adults to quit smoking.

Does an existing service need to be improved or enhanced? For example, what if customer surveys indicate that an estimated 50% of callers to the state's 800 number for questions about recycling hang up because they typically have to wait more than 5 minutes on hold? Relative to enhanced services, what if customer feedback also indicates that residents would be interested in (and would pay for) recycling of yard waste in addition to glass, paper, and aluminum?

Decisions regarding tangible objects to accompany the campaign are similar. Some examples follow.

Should we develop (or encourage the development of) a new product that would greatly benefit the behavior change? For example, many adult diabetics conduct finger-prick blood tests to monitor their blood sugar levels. A *painless, needle-free mechanism* that would provide reliable readings would be a welcome innovation and might result in more regular monitoring of blood sugar levels. Not all new products will require retooling or significant research and development costs. For example, a recent announcement in the news discussed the possibility of a "National Organ Donor Card" that would facilitate identification of individuals as well as needed communications with families, which might help dispel some of the myths around organ donation.

Does a current product need to be improved or enhanced? For example, typical compost bins require the gardener to use a pitchfork to regularly turn the yard and food waste to enhance compost development. New and improved models are suspended on brackets that only require a regular "tumble." (See Figure 9.4.)

Relative to product enhancement, until recent years, most users (and especially non-users) have perceived life vests as bulky and uncomfortable. For teens, concerns with tan lines and the "ugly" orange color were also raised. New options are vastly improved, with a look similar to suspenders and a feature for automatic inflation using a pull tab.

Is there a need or opportunity for a substitute product?[8] A substitute product is one that offers the target audience a "healthier and safer" way to satisfy a want, fulfill a need, or solve a problem. The key is to understand the real benefit (core product) of the *competing* behavior and to then develop and/or promote products offering the same, or at least some of the same, benefits. These include, for example, food and beverages

Figure 9.4. A Product Improvement for Composters

such as nonalcoholic beers, garden burgers, fat-free dairy products, and decaffeinated coffee; natural fertilizers, natural pesticides, and ground covers to replace lawns; an older sibling (versus a parent) taking a younger teen to a community clinic for STD screening; a package containing a can of chicken soup, tissues, and aspirin "prescribed" to patients suffering from colds, in an effort to reduce the overuse of antibiotics.

Chakravorty defines substitute products as "a product offered to a market that is thought of and used by those in the market as a replacement for some other product."[9]

She further surmises,

> An acceptable and accessible substitute product may promote desirable behaviors by enhancing the user's perceived self-efficacy. Self-efficacy is expected to be strengthened to the extent that many of the behaviors required in using a substitute are similar to behaviors associated with reference product use.[10]
>
> For example, a heavy coffee drinker may come to believe that eliminating coffee will lead to improved cardiac health. The prospective former coffee drinker may decide that she is very likely to quit coffee if she replaces it with decaffeinated coffee. A variety of factors may have contributed to this perception. First, she may feel that as a result of her coffee drinking behavior, she "knows how" to execute the behaviors required in drinking decaf. The beverage will be consumed in the same container, at the same temperature, and she will not have to make great adjustments to the flavor of the substitute. If she is able to consume decaf in all the same situations where she usually drinks coffee (i.e., at home, work, or a favorite restaurant) her efficacy for "decaf drinking" behavior may rise as she estimates that she will be able to perform the new behavior across a wide variety of settings.[11]

These accompanying services and tangible objects will also face *branding* and *packaging* decisions. Kotler and Armstrong define a *brand* as "a name, term, sign, symbol, or design, or a combination of these, intended to identify the goods or services of one seller or group of sellers and to differentiate them from those of competitors."[12] Kotler and Roberto recommend four desired characteristics for a brand name:[13]

1. It should be easy to pronounce, recognize, and remember.
2. It should capture or define the product's benefits.
3. It should define a product's qualities or appeal.
4. It should be distinctive.

They identify packaging as consisting of "several elements or dimensions, including the material, shape, color, size, weight, symbols, label, and copy."[14]

At subsequent steps in the planning process, additional decisions regarding services and tangible objects will be made to include pricing, distribution channels, and promotions.

HOW ARE THESE DECISIONS MADE AND HOW DO THEY AFFECT THE PRODUCT'S POSITIONING?

Decisions regarding the product platform (core, actual, and augmented) are made with two guiding principles:

1. *Make choices that are based on a clear understanding of your competition.* Know the needs, wants, and preferences that your target market associates with their current behavior (i.e., your competitor).

2. *Make choices that ensure that your target audience will see your product as offering more and greater benefits than the ones they associate with their current behavior.* Kotler and Armstrong suggested that the product's positioning be thought of as "the way the product is defined by consumers on important attributes—the place the product occupies in the consumers' minds relative to competing products."[15]

   One way to develop a positioning statement is to fill in the blanks to the phrase: "I want my target audience to see _____ (desired behavior) as _____ (a phrase describing positive benefits of adopting the behavior) and as more important and beneficial than _____ (the competing behavior)." For example, "I want my target audience to see *moderate physical activity* as *easy and something they can fit into their everyday lives* and as more important than *sleeping in*." Or "I want my target audience to see *breastfeeding* as *loving and healthy* and as more important than *concerns with nursing in public*."

Decisions regarding the core product (benefits that will be highlighted), the actual product (behaviors that will be promoted and associated sponsors and endorsements), and augmented products (quality, features, names, and packaging) will determine this positioning, "the perceptions, impressions and feelings that consumers have for the product."[16]

Smith advocates the following positioning for consideration:

Make the behavior **Fun, Easy, and Popular** for the audience. These three words focus program managers on how to change behavior by giving people what *they want*, along with what *we feel* they need.

Safety Tips

1: Wear protective gear, including a helmet, pads or guards on the arms, wrists and knees, and be sure to wear proper shoes, not flip-flops or bare feet

2: Never ride a scooter at night. Unlike bikes, scooters don't have reflectors.

3: Children under 8 should always be supervised by an adult when riding a scooter. Older kids should be supervised if crossing streets on a scooter.

Figure 9.5. Positioning of Wearing Protective Gear as Fun, Easy, and Popular

- FUN in this context means to provide your audience with some perceived benefits they care about.

- EASY means to remove all the possible barriers to action and make the behavior as simple and accessible as possible.

- POPULAR means to help the audience feel that this is something others are doing, particularly others who the audience believes are important to them.[17]

He further describes that he uses "these three words to summarize three social science determinants—perceived consequences, self-efficacy, and social norms . . . making a bridge between theory and practice."[18]

An example of an effort that reflects several elements of this approach is illustrated in Figure 9.5, in which a magazine article uses a visual image that reflects the desired positioning of wearing protective gear as fun, easy, and popular.

For some social issues and campaign focuses, other positioning strategies might be more appropriate and effective. On the basis of target audience input and a competitive analysis, we may want to plan and make choices to create the following positions:

- Position consequences of tobacco use as *gross, realistic, and shocking*. (See Figure 9.6.)

LUNG CANCER (Smoker)   NORMAL LUNG (Non-Smoker)   EMPHYSEMA (Smoker)

Figure 9.6. Positioning Tobacco Use

Here's one good reason for giving blood.
Officer R.D. Tuggle
Puget Sound Blood Center

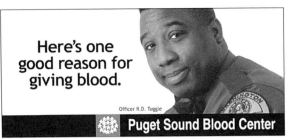

Figure 9.7. Positioning Blood Donation

- Position blood donation as a *generous, humanitarian act.* (See Figure 9.7.)
- Position drinking and driving as potentially *tragic,* as is the case in mock accident events often staged at high schools. (See Figure 9.8.)

MITCHELL
SENIOR
HIGH SCHOOL

Figure 9.8. Positioning Drinking and Driving

- Position counselors for domestic violence assistance as *compassionate, helpful, and nonjudgmental.* (See Figure 9.9.)

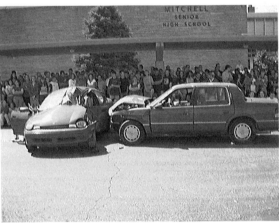

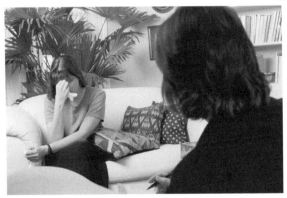

Figure 9.9. Positioning Domestic Violence Assistance

- Position conserving electricity as *smart and responsible.* (See Figure 9.10.)

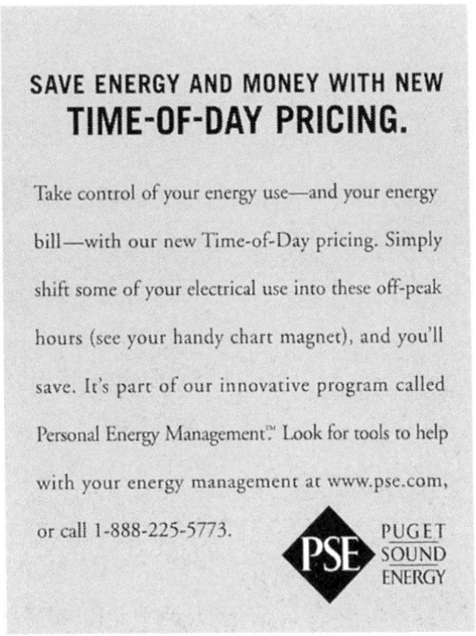

SAVE ENERGY AND MONEY WITH NEW
TIME-OF-DAY PRICING.
Take control of your energy use—and your energy bill—with our new Time-of-Day pricing. Simply shift some of your electrical use into these off-peak hours (see your handy chart magnet), and you'll save. It's part of our innovative program called Personal Energy Management.℠ Look for tools to help with your energy management at www.pse.com, or call 1-888-225-5773.
PSE
PUGET SOUND ENERGY

Figure 9.10. Positioning Conservation

Figure 9.10. Energy Conservation

The important point is that the positioning of the product should be deliberate, not accidental. "Marketers must plan positions that will give their products the greatest advantage in selected markets, and they must design marketing mixes to create these planned positions."[19]

CHAPTER SUMMARY

1. The product in a social marketing campaign is what we are selling: *the desired behavior and the associated benefits of that behavior.* It also includes any *tangible objects* and *services* developed to support and facilitate the target audience's behavior change.

2. The *product platform has three levels:* the core product (the benefit of the behavior), the actual product (the specific behavior being promoted), and the augmented product (any tangible objects and services associated with the program).

3. Decisions are faced at each level. At the *core product level,* decisions will need to be made regarding what potential benefits should be stressed. Although major decisions regarding the *actual product* were made in Step 3 when the behavior objective was established, additional decisions may need to be made, including choosing a name and identification of sponsors and endorsements for campaign communications. At the third level, the social marketer is faced with several decisions related to the *augmented product,* including whether to develop new products and services, as well as needs for improving existing ones.

4. Decisions regarding the core product, actual product, and augmented products will determine the *positioning* of the social marketing product in the minds of the target audience and will influence how the target audience thinks and feels about the proposed behavior. This positioning should be carefully planned on the basis of target audience preferences, as well as the positioning of competing behaviors.

KEY TERMS AND CONCEPTS

Product platform   Tangible objects
Core product   Services
Actual product   Positioning
Augmented product

ISSUES FOR DISCUSSION

1. In a campaign promoting use of condoms to drug users, describe hypothetical levels of the product platform: core, actual, and augmented.

2. Similarly, in a campaign promoting carpooling, describe a potential product platform.

3. In Figure 9.11 a-d, four different approaches to litter prevention are presented. How would you describe the positioning strategy for each approach?

Figure 9.11a. Don't Mess With Texas

Figure 9.11b. Litterbug Service Mark of the Pennsylvania Resource Council. Used with permission.

Figure 9.11c. On the Spot Littering

Figure 9.11d. A Sign at a Waterfront Restaurant

RESEARCH HIGHLIGHT: FOCUS GROUPS FOR INCREASED CONTRACEPTIVE USE

Improving Services and Communications, North Carolina Family Planning Program

Michael Newton-Ward
North Carolina Division of Public Health

Background

North Carolina's Division of Health Services, Women's Preventive Health Unit, which manages the state's family planning program, utilized focus groups to gather information to improve services for males. In 1997, Pharmacia and Upjohn offered the unit funding to conduct a special project, provided it related in some way to the use of Depo-Provera. Staff proposed investigating factors that influence male support of their partners' contraceptive use. Brown and Eisenberg (1995) state that partner support is a major predictor of female contraceptive compliance. The unit proposed conducting focus groups of men, aged 15-25, to better understand how they see their role in supporting contraceptive use. Staff hypothesized that programs to increase male support could lead to an increase in contraceptive use, including Depo-Provera.

Staff from the Regional Training Center at Emory University, who were conducting female focus groups related to chlamydial infections and infertility, helped conduct the male groups in exchange for including questions about chlamydia.

Methodology

Because of the paucity of information on males' attitudes and knowledge related to reproductive health issues, the investigators wanted to use an open-ended methodology that would generate as much information as possible from participants. Consequently, the investigators chose a focus group format because of its ability to generate program concepts and identify the scope of issues important to participants.

Researchers recruited participants from the community using a convenience sampling technique, which is useful for exploratory research. Researchers selected 10 sites based on their high incidence of teen pregnancy and low use of Depo-Provera, which represented all regions of the state. Researchers instructed each site to recruit participants from one of the specified age groups, 15-17 or 18-25. The recruiters, who were employees of that site's local health department, typically resided in the area and frequently had resourceful ideas for recruitment. Since the study sought to assess knowledge of, and attitudes towards, STI prevention and contraceptive use, individuals were eligible for the study if they had been sexually active since April 1997. Recruiters asked potential participants their age and whether they lived in an urban or rural area. Investigators obtained consents prior to the study. (Parents of participants younger than 18 years gave consent for their sons.) Participants received a study description. They were paid $20 for their participation and were served dinner.

Investigators conducted the groups from January-June 1998. Groups averaged 2 hours in length, ranged in size from 1 to 12 participants and were divided by age and by rural/urban locality. Fifty-six males comprised the 10 groups.

Data Collection and Analysis

Staff designed a background questionnaire and a semi-structured, open-ended focus group guide. The questionnaire explored demographic characteristics; experiences regarding sexual behavior, contraceptive use, and STIs; and "psychographic" factors. The focus group guide addressed: 1) health care access; 2) involvement and attitudes toward risk taking generally and sexual activity specifically; 3) exposure to and attitudes toward contraceptive use, STIs generally and chlamydia specifically; 4) modes of communication/media; and 5) recommendations for creating PSAs about contraceptive use and STI prevention.

Researchers tape-recorded group discussions, with a note taker present. Transcripts were typed from the recordings. Researchers developed a coding key to categorize the findings, then conducted a line-by-line transcript coding. Major themes emerged early and were confirmed by the remaining groups.

Findings

1. Participants believed males don't seek health care unless they are very sick.
2. They have concerns about the health care system—confidentiality, provider trust/caring,

waiting time, cost—that are barriers to utilization. However, most participants viewed local health departments positively.

3. Partner relationships influence the choice and use of contraceptive methods and the disclosure of STIs.
4. There was a general lack of knowledge about contraceptives and STIs, especially chlamydia.
5. All participants identified contraceptive use for STI prevention as more important than contraceptive use for pregnancy prevention.
6. Many participants would be reluctant to disclose an STI to their partners. Reasons included embarrassment, fear of losing the relationship, and fear that others would find out. They believed their partner would be reluctant for the same reasons and that she would lose respect and her reputation by disclosing.
7. Participants viewed shared responsibility for contraceptive use as the ideal. In practice, they tended to believe that each partner needs to take care of him/herself.
8. Mothers of the participants (and to a lesser extent, partners) have a major influence on their decisions to seek health care, regardless of the participant's age.
9. Health Information Channels: Participants preferred information via television, radio, the Internet, magazines, and personal speakers/interactions versus written materials, especially brochures.
10. Health Information Approaches:
   - Brief, concise;
   - Factual (e.g., disease symptoms or steps for using contraceptives) but personalized (from someone like themselves or from someone seen as a hero, such as Michael Jordan);
   - In a visual format;
   - Presented creatively, using humor.

Cluster analysis performed on the psychographic questions concluded that (a) men who report **always using** contraceptives tend to place a low value on risk (as related to sexual activity), tend toward self-efficacy, value the opinion and well-being of their partners, and recognize the importance of taking care of their health; whereas (b) men who report **not using** contraceptives are most likely to be less than 18 years old, value risk taking, need excitement in their lives, tend to be self-absorbed and conscious of fads or trends.

Recommendations

The groups generated the following recommendations for the major themes that emerged.

1. *Health messages—Many health messages are ineffective; there is a general lack of knowledge about contraceptives and STIs*
   - Make health education messages factual, humorous
   - Use heroes and friends to personalize
   - Use multiple channels. . . . Don't rely on brochures alone
   - Present contraceptive messages with an STI angle
2. *Relationship—Partner relationships influence males' behaviors such as:* choice/use of contraceptives, comfort discussing STIs, decisions to seek health care
   - Ask the males in your program: Are they in a relationship? What is the quality of the relationship?
   - Consider including a component for their partners
3. *Partner notification—The current partner notification process for STIs lacks effectiveness*

   - Try alternative approaches for partner notification. (Investigators quizzed participants about improvements and different approaches. Participant Bottom Line: "*Nothing can make this easier!*")
4. *Service provision—the current service delivery system is not reaching males effectively*
   - Provide confidential, timely, affordable services. (Females also cite these factors. However, males' aversion to seeking health care makes these critical considerations for them.)
   - To reach males, staff must reach outside the clinic
   - Consider the influence of mothers and partners on health care decisions

Limitations

The external validity of this study may be affected by the use of convenience sampling of only 15-25 year olds. There were small sample sizes in three of the groups. The fact that moderators were female may have affected responses.

Lessons Learned

► Focus groups *can* yield a wealth of information that staff would not have considered.

► Partnering (with Emory University) benefited both organizations, leveraging the work that could be accomplished.

► Psychographic questions can be asked in a focus group setting using paper-and-pencil measures.

► Although the investigators included a psychographic component and had access to statistical analysis, a program *can* utilize focus groups without having advanced statistical capabilities.

▶ This project promoted acceptance of formative research methods and the further integration of social marketing principles into a statewide public health program.

Reference

Brown, Sarah S., & Eisenberg, Leon (Eds.). (1995). *The Best Intentions.* Washington, DC: National Academy Press.

Contributing investigators include: April Privett, North Carolina Division of Health and Human Services, Women's Preventive Health Unit; Yvonne Hamby and Rachel Newman, Regional Training Center, Emory University, Atlanta, Georgia.

Notes

1. Shute, N. (2001, February 5). "The Weather Turns Wild." *U.S. News & World Report,* p. 52.
2. Kotler, P., & Armstrong, G. (2001). *Principles of Marketing* (p. 294). Upper Saddle River, NJ: Prentice Hall.
3. Ibid.
4. Ibid.
5. Kotler, P., & Roberto, E. L. (1989). *Social Marketing: Strategies for Changing Public Behavior* (p. 156). New York: Free Press.
6. Kotler & Roberto, *Social Marketing,* p. 155; Assael. (1981). *Consumer Behavior and Marketing Action.* Boston: Kent.
7. Kotler & Roberto, *Social Marketing,* pp. 155-157.
8. Ibid., p. 20.
9. Chakravorty, B. (1992, April/May). "Smokeless Tobacco Substitute Tested With Southern Illinois Youth." *Public Health Reports.* As quoted in *Social Marketing Quarterly,* 1996, "Product Substitution for Social Marketing of Behavior Change: A Conceptualization," p. 5.
10. Ibid., p. 10.
11. Ibid., pp. 9-10.
12. Kotler & Armstrong, *Principles of Marketing,* p. G-1.
13. Kotler & Roberto, *Social Marketing,* p. 153.
14. Ibid.
15. Kotler & Armstrong, *Principles of Marketing,* p. 269.
16. Ibid.
17. Smith, B. (1999, June). "Social Marketing: Marketing With No Budget." *Social Marketing Quarterly,* 5(2), pp. 7-8.
18. Ibid.
19. Kotler & Armstrong, *Principles of Marketing,* p. 270.

KEY CHAPTER QUESTIONS

1. What is the price of a social marketing product?

2. What are major categories and types of costs?

3. What are major strategies for managing costs?

4. What pricing-related tactics are used to manage costs?

5. What are considerations when setting prices for tangible objects and services?

CHAPTER 10

Price: Managing Costs of Behavior Change

In an effort to make people behave better, societies have tried some brutal measures throughout history: Decapitation. Disembowelment. Amputation. And now, in Fort Lupton, Colorado, yet another gruesome fate awaits. Barry Manilow. Bagpipe music. The theme song from Barney.

Municipal Court Judge Paul Sacco, 45, is a firm believer in making the punishment fit the crime. "Sentencing is an art," he says, "not a science." So whenever a teenager—or even an adult—violates the town's ordinance against loud music, Sacco sentences them to a dose of their own medicine—a full hour of listening to music they hate.

—*People* Magazine[1]

MARKETING HIGHLIGHT: LITTER PREVENTION

The following summary of a social marketing plan to reduce litter focuses on the element of pricing, with an emphasis on potential monetary (fines) and non-monetary (community service) costs associated with current behavior.

Litter and It Will Hurt

Megan Warfield
Litter Programs Coordinator
Washington State Department of Ecology

Campaign Background and Purpose

Litter hurts. Every year in Washington State, more than 16 million pounds of "stuff" are tossed and blown onto interstate, state, and county roads alone. The Washington State Department of Ecology spends more than $4 million dollars to pick up just a fourth of it. It creates an eyesore for motorists, harms wildlife and their habitats, and is a potential hazard for motorists who may be struck by anything from a lit cigarette to an empty can of beer, even a bottle of "trucker's pee." Many of us (about 25%) would never consider littering. Some of us (about 25%) litter most of the time. Almost half of us litter occasionally but can be persuaded not to.

This plan presents a recommended 3-year marketing strategy to help reduce intentional littering on roadways. It is designed to reach a broad audience to raise and maintain awareness and to reach targeted audiences contributing to a majority of the problem. It relies heavily on the partnership and involvement of state agencies, local governments and (litter) tax-paying businesses. It plans for media sponsorships and leverages their advertisers. It includes a system to measure campaign outcomes and implementation processes. It reinstitutes a Litter Hotline to send the message that people care enough about litter to make a call and that littering is not the norm in Washington. It includes a short-term plan to raise awareness and requires a long-term plan for behavior change.

Target Audiences

There are two major audiences for the campaign: litterers and non-litterers. Target audiences for littering include the five segments creating the majority of intentional litter on roadways: those who toss cigarette butts, alcoholic beverage containers, food wrappers, and other beverage containers out the window and those who drive pickup trucks and do not properly cover and secure their loads or clean out the back of their pickup trucks prior to driving on roadways.

Campaign messages will also be aimed at members of the general public traveling on Washington State roadways so that they will report litterers.

Objectives

Campaign strategies have been designed to support three separate objectives: (a) a short-term objective to create awareness that there are significant fines associated with littering and that there is a toll-free "800 number" to report littering; (b) a longer-term objective to convince litterers to believe that their littering will be noticed and they could be caught; and (c) a long-term objective to *influence litterers to change their behaviors:* to dispose of litter properly, cover and secure pickup truck loads, and clean out the back of their trucks prior to driving on roadways.

Strategies

To *create awareness,* activities will focus on major promotional channels used to "spread the word" that there are significant fines for littering and that there is a toll-free number to report littering. Channels include signage, advertising, publicity, special events, and messages on state collateral pieces, including litterbags, tab renewal envelopes and driver's education materials.

To *alter beliefs* that their littering isn't noticed and that people don't care, additional strategies will need to be implemented, including letters from toll-free calls signed by the Washington State Patrol; state troopers asking people during designated awareness periods whether they have litterbags and reminding them that "it's the law"; ongoing publicity featuring stories of people who get caught littering; imposing and publicizing additional community service

penalties for littering; creating demonstration piles of litter, to make what is being collected seem real; and vinyl-wrapped vehicles, window decals, and bumper stickers as frequent, constant reminders on the road.

To *change behavior,* we will also need to provide *tangible mechanisms* to make it easier to dispose of litter and prevent litter from blowing out. We'll need even more extensive distribution of litterbags, promotions of tarps and cargo nets, availability of disposable cigarette pouches, and more (and "cooler") litter receptacles. With all three strategies in place, we think we can "surround the enemy." (See Figure 10.1.)

It is important to note, and is emphasized throughout this plan, that to achieve each of these objectives, it will be necessary to implement the accompanying recommended strategies. As illustrated in Figure 10.1, all strategies play a role in "surrounding" the litterer. The communications goal of the campaign is to make litterers understand that

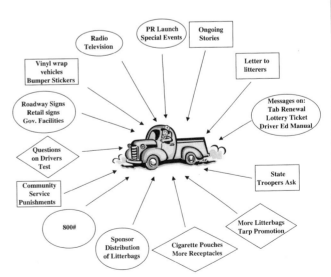

(Oval) Creating Awareness (Rectangle) Altering Beliefs (Diamond) Changing Behavior

Figure 10.1. Using All Elements of the Marketing Mix to Create Awareness, Alter Beliefs, and Change Behaviors

littering will not only hurt the environment but will also hurt them personally because of the risk of fines.

Sponsors

To achieve the awareness goals established for the Ecology Litter Prevention campaign, it is critical to get litter messages exposed to our target audiences over a sustained time period in an effective way. In addition, we need to identify cost-effective ways of distributing materials (litter bags, disposable ashtrays, tarps, etc.) and extend our campaign message at the retail level through signage, point-of-sale, collateral, and special events.

The Litter Prevention Campaign has limited funding to produce and run advertising to achieve its awareness goals. Extending the campaign to a wide audience through corporate sponsorships is critical to success. To this end, the Washington State Department of Ecology has formed a marketing partnership with two major Washington broadcast media partners. Together, they represent the most powerful broadcast network in the state.

Beginning in the fall of 2001, these media partners and their sales teams will identify, contact, and sign up corporate sponsors who will help underwrite the Litter Prevention Campaign elements (advertising and collateral production/distribution) between April 2002 and September 2003. In addition, they will support the campaign with public service announcements and editorial vignettes throughout the effort.

Partnerships

A Litter Task Force, convened in 1997 and representing businesses, state agencies, and local governments, recommended that Ecology conduct this statewide litter prevention campaign in *partnership* with other state agencies, local governments, and businesses that pay the litter tax. Support and involvement of these stakeholder groups is key.

Evaluation

A baseline survey of Washington state residents is planned to measure (a) awareness of stiff fines associated with littering and (b) awareness of the toll-free number for reporting littering.

Assuming that additional strategies to support belief and behavior objectives are implemented, it will also be appropriate to include questions regarding littering behavior in this baseline and follow-up survey. In addition, periodic litter composition surveys can be used to measure changes in targeted categories of roadway litter.

Several additional important measurements of efforts are recommended, including quantifiable reporting on reach and frequency data from media, sponsorship and in-kind contributions, press coverage, numbers of litterbags distributed, and participation levels of other state agencies. Several of these measures will then be combined with other campaign data (e.g., number of signs and associated visibility and traffic) to create overall numbers of campaign "impressions" with target audiences.

Budgets and Time Lines

Four phases have been identified for this 3-year campaign. In summary, first-year efforts are concentrated on awareness building. Years 2 and 3 will sustain this effort, as well as add elements key for belief and behavior change. Major costs will be associated with advertising (television and radio). Additional major costs will include signage at governmental facilities (e.g., department of transportation rest stations, truck weigh stations, department of licensing registration and licensing offices, and vehicle emission test stations) and operating the toll-free 800 number. Funding for litterbag printing, distribution, and retail signage is anticipated to be provided by media partners and corporate sponsors, who will also augment advertising (television and radio) media buys.

CHAPTER OVERVIEW

In social marketing, pricing is a two-part discussion, beginning with an exploration of what price the target market will pay for the social marketing product (desired behavior) and then exploring monetary and nonmonetary incentives and rewards to minimize these perceived costs. Several guidelines are also discussed in this chapter for developing and setting pricing objectives and tactics.

WHAT IS THE PRICE OF A SOCIAL MARKETING PRODUCT?

The price of a social marketing product is the cost that the target market associates with adopting the new behavior. Traditional marketing theory has a similar definition: "The amount of money charged for a product or service, or the sum of the values that consumers exchange for the benefits of having or using the product or service."[2]

Adoption costs may be *monetary* or *nonmonetary* in nature. Monetary costs are most often related to *tangible objects and services* associated with adopting the behavior. Nonmonetary costs are more intangible but are just as real for our target audience: They are costs associated with *time, effort, and energy* to perform the behavior; *psychological risks and losses* that might be perceived or experienced; and any *physical discomforts* that may be related to the behavior.

The social marketer's *pricing objective* is best described by the exchange theory, which states that *what we offer the target market (benefits) has to be equal to or greater than what they will have to give (costs).*[3]

A 2-step process is involved, first, identifying the monetary and nonmonetary costs associated with adopting the new behavior and second, developing strategies to decrease costs and increase benefits, an effort to "balance the scale."

WHAT ARE MAJOR CATEGORIES AND TYPES OF COSTS?

The first step in developing pricing tactics is to identify costs associated with adopting the new behavior. There may be *exit costs* associated with abandoning the old behavior (e.g., nicotine withdrawal) as well as *entry costs* associated with adopting the new behavior (e.g., getting up earlier to exercise).[4] Many of these costs, especially nonmonetary ones, were identified in Step 4 when we analyzed perceived benefits and costs of the proposed behavior relative to the competition. Potential monetary costs will also need to be identified, especially for any tangible objects and services that will be promoted in the campaign.

Monetary Costs

Most commonly, monetary costs are the *prices charged for purchasing tangible objects and services* that accompany the campaign. In some cases, it is the actual cost of the product or service, and in others, it is any increases in price relative to current products and services being used.

Examples of tangible objects with potential monetary costs include the following:

Bike helmets, life vests, and booster seats

Earthquake preparedness kits

Blood pressure monitoring equipment

Sunscreen

Condoms

Birth control pills

Garbage compost tumblers

Natural fertilizers (versus regular fertilizers)

Recycled paper (versus regular paper)

Breathalyzers

Special ashtrays for cars that reduce smoke

Energy-saving lightbulbs

Electric mulch mowers (versus gas or push mowers)

Energy-saving appliances

Examples of services with potential monetary costs include the following:

Fees for family planning services

Swimming classes

Parenting classes

Smoking cessation classes

Suicide prevention workshop

Athletic club fees

Nurse consultations

Immunizations

Monitoring service for seniors at risk for falls

Taxi rides

Nonmonetary Costs

Target audiences will also face nonmonetary costs that will be associated with adopting the new behavior, and examples have been organized in three major categories.

Time, effort, and energy involved in behaviors such as the following:

Sorting garbage

Pulling over to use the cell phone

Cooking a balanced meal

Getting rid of weeds by hand

Driving to a car wash versus washing the car in the driveway

Finding the box at the office for mixed paper recycling

Putting together an earthquake preparedness kit

Reusing grocery bags

Driving to the local farmers' market to cash WIC coupons

Waiting for a bus and then transferring to get to work

Delaying tossing the cigarette until finding a receptacle

Cleaning out trash in the back of an open pickup truck

Sweeping a sidewalk instead of using a gas blower

Psychological risks (e.g., embarrassment, rejection, or fear) and losses (e.g., aesthetics or familiarity) associated with behaviors such as the following:

Finding out whether a lump is cancerous

Letting a lawn go brown in the summer

Saying no to a second glass of wine

Having a cup of coffee without a cigarette

Listening to the chatter of others in a car pool

Asking your son whether he is considering suicide

Telling your husband you think he drinks too much

Using sunscreen and coming back from Hawaii "pale"

Physical discomfort or loss of pleasure from activities such as the following:

Taking shorter showers

Having a mammogram

Pricking a finger to monitor blood glucose

Exercising

Craving a cigarette

Lowering the thermostat

Wearing a life vest

WHAT ARE MAJOR STRATEGIES FOR MANAGING COSTS?

At this point, we know what potential costs the target audience perceives relative to adopting the new behavior. Now, we want to develop strategies that will balance the scale, ensuring that they believe our offer is equal to or greater than the costs they perceive. Looking at the task simply, we have two major strategies:

1. Decrease costs of adopting the new behavior, those associated with exiting the current behavior as well as entering the new one.
2. Increase benefits of adopting the new behavior.

Our tools to accomplish this include pricing tactics and other familiar elements of the marketing mix: product, place, and promotion. In the case of mammograms, for example, we may have identified costs and potential strategies to "balance the scales," as presented in Figures 10.2 and 10.3.

WHAT PRICING-RELATED TACTICS ARE USED TO MANAGE COSTS AND BALANCE THE SCALE?

We have identified and provided examples of five major pricing-related tactics that can be used to manage costs:

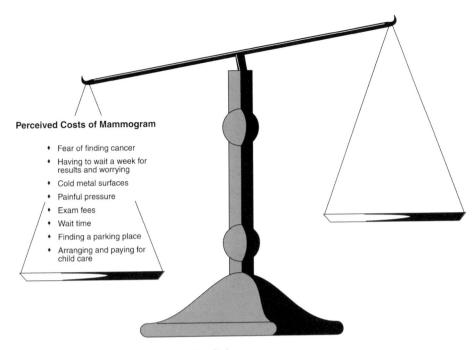

Figure 10.2. Perceived Costs for Adopting the Behavior

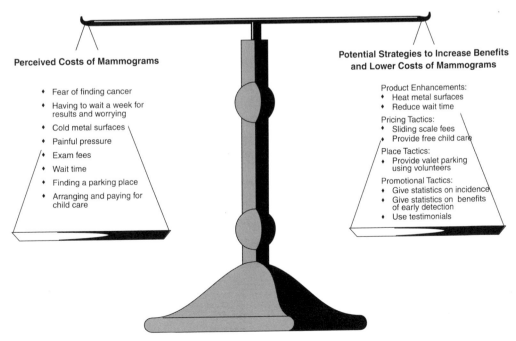

Figure 10.3. Perceived Costs for Adopting the Behavior Are Balanced With All Elements of the Marketing Mix

1. Decrease monetary costs.
2. Decrease nonmonetary costs.
3. Decrease costs relative to the competition.
4. Increase monetary benefits.
5. Increase nonmonetary benefits.

In most cases, these examples have implications for pricing, as well as other elements of the marketing mix.

Decreasing Monetary Costs

Methods to decrease monetary costs are familiar to most consumers: *discount coupons, cash discounts, quantity discounts, seasonal discounts, promotional pricing* (e.g., a temporary price reduction), and *segment pricing* (e.g., price based on geographic locations). Many of these tactics are available to the social marketer and can increase sales, as illustrated in the following example.

Example: Bike Helmet Coupons[5]

Harborview Injury Prevention and Research Center's Web site reported in February 2000 that "more bicyclists in Seattle wear helmets than bicyclists in any other major city in the country where laws do not require it...." The Washington Children's Helmet Bicycle Campaign was launched in 1986 by physicians at Harborview Medical Center in Seattle, who were alarmed at the nearly 200 children they were treating each year with bicycle-related head injuries.

"Although bicycle helmets were available in 1985, just one child in 100 wore one." HIPRC physicians conducted a study to understand why parents didn't buy bike helmets for their children and what factors influenced whether children actually wore them. "The results, from a survey of more than 2,500 fourth graders and their parents, shaped the eventual campaign. More than two thirds of the parents said they had never thought of providing a helmet and *another third cited cost as a factor.*"

A campaign was designed around "four key objectives: increasing public awareness of the importance of helmets, educating parents about helmet use, overcoming peer pressure among children against wearing helmets, and *lowering helmet prices.*"

The HIPRC formed a coalition of health, bicycling, helmet industry, and community organizations to design and manage a variety of promotions. As a result, parents and children heard about helmets on television, on the radio, in the newspapers, in their doctors' offices, at school, and at youth groups. These sources also advertised *discount coupons that cut helmet prices by half, to $20. Nearly 5,000 helmets were distributed at no or low cost to needy families.* [See Figure 10.4.]

BIKE HELMET
Discount Coupon
. . . .
Valid April 15–August 31, 1993

This coupon entitles you to purchase one of the helmets listed below at a discount price, courtesy of Troxel Cycling and Fitness and participating retailers (see back of coupon). For additional coupons, call the Bicycle Helmet Hotline at 1-800-537-4756.

Check the box below to indicate which helmet was purchased:

   ❑ Coronado Youth Helmet $19.99
   ❑ Coronado Adult Helmet $19.99
   ❑ Niño Toddler Helmet $19.99

All helmets are hardshell and Snell approved.

Distributed in cooperation with:

Washington Children's Bicycle Helmet Coalition

 **PEMCO** Insurance Companies

 Group Health Cooperative of Puget Sound

 HARBORVIEW INJURY PREVENTION & RESEARCH CENTER

 BARTELL DRUGS

Children's Hospital & Medical Center

BE HEAD SMART!

Figure 10.4. Bike Helmet Coupon Used to Encourage Purchase

By September 1993 (7 years later), helmet use had jumped from 1% to 57% among children in the greater Seattle area, and adult use increased to 70%. Five years into the campaign, an HIPRC evaluation revealed its ultimate effectiveness: Admissions at five Seattle-area hospitals for bicycle-related head injuries dropped by approximately two thirds for children 5 to 14 years old.

Decreasing Nonmonetary Costs

Strategies are available for decreasing *time, effort, physical,* or *psychological* costs.

Usage time can be reduced, according to Karen Fox, by "embedding" a new behavior into present activities.[6] Thus, people might be encouraged to floss their teeth while they watch television. People can also be encouraged to "anchor" a new behavior to an established habit.[7] To encourage physical activity, for example, the social marketer can recommend that people climb the stairs to their third-floor offices instead of taking the elevator.

Gemunden proposed several potential tactics for reducing other nonmonetary costs in this model:

1. Against a perceived psychological risk, provide social products in ways that deliver *psychological rewards.*

2. Against a perceived social risk, gather *endorsements from credible sources* that reduce the potential stigma or embarrassment of adopting a product.

3. Against a perceived usage risk, provide target adopters with *reassuring information* on the product or with a free trial of the product so they can experience how the product does what it promises to do.

4. Against perceived physical risk, solicit *seals of approval* from authoritative institutions, such as the American Dental Association, the American Medical Association, or other highly respected organizations.[8]

Example: Redeeming Farmers' Market Checks

Women and Infant Children (WIC) offices often distribute checks to qualifying families to purchase fresh fruits and vegetables at local farmers' markets. Yet clients often face several nonmonetary costs that lead to lower redemption rates than many WIC offices would like to see, for example: *effort* to find the market and parking; *embarrassment* around other shoppers when using coupons; *difficulty* in identifying qualified produce when signs are inconsistently displayed or difficult to see; *concern* with not getting change back from checks; *frustration* with misplacing checks that are often stored or forgotten in drawers or strollers; and *fear* of what the WIC counselor will think if they decline the checks, even though their chances of using them are minimal given work schedules that conflict with market hours.

These costs could be overcome with a variety of tactics:

◆ Detailed maps to the market and for parking printed on the back of checks

◆ Electronic debit cards in place of the checks

◆ Signs on poles above the stands that display some recognizable logo that doesn't "brand" the client, such as the 5 A Day logo

◆ Printing checks in lower amounts, such as $1 denominations

◆ Packaging checks in sturdy check folders

◆ Offering hesitant clients fewer checks, and more if they use them all

Decreasing Costs
Relative to the Competition

Cost-comparison strategies can be as effective in the social marketing environment as they are in the commercial sector, especially when the cost difference is great and in our favor.

Example: Booster Seats as a Better Alternative[9]

While great strides have been made to protect infants and toddlers in a motor vehicle crash, preschoolers and young children remain at high risk of injury. Most of the nation's 20 million children aged 4 to 8 ride in motor vehicles either unprotected or using adult seat belts that do not fit them properly. Seat belts alone can cause serious internal injuries and even death. [See Figure 10.5.] Booster seats raise the child up so that the lap and shoulder belts fit the child. A booster seat provides a safe transition from child seats that have their own harness systems to adult lap and shoulder belts. Children 40 to 80 pounds and 4 to 8 years of age should use a belt-positioning booster seat.

Figure 10.5. Reducing Perceived Costs of the Desired Behavior

The Washington State Booster Seat Coalition has two goals. The first is to increase the use of belt-positioning booster seats among preschoolers and young children 4 to 8 years old by the end of 2001. The second is to establish a multifaceted public education program that can serve as a model for other communities.

Prior to campaign development, a series of focus groups were conducted to assess parental attitudes toward booster seats and to test market potential public health messages.

Activities and services planned to accomplish goals include the following:

- Development of a community coalition of agencies and organizations to promote the use of booster seats

- Creation of a citizen advisory group of parents and caregivers to provide feedback on campaign messages and materials and to develop strategies to ensure community involvement

- A broad-based community education program to increase knowledge and awareness of the importance of booster seat use, which will include the following:

  Newspaper articles
  Organization and group newsletter articles
  Booster seat Web site
  Tip sheet, brochures, and flyers
  Telephone information line
  Resource kits for preschools and health care providers
  Radio public service announcements
  Television public service announcements
  Local news reports
  Educational programs to address barriers to booster seat use, including defining types of booster seats, identifying where devices are available, and providing alternatives for automobiles with lap-only belts
  Distribution of discount coupons
  Expansion of successful car seat training programs developed by the Washington Traffic Safety Commission and Safety Restraint Coalition: Implement training for child care providers, educators, law enforcement, emergency medical service personnel, and child passenger safety advocates. Training will include hands-on workshops, electronic training seminars and an e-mail information exchange.

Integral to the booster seat campaign is an evaluation component. Baseline observations were conducted to measure booster seat use in intervention and control areas. A follow-up observational study was conducted after one year, showing that booster seat use in King County had risen from 13% to 25%. The evaluation also included information on where parents were getting their information about booster seats, to better target future campaign efforts.[10]

Increasing Monetary Benefits

Monetary rewards and incentives for buying the product can take many forms and would include *rebates, allowances, cash incentives,* and *price adjustments* that reward customers for adopting the proposed behavior. Some have been rather "tame" in nature (e.g., 4¢ credit for reusing grocery bags), whereas others have been quite bold (e.g., offering drug-addicted women a $200 incentive for voluntary sterilization).

Example: Bargain Prices for Electricity at Nonpeak Hours

Communications to customers of Puget Sound Energy during the 2001 energy crunch used monetary incentives to help convince customers to conserve electricity:

1. *Shift your use of electricity to economy and bargain times.* "It's better for the environment and for you." Bill inserts contained charts that displayed the customer's distribution of energy use by time of day. Bar graphs displayed the customer's usage (e.g., showing that 2,830 kilowatt hours were used in the past 30 days, 36% in the most expensive time frames (6 a.m. to 11 a.m. and 5 p.m. to 9 p.m.). The utility explained that proposed policies would offer decreased rates during "Economy Hours" and even more so during "Real Bargain Times."

2. *Look for savings by reducing use of the heaviest users of electricity.* A pie chart highlighted the fact that water heaters represented 34% of the average household's electrical use. Real savings could occur by reducing the temperature by only a few degrees. (See Figure 10.6.)

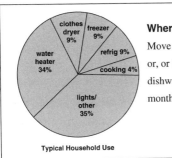

Where electricity is used...and where to look for savings.

Move as many activities as you can that use appliances to the "economy" or, or better yet, the "bargain" times. Maybe you can wait to start your dishwasher until just before bedtime, for example. Then compare this month's information with the next month's to see how you did.

Figure 10.6. Bill Insert From Utility Encouraging Electrical Use During Economy Times

Increasing Nonmonetary Benefits

Nonmonetary tactics, such as *recognition* and *appreciation,* can be employed to increase perceived benefits of the desired behavior and often include recognition programs.

Example: Backyard Wildlife Sanctuary Recognition Programs

Some state and local agencies, such as the Washington State Department of Fish and Wildlife, recognize good environmental stewardship by providing homeowners with impressive weatherproof plaques for the yard and frameable certificates for inside the

Figure 10.7. Plaque Given to Homeowners Completing Application and Agreeing to Practices

home. (See Figure 10.7.) Programs typically include filling out a habitat inventory application that ensures the presence of numerous trees and shrubs, birdbaths or some other source of water, bird feeders, and birdhouses or shelters. Applicants "promise" (in writing) to minimize their use of dangerous chemicals in fertilizers and pesticides.

This recognition program not only increases perceived benefits of being a habitat manager but also makes it more likely that homeowners will know and practice the desired environmental behaviors that protect wildlife. Packets of information sent to the homeowner along with the plaque and certificate include the following:

- Lists of plants to attract butterflies
- How to best feed birds
- Types of natural fertilizers and pesticides
- How to design a small wildlife pond
- Tips for attracting hummingbirds

- References for landscaping
- Instructions on building a songbird nest box

CONSIDERATIONS WHEN SETTING PRICES FOR TANGIBLE OBJECTS AND SERVICES

Prices for tangible objects and services involved in social marketing campaigns are typically set by manufacturers, retailers, and service providers. The social marketer primarily promotes the use of the products or distributes discount coupons and related incentives.

When a social marketer gets involved in the price setting, several principles guide decision making. The first task is to determine *pricing objectives.* Kotler and Roberto[11] outline several potential objectives:

- *Maximizing profits* where the primary consideration is money making

- *Recovering costs* where revenue is expected to offset a portion of costs

- *Maximizing the number of target adopters* where the primary purpose is to influence as many people as possible to use the service and/or buy the product

- *Social equity* where reaching underprivileged or high-risk segments is a priority and different prices might be charged according to ability to pay

- *Demarketing* where pricing strategies are used to discourage people from adopting a particular social product

Once the pricing objective is clarified, specific prices can be set. Three options are available:[12]

- *Cost-based pricing* where prices are based on a desired or established profit margin or rate of return on investment (e.g., condoms are sold at community clinics at prices to cover purchase costs)

- *Competitive-based pricing* where prices are more driven by the prices for competing (similar) products and services (e.g., a life vest manufacturer partnering on a drowning prevention campaign offers discount coupons to make pricing similar to less expensive vests that are not coast guard approved)

- *Value-based pricing* where prices are based on an analysis of the target adopters' "price sensitivity," evaluating demand at varying price points (e.g., food waste composters that require simple spinning are priced higher than those requiring manual tossing)

CHAPTER SUMMARY

1. *The price of a social marketing product is the cost that the target audience associates with adopting the new behavior.* Costs may be monetary or nonmonetary in nature. They may be costs associated with exiting the old behavior, as well as entering the new one.

2. The marketer's task is to ensure that what we offer the target market (benefits) is equal to or greater than what they will have to give up (costs).

3. Two steps are involved in this process: (a) identifying the monetary and nonmonetary costs associated with adopting the new behavior and (b) developing product, price, place, and promotional tactics to decrease costs and increase benefits.

4. Monetary costs are those associated with the prices charged for tangible objects and services that accompany the campaign. Nonmonetary costs are typically related to time, psychological risks and losses, and physical discomfort or loss of pleasures.

5. Although most prices for tangible objects and services are established by manufacturers, retailers, and service providers, several principles can guide a social marketer faced with price-setting decisions, beginning with establishing pricing objectives.

KEY TERMS AND CONCEPTS

Adoption costs   Exit costs
Monetary costs   Entry costs
Nonmonetary costs   Pricing objective
                              Price-setting

ISSUES FOR DISCUSSION: EXIT COSTS

1. In the opening case on litter prevention, a toll-free 800 number for reporting littering was a key strategic element of the campaign. In reality, most of the time violators merely receive a letter stating that someone saw them littering and where

and when. They are not mailed a ticket or a fine. Why do you think planners included this element?

2. What are potential costs associated with deciding not to binge drink and to drink moderately instead? What strategies would you use to balance these costs?

3. How could a desired behavior of drinking eight glasses of water a day be embedded in or anchored to a current habit?

RESEARCH HIGHLIGHT:
INFORMAL INTERVIEWS FOR TEEN SEXUAL ABSTINENCE

This research example highlights the potential effectiveness of *brief, informal interviews* as a research instrument. We often think that we need to organize and implement a series of formal focus groups to explore audience perceptions (and sometimes that is exactly what is needed). In this case, however, major insights were gained with a few simple questions and a few minutes with members of the target market.

Teen Aware:
A Youth Driven Abstinence Campaign

The Teen Aware Project is a part of a statewide effort to reduce teen pregnancy and is sponsored by the Washington State Office of Superintendent of Public Instruction. Funds are allocated through a competitive grant process to public middle/junior and senior high schools for the development of media campaigns to promote sexual abstinence and the importance of delaying sexual activity, pregnancy, and childbearing.

These campaigns are substantially designed and produced by students. Student media products include video and radio productions, posters, theater productions, print advertising, multimedia, T-shirts, buttons, Web sites, and more. Campaign messages are distributed in local project schools and communities.

This particular research effort was conducted by teens at Mercer Island High School, a grant recipient in 1994. A team of nine students from marketing, health, and communication classes volunteered to develop the campaign, from start to finish. Several teachers and outside consultants served as "coaches" on the project.

At the time this research effort was undertaken, the team had chosen their campaign focus (abstinence), purpose (reducing teen pregnancies), target audience (eighth graders), and their campaign objective (to persuade students to "pause and think in a heated moment"). Information from existing student surveys indicated that about 75% of eighth graders—but only 25% of seniors—were abstinent. It was decided that the campaign "bull's-eye" would be eighth graders, who were seen as being the most vulnerable for making choices regarding sexual activity.

The team of juniors and seniors wanted to refresh their memories about middle school years. As one student expressed, "It's been a long time since I was an eighth grader, and I don't have a clue what they know and think about sex these days."

Research Purpose and Objectives

Two primary purposes were identified for their research:

1. To help make decisions regarding which benefits of abstinence and costs related to sexual activity should be highlighted in the campaign
2. To provide input for *selecting a slogan* for the campaign

The students then developed the following informational objectives:

▶ Major perceived benefits of abstinence

▶ Major perceived costs of being sexually active

▶ What messages (and tone) would be most effective in influencing an eighth grader to consider abstinence

Methodology

Each of the nine students agreed to conduct casual interviews with at least five eighth graders over a 1-week period. They used an informal script that explained the project and assured respondents that their comments would be anonymous. They recorded and summarized responses to the following three open-ended questions:

1. "What's the most important reason you can think of for delaying having intercourse until you are older?"
2. "What are the worst things you can think of that can happen to you if you have intercourse before you are ready?"

3. "What would you say to your best friend if she or he told you that they thought they were going to have sex for the first time tonight?"

Interviews were conducted with district permission, before and after classes at the middle schools, as well as in informal settings such as sports events, after-school programs, and in friends' homes.

Findings

Students returned to class the following week, shared their summary findings, and were guided to identify the following themes for each of the informational areas:

Major Reasons for Delaying Sex:

▶ You won't get pregnant.

▶ You won't get Sexually Transmitted Diseases (STDs).

▶ You can save it for someone special.

The Worst Things That Can Happen:

▶ They could drop you later for someone else.

▶ You could get pregnant, and childbirth really hurts.

▶ You can get really bad STDs, like "crabs."

Words for a Friend:

▶ You should wait until you are older.

▶ Are you sure he really loves you?

▶ Do you have protection?

▶ Are you ready for all the things that could happen?

Figure 10.8. Abstinence Campaign Poster

Campaign Implications

The team used this input to develop a campaign centered around emphasis on three "gross" consequences of having sex before you're ready.

They developed a campaign slogan "Are you ready?" and followed the question with each of the three consequences. Graphic, in-your-face images were reflected on the posters and depicted in radio scripts. (See Figures 10.8, 10.9, and 10.10.)

Radio spots that were played on the high school radio station followed the three "gross" consequence themes. In one, a male voice says,

> I remember the day I learned what an STD really was. I had seen little things crawling around in my . . . hair. I woke up in the middle of the night, my . . . you know . . . was burning from an itch. My entire crotch was swarming with miniature crabs. Finally, I had to get help.
>
> If you think you're going to have sex, ask yourself: "Are you ready for that?" (See Figure 10.8.)

In another radio ad, a girl graphically recounts the pain of giving birth. (See Figure 10.9.)

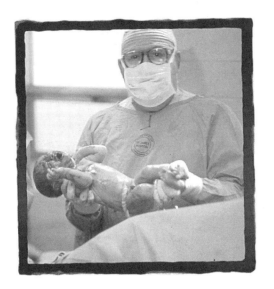

Figure 10.9. Abstinence Campaign Poster

Are you ready?

Mercer Island Teens For Delaying Sex

Figure 10.10. Abstinence Campaign Poster

In the third ad, a girl sadly yet frankly relates how the guy she slept with immediately told everyone at school and found a new girlfriend. It took her years to trust a guy again. (See Figure 10.10.)

NOTE: Students received creative and production assistance from: Cynthia Hartwig (Creative Director), Shelley Baker (Art Director) at Cf2gs Advertising, Marlene Liranzo (Mercer Island High School Teacher), Gary Gorland (Teen Aware Program Manager), and Nancy Lee (Consultant).

Notes

1. *People* Magazine (1999, April 19), p. 83.
2. Kotler, P., & Armstrong, G. (2001). *Principles of Marketing* (p. 371). Upper Saddle River, NJ: Prentice Hall.
3. Kotler, P., & Andreasen, A. (1991). *Strategic Marketing for Nonprofit Organizations* (p. 125). Englewood Cliffs, NJ: Prentice Hall; for additional discussion of the concept of exchange in marketing, see Richard P. Bagozzi, "Marketing as an Organized Behavioral System of Exchange," *Journal of Marketing,* October 1974, 77-81, and "Marketing as Exchange," *American Behavioral Scientist,* March-April 1978, 535-556.
4. Porter, Michael E. (1998). *Competitive Advantage: Creating and Sustaining Superior Performance.* New York: Free Press.
5. Information in this example is from Harborview Injury Prevention and Research Center. University of Washington, Seattle, Washington. Retrieved 10/01/01 from Harborview Injury Prevention and Research Center Web site at http/www.hiprc.org
6. Kotler, P., & Roberto, E. L. (1989). *Social Marketing: Strategies for Changing Public Behavior* (p. 182). New York: Free Press, citing: Fox, K. F. (1980). "Time as a Component of Price in Social Marketing" (pp. 464-467). In Richard P. Bagozzi et al. (Eds.). *Marketing in the 1980s.* Chicago: American Marketing Association.
7. Ibid.
8. Kotler, P., & Roberto, E. L. (1989). *Social Marketing: Strategies for Changing Public Behavior* (pp. 182-183). New York: Free Press, citing: Gemunden, H. G. (1985). "Perceived Risk and Information Search: A Systematic Meta-Analysis of the Empirical Evidence," *International Journal of Research in Marketing, 2,* 79-100.
9. Harborview Injury Prevention and Research Center. University of Washington. Seattle, Washington. Retrieved 10/01/01 from Harborview Injury Prevention and Research Center Web site at www.hiprc.org
10. The Washington State Booster Seat Coalition and the King County Booster Seat Campaign is coordinated by Harborview Injury Prevention and Research Center, Children's Hospital and Regional Medical Center, the Washington Traffic Safety Commission, and the Safety Restraint Coalition. It is funded in part by a grant from the National Highway Traffic Safety Administration. Information for this example was taken from their Web site 5/2/2001 at: http://www.depts.washington.edu/booster/coalition_info.htm
11. Kotler & Roberto, *Social Marketing,* pp. 176-177.
12. Ibid., pp. 177-181.

1. What is place in a social marketing environment?

2. What is the objective when developing a place strategy?

3. How do we make access to our social marketing product more convenient?

CHAPTER 11

Place: Making Access Convenient

Store-based retailers say that the three most important things in the success of their business are "Location, location, location!"

MARKETING HIGHLIGHT: SAFE GUN STORAGE

This case employs all elements of the marketing mix to persuade firearm owners to "lock them up." Efforts to make storage and safety devices easy to purchase stand out as an essential core strategy.

LOK-IT-UP

John Britt, RN, MPH
Injury Prevention Specialist
Tacoma/Pierce County Health Department

Background

During the years 1994-1998, an average of 14,000 firearm homicides and 18,000 firearm suicides occurred each year in the United States. In addition, hundreds of children and teens die each year from unintentional firearm discharge. A recent study of adolescent suicides found that over half were committed with firearms from the adolescents' homes.

The LOK-IT-UP campaign was developed for Pierce County, Washington, where 36% of households own firearms and 62% of firearm owners own handguns. Fifty-seven percent of firearm owners report that a firearm is stored unlocked and 22% report keeping a firearm loaded. It is estimated that 75,000 children and adolescents under the age of 18 live in homes where there is at least one firearm. An estimated 23,000 reside in homes where a firearm is kept unlocked, 11,000 where a firearm is kept loaded, and 3,000 where a firearm is kept unlocked and loaded.

Purpose and Objectives

The primary purpose of the LOK-IT-UP campaign is to reduce injuries and deaths due to firearms.

To effect this, campaign planners wanted to influence firearm owners *to purchase and use one of several trigger-locking or gun storage devices,* to *know* what devices are available and where they can obtain these devices locally, and to *believe* that there is a device that will meet their locking and storage requirements.

Target Audiences

Men

National studies indicate that about 42% of men and about 9% of women personally own firearms. Initial LOK-IT-UP campaign strategies were developed to directly influence men.

Handgun Owners

The vast majority of firearm injuries in the United States involve handguns. While overall household firearm ownership has declined in recent years, the proportion of household firearms that are handguns has increased. Use of handgun images and safety products uniquely suited to handguns were selected to be used in all materials.

Adults With Children at Home

National and state studies confirm that households with children present lock up their firearms more consistently. This suggests that most parents recognize the risk of an unlocked firearm and would be more receptive to a safe storage message. Homes with children and adolescents present a triple threat from an unsecured firearm (gun theft, unintentional injury/death, and suicide).

Self-Protection Advocates

Some firearm owners were too concerned about having ready access for self-protection to ever consider locking up their guns. Others were quite concerned about safety issues and already make use of reliable storage practices and products. A third group of focus group participants moved back and forth between concerns for safety and concerns about access. It was this "swing" group that was selected for major conversion efforts.

Audience Attitudes

Most campaigns intending to change the habits of firearm owners emphasize the hazards of firearm ownership. A typical message, represented by a current national campaign, is "A gun in your home is a hazard to your family." While also addressing safe storage, the dominant theme is that families with guns in their homes should consider getting rid of them. Material distributed to pediatricians, who see mostly female clients, has the implicit strategy that women will take this information back to their homes and influence the ownership and storage practices of their male partners. Other common advice is to store all firearms unloaded and locked with ammunition locked in a separate location. This message has not addressed almost half of firearm owners, who claim "self-defense" as a reason for ownership. These individuals want quick access to their firearms.

The LOK-IT-UP campaign adopted a different marketing perspective to reach its objectives. Most firearm owners will not relinquish ownership because of statistics and emotional appeals, and some will keep at least one handgun for self-protection. It was decided that a campaign beginning with understanding firearm owners' perspectives would have the best chance of success promoting safe firearm storage. Focus groups were designed to gather an understanding of firearm owner perspectives and how to best influence their current practices.

Product Strategies

The LOK-IT-UP campaign promoted several devices for handgun locking: lockboxes, trigger locks, chamber locks, and personalized locks. Materials described each device, provided price ranges, and noted advantages and disadvantages. (See Figure 11.1.) Several benefits were also stressed: Prevent children from being injured or killed, prevent crimes from being committed with your gun, prevent depressed teens from committing suicide, and keep schools gun-free.

Pricing Strategies

Locking devices ranged from $5 to over $300.

Discount Coupon

Some focus group members suggested that a simple reduction in price might result in increased purchases. Local gun shops, sporting goods stores, and other retailers that carried locking and storage devices were approached and asked to honor a 10% to 15% discount on selected locking and storage products. The coupon was inserted in the LOK-IT-UP brochure, sent out with utility mailings and included in weekly newspapers near sports sections. (See Figure 11.2.) The politically neutral stance of the campaign has been essential to gaining retailer support.

Figure 11.1. Brochure Presents Options

Figure 11.2. Coupon Used to Promote Action

Place Strategy

Retail Outlets

Campaign materials provided detailed listings of where products could be purchased throughout the county, including major retail chains, as well as gun shops, gun supply stores, and ranges. More than 30 locations were listed on most materials, with phone numbers to call for more information and addresses. (See Figure 11.3.)

PULL ←—

Where can I buy locking & storage devices?

Call for product availability and prices.

Bonney Lake
Fred Meyer — 253-891-7300

Eatonville
High Country Guns — 360-832-3280

Edgewood
Great Guns — 253-952-4992

Fife
SportCo — 253-922-2222

Gig Harbor
Big 5 Sports — 253-851-2172
Coast to Coast — 253-857-6300
Russ Haydon Shooters Supply — 253-857-7557

Graham
John's Guns — 253-846-1275
Richard's Smoking Guns — 360-893-3468

Lakewood
AA Loans & Gun Shop — 253-582-4000
Big Kmart — 253-582-5406
Duffle Bag — 253-588-4433
Rainier Guns — 253-584-8560

Puyallup
Big 5 Sporting Goods — 253-848-9898
Big Kmart — 253-848-8751
Fred Meyer -Meridian E — 253-445-7840

PULL ←— **More locations on other side**

Figure 11.3. Brochure Provides Lists of Several Locations to Purchase a Device

Personal Distribution of Locks to High-Risk Audiences

Health department nurses visit over 800 low-income, high-risk families each year in the county. They have been trained to use a brief protocol to ask families they visit about firearm ownership and storage. If appropriate, the nurse demonstrates the use of lockboxes or trigger locks with the help of a realistic plastic handgun and offers the family a free device. These families have lower-than-average firearm ownership, about 20%, as compared with 36% in the county. On the other hand, a higher proportion of those who own firearms store them unlocked and/or loaded (about 65%).

Free lockboxes are provided to licensed psychiatrists and psychologists who indicate that they are treating adolescents at risk for self-harm and believe firearms are present in the home.

1-877-LOK-IT-UP

A statewide toll-free line was set up. Callers leave their requests on an answering machine, and brochures and coupons are sent out later.

Promotion Strategy

Printed Materials

Focus groups indicated that firearm owners wanted straightforward information that was untainted with antifirearm language and excessive emotional "hype." A brochure was developed which showed the four most common types of handgun locking and storage devices (trigger locks, cable locks, lockboxes, and personalized locks), price ranges, pros and cons, and where they can be purchased locally. The brochure has the look and feel of a *Consumer Reports* style of publication. Several cover designs were developed and tested with owners of gun shops, managers of firearm ranges, and staffs of concealed-weapons permit offices. The clear favorite was a bold design that showed the salient features of the four device types. Other designs with more sophisticated layouts and subtle colors were discarded as not attention-getting or too "feminine." A large four-color poster was also developed, showing an abbreviated form of the same information.

Radio

The favorite of several spots, titled "The Whole Purpose," features a representative from law enforcement. The piece is direct, presenting simple facts about the risk of firearm injury, extolling the two primary virtues of lockboxes (quick access in time of need and security against the "wrong hands"), while acknowledging the self-protection purpose behind some firearm ownership. It concluded by directing listeners to the LOK-IT-UP line. Spots using female voices were universally disparaged, as were spots that were deemed "too cute," "too emotional," or "statistically manipulative."

Outdoor

The favorite billboard ad is a picture of a lockbox with the handgun visible inside, with the phrase "It protects something valuable—your family." The double meaning of "It," linked to the perceived importance of owning a firearm for home protection, was recognized and embraced by the focus group members. As expected, this ad does not find favor with antigun advocates.

Gun Shows

LOK-IT-UP has explicitly sought the support of firearm owners, firearm safety instructors, law enforcement, and gun range and gun shop owners. Hosting a monthly booth at a large local gun show allows regular interaction with many firearm owners, distribution for materials, testing acceptance of campaign messages, and an invitation for comments and suggestions for new strategies. Free cable locks are distributed to participants in return for completed survey and opinion polls.

Evaluation

Although the primary motivation behind LOK-IT-UP is to reduce the incidence and prevalence of firearm injuries and death, using firearm injury rates to measure the effectiveness of the campaign is problematic. As serious as these incidents are, they are relatively rare for a small population such as Pierce County, and there is too much year-to-year fluctuation to provide a reliable measure of success. Also, firearm injuries are only partially related to storage practices. Therefore, it is necessary to identify other measures linked with campaign activities that can serve as reasonable proxies for injury and death reduction. Surveys used are described in the next section.

Surveys

Change in awareness. A commercial marketing data research firm was contracted to include questions on one of their monthly random sample telephone surveys to assess whether respondents were aware of the LOK-IT-UP campaign. The baseline (prior to outdoor advertising) survey showed that about 5% of respondents were aware of the campaign. Men were twice as likely to be aware of and correctly identify the purpose of the campaign. This survey will be repeated annually to determine whether promotional efforts do result in an increased campaign awareness by the target audience. The survey provides demographic information and also asks about firearm ownership.

Changes in behavior. In addition to county surveys, the state department of health conducts an annual behavioral risk factor surveillance survey that includes a set of standardized questions about firearm ownership and storage. A statistically significant number of respondents from Pierce County are included to provide reliable percentage estimates of residents who own firearms and who store them in a locked and/or loaded manner.

Awareness: Calls to the LOK-IT-UP line. The state Department of Health Injury Prevention Program distributes call reports on a monthly basis that indicate the number of calls to the line and the city and zip code of the caller. This method of tracking the campaign is most useful to assess the utility of new outdoor advertising and radio spots that promote 1-877-LOK-IT-UP.

Action: Discount coupon redemption. Health department staff made arrangements with participating retail personnel for monitoring the number of redeemed coupons.

Action: Sales data. One discount program participant is also a wholesale distributor for many of the locking and storage devices being promoted. For popular lockbox brands, this business has 100% of the Pacific Northwest market share. The numbers of locking devices sold from year to year are provided through the generosity of this retailer. Baseline sales data for the year 2000 have been established.

CHAPTER OVERVIEW

In the process of developing pricing strategies, we identified monetary and nonmonetary costs that our target audience might pay or experience while adopting the desired behavior. It was also noted that we would eventually be exploring *place* strategies to help reduce costs, remove access barriers, and increase perceived benefits. As illustrated in the LOK-IT-UP case, program managers worked closely with retailers and gun shop owners to ensure ease of access to locking devices, as well as personally distributing devices to high-risk audiences.

WHAT IS *PLACE* IN A SOCIAL MARKETING ENVIRONMENT?

Place is where and when the target market will perform the desired behavior, acquire any related tangible objects, and receive any associated services.

We live in a convenience-oriented world in which many of us place an extremely high value on our time, trying to save some of it for our families, friends, and favorite leisure activities. As social marketers, we need to be keenly aware that our target audience will evaluate the convenience of our offer relative to other exchanges in their lives. And the convenience "bar" has been raised over the past decade for all marketers by companies such as Starbucks, McDonald's, Federal Express, amazon.com, Lands' End, 1-800-Flowers, and innovations such as microwaves, movie channels, cell phones, ATM machines, and of course, the Internet.

In commercial sector marketing, place is often referred to as the marketing or *distribution channel* and is defined by Kotler and Armstrong as "a set of interdependent organizations involved in the process of making a product or service available for use or consumption by the consumer or business user."[1] Therefore, we have included at the end of this chapter a brief discussion of decisions regarding any "middlemen" that will be involved in providing services and distributing and selling products.

It is also important to clarify that place is *not the same as media channel*, which is where our communications will appear (e.g., brochures, radio ads, news stories, and personal presentations). Chapter 13 presents a detailed discussion of media channels.

WHAT IS THE OBJECTIVE WHEN DEVELOPING A PLACE STRATEGY?

Our objective with the *place marketing tool* is to develop strategies that will make it as convenient and pleasant as possible for our target audience to perform the behavior, acquire any tangible objects, and receive any services. We also want to do anything possible and within reason to make the competing behavior (seem) less convenient.

HOW DO WE MAKE ACCESS TO THE SOCIAL MARKETING PRODUCT MORE CONVENIENT?

Numerous access strategies are potentially available, including the following: increasing the *number and location of outlets;* moving outlets *closer* to target audiences; providing *mobile units* that come to neighborhoods or worksites; offering the option of *purchasing on-line,* over the *phone,* or through the *mail;* providing *pickup and delivery* services to homes or offices; *extending hours and days* of the week; improving the *ambiance* of a location; reducing *wait time;* improving *parking;* and increasing prominence of products displayed on *aisles and shelves.*

Creative and, we hope, cost-efficient means should be explored to find ways to accomplish the following:

- Make the location closer

- Extend hours

- Make the location more appealing

- Be there at the point of decision making

- Make performing the desired behavior more convenient than the competing behavior

Each of these strategies is described further in the following sections.

Find Ways to Make the Location Closer

Example: A Dental Office on Wheels

Many children don't get the regular dental care they need. They may be struggling with language barriers, poverty, rural isolation, or homelessness. A mobile clinic called the SmileMobile travels to communities all across Washington State. This modern dental office on wheels brings dental services directly to children aged 13 and younger who don't otherwise have access to care. Children enrolled in Medicaid have no out-of-pocket expenses, and other children are charged on a sliding fee schedule. Families may even enroll in Medicaid at the SmileMobile.

The brightly painted clinic features three state-of-the-art dental operatories and includes X-ray facilities. A full-time dentist and teams of local volunteer dentists and their staffs provide a range of dental services, including diagnostic services (e.g., exams and X rays), prevention services (e.g., cleaning and sealants), acute and emergent relief of pain (e.g., extractions and minor surgical procedures), and routine restorative services (e.g., fillings and crowns).

The SmileMobile was developed by the Washington State Dental Service (WDS), the Washington State Dental Association (WSDA), and the Washington Dental Service Foundation (WDSF). (See Figure 11.4.) Staff work closely with local health departments and community, charitable, and business organizations to coordinate visits to cities and towns throughout the state. Every effort is made to reach the neediest children and provide translators for non-English-speaking patients and their families.[2]

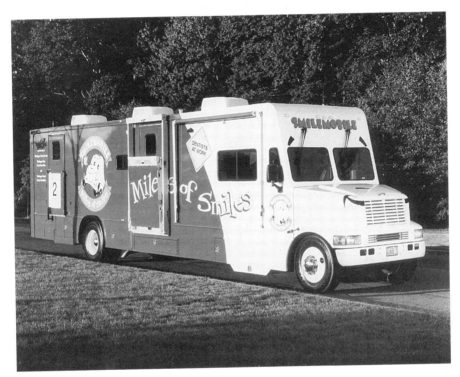

Figure 11.4. Making Dental Care for Children More Accessible

Additional examples illustrating time and effort savings for the target adopter include:

- Exercise facilities at worksites
- Flu shots at grocery stores
- Needle exchange tables on street corners
- Breastfeeding consultation provided during home visits
- Hazardous waste mobiles routed through neighborhoods
- Organics included in curbside recycling programs
- Print cartridges recycled at office supply stores

- Litter receptacles that make it easy to drive by and deposit litterbags

- Breathalyzers purchased over the Internet

- Dental floss kept in the TV room

- Xmas tree recycling drop-off at local schools

- Blood pressure checks at the mall

Find Ways to Extend Hours

Example: "Pets on the Net"

It is estimated that close to 10 million dogs end up in shelters across America every year, and only about 25% get adopted.[3] Potential pet owners have several considerations (perceived costs) associated with visiting animal shelters to see what pets are available. In addition to the time it takes to travel to a center, some describe the psychological risk, a concern that they might take home a pet that isn't what they are really looking for. They worry they won't be able to say "no." Viewing pets available for adoption on the Internet can help reduce both of these costs.

Many humane societies across the country have created Web sites where all or some of the pets currently available for adoption are featured, 24 hours a day, 7 days a week. As illustrated in the photo on Sacramento's "Pets on the Net" Web site, detailed information on the pet includes a personality profile based on the information provided by the previous owner. (See Figure 11.5.) Web site visitors are told that adoptions are on a first-come, first-serve basis, and directions to the facility are provided.[4]

Some Web sites include features such as daily updates, an opportunity to put a temporary hold on an animal, information on how to choose the right shelter pet, and reasons the pet was given up for adoption. A few national sites offer the ability to search nationwide for a pet by providing criteria including desired breed, gender, age, size, and geographic locales.

Additional examples of strategies that offer target adopters more options in terms of time and day of the week include the following:

- Child care searches online (versus calling a telephone center during normal business hours)

- Absentee ballots that are clearly offering more than a "one-day" option

- 24-hour help lines for counseling and information

Name: **Jake**

Sex: Neutered Male

Age: 3 yrs

Breed: German
Shepherd/Boxer

Color: Brown/Black,
Bicolor

Personality Profile:
Hey there! I'm Jake. I'm
a friendly and playful
young dog in need of a
good home, and a little
love and guidance from
someone special like
you! I walk well on a
leash and I like to ride in
the car, so maybe we
could run errands
together! Please come
and adopt me and give
me the chance I
deserve.

CASE: 47862A

Figure 11.5. Pets on the Net: Making Finding a Pet More Accessible

Find Ways to Make the Location More Appealing

Example: Mammograms at the Mall

The following article, from the *Detroit Free Press*, provided an example of reducing costs through improving access and location appeal.[5]

Many women already pick up birthday gifts, grab dinner, and get their hair cut at the malls, so why not schedule their annual mammograms there, as well?

With a concept that screams "no more excuses," the Barbara Ann Karmanos Cancer Institute will open a cancer prevention center at the Somerset Collection South in Troy in September.

A first for Michigan and the Detroit Institute, the mall-located screening center will provide a comfortable, spa-like atmosphere for patients in a less intimidating setting than a traditional doctor's office or hospital.

Targeting shoppers, mall workers—including about 3,000 women—and the 100,000 employees near the mall, Karmanos is renovating a 2,000-square-foot space in the lower level of the mall.

The center initially will focus on breast cancer prevention, with clinical breast exams and mammography available. However, services could expand to prostate, lung and gastrointestinal cancer screenings and bone-density testing, said Yvette Monet, a Karmanos spokeswoman.

Taking its cues from the spas, the Karmanos Prevention Center will pamper patients with privacy, peace and quiet, and warm terry-cloth robes.

The center is expected to encourage regular mammograms and breast exams. Nearly 44,000 women in the United States died last year from breast cancer—including 1,500 in Michigan—even though American Cancer Society studies show early diagnosis can mean a 97-percent survival rate.

The Karmanos Center is expected to reach women who think they are too busy to get mammograms or are afraid to do so. "This is intended to be a nonclinical-type setting that will feature soothing shades of blue and comfy couches," Monet said.

The Karamanos Center is not the first in a mall. Five Rich's/Lazarus/Goldsmith department stores—in Pittsburgh; Atlanta; Cincinnati; Columbus, Ohio and soon Indianapolis—have mammography centers tucked inside them. The department store chain, a division of Federated Department Stores Inc., supplies the space and nearby health care providers operate the facilities.

At Somerset, mall partners Forbes Cohen Properties and Frankel Associates are providing the lower-level space rent-free. Karmanos is footing the renovation costs and will be responsible for center-related expenses. The space formerly housed mall management, which has moved to the north end of Somerset.

Donating the space is "our opportunity to give back," said Rebedda Maccardini, director of operations for Forbes Cohen Properties.

Somerset considered a cancer prevention center for years but worried available spaces didn't provide enough privacy, Maccardini said.

The Somerset prevention center will join Karmanos' Breast Cancer Detection Center in Berkeley—which opened in 1993—as the institute's only nonhospital centers. Karmanos plans to open more community prevention sites, but no other mall locations are planned at this time, Monet said.

The Somerset facility will include one mammography room and several exam rooms and will be staffed by radiologists, clinical nurse practitioners and mammography technicians.

"Anybody will be able to make an appointment at the center with or without a doctor's referral," Monet said. Walk-ins will be welcome.

Mammograms at the center will cost between $100 and $125. Insurance coverage will depend on each patient's carrier.

Additional examples of enhanced locations include the following:

- Organized walking groups in malls and on community trails
- Community clinics instead of hospitals
- Conveniently located teen clinics that have reading materials and decor to which the market can relate

Find Ways to Be There at the Point of Decision Making

Example: Ecstasy Pill Testing at Nightclubs

DanceSafe is a nonprofit organization promoting health and safety within the rave and nightclub community. They report that they neither condone nor condemn the use of any drug. Rather, they engage in efforts to reduce drug-related harm by providing health and safety information and on-site pill testing to those who use.[6] They currently have chapters in 24 cities throughout the United States and Canada.

Among other programs and services, volunteers in communities with chapters offer *on-site pill testing* to ecstasy users at raves, nightclubs, and other public events where ecstasy is being used socially. Users who are unsure of the authenticity of a pill they possess can bring it to a booth or table where trained harm reduction volunteers will test it for use.

DanceSafe reports on their Web site that volunteers staff booths at raves, nightclubs, and other dance events where they also provide information on drugs, safe sex, and other health and safety issues concerning the dance community (such as driving home safely and protecting one's hearing).[7]

They cite two fundamental operating principles: *harm reduction and popular education.* They believe that "combining these two philosophies enables them to create successful, peer-based educational programs to reduce drug abuse and empower young people to make healthy, informed lifestyle choices."[8]

They elaborate,

> While abstinence is the only way to avoid all the harms associated with drug use, harm reduction programs provide non-abstentionist health and safety information under the recognition that many people are going to choose to experiment with drugs despite all the risks involved. Harm reduction information and services help people use as safely as possible as long as they continue to use.[9]

Other creative solutions to influence "just in time" decision making include the following:

- Placing a glass bowl of fruits and vegetables at eye level in the refrigerator, versus in closed drawers on the bottom shelf

- Providing pet waste bags and receptacles at parks and walking trails

- Offering an opportunity to sign up for organ donation when getting a driver's license

- Including condoms in vending machines located in bar restrooms

- Placing watercoolers in copy rooms at worksites

- Loaning life vests to toddlers at public beaches

- Making free litterbags available at gas pumps

- Positioning natural fertilizers in a prominent display at the end of the aisle

Find Ways to Make Performing the Desired Behavior More Convenient Than the Competing Behavior

Example: Converting an SOV to an HOV

Convenience is the focus of many strategies to influence a single-occupancy vehicle (SOV) to join a car pool or vanpool (the core product and desired behavior). Motorists can then use high-occupancy vehicle (HOV) lanes that can significantly *cut commute time.* Most rideshare programs offer the ability to *register by phone or find a match online.* Businesses often reserve *parking spots close to workplace entrances* for vans and car pools. Some will even remove barriers to carpooling by offering a *free taxi ride* home in the event of an emergency or need to work late.

Results from providing increased convience can pay off as it did in Texas. "HOV lanes in Houston and Dallas have proven to be successful with 72 to 180 percent more people per lane moving on HOV lanes than general-purpose lanes. Also, the average number of people per vehicle has increased by more than 15 percent. Depending on conditions and length of the HOV lanes, travel time reductions have ranged from 5 to 18 minutes."[10]

Local Web sites in many cities around the country provide information on specific HOV locations, hours, and the number of people required in the car in order to use the HOV lane. Many Web sites also offer "instant" matching services to find car pool part-

Figure 11.6.
This Ridematching
Service Is Available
Online

ners or vanpools, taking into consideration work hours, as well as preferences for travel routes and interest in being a driver or passenger. (See Figure 11.6.)

Other examples in which the desired behavior is made more appealing relative to the competition include the following:

- Family friendly lanes in grocery stores where candy, gum, and adult magazines have been removed from the checkout stand

- Smoking locations that have been limited to standing outside buildings or in small smoke-filled rooms at airports

WHAT ARE GUIDELINES FOR MANAGING MORE FORMAL DISTRIBUTION CHANNELS?

In situations in which tangible objects and services are included in a campaign or program, a more formal network of intermediaries may be needed to reach target audiences through the distribution channel.

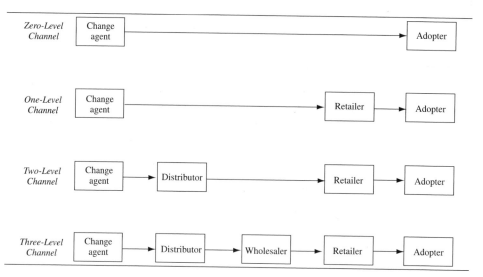

Figure 11.7. Distribution Channels of Various Levels

Kotler and Roberto describe four types of distribution levels to be considered, which are illustrated in Figure 11.7.[11] In a *zero-level channel,* there is direct distribution from the social marketer to the target audience. Tangible objects and services are distributed by mail, over the Internet, door-to-door, or through outlets managed by the social marketing organization (e.g., the health department providing immunizations at community clinics). In a *one-level channel,* there is one distribution intermediary, most commonly a retailer (e.g., grocery stores where health care officials set up tables for flu shots). In a *two-level channel,* the social marketer may need to deal with the local distributor as well as the retailer (e.g., working with distributors of life vests to include safety tips attached to the product). In a *three-level channel,* a national distributor finds local distributors.

Choices regarding distribution channels and levels are made on the basis of variables such as the number of potential target adopters, storage facilities, retail outlet opportunities, and transportation costs, with a focus on choosing the most efficient and cost-effective option for achieving program goals and reaching target audiences.

The process of selecting and managing distribution channels can be guided by several principles offered by Coughlan and Stern:[12]

♦ The purpose of channel marketing is to satisfy end users, which makes it critical that all channel members have their attention on this focus and that channels are selected on the basis of the unique characteristic of each market segment.

♦ Marketing channels "play a role of strategic importance in the overall presence and success a company enjoys in the marketplace."[13] They contribute to the product's positioning and the organization's image, along with the product's features, pricing, and promotional strategies.

◆ Marketing channels are more than just a way to deliver the product to the customer. They can also be an effective means to add value to to the core product. This is evidenced, for example, by the fact that employees are often willing to pay a slightly higher price for the convenience of bottled water at a vending machine at a worksite than they would in a retail location.

◆ Issues currently challenging channel managers include increasingly demanding consumers, management of multiple channels, and the globalization of markets.

CHAPTER SUMMARY

1. *Place* is where and when the target market will perform the desired behavior, acquire any related tangible objects, and receive any associated services.

2. Our objective as we develop the place strategy is to make it as convenient and pleasant as possible for our target audience.

3. Access strategies available for consideration are similar to those used by commercial sector marketers, including physical locations, hours, mobile units, ambiance, wait time, parking, and retail displays.

4. Cost-efficient means should be explored to make locations closer and more appealng, extend hours, be there at the point of decision making, and make performing the desired behavior more convenient than the competing behavior.

5. In situations where tangible objects and services are included, a more formal network of intermediaries may be needed to reach target audiences. Choices will focus on the most efficient and cost-effective options.

KEY TERMS AND CONCEPTS

Distribution channel
Access strategies
Be there at the point of decision making, "just in time"

One-level channel
Two-level channel
Three-level channel
Zero-level channel

ISSUES FOR DISCUSSION

1. What place strategies could be considered to influence each of the following desired behaviors:

   a. Using sunscreen
   b. Breastfeeding for at least 6 months
   c. Calling for help in cases of domestic violence
   d. Measuring pesticides properly
   e. Disposing of cigarettes properly
   f. Donating blood
   g. Volunteering to be a mentor

2. As a social marketer, how would you defend the ecstasy pill testing at nightclubs to an audience concerned that this will increase drug use? Or could you?

3. Assume that you work as a marketing manager for a community health clinic and have been asked to comment on the idea of a special mall facility for mammograms. What questions would you have for the managers of the mall program in Michigan that was described in this chapter?

RESEARCH HIGHLIGHT: OBSERVATION RESEARCH FOR NEEDLE EXCHANGE PROGRAMS

This research highlight demonstrates the remarkable insight that can be gained when researchers observe the distribution channel "in action," highlighting the powerful influence of access, as well as channel intermediaries on target adoption.

From *The Tipping Point*[14]

Malcolm Gladwell

In Baltimore, as in many communities with a lot of drug addicts, the city sends out a van stocked with thousands of clean syringes to certain street corners in its inner-city neighborhoods at certain times in the week. The idea is that for every dirty, used needle that addicts hand over, they can get a free clean needle in return. In principle, needle exchange sounds like a good way to fight AIDS, since the reuse of old HIV-infected needles is responsible for so much of the virus's spread. But, at least on first examination, it seems to have some obvious limitations. Addicts, for one, aren't the most organized and reliable of people. So what guarantee is there that they are going to be able to regularly meet up with the needle van? Second, most heroin addicts go through about one needle a day, shooting up at least five or six times—if not more—until the tip of the syringe becomes so blunt that it is useless. That's a lot of needles. How can a van, coming by once a week, serve the needs of addicts who are shooting up around the clock? What if the van comes by on Tuesday, and by Saturday night an addict has run out?

To analyze how well the needle program was working, researchers at Johns Hopkins University began, in the mid-1990s, to ride along with the vans in order to talk to the people handing in needles. What they found surprised them. They had assumed that addicts brought in their own dirty needles for exchange, that IV drug users got new needles the way that you or I buy milk; going to the store when it is open and picking up enough for the week. But what they found was that a handful of addicts were coming by each week with knapsacks bulging with 300 or 400 dirty needles at a time, which is obviously far more than they were using themselves. These men were then going back to the street and selling the clean needles for one dollar each. The van, in other words, was a kind of syringe wholesaler. The real retailers were these handfuls of men—these *super-exchangers*—who were prowling around the streets and shooting galleries, picking up dirty needles, and then making a modest living on the clean needles they received in exchange. At first, some of the program's coordinators had second thoughts. Did they really want taxpayer-funded needles financing the habits of addicts? But then they realized that they had stumbled inadvertently into a solution to the limitations of needle exchange programs. "It's a much, much better system," says Tom Valente, who teaches in the Johns Hopkins School of Public Health. "A lot of people shoot on Friday and Saturday night, and they don't necessarily think in a rational way that they need to have clean tools before they go out. The needle exchange program isn't going to be available at that time—and certainly not in the shooting galleries. But these (super-exchangers) can be there at times when people are doing drugs and when they need clean syringes. They provide twenty-four seven service, and it doesn't cost us anything."

One of the researchers who rode with the needle vans was an epidemiologist by the name of Tom Junge. He would flag down the super-exchangers and interview them. His conclusion is that they represent a very distinct and special group. "They are all very well connected people," Junge says. "They know Baltimore inside and out. They know where to go to get any kind of drug and any kind of needle. They have street savvy. I would say that they are unusually socially connected. They have a lot of contacts. . . . I

would have to say the underlying motive is financial or economic. But there is definitely an interest in helping people out."

Does this sound familiar? The super-exchangers are the Connectors of Baltimore's drug world. What people at Johns Hopkins would like to do is use the super-exchangers to start a counter-drug epidemic. What if they took those same savvy, socially connected, altruistic people and gave them condoms to hand out, or educated them in the kinds of health information that drug addicts desperately need to know? Those super-exchangers sound as though they have the skills to bridge the chasm between the medical community and the majority of drug users, who are hopelessly isolated from the information and institutions that could save their lives. They sound as if they have the ability to translate the language and ideas of health promotion into a form that other addicts could understand.

Notes

1. Kotler, P., & Armstrong, G. (2001). *Principles of Marketing* (p. 432). Upper Saddle River, NJ: Prentice Hall.
2. Information from *SmileMobile* brochure, an effort of the Washington State Dental Service (WDS), the Washington State Dental Association (WSDA), and the Washington Dental Service Foundation (WDSF).
3. Pasadena Humane Society. From "Choosing A Dog" section of Web site. Statistic cited in summary of "The Adoption Option: Choosing and Raising the Right Shelter Dog for You," by Eliza Rubenstein and Shari Kalina. Retrieved 10/01/01 from: http://www.phsspca.org/store/choosingadog.htm
4. Sacramento Society's Prevention of Cruelty to Animals (SSPCA). Retrieved Fall 2001 from their "Pets on the Net" Web site at http://www.sspca.org/adopt.html
5. Bott, J. (2001). "Karmanos Site to Offer Mammograms at Mall." *Detroit Free Press*, April 28, 1999. Retrieved from www.freep.com/news/health/qkamra28.htm
6. DanceSafe. (2001). Retrieved 5/15/01 from http://www.dancesafe.org
7. Ibid.
8. Ibid.
9. Ibid.
10. Texas Transportation Institute. (2001, May 15). Retrieved 5/15/2001 from: http://tti.tamu.edu/product/ror/hov.stm
11. Kotler, P., & Roberto, E. L. (1989). *Social Marketing: Strategies for Changing Public Behavior* (p. 162). New York: Free Press.

12. Coughlan, A. T., & Stern, L. W. (2001). "Marketing Channel Design and Management." In *Kellogg on Marketing* (Chap. 11, pp. 247-267). New York: John Wiley & Sons, Inc.

13. Ibid., p. 250.

14. From *The Tipping Point: How Little Things Can Make a Big Difference* (pp. 203-206), Copyright by Malcolm Gladwell. By permission of Little, Brown and Company, Inc.

KEY CHAPTER QUESTIONS

1. What is the role of promotion, and what are two major components?

2. What are major elements of a creative brief, and how is it used to develop message strategy?

3. What options are considered when developing message executions?

4. In addition to the creative brief, what other principles and theories can guide the process of creating messages?

5. What are important considerations when planning and conducting pretests?

CHAPTER 12
Promotion:
Creating Messages

People don't buy products. They buy expectations of benefits.

—Roman & Maas[1]

MARKETING HIGHLIGHT: SEXUAL ASSAULT PREVENTION

This case highlights the process one campaign used to develop key messages for a campaign to prevent sexual assault among teens, as well as key strategies to implement and evaluate campaign elements.

Youth Sexual Assault Prevention Campaign

Katharine Fitzgerald
Senior Vice President
DeLaunay/Phillips Communications, Inc.

Background

Washington State's Office of Crime Victims Advocacy (OCVA), the Department of Health (DOH), and members of the statewide Sexual Assault Prevention Advisory Committee worked with DeLaunay/Phillips Communications, Inc., to design and implement a statewide youth-oriented sexual assault prevention media campaign.

Target Audience

The state chose teens 14 to 17 years old as the primary target audience for the campaign. Preteens and older youth (18–22) were seen as important secondary audiences, and parents and teachers, as important influencers.

Formative Research for Message Development and Ad Pretesting

Ten focus groups were conducted with teens in urban and rural areas around the state to provide input for developing key messages and to determine whether any existing campaigns from other states would work well in Washington. Findings regarding awareness and attitudes regarding sexual assault, teens' recommendations on key messages, and pretesting of other state campaigns follow:

Awareness and Attitudes Regarding Sexual Assault

▶ Most teens knew what behaviors constituted sexual assault and freely listed them: rape, forced/unwanted touching, verbal harassment, and "flashing."

▶ Many knew that teen girls aged 14 to 18 were the number one target of rape; a few thought that younger girls were the more common victims, elaborating that this is what they hear about most.

▶ Most were surprised that the major offenders were teen boys aged 14 to 18, thinking it would be older boys with more power and influence. A common belief was that girls in the target market range tended to date older guys.

▶ Although most were aware of acquaintance or date rape, the vast majority were very surprised that the incidence (close to 80% of teen sexual assaults) is so high.

▶ Although the majority of girls and boys believed (theoretically) that victims are never at fault, there was confusion and some discomfort about where the girl's responsibility begins and ends.

▶ One of the bigger surprises for the youth was that verbal pressure was the most common "weapon" involved in rape among teens.

Ideas on Key Messages

▶ Most youth were "sure" that there needed to be separate messages for teen boys and for teen girls.

▶ For boys, they suggested that the emphasis should be on the fact that if you force a girl to have sex when she doesn't want to, it's rape, and that there are serious consequences.

▶ For girls, they felt that messages should educate about the circumstances and high incidence of date rape, the power of verbal pressure, and most important, the need to be more assertive.

Reaction to Other State Campaigns

The Wisconsin campaign was a "big hit":

▶ The boys' radio spot and slogan were "right on" for most of the youth. They found it entertaining and they liked the fact that it stressed (all) the serious consequences of rape. They felt it related well to youth, using their language ("you're screwed") and music.

▶ The girls' radio spot had several good messages, including the slogan "No is never wrong. It's your right."

▶ The Mylar posters developed by Wisconsin were also a "hit." Teens liked the idea of using a reflective surface to easily convey the message that *anyone* could be a victim or perpetrator of date rape. And, they pointed out that all teens like to look at themselves in the mirror at any opportunity!

Campaign Strategies

Based on the focus group input, the Wisconsin materials were then refined and revised for use in Washington State. The campaign included two separate messages, one aimed at boys with the tag line: "If you force her to have sex, you're screwed." A second message aimed at teen girls says, "No is never wrong, it's your right."

Two sixty-second radio spots featuring real teens were produced and began airing in September 1998. The radio spots ran on top teen-oriented stations statewide through June 2001. Mylar posters were produced and distributed statewide to schools, community centers, malls, clubs, health clinics, and Community Sexual Assault Prevention Programs (CSAPs). Radio spots and posters were also translated and produced in Spanish.

The radio spots and Mylar posters and flyers also accomplished another campaign objective—to get teens talking about sexual assault and prevention tips among their peer groups. The graphic nature of the radio spots helped teens engage in a conversation about the topic of sexual assault and sexual harassment.

Radio Advertising Strategy and Tactics

Efforts focused on leveraging the combination of paid advertising and nonpaid bonus exposure to reach the target market (teens aged 14-17) and maximize the state's investment.

Station selection for radio spots was based on their ability to reach teens (i.e., their listener demographics matched our target audience, and their willingness to provide no-charge or matching bonus spots.)

The radio buy was negotiated by a professional media-buying service, with the goal that stations provide at least one nonpaid or bonus radio spot for every spot purchased, providing the ability to extend the length of time the radio spots aired and increase reach and frequency for the campaign.

Results

Over the course of the campaign (3.5 years), we estimate the radio spots reached approximately 60% of the target audience (youth aged 14-17) an average of 11 times. We achieved a two-for-one return on investment overall, meaning that for every dollar spent on paid radio, we generated another $2 in nonpaid and bonus spots for the campaign.

Posters & Flyers

There were a couple of challenges with the posters and flyers. The first was distribution. We enlisted the help of the Office of the Superintendent of Public Schools (OSPI) to direct mail two posters to every high school in the state, encouraging the principal or administrator to post these samples and order more posters. The cover memo told school administrators that despite the language used in the posters, the state was supporting the campaign. This gave individual schools "cover" if they encountered any resistance to putting up the posters.

The second challenge was keeping the posters up. Many students liked the message and the reflective surface of the poster so well that they took the posters home! This led to the campaign developing a 9"-by-12" version of the poster, with prevention tips on the back, for distribution to individual students and teens.

Ongoing distribution of the posters and flyers was handled by individual CSAPs and coordinated by the Washington Coalition of Sexual Assault Programs (WCSAP) office.

Results

Overall, 20,000 posters and 35,000 flyers were distributed to the target audience through local sexual assault prevention agencies, community partners, radio stations, and schools.

Earned News Media

An aggressive news media relations component complemented the paid media buy. The media effort was aimed at an adult audience, as well as teens. The main objective was to reinforce the sexual assault prevention messages among adults and to highlight that the state was taking on this issue in a novel way.

The following items assisted in implementation of the media strategy to publicize the statewide media campaign:

▶ *Launch Events:* To generate media interest and coverage of the state's youth sexual assault prevention campaign, press conferences were held in three Washington cities on the same day. Spokespersons from OCVA, local agencies, and teens were on hand to talk with media about the campaign.

▶ *Launch News Release:* A news release about the youth-oriented campaign was distributed via Business Wire statewide on September 8. For media who could not attend briefings, the release gave them the information they needed to write or broadcast a story about the Sexual Assault Prevention campaign.

▶ *Sexual Assault Awareness Week:* In April 1999 and again in April 2000, the campaign worked to generate media interest and coverage during National Sexual Assault Prevention Week. Coverage focused on the pilot projects and local activities planned for Washington State.

▶ *Teen Section Editors:* Tailored releases and story ideas were pitched to teen section editors statewide. This results in sexual assault prevention stories in several teen columns and sections in newspapers around the state.

▶ *High School News Bureau:* A high school bureau was developed so that teens could write about the issue of sexual assault in their high school newspapers. Overall, more than 100 high schools in Washington State participated in the news bureau.

Results

Between the campaign launch on September 8, 1998, through June 30, 2001, more than 150 news stories were generated about the statewide Youth Sexual Assault Prevention Campaign.

Pre- and Post-Awareness and Attitude Survey Results

Highlights of a comparison of baseline and 2-year follow-up data at four survey sites include the following:

▶ There was evidence across survey sites of a significant increase in perception of the serious consequences of sexual assault.

▶ Of the 846 students surveyed in 2000, 56.2% reported they had seen media campaign posters in their schools or communities, and 60.1% indicated they had heard media campaign radio spots.

▶ The majority (82.1%) of the students who had seen the media campaign posters were able to identify the girls' key message of the posters. Of those who had heard the media campaign radio spots, 77.2% were able to identify the girls' key message in the radio spots. A smaller proportion of the sample were able to identify the boys' key message

(44.5% for the posters and 56.5% for the radio spots). (See Figures 12.1 and 12.2.)

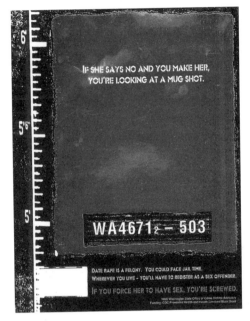

Figure 12.1. Reflective Poster for Teen Boys

Figure 12.2. Reflective Poster for Teen Girls

CHAPTER OVERVIEW

Now that our *product* is developed, *prices* are established, and distribution channels are in *place*, we are ready to create *promotions*, persuasive communications designed and delivered to highlight the following:

- ◆ Product benefits, features, and associated tangible objects and services
- ◆ Pricing strategies, including an emphasis on value relative to the competition, as well as any incentives, recognition, and rewards
- ◆ Place components that offer convenience of access

The communicator's job is to ensure that the target audience knows about the offer, believes they will experience the stated benefits, and are inspired to act. This is perhaps the marketing mix tool that we rely on most to move target adopters to the next stage of behavior change.

Developing a communication strategy consists of two major elements: *creating messages* and *selecting media*. Messages are further defined as both *what* we are trying to communicate (message strategy) and *how* we will communicate (execution strategy).[2] Media decisions include selection of *where* communications will be delivered, *when,* and by *whom.*

This chapter presents strategies for creating messages, and Chapter 13 discusses the process of selecting media channels.

MESSAGE STRATEGY:
WHAT DO WE WANT TO SAY?

Siegel and Doner describe creating messages as "a complex art. The final message a target audience member receives is a combination of the communication strategy, how the message is executed in the materials, and how it is processed by the sender."[3] Reeves recommends, "Think of an ad not as what you put into it, but as what the consumer takes out of it."[4]

One of the most effective ways to establish clear message objectives and select effective execution and media strategies is to develop a document that will provide direction for message design and media selection. A useful tool is a creative brief, typically one to two pages in length.[5] It helps ensure that communications will be *meaningful* (pointing out benefits that make the product desirable), *believable* (the product will deliver on the promised benefits), and *distinctive* (how it is a better choice than competing behaviors).[6] It will ensure that all team members working on the campaign are in agreement with communication objectives and strategies prior to more costly development and production of communication materials. Typical elements of a creative brief are illustrated in the following section:

Key Message:

This is a brief statement that summarizes the bottom-line message. This is not the actual slogan, tagline, or headline.

Target Audience:

This section presents a brief description of the target audience in terms of key variables determined in Step 2. Most commonly, it will include a demographic and geographic profile of the target audience. It will also, we hope, summarize the audience's current knowledge, beliefs, and behaviors relative to the desired behavior, as well as to competing ones. Ideally, it describes the target's current stage of change.

Communication Objectives:

This section specifies what we want our target audience to *know* (think), *believe* (feel), and/or *do,* based on exposure to the communications. This can be taken directly from decisions made in Step 3. (Individual campaigns may or may not have all three types of objectives.)

What we want them to know (think):
These are brief statements of facts and information the audience may need in order to be motivated to act.

What we want them to believe (feel):
This is something we know they need to believe or feel (or not) in order to act.

What we want them to do:
This describes the *specific actions* we want the audience to take as a result of exposure to campaign communications. This may or may not differ from the key message above. For example, a key message to "Get help if you are suicidal" may have a specific desired action such as "Call this 24-hour help line." A "Wear a seat belt" key message would be the same as what we want them "to do."

Benefits to Promise:

Key benefits the audience hopes they will receive from adopting the behavior were identified as the *core product* when developing the product platform in Step 5. The primary benefit may be expressed in terms of a cost that the audience can avoid by adopting the desired behavior (e.g., stiff penalties for drinking and driving).

Support for Promise:

This section refers to a brief list of additional benefits and highlights from product, price, and place strategies established earlier in Step 5. The ones to be highlighted are those that would most help convince the target audience that they can perform the desired behavior, the benefits are likely, and that they exceed perceived costs.

Openings:

This section will be helpful to selecting and planning media channels. Siegel and Doner describe openings as "the times, places, and situations when the audience will be most attentive to, and able to act on, the message."[7] Input for this section will come from profiles and audience behaviors explored in Step 3 and Step 4. Additional input may come from secondary and expert resources on the target market's lifestyle and media habits.

Position:

The product positioning established earlier in Step 5 (Product) is summarized here, describing the desired way that we want our target audience to think of and feel about performing the desired behavior relative to the competition. This provides guidance to those selecting images and graphics and developing script and copy points.

A sample of a typical creative brief is featured in Table 12.1.

MESSAGE EXECUTION STRATEGY: HOW DO WE WANT TO SAY IT?

Now that we know what we want to say and why, our attention is turned to how we will say it. Our goal is to develop communications that will capture the attention of our target audience and persuade them to adopt the desired behavior. Our task is to consider and choose from a variety of potential communication *elements, styles, tones, words,* and *formats*.[8]

Kotler and Andreasen suggest different ways to generate potential messages.[9] Target markets can be interviewed, and ideas can be generated from their com-

---

TABLE 12.1 Creative Brief for a Youth Tobacco Prevention Campaign

Key Message:

Don't start to smoke or chew tobacco.

Target Audience:

Middle school and high school youth who don't currently smoke or chew tobacco, although they may have experimented with it in the past. They are vulnerable, however, to using tobacco because they have family members and friends who smoke or chew. They know many of the facts about the consequences of using tobacco. They've been exposed to them in health classes and may even have experienced the reality with family members who have smoking-related illnesses or who have died from smoking. The problem is, they don't believe it will happen to them. They don't really believe they will get addicted. There are many peer pressures to fit in by smoking. They also have heard that smoking is a great stress relief and is appealing to pass the time. Some think kids who smoke look older and cool.

Communication Objectives:

To Know: Addiction is real and probable.

To Believe: Smoking-related illnesses are shocking, "gross," and painful.
            If you die from tobacco someday, your family will hurt too.

To Do: Refuse to try cigarettes or chew.

Benefits to Promise:

You will have a longer, healthier, and happier life, free of tobacco addiction.

Supports to Promise:

- Real stories from real people who started smoking at a young age
- Stories of personal loss about having a family member die or about living with or dying from a smoking-related illness
- Graphic visuals depicting real, shocking, and "gross" consequences to the body
- Real facts from the American Cancer Society and Surgeon General

Openings:

- Listening to the radio
- Watching television
- Surfing the Internet
- Talking with friends

Positioning:

People who smoke are risking their health and hurting their future families and friends. It's not worth it.

---

ments. A second approach might use creative brainstorming sessions, a common practice in advertising and marketing communication firms. A third method uses "formal deductive frameworks to tease out possible advertising messages."[10] Discussions and examples for two such frameworks follow.

Rational, Emotional, Moral, and Nonverbal Elements

This first framework identifies four elements that can be considered for an execution strategy: (1) rational, (2) emotional, (3) moral, and (4) nonverbal.[11]

1. *Rational elements* focus on delivering straightforward information and facts. An example would be a litter campaign that has messages on roadway signs and litterbags that inform motorists about laws and fines for littering.

   Decisions may need to be made as to whether to use *one-sided or two-sided messages.* "One-sided messages usually present a major benefit, but do not directly address any major drawbacks. Two-sided messages address both drawbacks and benefits."[12] For example, an immunization campaign that is one-sided would emphasize the disease prevention benefits of immunizing on time. A two-sided message strategy would also mention any potential side effects from specific immunizations. Kotler and Roberto noted that each type of message is appropriate for different audiences: "Studies have identified that one-sided messages appear to work best with people who are already favorably predisposed to an idea or practice and who have a low level of education but that two-sided messages work best when people are not predisposed to the product and have a higher level of education."[13]

2. *Emotional elements* are designed to elicit some negative feeling (e.g., fear, guilt, or shame) or positive emotion (e.g., humor, love, pride, or joy) that will motivate the desired behavior. A litter prevention campaign for Texas, for example, uses the slogan "Don't Mess With Texas." For many, it engenders emotions of pride as well as humor.

   Kotler and Roberto discuss research that has shown that "negative messages work better when a social product presents a real solution to a problem, while positive messages are appropriate to social products that offer a means of satisfying a personal goal or objective."[14] They emphasize, however, that each situation will be unique and that it will be important to determine whether a particular segment is more responsive to appeals to fear or to positive messages.

   They further advise that *humorous* messages (a) are more effective when they represent a unique approach for the social issue, (b) become "stale" if repeated too frequently, and (c) are not as appropriate for complex messages.[15] They suggest that *fear-based* messages (a) work best when accompanied by solutions that can be easily implemented, (b) are most persuasive to those who have been previously unconcerned about a particular problem, and (c) may be more effective when directed toward someone who is close to a potential target adopter rather than to the actual target adopter and when a credible source is used for endorsement.[16]

3. *Moral elements* are "directed to the audience's sense of what is right and proper."[17] This "Keep America Beautiful" litterbag appears to be designed to appeal to patriotic citizens. (See Figure 12.3.)

4. *Nonverbal elements* rely on visual cues, graphic images, and symbols and on the body language of actors and models, including vocal expressions, facial expressions, body movement, eye contact, spatial distance, and physical appearance.[18]

Figure 12.3. Featuring a Moral Element

Figure 12.4. Featuring a Nonverbal Element

Even though many campaigns include several of these elements, most executions choose one as the dominant approach. For example, the Ad Council's famous anti-litter campaign featuring an image of a Native American with a tear in his eye is widely remembered by many to this day. It includes elements that are rational (don't litter), emotional (disappointment), and moralistic (responsibility). But the nonverbal element (the tear) is recalled most often, even decades later. (See Figure 12.4.)

Types of Execution Styles

This second framework presents nine different execution styles.[19] Examples using the Youth Tobacco Prevention Creative Brief (see Table 12.1) illustrate how a variety of executional styles can be used to deliver on the same message strategy.

♦ *Slice of life (shows "typical" people in a normal setting):* A young boy and his teen brother are sitting in their bedroom talking about how much they miss their dad, who died from smoking, and how sad their mom seems.

♦ *Lifestyle (highlights how the product fits with a particular lifestyle):* Teens are shown on snowboards and then on skateboards and then smoking. The ad discusses the impact of smoking on athletic ability, showing footage of clogged arteries.

♦ *Fantasy (creates a fantasy around the product or its use):* A group of teen girls are shown applying makeup to cover up a "zit." A girl's face catches on fire and the announcer talks about how no other product on the market kills one out of three users. (This is the actual story line of one of the "Truth" campaign ads.)

Figure 12.5. A Counter-Advertising Campaign Using a Familiar Character

♦ *Mood or image (builds a mood or strong image):* A woman is shown smoking out of a hole in her neck and talks about how she started smoking at the age of 10 but thought she'd be able to quit.

♦ *Musical (uses songs or musical performances to deliver messages):* A rap song highlights the types of poisons found in cigarettes.

♦ *Personality symbol (creates or uses a well-known character):* Joe Camel is featured as "Joe Chemo" in a graphic ad in Figure 12.5.

♦ *Technical expertise (uses experts in the company or industry):* A television spot features a physician showing two lungs, one of a non-smoker and one of a smoker, side by side.

♦ *Scientific evidence (presenting statistics and evidence):* Statistics are featured in television and magazine ads showing the number of teens who start smoking each day, how many of them will get addicted, and how many of them will die early of a smoking-related disease.

♦ *Testimonial or endorsement (featuring a highly believable character who has experience with the product):* A young girl talks about how much she will miss her mom, who is dying from emphysema and can only breathe using an oxygen mask.

Figure 12.6a. Approach A

Additional important decisions regarding execution include those related to *tone* (e.g., whether to be serious or lighthearted or straightforward), choice of *words* (e.g., program names, slogans, tag lines, copy and scripts), and *format* (e.g., use of illustrations, layout, graphics, and color). Once again, decisions should be based on appropriateness and appeal to the target audience—always relative to the intended communications.[20]

Figure 12.6 presents different approaches in *tone* for a variety of public behaviors. An issue for discussion at the completion of this chapter is to describe the tone of each of these approaches.

Figure 12.6b. Approach B

Figure 12.6.c
Approach C

Figure 12.7. One Approach for Slogan and Copy

In Figure 12.7, a poster for an abstinence program demonstrates one approach to slogans and copy. Other slogans and tag lines demonstrating the power of simple, clear words include those that have been used for promoting water and electricity conservation: "Clean plates after eight," "Take one minute off your shower," "Turn off your computer monitor at night," and "Flush toilets one less time each day."

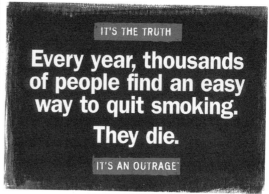

Figure 12.8a. A Strong Copy-Oriented Format

Figure 12.8b. A Strong Photography-Oriented Format

Format decisions for print communications include choosing headlines, copy, illustrations, images, layout, font style, and color; for radio, scripts, sound effects, and voices; and for television, settings, props, scripts, and talent. The two print ads in Figure 12.8 illustrate different format choices for the same issue, tobacco prevention.

TABLE 12.2 Stages of Change and Message Development

Stage of Change	Recommended Types of Messages
Precontemplation	• Enhance knowledge of and expectations about the consequences—good or bad—of the risk behavior. • Personalize the risk. • Emphasize the benefits of the new behavior and encourage a reevaluation of the costs and benefits (or outcome expectancies) that includes the new benefits.
Contemplation	• Encourage gaining experience with the new behavior (e.g., through trying the new behavior or trying to refrain from the risk behavior). • Continue promoting new expectations of positive consequences and reinforce existing positive expectations. • Consider disputing commonly believed but untrue negative consequences and suggesting ways to minimize bona fide negative consequences, though it is typically easier to promote advantages than to challenge perceived disadvantages. • Enhance self-efficacy by identifying how to effectively overcome barriers to change.
Preparation	• Encourage people to restructure their environments—and instruct them on how to do so—so that important cues for practicing the new behavior are obvious and supported socially. • Encourage people to identify and plan solutions to relevant obstacles they are most likely to face. • Help people maintain their motivation by encouraging them to set a long-term goal and instructing them on appropriate ways to set short-term goals to keep them progressing to the long-term goal. • Increase self-efficacy to cope with specific situations and other obstacles that people are likely to encounter in their change efforts. • Model social reinforcement of appropriate behaviors.
Action	• Encourage refining skills, especially those that will help avoid relapse and that allow productive coping with setbacks to prevent full relapse. • Bolster self-efficacy for dealing with new obstacles and setbacks in the behavior change process. • Encourage people to feel good about themselves when they make progress, especially in the face of temptation. • Make explicit or reiterate the long-term benefits of the behavior change.

SOURCE: Reprinted by permission from Siegel and Doner, *Marketing Public Health: Strategies to Promote Social Change*, pp. 314-315. © 1998 by Aspen Publishers, Inc.

PRINCIPLES AND THEORIES FOR DECISION MAKING: DESIGNING MESSAGES AND CHOOSING AN EXECUTIONAL STRATEGY

Designing messages and choosing an executional strategy can be guided by several theories and principles developed by experts in behavior change and communication theory.

In the first discussion, we return to the stages of change model. Siegel and Doner summarize Maibach and Cotton's "Moving People to Behavior Change," highlighting recommended message strategies to help target audiences move to the next stage. (See Table 12.2.)[21]

TABLE 12.3 Effective Communications (Partial List From McKenzie-Mohr and Smith)

✓ Make sure your message is vivid, personal, and concrete. (See Example A, Figure 12.9.)

✓ Have your message delivered by an individual or organization who is credible with the audience you are trying to reach. (See Example B, Figure 12.9.)

✓ Frame your message to indicate what the individual is losing by not acting, rather than what he/she is saving by acting (See Example C, Figure 12.9.)

✓ If you use a threatening message, make sure that you couple it with specific suggestions regarding what actions an individual can take. (See Example D, Figure 12.9.)

✓ Make your communication, especially instructions for a desired behavior, clear and specific. (See Example E, Figure 12.9.)

✓ Make it easy for people to remember what to do, and how and when to do it. (See Example F, Figure 12.9.)

SOURCE: From *Fostering Sustainable Behavior*, p. 101, by Doug McKenzie-Mohr and William Smith. © 1999. New Society Publishers. Reprinted by permission of the publisher.

McKenzie-Mohr and Smith suggest a checklist for effective communications.[22] A partial list is included in Table 12.3 with examples from a variety of social marketing campaigns in Figure 12.9.

Figure 12.9. Illustrating Effective Message Techniques
Example A. A Vivid, Personal, Concrete Example

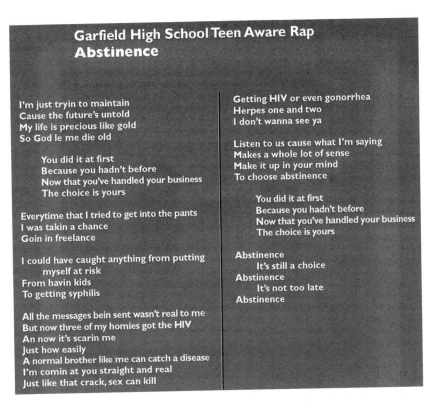

Garfield High School Teen Aware Rap
Abstinence

I'm just tryin to maintain
Cause the future's untold
My life is precious like gold
So God le me die old

> You did it at first
> Because you hadn't before
> Now that you've handled your business
> The choice is yours

Everytime that I tried to get into the pants
I was takin a chance
Goin in freelance

I could have caught anything from putting
    myself at risk
From havin kids
To getting syphilis

All the messages bein sent wasn't real to me
But now three of my homies got the HIV
An now it's scarin me
Just how easily
A normal brother like me can catch a disease
I'm comin at you straight and real
Just like that crack, sex can kill

Getting HIV or even gonorrhea
Herpes one and two
I don't wanna see ya

Listen to us cause what I'm saying
Makes a whole lot of sense
Make it up in your mind
To choose abstinence

> You did it at first
> Because you hadn't before
> Now that you've handled your business
> The choice is yours

Abstinence
    It's still a choice
Abstinence
    It's not too late
Abstinence

Example B. Messages Delivered by Peers

Example C. An Emphasis on Personal Loss

Example D. Fear Followed by Solutions

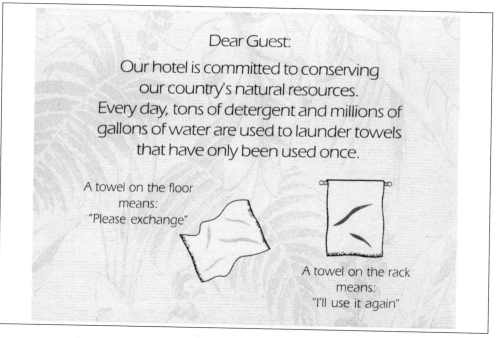

Example E. Visual Graphics Make It Easy to Know What to Do

Duck, Cover, and Hold

DUCK
DUCK or DROP down on the floor

COVER
Take COVER under a sturdy desk, table or other furniture. If that is not possible, seek cover against an interior wall and protect your head and neck with your arms. Avoid danger spots near windows, hanging objects, mirrors or tall furniture.

HOLD
If you take cover under a sturdy piece of furniture, HOLD on to it and be prepared to move with it. Hold the position until the ground stops shaking and it is safe to move.

Example F. A Memorable Instruction

Try for a "Big Idea"

As Kotler and Armstrong describe,

Message strategy statements tend to be plain, straightforward outlines of benefits and positioning points that the advertiser wants to stress. The advertiser must next develop a compelling creative concept—or "big idea"—that will bring the message strategy to life in a distinctive and memorable way.[23]

Examples in the commercial sector to model include the well-known "got milk?" campaign that has been adopted for a variety of celebrities and occasions for product usage. Evian's natural spring water campaign vividly demonstrates the use of a big idea to capture the supreme positioning for "L'original." Each of the ads in Figure 12.10 shows a variation of the same core concept.

Figure 12.10. A Campaign With a Big Idea

TABLE 12.4 Pitfalls to Avoid When Developing Communication Strategies

- Focusing on very small audiences
- Targeting too many or too diverse audiences
- Including multiple actions or framing an issue multiple ways rather than focusing on one
- Focusing on long-term public-health benefits rather than short-term consumer benefits
- Appealing to noncritical values (e.g., good health) rather than core values (freedom, autonomy, control, independence)
- Supporting the message with facts alone when an emotional appeal would be more compelling
- Using mass media to convey complex messages
- Developing strategies for different audiences that conflict or send mixed messages

SOURCE: Reprinted by permission from Siegel and Doner, *Marketing Public Health: Strategies to Promote Social Change*, p. 332. © 1998 by Aspen Publishers, Inc.

Pitfalls to Avoid

Siegel and Doner identified several pitfalls to avoid while developing communication strategies, presented in Table 12.4.

PRETESTING

Appropriate Reasons for Pretesting

The primary purpose for pretesting potential messages and executions is to *assess their ability to deliver on the strategies and objectives developed in the creative brief.* When faced with several potential executions, the process can also help *choose the most effective options* or eliminate the least effective. It provides an opportunity to *refine materials* prior to production and distribution.

In addition, it helps identify any "red flags," something about the potential ad that might interfere with communications or send the wrong message. This often happens when planners and campaign developers are too close to their work or don't have the same profile and characteristics as the target audience. For example, a potential tobacco prevention ad targeting teens with the fact that "all it takes is 100 cigarettes to become addicted" raised a couple of red flags when several youth commented, "Well, then I'll just have 99," and others expressed the idea that 100 cigarettes (to a nonsmoker) "sounds like a lot!"

Potential Pretesting Techniques

Techniques used for pretesting are typically qualitative in nature and most often include *focus groups* or *personal interviews* and *professional review* of materials for technical accuracy and readability (i.e., literacy levels). When a more quantitative, controlled approach is required, methodologies may include *theatre or natural exposure testing* (e.g., ads are embedded between other spots or in the middle of programming) and/or a *larger number of focus groups, intercept interviews,* and *self-administered surveys.* This more extensive testing is often warranted when (a) interested parties are divided on their initial assessments of creative executions, (b) there will be significant economic and political implications to choices, and (c) the campaign needs to have a longer-term shelf life (e.g., years versus months).

Often, these techniques vary according to stages in the pretest process. At early stages, when concepts and draft executions are being tested, qualitative instruments are usually most appropriate. After concepts have been refined, quantitative techniques may be important to help choose from several potential executions.

Typical topics explored with respondents to assess the ability of potential executions to deliver on the creative strategy are listed as follows. Responses will then be compared with intentions developed in the creative brief.

1. What is the main message you get from this ad?
2. What else are they trying to say?
3. What do you think they want you to know?
4. What do you think they want you to believe or think?
5. What action do you think they want you to take?
6. If the respondent doesn't mention desired action, say, "Actually, the main purpose of this ad is to persuade you and people like you to . . ."
7. How likely do you think it is that this ad will influence you to take this action?
8. What about this ad works well for that purpose?
9. What doesn't work well for that purpose?
10. How does the ad make you feel about (doing this behavior)?
11. Where is the best place to reach you with this message/ad? Where would you most likely notice it and pay attention to it? Where are you when you make decisions about (this behavior)?

Words of Caution About Pretesting

The idea of pretesting potential messages, concepts, and executions is often dreaded among creative professionals. Many of their concerns are legitimate, grounded in experiences with respondents who typically don't like advertising, don't really want to adopt the desired behavior we're promoting, want to be art directors, want to meet expectations to be an ad critic, can't imagine what the finished ad will really be like, or seize the opportunity to vent about the campaign's sponsor.

Principles and practices that can help to assuage these concerns and produce more effective results from testing efforts include the following:

1. *Inform respondents up front that this testing has nothing to do with whether they like or dislike the ads.* We are trying to find out whether they think the ad will work relative to stated objectives and why or why not. Respondents should be told (at some point) what the intended purpose of the ads are and then be asked to comment relative to that intention. (One successful technique is to put the objective on a flipchart or whiteboard and continue to refer to the statement throughout discussions.)

2. *Consider testing concept statements* that describe the theme and ad, instead of using storyboards or illustrations, especially when dealing with executions that involve fantasy, humor, or other styles that are difficult to convey with two-dimensional descriptions.

3. *Test conceptual spots in the lineup before finished ads* when evaluating several potential executions at the same time relative to each other.

4. *Ask respondents to write down their comments first before discussing reactions to ads.* They should be instructed that they can ask for points of clarification if needed, but to hold their comments until they have had a chance to capture them in writing.

5. *Thoroughly brief clients and colleagues not familiar with the creative testing process* on the limitations of this type of research and the potential pitfalls. Emphasize the importance of listening for what the ads are communicating and what components work and don't work relative to the intended objectives. Warn them not to be surprised or discouraged if participants don't like an ad and not to celebrate just because they do.

CHAPTER SUMMARY

1. *Promotion* is persuasive communication and is the tool we count on to ensure that the target audience knows about the offer, believes they will experience the stated benefits, and is inspired to act.

2. Promotion has two major components, message and media. Message is *what* will be said, *why* (message strategy), and *how* (message execution). Media is *where* it will be said, *when,* and *by whom.*

3. Message strategy is developed using a *creative brief,* a one- to two-page document describing the key message, target audience, and communication objectives;

benefits to promise; support for promise; and openings to guide media planning and positioning.

4. Message execution will be determined by choices relative to communication elements, style, tone, words, and format.

5. Pretesting messages and potential executions is advised, especially when economic and political implications are significant. Potential pitfalls in testing are real and can be minimized with careful construction of questioning and briefing of respondents, as well as colleagues and clients.

KEY TERMS AND CONCEPTS

Persuasive communication	Nonverbal elements
Message strategy	Execution style
Execution strategy	Tone
Media strategy	Words
Creative brief	Format
Rational elements	Big idea
Emotional elements	Pretest
Moral elements	Red flags

ISSUES FOR DISCUSSION

1. In the opening case on sexual assault prevention, assume that you were asked at the governor's office briefing to change the tag line "If you force her to have sex you're screwed." Concern was expressed that there might be negative public reaction to the strong language. What would you say?

2. Why is it important to determine message strategies before media strategies?

3. In developing a creative brief, what are potential supports to a promise that safe gun storage will keep your family safe and prevent your gun from getting into the wrong hands?

4. Assume that program managers have decided, on the basis of research and advice of experts, to use a fear-based strategy for a youth tobacco prevention campaign. What recommendations would you make to ensure the effectiveness of this strategy?

5. How would you describe the tone of each of the three different approaches to public signage in Figures 12.6a, 12.6b, and 12.6c?

RESEARCH HIGHLIGHT:
TELEPHONE SURVEY FOR PREVENTION OF SUDDEN INFANT DEATH SYNDROME (SIDS)

The following research highlight used telephone surveys to provide feedback and input for a new public awareness campaign.

Benchmark Survey on Awareness, Knowledge and Behaviours Relating to Sudden Infant Death Syndrome (SIDS)

Prepared by Environics Research Group
for Health Canada

In February 1999, Health Canada retained Environics Research Group Limited to conduct survey research among new parents, caregivers, and those expecting to become parents, to examine awareness, knowledge, and behaviours relating to Sudden Infant Death Syndrome (SIDS). This was a benchmark survey to test awareness and knowledge prior to the launch of a new public awareness campaign about SIDS.

Environics conducted a nationwide survey of 600 respondents who were part of the target group (parents of an infant under one year old, those planning to become a parent within the next year and those who work as caregivers of any child under one year old). The sample design involved sampling from the general population across the country among households with women between the ages of 18 and 35 years, as well as sampling from the general population as a whole. Within households, respondents were screened according to the criteria established for the target group. The margin of error for a sample of this size is plus or minus four percentage points, 19 times out of 20.

The survey was conducted by Environics between February 15 and 27, 1999.

The sample was composed of 86 percent women and includes respondents in all regions of the country. . . .

The survey finds that awareness of SIDS is very high among the target group. However, significant proportions of respondents are not knowledgeable about the up-to-date information on the recommended infant sleeping position to reduce the risk of SIDS. The survey also finds that respondents are open to various ways to learn more about SIDS, especially television advertising and brochures.

Here are some highlights of the survey:

- ► SIDS is mentioned, unaided, as the most prevalent cause of infant mortality in this country today.

- ► There is almost unanimous (94%) top-of-mind awareness about SIDS among the target group.

▶ About two-thirds of respondents who are aware of SIDS express some personal concern about their baby dying from SIDS; 34 percent are personally very concerned and 34 percent are somewhat concerned about SIDS.

▶ One-half of respondents (52%) are not aware of any progress that has been made in recent years in understanding and dealing with SIDS.

▶ Almost three-quarters of respondents believe there are ways to reduce the risk of SIDS. However, among these, the largest number (47%) say a side sleeping position reduces risk. Forty-four percent say a back sleeping position reduces risk.

▶ Three-quarters of parents or caregivers say they are taking or have taken action to reduce the risk of SIDS. Again, the largest proportion (45%) of these say their action involves placing the infant on her or his side to sleep; 41 percent say their action involves placing the infant to sleep on her or his back.

▶ Currently, 49 percent of parents or caregivers place infants on their side to sleep; 40 percent place them on their back.

▶ When asked specifically, a majority (57%) are unaware that laying a baby on his or her back to sleep reduces the risk of SIDS; 43 percent are aware.

▶ When asked specifically, large majorities of respondents are aware of the increased risk of SIDS related to secondhand smoke, smoking during pregnancy, and drug and alcohol use during pregnancy.

▶ Seven in ten respondents (71%) say they recall seeing informational material about SIDS. Most of these recall seeing a brochure or pamphlet.

▶ Among respondents who recall seeing brochures, pamphlets [or] posters about SIDS, the largest number have seen them in a clinic or hospital or a doctor's office. Most respondents (64%) who recall seeing any information about SIDS are unable to recall the sponsor. Five percent say this information was sponsored by Health Canada.

▶ Almost nine in ten respondents (88%) who recall seeing information about SIDS say this information was useful or helpful to them.

▶ Television advertising and brochures describing ways to reduce the risk of SIDS are seen as the most useful ways to learn more about SIDS; posters and radio advertising are seen as less useful ways to convey this information.

▶ Almost six in ten respondents (57%) report being given advice from a health professional about the sleeping position for an infant. Of these, a majority (61%) have been advised to place their infant on his or her side to sleep; only 21 percent of this group report being advised to place their infant on his or her back.

From previous research, we know that new and expectant parents are motivated to take positive action relating to their infants' or children's health, when they have the correct information. The survey indicates strong top-of-mind awareness of SIDS among the target group, and now the challenge for Health Canada and its partners is to disseminate the new information about SIDS effectively, especially with regard to infants' sleeping position. Although there is certainly some level of knowledge of the importance of a back sleeping position, there remains a stronger belief and practice emphasizing a side position.

This research also suggests that health professionals should be a target of an informational campaign, given their key role in providing health information to new parents and given the survey findings that only a minority of respondents report receiving the most accurate advice (baby on back, not side) from their doctor or nurse.

SOURCE: *Benchmark Survey on Awareness, Knowledge and Behaviours Relating to Sudden Infant Death Syndrome (SIDS)*. (March, 1999). Final Report. Prepared for Health Canada by Environics Research Group. Reprinted with permission. Retrieved 4/30/01 from Case Studies on the Social Maraketing Web site at: www.hc-sc.gc.ca/hppb// socialmarketing

Notes

1. Roman, K., & Maas, J. M. (1992). *How to Advertise* (2nd ed.). New York: St Martin's.
2. Kotler, P., & Armstrong, G. (2001). *Principles of Marketing* (p. 543). Upper Saddle River, NJ: Prentice Hall.
3. Siegel, M., & Doner, L. (1998). *Marketing Public Health: Strategies to Promote Social Change* (pp. 332-333). Gaithersburg, MD: Aspen.
4. Reeves, R. (1961). *Reality in Advertising*. New York: Knopf.
5. Siegel & Doner, *Marketing Public Health*, p. 506.
6. Kotler & Armstrong, *Principles of Marketing*, p. 548.
7. Siegel & Doner, *Marketing Public Health*, p. 321.
8. Kotler & Armstrong, *Principles of Marketing*, p. 549.
9. Kotler, P., & Andreasen, A. (1991). *Strategic Marketing for Nonprofit Organizations* (p. 512). Englewood Cliffs, NJ: Prentice Hall.
10. Ibid.
11. Kotler, P., & Roberto, E. L. (1989). *Social Marketing: Strategies for Changing Public Behavior* (pp. 196-202). New York: Free Press; and Kotler & Andreasen, *Strategic Marketing for Nonprofit Organizations*, p. 512.
12. Siegel & Doner, *Marketing Public Health*, p. 334.
13. Kotler & Roberto, *Social Marketing*, p. 196.
14. Ibid., p. 197.
15. Ibid., pp. 198-199.
16. Ibid., p. 198.
17. Kotler & Andreasen, *Strategic Marketing for Nonprofit Organizations*, p. 512.
18. Kotler & Roberto, *Social Marketing*, pp. 200-201.
19. Kotler & Armstrong, *Principles of Marketing*, pp. 549-552.
20. Kotler & Andreasen, *Strategic Marketing for Nonprofit Organizations*, pp. 522-527.
21. Maibach, E. W., & Cotton, D. (1995). "Moving people to behavior change: A staged social cognitive approach to message design." In E. Maibach & R. L. Parrott (Eds.), *Designing Health Messages* (pp. 41-64). Thousand Oaks, CA: Sage.
22. McKenzie-Mohr, D., & Smith, W. (1999). *Fostering Sustainable Behavior* (p. 101). Gabriola Island, British Columbia, Canada: New Society.
23. Kotler & Armstrong, *Principles of Marketing*, p. 548.

KEY CHAPTER QUESTIONS

1. What decisions are needed to complete the promotional plan?

2. What are the major types of media channels?

3. What specific media vehicles can be considered?

4. What timing decisions need to be made?

5. What factors influence media strategies?

6. What principles can guide media decision making?

CHAPTER 13

Promotion: Selecting Media Channels

I know that half the money I spend on advertising is wasted; but I can never find out which half.

—John Wanamaker[1]

MARKETING HIGHLIGHT: AIDS PREVENTION

The following case highlights examples of three major forms of communication discussed in this chapter: mass, selective, and personal.

AIDS Communications Around the World

Daniel Garzia
Student, Seattle University

AIDS affects all of us: our friends, our families, and our communities. As many as 36 million people are living with AIDS and HIV, and more than 20 million have died from the virus.[2] The Sub-Saharan region of Africa contains the majority (more than 25 million) of the reported HIV/AIDS cases. The overwhelming growth of this internationally sexually transmitted virus has prompted many organizations to implement social marketing campaigns to educate people on safe sex and the AIDS epidemic. Here, we describe the national campaigns launched by Switzerland, the United States, and South Africa as examples of the use of mass, selective, and personal channels of communication.

Switzerland: Use of Mass Media

Background

The Swiss AIDS Foundation, in cooperation with the Swiss government, introduced the first-ever Swiss AIDS campaign. The campaign was titled "STOP AIDS," with the "O" of the word "STOP" in the form of a pink, rolled-up condom. (See Figure 13.1.)

The campaign pledged to spread two golden rules of AIDS prevention: to use condoms during sexual contacts and to never swap needles. The foundation targeted the Swiss population as a whole, focusing on intravenous drug users, males with homosexual contacts, and adolescents. The objective of the campaign was to prevent initial infection and reduce the impact of the AIDS epidemic. In addition, intentions were to create solidarity and to maintain high ethical standards. Messages concerned everyone, those with and without HIV/AIDS.

Promotion

To reinforce the message, The Swiss AIDS foundation created its own brand of condoms, *"Hot Rubber,"* and its own distribution channels. The sales of the condoms reached more than 75,000 per month. Mass media campaign components included print ads, television, radio, motion picture theaters, and billboards. Billboards and posters were produced in

Figure 13.1. Promoting Condom Use, a Core Strategy for the Swiss Campaign

three different languages: French, German, and Italian. They carried simple slogans such as: "Condoms protect—so does faithfulness." Billboards were posted in 1,250 sites throughout Switzerland. Television commercials throughout the 1980s were broadcast free of charge by the three major Swiss networks. Beginning in the early 1990s, however, the foundation had to buy 42 minutes of television airtime per language area; this provided a net reach of 72.6% of the Swiss population. Movie theater advertising reached a significant portion of the 15 to 24 age group. The advertisements were produced to be both fun and exciting in order to hold the attention of the general viewer. Print ads in newspapers and magazines were used, but less extensively. Over 592 press releases were published, with a combined circulation of 23 million. Sporting events were also used. Although campaign content changed over time, the general message and logo persisted: "STOP AIDS."

Results

The Swiss AIDS Foundation estimated through spot checks that the logo had a 90% recognition factor. From 1986 to 1992, condom sales had risen from 7.6 million to 15 million units. Approximately 50% of those involved in occasional sexual contacts aged 17 to 30 reported use of condoms (always) in 1990, compared with the previous 8% in 1987. Condom use among individuals between the ages of 31 to 45 also increased from 22% in 1989 to 52% in 1992.

The success of this campaign prompted The Swiss AIDS Foundation and the Swiss government to continue these educational efforts to combat the growing AIDS epidemic.[3]

United States: The Use of Selective Communication Media

Background

In the late 1990s, a Prevention Marketing Initiative (PMI) was launched in Sacramento, California,

with the title "Teens Stopping AIDS."[4] The campaign aimed to reduce the sexual transmission of HIV infection among sexually active adolescents. PMI advocated condom use, targeting sexually active adolescents between the ages of 14 and 18 who were using condoms inconsistently. The campaign focused on 15 zip code areas with high rates of STD and pregnancy among adolescents. This group represented 6,000 to 10,000 teenagers.

Promotion

PMI's campaign focused on the teenager's future, using messages, including "You've got dreams—don't lose them" and "It's okay to carry and use condoms; me and my friends do." Messages were relayed through radio, posters, workshops, outreach programs, and telephone information lines. All of the media channels featured the campaign title "Teens Stopping AIDS." The year-long radio campaign consisted of 2,000 30-second spots, aired on four stations, which were all popular with teens. Radio stations estimated that the spots reached as many as 7,000 adolescents. Posters and promotional material were displayed in many high schools, retail outlets, community centers, and on the sides of city buses. The material pictured adolescents of multiple ethnic backgrounds. PMI also produced hats, mugs, dog tags, T-shirts, temporary tattoos, and condom packets, all marked with the "Teens Stopping AIDS" logo. These promotional items were distributed at teen events, such as concerts. PMI introduced skill-building workshops for small groups of adolescents. Each program lasted 6 to 7 hours and included lectures, discussions, role-playing, videotapes, and a behavioral contract. The behavioral contract consisted of workshop graduates pledging to convey the basic PMI message to at least three friends. Last, PMI introduced an automated telephone information line (800-TEEN) where teens could get HIV facts and other information, such as where to go for free condoms. The information line also included a directory for parents concerned with unsafe sex among teens.

Results

Over 1,400 telephone interviews were completed between December 1996 and October 1998 with a random sample of adolescents within the 15 zip code areas. Results indicated that the percentage of adolescents who reported exposure to the "Teens Stopping AIDS" campaign increased significantly during this period. Eventually, over half of the target population had been exposed to the program's message through at least one media channel.

Findings also indicated that the more channels an adolescent had been exposed to, the more likely he or she would have been to have used a condom during the last sexual encounter; reported condom use was increased 26% with each additional media channel. The proportion of adolescents who had used a condom at their last sexual encounter increased 4.3 percentage points (from 68.6% to 72.9%) over a 1-year period of the campaign (after statistical adjustments for sex, age, and race/ethnicity).[5]

South Africa: The Use of Personal Media

Background

During the year of 1992, The Society for Family Health (SFH) and Population Services International (PSI) launched a pilot project in Natal, South Africa, to promote safe sex. The nationwide promotion targeted the general public with a focus on adolescents and mineworkers. The goal was to provide quality condoms to the general public for an affordable price. The condom, *Lovers Plus,* was available in a three-pack for US $0.30. The price was believed to be affordable for low-income South Africans, in contrast with commercial brands commonly priced at US $2.30 per three-pack. The packaging upgrade of

Figure 13.2. More Recent "Lovers Plus" Packaging

"Lovers Plus" male condoms increased the quality perception and appealed to a sense of style among the target market of black youths between the ages of 16 and 24. (See Figure 13.2.)

Promotion

PSI worked hard to make the *Lovers Plus* product widely available in both traditional outlets, such as pharmacies, hotels, and supermarkets, and nontraditional outlets, such as spaza shops, bars, nightclubs, petrol stations, and through traditional healers. Many nontraditional outlets were open late, when access to condoms is most needed. PSI/SFH used an educational approach to communicate the necessity of using condoms to protect against HIV/AIDS. The strategy included training South African vendors who sold condoms. PSI/SFH also used traditional media channels, including call-in radio programs, informational booklets, a 6-foot condom mascot, and promotional items (T-shirts, calendars, and bumper stickers). All of the promotional items were branded with the *Lovers Plus* logo. Two educational booklets were also produced to coincide with the call-in radio programs; the first booklet was "Lovers' Straight Talk: A Teenager's Guide" to safe sex; the second booklet explained the correct way to use a condom. "Mr. Loverman," the 6-foot condom mascot, was used to promote safer sex at sporting events, such as The Africa Cup of Nations soccer tournament in South Africa. (See Figure 13.3.) There was also a television-broadcasted educational video, "The Rubber Revolution," which promoted safer sex and condom use.

Results

PSI first launched *Lovers Plus* condoms in October 1992. By 2001, more than 19 million Lovers Plus condoms had been sold. The PSI/SFH campaign has led to a significant increase in the percentage of women using condoms and a significant increase in the number of young women receiving information about pregnancy, contraceptives, STDs, and HIV/AIDS. There have also been increases in condom use during sexual encounters among mineworkers.[6]

Figure 13.3. "Mr. Loverman," the 6-Foot Condom Mascot

CHAPTER OVERVIEW

This chapter discusses selection of media channels and vehicles to carry out promotional strategies. The major decisions are (a) *choosing types of media channels,* (b) *selecting specific media vehicles,* and (c) *determining campaign timing.*

Media selection often has the most impact on program budgets and requires some of the most thoughtful analysis and evaluation of options. Media decisions must be made on the basis of a variety of criteria, including campaign goals, communication objectives, advantages and limitations of each media channel, target audience profiles, and the realities of budgets and funding. Principles to guide this decision making and to maximize media budgets are presented in the final section of the chapter.

WHAT ARE MAJOR MEDIA CHANNELS TO CONSIDER?

Media categories and specific channels for each are listed in Box 13.1. The following section describes each type. (Also see Figures 13.4-13.19.)

Advertising: Most advertising is nonpersonal and is paid for by the sponsor. Major categories include mass media, such as television, radio, newspapers, magazine, direct mail, and the Internet, and a variety of outdoor (out-of-home) channels, such as billboards, transit signage, and kiosks. The social marketer may also have opportunities for *unpaid advertising;* messages are placed in these channels for free, as a public service.

Major advertising activities will include determining advertising goals, selecting specific media vehicles on the basis of target audience profiles and media habits, and then placing media buys.

Public Relations: Successful public relations efforts generate *free, positive mention of the social marketer's program in the media,* most commonly as news and special programming on radio and television, and as stories, articles, and editorial comments in newspapers and magazines. Additional typical efforts may include planning for *crisis communications* (e.g., responding to adverse or conflicting news), *lobbying* (e.g., for funding allocations), managing *public affairs* (e.g., issue visibility), and organizing *special events,* such as demonstrations (e.g., car seat checks), fairs (e.g., health screenings), or some other activity designed to increase media coverage (e.g., advocacy march for safe gun storage).

BOX 13.1
Major Social Marketing Media Types

A. ADVERTISING (PAID MEDIA AND UNPAID PUBLIC SERVICE ANNOUNCEMENTS)

Broadcast:
    Television
    Radio
    Internet: banner ads
Print:
    Newspaper
    Magazine
Direct Mail:
    Separate mailings
    Paycheck and other stuffers
    Internet/Web sites
Backs of tickets and receipts

Outdoor/Out of Home:
    Billboards
    Busboards
    Bus shelter displays
    Subways
    Taxis
    Vinylwrap cars and buses
    Sports events
    Banners
    Postcard racks
    Kiosks
    Restroom stalls
    Truckside advertising
    Airports billboards and signage

B. PUBLIC RELATIONS

Stories on television and radio
Articles in newspapers and magazines
Op-eds
Public affairs/community relations
Lobbying
Videos
Media advocacy

Special Events:
    Meetings
    Speakers bureau
    Conferences
    Exhibits
    Health screenings
    Demonstrations

C. PRINTED MATERIALS

Brochures
Newsletters
Flyers
Posters
Catalogs

Calendars
Envelope messages
Booklets
Bumper stickers
Static stickers

D. SPECIAL PROMOTIONAL ITEMS

Clothing:
    T-shirts
    Baseball hats
    Diapers
    Bibs
Temporary Items:
    Coffee sleeves
    Bar coasters
    Lapel buttons
    Temporary tattoos
    Balloons
    Stickers
    Sports cards

Functional Items:
    Key chains
    Flashlights
    Refrigerator magnets
    Water bottles
    Litterbags
    Pens and pencils
    Bookmarks
    Book covers
    Notepads
    Tote bags
Mascots
Door hangers

E. SIGNAGE AND DISPLAYS

    Road signs
    Signs and posters on government property
    Retail displays and signage

F. PERSONAL SELLING

    Face-to-face meetings, presentations, speakers bureau
    Telephone
    Workshops, seminars, and training sessions

G. POPULAR MEDIA

    Songs
    Movie scripts, television, radio programs
    Comic books and comic strips

Figure 13.4. Magazine Ad

Figure 13.5. Outdoor Billboard

Figure 13.6. Magazine Insert

Figure 13.7. Newspaper Ads

DATE RAPE

By Nora Doyle
Mercer Island Reporter

Looking forward to a night out last August, Lisa Johnson (not her real name) and a girlfriend planned to meet for a drink on Mercer Island and then decide where they'd go for dinner.

They met early in the evening, took a table and began catching up with each other over drinks, a Jack Daniels and Coke for Johnson. The talk continued to flow, so Johnson ordered another drink. It tasted weak, a fact she mentioned to the bartender.

She kept the drink anyway, and was surprised when a man at the bar said, "Here, Lisa, try this one."

Johnson didn't know the man, although he claimed to know her. Thinking the bartender had made her a new drink and passed it down through the man at the bar, Johnson took it and noted aloud that it was a double. Ignoring the man's advances and familiarity, Johnson continued to devote her attention to her friend.

After a while longer, she walked her friend to her car and told her she'd call her shortly to meet for dinner. Johnson went back inside to settle her tab and collect her belongings.

That's the last thing she remembered until three hours later,

Please see **Rape** on A7

Photo illustration by Marta Storwick/Mercer Island Reporter
More than 50 percent of rapes occur on dates, and in most cases of date rape, drugs or alcohol are involved.

Figure 13.8. Newspaper Story

Figure 13.9. Community Relations

Figure 13.10. Bumper Sticker

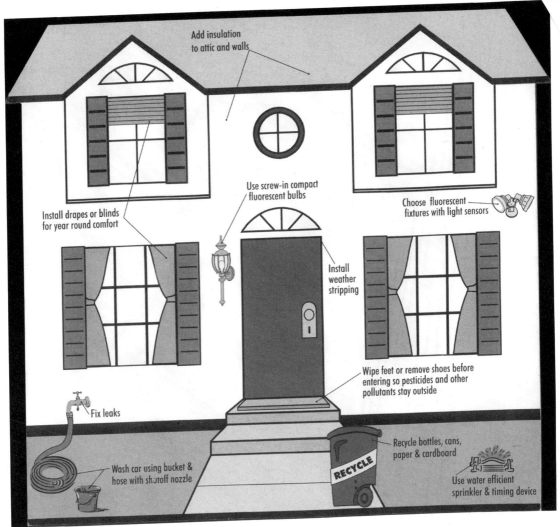

Figure 13.11. Brochure

Publicity is a powerful messenger for behavior change messages; it provides more in-depth coverage of the issue than is often possible with a brief commercial and is often seen as more objective than paid advertising. Tools used to generate news coverage include press releases, press kits, news conferences, editorial boards, letters to the editor, and strong personal relationships with key reporters and editors.

Printed Materials: Most social marketing campaigns use some type of printed materials. *Brochures, newsletters, booklets, flyers, posters, calendars, bumper stickers,*

Figure 13.12. Door Hanger

Figure 13.13. Sticker

and catalogs provide opportunities to present more detailed information regarding the desired behavior and the social marketing program. Often, target audiences hold on to these materials and, ideally, even share them with others. In some cases, special materials are developed and distributed to other key internal and external groups, such as program partners and the media. Included in this media category are any collateral pieces associated with the program, such as *letterheads, envelopes, and business cards.*

Major decisions and activities relative to printed materials will include selecting designs and formats, managing production, and implementing distribution plans.

Special Promotional Items: Campaign messages can be reinforced and sustained through the use of special promotional items, referred to by some in the industry as "trinkets and trash." Among the most familiar are messages on *clothing* (e.g., T-shirts, baseball hats, diapers, and bibs), *functional items* (e.g., key chains, water bottles, litterbags, pens and pencils, notepads, bookmarks, book covers, and refrigerator magnets), and more *temporary mechanisms* (e.g., bar coasters, stickers, temporary tattoos, coffee sleeves, and lapel buttons).

Major decisions and activities relative to promotional items are similar to those for printed materials, including

Figure 13.14. Mascot for Natural Lawns: Bert the Salmon

choosing among the many options that are available, selecting designs and message components, managing production, and implementing distribution plans.

Signage and Displays: Many social marketing campaigns rely on signage and displays to launch and, especially, sustain campaign messages. Examples of those more permanent in nature include *road signs* warning against drinking and driving, reminding people to use a litterbag, and asking motorists to "Move right for sirens and lights." *Signs on government property and establishments regulated by the government* can be used to target messages, such as those in forests asking people to stay on the path, plaques in bars with messages warning about the dangers of alcohol when pregnant, and those in subways asking us not to run. Displays and signage can also be used in *retail environments,* for example, for life vests, tarps for covering pickup loads, energy-saving lightbulbs, and natural pesticides.

Efforts related to signage and special displays will include selling the idea to distribution channel decision makers and coordinating distribution of any special signage and accompanying materials.

Figure 13.16. Road Sign

Figure 13.15. T-Shirt Imprinting Discouraging Binge Drinking

Figure 13.17. Retail Energy Saving Lightbulb Display

Figure 13.18. Comic Book

Figure 13.19. Comic Strip

Personal Selling: In the social marketing environment, this classic media tool is most often found in *face-to-face meetings and one-on-one presentations* (e.g., Women and Infant Children Program (WIC) counselors describing the benefits of using farmers' market coupons), in *workshops, seminars, and training sessions* (e.g., a presentation at a PTA meeting on the benefits of caring adult relationships), over the *telephone* (e.g., when explaining the warning signs of suicide to a concerned parent), and through the *Internet* (e.g., chat rooms where participants can pose questions and get advice on topics such as diabetes maintenance and control).

Activities for the social marketer may include selecting, organizing, and/or training personal communicators who will play key roles in delivering behavior change messages. They may include outreach workers, facilitators, field workers, volunteers, health care providers, professionals, recruiters, educators, counselors, missionaries, community organizers, extension workers, social workers, and more.[7]

Popular Media: A less well-known and perhaps underused media category employs popular forms of entertainment to carry behavior change messages, including *movies, television series, radio programs, comic books, comic strips, songs, theatre, and traveling entertainers, such as puppeteers.* Social marketing messages integrated into programming have included topics such as drinking and driving, use of condoms, eating disorders, recycling, youth suicide, and sudden infant death syndrome.

According to Andreasen,

This approach has been very effective in overcoming the problems of selective exposure and selective attention on the part of indifferent target audiences. This has come to be called the Entertainment Education Approach.[8] It began in the 1960s with a soap opera in Peru called *Simplemente Maria,* which discussed family planning, among other topics.[9]

More recently, the news reported that a 10-year-old boy saved his mother, who was choking from a piece of meat, by using the well-known Heimlich maneuver. The mother believes one of her son's favorite cartoon shows helped him save her life: He had seen and remembered how the character performed the maneuver on a friend.[10]

Efforts to make this happen on a large scale are likely to be substantial and may include lobbying efforts with the entertainment industry. On a smaller, more local level, social marketers might persuade local entertainers popular with the target audience to develop special promotional products, such as songs on their

CDs, to perform at special events or to be featured in advertisements. The successful "Don't Mess With Texas Campaign" against litter, for example, featured Willie Nelson singing about litter, at events and in commercials.

CHOOSING SPECIFIC MEDIA VEHICLES

Those responsible for media planning will also be faced with decisions on choosing the best *specific media vehicles* to carry the message, including selecting *television shows, radio programs, magazines, sections of the newspaper, locations of billboards, transit routes, Web sites, and direct mail lists.*[11] Vehicles for public relations will also include targeted television stations, sections of the newspaper, specific magazines, and venues for special events. Vehicles (distribution sites) will need to be chosen for printed materials and promotional items, and locales will need to be identified for any signage and displays.

Planners will review and compare costs, size, and profiles of audiences reached by the vehicle and compare the compatibility of the vehicle with the social change objectives, messages, and positioning. Most often, the social marketer will be able to rely on representatives from the various media organizations to recommend specific media vehicles.

WHAT TIMING DECISIONS NEED TO BE MADE?

The social marketer will also need to make choices regarding the timing and phasing of the campaign.[12]

Specific timing elements will include decisions regarding *months, weeks, days,* and *hours* when campaign elements will be launched, distributed, implemented, and/or aired in the media. The marketer will make decisions on the basis of when the target audience is most likely to be reached, as well as influenced, by campaign messages. For example, a drinking and driving campaign aimed at teens might be most effective immediately prior to and during prom and graduation nights.

In some cases, a phased approach to campaigns should be considered. This approach may be appropriate when *various and different target audiences* will be targeted during a campaign. For example, a drowning prevention campaign might target toddlers the first year, elementary school age kids the second year, and teens the third year, given the different approaches for messages and media. Phases may be appropriate when target audiences will need to be "moved" through *several stages of change* over a period of time. For example, a campaign to reduce waste use might have a first-year goal to create awareness and education regarding the severity of the problem and then follow this with campaigns promoting specific, desirable behaviors. Finally, a phased approach might be the answer when *funding sources and amounts are spread out over a period of years.* For example, a physical activity campaign that only has enough funding the first year to target one community in the state could pilot the program the first year, make enhancements to the project, and then roll it out to other communities in subsequent years.

WHAT FACTORS INFLUENCE MEDIA STRATEGIES?

Clearly, the social marketer has numerous options available for media channels, media vehicles, and media timing. Choices and decisions will be based on a variety of considerations: *communication objectives and campaign goals; desired reach and frequency* needed to meet these objectives and goals; *advantages and limitations* of each media type; *target market* size, media habits, "openings," and compatibility with the media type and vehicle; and comparative costs and available *budgets* for the program.

Make Choices That Support Communication Objectives and Campaign Goals

Kotler and Roberto discuss three major approaches to consider when choosing media channels: *mass, selective,* and *personal.* Each approach may be appropriate, depending on communication objectives established in the creative brief and campaign goals established in Step 3. Many campaigns and programs may warrant all three, as they are mutually reinforcing.[13]

Mass media is most often called for when large groups of people need to be quickly informed and persuaded regarding an issue or desired behavior. There is a need, and perhaps a sense of urgency, for audiences to "know, believe, and/or do something." Typical media types would include (a) *advertising on television, radio, newspapers, billboards, and transit signs* and (b) *publicity on television and radio and in newspapers, magazines, and governmental signage.* Examples of situations in which mass communications would be most appropriate include those exhibiting *imminent threats or dangers* (e.g., airport security checks, an energy shortage, a measles outbreak in a community, the spread of mad cow disease, or an increased danger of forest fires); *new important findings and information* (e.g., benefits of moderate physical activity, an increase in the number of heterosexual women who are HIV positive, or recent findings on the percentage of obese children); *changes in laws with widespread impact* (e.g., for booster seats, life vests, blood alcohol levels when driving, or outdoor burning); *increasing and widespread concerns* in a community, and people wanting to know more about what they can do (e.g., shootings in schools, drug use among teenagers, or how to prepare for another earthquake). Media plans will be developed to ensure broad exposure to the communication and to create awareness of the issue, recall of specific messages, and a favorable attitude and image of the program.[14]

Selective media are used in cases in which target markets can be reached more cost-effectively through targeted media channels, target audiences need to know more than is available in mass media formats, and/or target audiences need an opportunity to interact with communicators. Typical appropriate media types include *direct mail, flyers, brochures, posters, special events, telemarketing,* and the *Internet.* Examples of target audiences that might be targeted with selective media regarding specific issues are homeowners with waterfront property, parents of high school students in a community, senior citizens in retirement communities, small farm owners, families on Medicaid, and boaters. Selective media may be used to supplement mass media efforts, both as a follow-up technique that offers more intensive information and as a market-segmenting technique that more precisely targets segments of the mass audience a social marketer is seeking to reach.[15]

In some cases, media plans will need to include *personal media* to successfully achieve behavior change objectives. In this case, personal contact is delivered in the form of *face-to-face meetings and presentations, telephone conversations, workshops, seminars, and training sessions.* This approach is most warranted when some form of personal intervention and interaction is required in order to deliver detailed information, address barriers and concerns, build trust, and gain commitment. Costs (per contact) are often greatest for this approach and must be evaluated and justified relative to campaign objectives and budgets.

Use Desired Reach and Frequency as a Guide

Another consideration when making media decisions will be the desired reach and frequency needed to achieve campaign goals. Kotler and Armstrong define *reach* as

> A measure of the percentage of people in the target market who are exposed to the ad campaign during a given period of time. *Frequency* is a measure of how many times the average person in the target market is exposed to the message.[16]

For example, a state health department may want radio and television spots to reach 75% of youth aged 12 to 18 living in major metropolitan areas at least 9 times during a 2-month campaign. Media representatives will then use computer programs to

TABLE 13.1 Profiles of Major Media Types

Medium	Advantages	Limitations
Newspapers	Flexibility, timeliness, good local market coverage, broad acceptability, high believability	Short life, poor reproduction quality, small pass-along audience
Television	Good mass-market coverage; low cost per exposure; combines sight, sound, and motion; appealing to the senses	High absolute costs, high clutter, fleeting exposure, less audience selectivity
Direct mail	High audience selectivity, flexibility, no ad competition within the same medium, allows personalization	Relatively high cost per exposure, "junk mail" image
Radio	Good local acceptance, high geographic and demographic selectivity, low cost	Audio only, fleeting exposure; low attention ("the half-heard" medium); fragmented audiences
Magazines	High geographic and demographic selectivity, credibility and prestige, high-quality reproduction, long life and good pass-along readership	Long ad purchase lead time, high cost, no guarantee of position
Outdoor	Flexibility, high repeat exposure, low cost, low message competition, good positional selectivity	Little audience selectivity, creative limitations
Internet	High selectivity, low cost, immediacy, interactive capabilities	Small, demographically skewed audience; relatively low impact; audience controls exposure

SOURCE: From *Principles of Marketing* (p. 553), by P. Kotler and G. Armstrong, 2001, Upper Saddle River, NJ: Prentice Hall. Reprinted with permission.

produce media schedules and associated costs to achieve these objectives. The media planner then looks at the total cost of the plan and calculates the cost per contact or exposure (often expressed as the *cost per thousand,* the cost of reaching 1,000 people using the medium).

Know Advantages and Limitations of Media Options

Media decisions should be based on advantages and limitations of media types and should take into consideration the nature and format of key messages established in the creative brief. For example, a brief message such as "Choose a designated driver" can fit on a key chain or bar coaster, whereas a complex one such as "How to talk with your teen about suicide" would be more appropriate in a brochure or on a special radio program. Table 13.1 presents a summary of advantages and limitations for each of the major advertising categories.

Match the Media to the Target Market

Perhaps the most important consideration when planning media strategies will be the *target market's profile* (demographics, psychographics, geographics, and behaviors) and *media habits*. This will be especially important when using paid advertising and selecting specific media vehicles such as radio stations, television programs, sections of the newspaper, magazines, and direct mail lists. These were, ideally, identified as "openings" when developing the creative brief. Again, media representatives will be able to provide audience profiles and recommendations. The goal will be to choose general media types, specific vehicles, and the timing most likely to reach, appeal to, and influence target audiences. *Compatibility* of the social marketing program and associated messages will also be key and will contribute to the ultimate impact of the given medium. For example, a message regarding safe gun storage is more strategically aligned with a parenting magazine than one on home decorating, even though both may have readerships with similar demographic profiles.

Allocate Funds Based on Budget Constraints

Simply stated, the more reach, frequency, and impact the marketer seeks, the higher the budget will need to be.[17] Ideally, media strategies and associated budgets are based on desired and agreed-upon campaign goals (e.g., reach 75% of youth at least 9 times). In reality, as is discussed further in Chapter 14, plans are more often influenced by budgets and available funding sources. For example, first estimates of a draft media plan to achieve the above goal may indicate that costs for the desired reach and frequency exceed actual and fixed budgets. In this (all too common) scenario, planners will then need to prioritize and allocate funding to media types and vehicles judged to be most efficient and effective. In some cases, it may then be necessary and appropriate to reduce campaign goals (e.g., reach 50% of youth at least 9 times) and/or create a phased approach to campaign implementation (e.g., achieve the reach and frequency goals in half the state).

WHAT PRINCIPLES CAN GUIDE DECISION MAKING?

Several principles can benefit decision making and maximize media budgets: an integrated approach, being there "just in time" or "in the event of," maximizing publicity and public service announcements (PSAs) opportunities, and exploring alternative media.

Develop an Integrated Approach

Experiences of commercial sector marketers routinely investing millions of dollars in marketing communications have led many companies to adopt the concept of *Integrated Marketing Communications (IMC),* "where a company carefully integrates and coordinates its many communication channels to deliver a clear, consistent, and compelling message about the organization and its products."[18]

Integrated marketing communications means achieving consistency in the use of slogans, images, colors, font types, key messages, and sponsor mentions in all media vehicles. It means that statistics and facts used in press releases are the same as those in printed materials. It means that television commercials have the same tone and style as radio spots and that print ads have the same look and feel as the program's Web site.[19]

In addition, IMC points to the need for a graphic identity and perhaps even a statement or manual describing graphic standards. The integrated approach also addresses the need for coordination and cooperation between those developing and disseminating program materials and, finally, calls for regular audits of all customer contact points.

Benefits of an integrated approach are significant, with (a) increased efficiencies in developing materials (e.g., eliminating the need for frequent debates over colors and typefaces and incremental costs for developing new executions) and (b) increased effectiveness of communications, given their consistent presentation in the marketplace.

Be There "Just in Time"

Many social marketers have found that an ideal moment to speak to the target audience is when they are about to choose between alternative, competing behaviors. They are at a fork in the road and the social marketer wants a last chance to influence this decision. Tactics demonstrating this principle include the following:

◆ The use of the ❤ symbol on menus signifying a smart choice for those interested in options that are low in fat, cholesterol, and/or calories

◆ The familiar forest fire prevention signs that give updates on the current level of threat for forest fires in the park

◆ A message on the backs of diapers reminding parents to turn their infants over, onto their backs, to sleep

◆ The idea of encouraging smokers (in the contemplation stage) to insert their children's photos under the wrappers of cigarette packs

- A sign at a beach that makes the benefit of a life vest clear (see Figure 13.20)

- A key chain for teens with the message "You Don't Have to Be Buzzed to Be Busted" (see Figure 13.21)[20]

- A handmade tent card next to a napkin holder suggesting customers take only what they need (see Figure 13.22)

Figure 13.20. A Sign at a Beach Shows the Benefit of a Life Vest

Figure 13.21. A Key Chain for Teens

Figure 13.22. A Handmade Tent Card

◆ A sign on an outdoor restaurant patio cajoling patrons into not feeding the birds (see Figure 13.23)

Be There "In The Event Of"

Communicators also want to prepare for events that are likely to motivate target audiences to listen, to learn more, and to alter their behaviors. Examples would include events such as an earthquake, a teen suicide in a small community, the listing of an endangered species, threats of drought and power blackouts, a famous female entertainer diagnosed with AIDS, a local teen killed in an automobile accident and not wearing a seatbelt, a college student

Figure 13.23. A Sign on an Outdoor Restaurant Patio

sexually assaulted after a rave party, or a celebrity diagnosed with prostate cancer. Events such as these often affect levels of awareness and belief relative to costs and benefits associated with behavior change. The amount of time it will take to learn about and prepare a home for a potential earthquake seems minor compared with suffering the costs and losses in a real earthquake. Though such events are often tragic, the "silver lining" is that target audiences in the precontemplation stage are often moved to contemplation, even action, and the social marketer can take advantage of the momentum created by heightened publicity and the need for practical information. Just as public relations professionals prepare for *crisis communications*, the social marketer also wants to prepare for these *opportunity communications*. (See Figure 13.24.)

KIDS AND GUNS: WHAT PARENTS CAN DO

GUN VIOLENCE IS SCARY, and there's no way to guarantee that your kid will be 100 percent safe. But you can significantly improve the odds. Here's some advice:

☑ **Talk to your** children about guns and violence. Explain that weapons are not toys and that kids should never play with them. Tell your kids that if they see an unlocked gun in a friend's house, they should stay away from it and inform you about it immediately.

If you have a gun in your home, unload it and lock it away; store the bullets in a separate place, also under lock. Hide the keys. When your children are older, make sure they get training in gun safety.

☑ **Get to know** the parents of your children's friends. The more you know, the easier it is to spot poten-

tial danger away from home. Ask other parents if they have a gun, and if they do, ask whether it's locked up. This is a difficult conversation, but it's important because nearly half of all accidental shootings of kids under 16 take place in the homes of friends and relatives.

Never leave young children home alone, even for just a few minutes. As your children get older, make sure you always know where they are and who their friends are.

ROLE MODEL: A Buell mom comforting her daughter

Studies show that unsupervised children have the most behavior problems and are most likely to resolve conflicts with violence.

☑ **Encourage your** local school to develop a violence-education program that includes information about gun safety as well as conflict resolution. These programs are not just for teenagers; even children in early elementary school can benefit.

☑ **Monitor what** your kids watch on TV and in the movies. Scenes of explicit violence should be off limits for school-age children. Young kids aren't able to distinguish between what looks like reality on screen and real life.

☑ **Remember that** you are your child's primary role model. If you carry a gun, you could send your kid the message that guns solve disputes.

RICHARD LEE—DETROIT FREE PRESS—ART

Figure 13.24. Practical Behaviors Presented in a Popular Magazine After a Crisis

Maximize Publicity

News and feature stories can have a strong impact on target audiences, often at a much lower cost than advertising (paid media) and with more credibility. Kotler and Armstrong argue,

The organization does not pay for the space or time in the media. Rather, it pays for a staff to develop and circulate information and to manage events. If the company develops an interesting story, it could be picked up by several different media, having the same effect as advertising that would cost millions of dollars.[21]

Siegel and Doner describe several tactics to obtain news coverage.[22] A few are summarized and quoted below:

Build relationships with the media by first finding out who covers what and then working to "position yourself and your initiative as an important, reliable source of information so that the reporters will call you when they are running a story on your topic."[23]

Frame the issues with the goals of the media in mind, "to appeal to the broadest number of audience members possible, and . . . tell a compelling story that is relevant to their audience and in the public's interest."[24]

Create news by convening a press conference, special event, or demonstration. Consider a technique mastered by The Center for Science in the Public Interest (CSPI) in which their studies create "news that applies pressure to decision makers. For example, after its analysis of the nutrient content of movie popcorn was reported in the media, many major movie chains began using oils lower in saturated fat or offering air-popped options."[25]

Know the Limitations of PSAs

The fact that some people refer to PSAs as "people sound asleep" instead of "public service announcements" reflects the concern that they will not be very effective. PSAs may appear in the middle of the night, they cannot easily be directed to target groups, and they have other disadvantages. Yet there is intense competition for public service airtime and free out-of-home and print media placement. Strategies to "win" and receive more favorable placements include (a) building strong relationships with community affairs staff by getting to know their priorities and recognizing them for contributions and efforts in the past; (b) finding media organizations interested in your issue, either because it is of interest to their audience or because they have chosen it as one of their areas of community focus; and (c) providing high-quality materials for reproduction and spots that stations will be proud to air. Some social marketers seeking more control over placement of ads have found success in getting paid sponsors for their announcements, or getting "one free spot for every paid spot."

Explore
Alternative Media

Today, one can find many new media for carrying messages: video cases, parking lot tickets, golf scorecards, delivery trucks, gas pumps, and municipal garbage cans. Social marketers are encouraged to think creatively to find places and people to carry messages that will surprise and appeal to target audiences. Consider the attention-getting potential of the following: temporary tattoos promoting "Don't Drink and Drive" on the midriffs of professional cheerleaders; posters in bathroom stalls in bar restrooms promoting condoms; recorded messages of celebrities played in the back of taxi cabs, reminding you to buckle up and be sure to take all your belongings; immunization schedules printed on bibs; messages to wear a life vest written in the sand on public beaches; and the grim statistics on organ donation that appeared in the "Vital Statistics" section of *U.S. News & World Report*.[26] (See Figure 13.25.) Consider the potential influence of these messengers, in these situations: lawyers suggesting to clients that they let family members know of their wishes for organ donation; physicians asking seniors if they know about medical alert devices; grocery store clerks asking kids if they've had their five fruits and vegetables for the day; child care providers reminding parents when their children are due for immunizations; peers knowing what to say to fellow students if they seem depressed; and a grandson persuading a grandfather to call a tobacco Quit Line "because I love you."

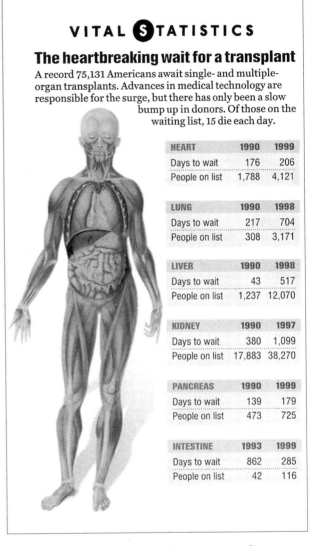

Figure 13.25. Social Marketing Message in a Prominent Section of a Popular Magazine

CHAPTER SUMMARY

1. Deciding where and when messages will appear includes choosing from a variety of media types (channels), selecting specific media vehicles, and determining timing for the launch and airing of communications.

2. More than a hundred *types of media channels* are available for the social marketer to consider; major categories include advertising (paid and unpaid), public relations, printed materials, special promotional items, signage and displays, personal selling, and popular media.

3. *Specific media vehicles* will also need to be selected and will include decisions such as television programs, radio stations, sections of the newspaper, and locations of brochure distributions.

4. Decisions will also need to be made on scheduling the communications over the course of a year. This will involve specifying months, weeks, days, and hours when communications will launch and be visible.

5. Media strategies will be developed on the basis of several considerations, including *communication objectives and campaign goals; desired reach and frequency* needed to meet these objectives and goals; *advantages and limitations* of each media type; *target market size,* media habits, "openings," and compatibility with the media type and vehicle; and comparative *costs* and available *budgets* for the program.

6. Several principles can benefit decision making and maximize media budgets. Those discussed in this chapter include using an integrated approach, being there "just in time" and "in the event of," maximizing publicity and PSA opportunities, and exploring alternative media.

KEY TERMS AND CONCEPTS

Media types	Mass media
Media vehicles	Selective media
Media timing	Personal media
Advertising	Media habits

Public relations
Printed materials
Special promotional
  items
Personal selling
Popular media
Campaign timing
Campaign phasing

Integrated marketing
  communications
Communications
  "just in time"
Communications
  "in the event of"
Crisis communications
Opportunity communications

ISSUES FOR DISCUSSION

1. Assume that you are a program manager for HIV/AIDS prevention in your county. How would you respond to strong feelings from your colleagues that a television spot should be included in the social marketing campaign being planned? What factors would you say should be considered in making this decision?

2. Relative to a statewide campaign to increase the number of fruits and vegetables that elementary age children consume each day, what types of media channels would you consider exploring?

3. What additional desired behaviors might benefit from "just in time" media channels? What specific media vehicles would you consider for these?

4. What additional desired behaviors might benefit from popular education? What specific media vehicles would you pursue for these?

RESEARCH HIGHLIGHT: CLINICAL TRIAL FOR SKIN CANCER DETECTION

This research highlight presents an example of the research techniques discussed in Chapter 4, the use of control and comparison groups in randomized clinical trials.

Skin Cancer Prevention: The *Skin Sense*® Educational Effectiveness Trial

Martin McCarthy Jr., Ph.D.
Edumedia, Inc.

Background

Following decades of over-promise and over-promotion, communication and computing channels have finally begun to converge, provide full interactivity, and supply sophisticated multimedia content to large numbers of people. The fusion of information processing and message distribution technologies has resulted in unprecedented levels of personalization and tailored functionality. Still higher levels of return on investment will be realized as continuing relationship with target audience members becomes commonplace using networked and wireless media.

Skin Sense® is an interactive health education program developed by the EduMedia Corporation of Evanston, Illinois. An evaluation study funded by the National Cancer Institute will compare the effectiveness of a Web-based skin cancer prevention initiative targeting middle-aged and elderly persons with videotape and print-based interventions in a randomized clinical trial format. This research project was begun in October 2001 and will be completed in December 2002.

Purpose

An undeclared epidemic of sun-damaged skin has been proceeding worldwide, as a result of behavioral and lifestyle factors and changes in the environment. (See Figure 13.26.) Many members of at-risk populations are not aware that their chances of developing skin cancer increase dramatically as they age and that a few simple and effective strategies can prevent sun damage and maintain healthy skin. The main purpose of this program is to educate people about these issues and motivate them to protect and examine and care for their skin on a continuing basis.

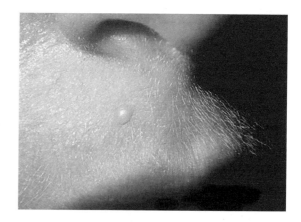

Figure 13.26. Basal Cell Cancer on the Upper Lip of Middle-Aged Woman

In addition to providing information, another purpose of the program is to assess user *readiness* (Prochaska & DiClemente, 1984) and sense of *self-efficacy* (Bandura, 1997) with regard to protecting their skin, conducting regularly scheduled skin examinations and participating in daily skin care. Stage of change appropriate interventions are then used to

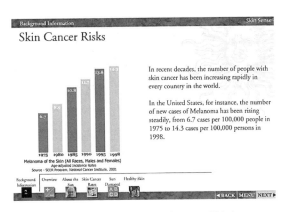

Figure 13.27. Increased Incidence of Melanoma

increase viewer motivation to begin these activities, and strategies are provided to promote continuation of both new and old self-care behaviors (DiClemente et al., 1998). Linkages to Internet-based resources provide additional relevant information and enable program users to purchase skin protection, skin care, and skin renewal products online. (See Figure 13.27.)

Long-standing research indicates that the combination of interactive media and behavioral technologies can be notably more powerful than traditional teaching methods (McCarthy et al., 1991). The randomized trial will provide a multidimensional comparison of the relative effectiveness of the three media in promoting behavior change in both short-term and longer-term time frames. The final purpose of the research study is therefore to provide well-founded and credible information regarding the impact of these three different approaches to education about skin care issues.

Methodology

About 1,000 subjects from three population groups are participating in the study. The *high-risk* group includes patients at a tertiary care Cancer Center who have previously been treated for either basal cell, squamous cell, or melanoma skin cancer. The *medium-risk* population includes patients from primary care office practice settings who have not had any form of skin cancer. The *low-risk* subjects are participants in a corporate wellness program who also do not have any history of skin cancer.

Subjects from each group are randomly assigned to either the Web-Based, Video-Only, or Print-Only intervention. All participants receive the same kind of information about skin cancer and skin care issues—the only difference between the conditions is in the medium of presentation. (See Figure 13.28.)

The Web-based program is organized around a book metaphor—a familiar frame of reference for members of our target audience. Individual chapters cover the following topics:

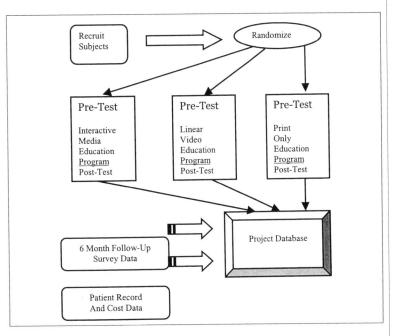

Figure 13.28. Schema Showing Research Design

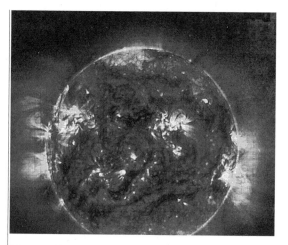

Figure 13.29. Ultraviolet Radiation From the Sun

▶ Background concerning the sun, environmental change, and skin cancer risks

▶ Descriptions of healthy skin, damaged skin, and skin cancers

▶ Instruction in how to conduct a skin examination

▶ Advice about how to prevent sun damage to skin

▶ Information about products to protect healthy skin and renew damaged skin

▶ Strategies help users manage their self-care behavior on a continuing basis. (See Figures 13.29 and 13.30.)

Program content includes text, graphics, charts, images, and animation on skin care and skin cancer topics, as well as digital video interviews with people who have healthy skin and with persons who have had skin cancer. (See Figure 13.31.) Links to Internet-based information and enabling resources are provided at the end of each chapter. Progress charts, body maps showing the location of lesions, and other

Figure 13.30. The A-B-C-D Rule

take-away materials can be printed after the user has completed the educational experience.

Prior to receiving any content information, subjects participate in an online assessment of their biological and behavioral risk factors, their sense of self-efficacy with regard to skin protection and skin examination, their readiness or stage of change for these behaviors, and their knowledge of skin care and skin cancer issues. (See Figure 13.32.) Immediately following completion of the educational session, the three groups of subjects are assessed again on these same dimensions.

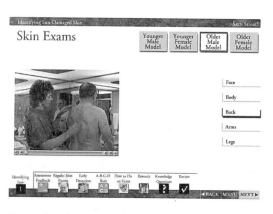

Figure 13.31. Identifying a Melanoma

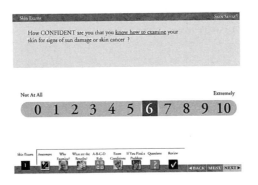

Figure 13.32. Self-Efficacy Scale for Skin Examinations

Subjects will participate in a telephone survey at 6-months postintervention as well. The survey will reassess their knowledge and attitudes about skin care topics and their skin protection and skin examination behaviors within this time period. Self-report data will be collected concerning the number of skin lesions identified and whether the lesions required treatment. Records from health care providers and health care institutions will also be reviewed. The patient records will provide information about specific diagnoses of skin-related disorders, treatments provided, treatment outcomes, and costs of care for study participants.

Future Plans

The results of the *Skin Sense*® randomized trial will be published in health care and social science venues. The evaluated product will be marketed to health information providers, managed care organizations, and high-risk population groups, among others.

NOTE: For more information, log on to skinsense.info, to edumedia.ws, or to the mythryn.com Web sites. Martin McCarthy can be contacted via email at: mmcc@northwestern.edu

References

Bandura, A. (1997). *Self-Efficacy: The exercise of control.* New York: W. H. Freeman.

DiClemente, C. C., & Prochaska, J. O. (1998). Toward a comprehensive transtheoretical model of change: Stages of change and addictive behaviors. In Miller and Heather (Eds.), *Treating Addictive Behaviors.* New York: Plenum Press.

McCarthy, M., Demakis, J., Zarada, S., Trimble, J., & Barone, R. (November 13, 1991). *Process and product: The development and formative evaluation of an interactive videodisc program for educating diabetic VA patients.* Annual Meeting, American Public Health Association, Atlanta, GA.

Prochaska, J. O., & DiClemente, C. C. (1984). *The transtheoretical approach: Crossing the traditional boundaries of therapy.* Chicago: Dow Jones/Irwin.

Notes

1. As cited in Boone, L. E. *Quotable Business* (1992, p. 151). New York: Random House. (Wanamaker lived 1838-1922)
2. The White House. *Summary Fact Sheet on HIV/AIDS.* Retrieved 10/02/01 from http://www.whitehouse.gov/onap/facts.html
3. Case Source: Kocher, K. W., cR Kommunikation AG, Zurich. (1993). *The STOP AIDS Story, 1987-1992* (1st ed.). STOP AIDS Campaign of the Swiss AIDS Foundation and the Federal Office for Public Health. Images retrieved from http://tecfa.unige.ch/tecfa/research/humanities/AIDS-campaign/campaign-themes.html
4. The Academy for Educational Development and the U.S. Centers for Disease Control and Prevention supported the development of PMI.

5. Case Source: Kennedy, M., Mizuno, Y., Seals, B., Myllyluoma, J., & Weeks-Norton, K. "Increasing Condom Use Among Adolescents With Coalition-Based Social Marketing." *AIDS* (2000) *14*(12), 1809-1818.

6. Case Source: Population Services International: "Social Marketing for AIDS Prevention in Post-Apartheid South Africa." Retrieved 10/9/2001 from PSI Web site at http://www.psiwash.org/psi_ops/profile/81_s_africa/s_africa.htm

7. Kotler, P., & Roberto, E. L. (1989). *Social Marketing: Strategies for Changing Public Behavior* (p. 221). New York: Free Press.

8. Rogers, E. M., et al. (1989). *Proceedings From the Conference on Entertainment Education for Social Change.* Los Angeles: Annenberg School of Communications.

9. Andreasen, A. R. (1995). *Marketing Social Change: Changing Behavior to Promote Health, Social Development, and the Environment* (p. 215). San Francisco: Jossey-Bass.

10. *The Seattle Times,* June 15, 2001, p. 1.

11. Kotler, P., & Armstrong, G. (2001). *Principles of Marketing* (p. 553.) Upper Saddle River, NJ: Prentice Hall.

12. Kotler & Roberto, *Social Marketing,* p. 202.

13. Ibid., pp. 190-237.

14. Ibid., p. 192.

15. Ibid., p. 212.

16. Kotler & Armstrong, *Principles of Marketing,* p. 552.

17. Ibid., p. 552.

18. Ibid., pp. 513-517.

19. Ibid., pp. 513-517.

20. DeLaunay Phillips Communications/Washington Traffic Safety Commission.

21. Kotler & Armstrong, *Principles of Marketing,* p. 566.

22. Siegel, M., & Doner, L. A. (1998). *Marketing Public Health: Strategies to Promote Social Change.* Gaithersburg, MD: Aspen.

23. Ibid., p. 393.

24. Ibid., p. 394.

25. Ibid., p. 396.

26. *U.S. News & World Report* (March 26, 2001). Vital Statistics Section, p. 10.

PART V

Managing
Social Marketing
Programs

KEY CHAPTER QUESTIONS

1. What are key components of an evaluation and monitoring plan?

2. What are key factors that might be measured?

3. What are options for measuring these factors?

4. What else should be taken into consideration when developing this plan?

CHAPTER 14

Developing a Plan
for Evaluation
and Monitoring

Marketing is a learning game. You make a decision. You watch the results. You learn from the results. Then you make better decisions.

—Philip Kotler[1]

MARKETING HIGHLIGHT: NUTRITION

This chapter's major case is divided into two parts. The first section, appearing here as a marketing highlight, describes a program evaluation plan. The second part discusses results from the evaluation, which are presented at the end of this chapter as a research highlight.

The Impact of Multiple Channel Delivery of Nutrition Messages on Student Knowledge, Motivation, and Behavior (Part I): Results From the Team Nutrition Pilot Study

R. Craig Lefebvre, Carol Olander, and Elyse Levine

Innovations in Social Marketing Conference,
Montreal, Canada, 1999

The USDA School Meals Initiative for Healthy Children, published in 1995, is a comprehensive plan that aims to ensure that children have healthy meals at school. A major part of this plan is an update of nutrition standards that requires school meals to meet the Dietary Guidelines for Americans. Recognizing that simply publishing a regulation is not likely to change children's diets, USDA established Team Nutrition to ensure that schools are able to implement the plan and that students avail themselves of the healthier meals offered. The goals of Team Nutrition include: eating less fat; eating more fruits, vegetables, and grains; and eating a variety of foods.

Team Nutrition supports the School Meals Initiative through two interrelated components:

Multifaceted Nutrition Education is delivered through the media, in schools, and at home to build skills and motivate children to make food choices for a healthful diet. The nutrition education approach and its components were developed and implemented following the tenets of social cognitive theory (SCT) and social marketing. The objectives of this component were to provide consistent and relevant messages through multiple channels that gain children's attention, motivate them to engage in desired behaviors, increase their self-efficacy in performing desired behaviors, and reinforce their actual performance of the behaviors (Bandura, 1986; Lefebvre & Flora, 1988).

Training and Technical Assistance is designed to ensure that school nutrition and food service personnel have the education, motivation, training, and skills necessary to provide healthy meals that appeal to children and meet the Dietary Guidelines for Americans. This component is also based on an SCT foundation of creating an environment in which to observe, practice, and receive reinforcement for healthy nutrition behaviors (i.e., "reciprocal determinism").

The Pilot Implementation of Team Nutrition

USDA launched a pilot implementation of Team Nutrition with two purposes: to systematically document the implementation process and to evaluate whether the initiative results in healthier food choices by students.

The pilot project was implemented in two phases—once in the Spring of 1996 and again in the Fall of 1996. The Fall implementation was essentially a replication of Spring with a new set of students. However, participating districts made changes in the activities conducted in Phase II based on their initial experiences. In addition, students who participated in the Phase I pilot were surveyed again during Phase II to ascertain whether any changes that occurred in Phase I were sustained over time.

Seven school districts were selected to participate in the pilot. Four of the seven school districts were selected to participate in an intensive process and outcome evaluation. The remaining three districts were the subject of a more limited process evaluation.

In the four districts participating in the intensive evaluation, one half of the school pairs were randomly assigned to the treatment condition (i.e., to implement Team Nutrition). The others became comparison sites and did not conduct nutrition lessons during the semesters in which the evaluation took place. In the remaining three districts, all of the nominated schools operated as Team Nutrition sites. Altogether, Team Nutrition was implemented at 18 schools and in over 140 classrooms in three grade levels during both phases.

Components of the Pilot Implementation

Each of the schools agreed to conduct a set of grade-specific classroom lessons developed by Scholastic, Inc. There are three grade-specific modules—Pre-K and K, Grades 1-2, and Grades 3-5. Each of the modules consists of a set of eight to nine lessons and

contains teacher guides, classroom and cafeteria activities, videos, posters, student magazines, and parent take-home pieces. In addition, the Team Nutrition schools committed to teacher and food service staff training, as well as a set of core school and community activities. Specifically, implementation schools were expected in each phase to:

- ▶ Conduct at least two schoolwide cafeteria events

- ▶ Conduct at least three parent contact activities

- ▶ Conduct at least two chef activities

- ▶ Conduct at least one districtwide Team Nutrition community event

- ▶ Conduct at least one districtwide media event

While some of those activities could overlap, all pilot schools were expected to conduct at least five core activities during each phase.

Methodology

The *process evaluation* was designed to measure the nature and magnitude of the Team Nutrition effort in all seven of the pilot districts. A number of data collection efforts were implemented as part of the basic process evaluation, including:

- ▶ Extant data on school and district characteristics including total student population, students' racial/ethnic background, and percentage of students receiving free or reduced school meals

- ▶ Interviews with school principals at the start of each phase in each implementation school

- ▶ Team Nutrition Core Activity Logs filled out by the person responsible for directing each school-based or community activity to document its key features, participation rates, and lessons learned

▶ Team Nutrition Teacher Activity Logs filled out by all implementing teachers for each scholastic lesson taught, including preparation time, actual classroom time, and which lesson components were utilized

In addition to the above data collection efforts, the teachers implementing Team Nutrition in their classrooms completed surveys that were conducted in group settings before and after the intervention.

The primary objective of the Team Nutrition *outcome evaluation* was to determine the degree to which the pilot implementation brings about changes in students' skills, motivations, and behavior as they relate to healthy eating. The focus of the outcome evaluation is on fourth-grade students. This grade level was chosen because children at this age (8 through 10 years) are capable of completing survey instruments and food frequency questionnaires.

Data used for this evaluation included:

▶ Self-administered questionnaires with fourth-grade students

▶ Telephone interviews with the parent/guardian most knowledgeable about the student's nutrition-related behavior and family's nutrition practices and attitudes

▶ Observation of these fourth-grade students' lunchroom food choice and consumption behavior

Description of Sample

Across the four intensive evaluation districts, about 1,650 fourth graders were eligible to participate during each phase, divided about evenly between implementation and comparison school students. The response rates for the self-administered surveys were between 85% and 91% over the two phases. In addition, over 1,400 students participated in the cafeteria observations during Phase I and over 1,300 students in Phase II. The majority of parents completed the telephone surveys. In Phase I, the response rates for the pretest and posttest were 87% and 79%, respectively. In Phase II, response rates were 74% and 72%.

Analytic Approach

Data were analyzed using a mixed models approach to regression analysis to control for clustering effects introduced by classroom and school assignment. Team Nutrition impact was calculated by totaling the change shown by students in the intervention schools minus the total change shown by students in comparison schools (i.e., double difference). Depending on the specific model that is used, that difference is the same as the regression coefficient representing Team Nutrition participation or the difference in the least square means when comparing intervention to comparison students.

Note: Results from the program evaluation of Team Nutrition appear at the end of this chapter as a research highlight, followed by the reference section.

CHAPTER OVERVIEW

We noted in Chapter 4 that "evaluation typically refers to a single final assessment of a project or program" and monitoring is associated with "ongoing measurement of program outcomes."[2] Our evaluation and monitoring plan includes several components and decisions. We will need to determine the following processes:

- What will be measured
- How it will be measured
- When it will be measured
- How results will be reported and used

WHAT WILL BE MEASURED?

Most commonly, we measure *outcomes* and *processes.* Outcome measures (sometimes referred to as *impact measures*) focus on specific results we can attribute (at least in part) to our program and campaign efforts (e.g., a 10% increase in registered organ donors). Process measures relate more to an assessment of campaign activities and executional elements (e.g., we distributed 1,000 organ donation brochures at a health fair and engaged 50 volunteers in our efforts). This chapter will focus on both of these measures.

Ethical outcomes, a third consideration, is discussed in our final chapter.

Outcome Measures

At this point, we refer back to the goals we established in Step 3, the specific measurable results we wanted our program to achieve. We stressed that goals would be the basis for evaluation of the campaign. Goals were stated as a "desired level of behavior change," and they may also include knowledge or belief change goals. Major indicators used for measuring outcomes (target audience impact) include the following:

- Changes in behavior
- Changes in behavior intent
- Changes in knowledge
- Changes in belief
- Responses to campaign elements
- Awareness of campaign
- Customer satisfaction levels

Intended Outcomes: Potential Indicators

1. Changes in Behavior

Change in behavior is most commonly measured and stated in terms of a *change in percentage* (e.g., adult binge drinking decreased from 17% to 6%), a *percentage increase or decrease* (e.g., seat belt usage increased by 20%), and/or a *change in numbers* (e.g., 40,000 new households signed up for food waste recycling bins, increasing the total number of households participating from 60,000 to 100,000).

2. Change in Behavior Intent

Some campaigns may measure and report changes in intention to adopt the desired behavior. This measure might be appropriate for campaigns with minimal exposure or when campaigns have been running for only short periods of time. It may be the most appropriate measure for campaigns targeting those in the precontemplation stage, when the social marketer's goal is to move them to contemplation and then (eventually) to the action stage.

3. Change in Knowledge

Typical indicators of changes in knowledge include changes in awareness of important *facts* (e.g., five drinks at one sitting is considered binge drinking), *information* (e.g., an estimated 75,000 people are on waiting lists for organ transplants), and *recommendations* (e.g., eat five or more servings of vegetables and fruit daily for better health).

4. Changes in Belief

Typical indicators of changes in beliefs include *attitude* indicators (e.g., my vote doesn't count), *opinions* (e.g., native plants are not attractive), and *values* (e.g., tanning is worth the risk).

5. Responses to Campaign Elements

Responses to campaign elements can be indicators of campaign reach and, in some cases, appeal. Typical measures include counting calls to an *"800 number"* (e.g., for a booklet on natural gardening), *redemption of coupons* (e.g., for a bike helmet), *mail or Internet orders or requests for more information* (e.g., for a free consultation on home earthquake preparedness), *purchases of tangible objects that were promoted* (e.g., number of new low-flow toilets sold or energy-saving lightbulbs compared with numbers in previous years), and *services provided* (e.g., number of blood pressure checks given at a mall event).

6. Awareness of Campaign

Though not necessarily an indicator of impact or success, measures of awareness of campaign elements provide some feedback on the extent to which the campaign was noticed and recalled. Measurements might include levels of *unaided awareness* (e.g., what you have seen or heard lately in the news about legal limits for blood alcohol levels while driving); *aided awareness* (e.g., what have you seen or heard lately in the news about our state's new .08% legal limit); or *proven awareness* (e.g., where did you read or hear about this change in the law).

7. Customer Satisfaction Levels

Customer satisfaction levels associated with service components of the campaign provide important feedback for analyzing results and for planning future efforts (e.g., ratings on levels of satisfaction with counseling at the Women and Infant Children Program [WIC] clinics).

Unintended Outcomes

Campaign evaluation may also include measuring and reporting on unintended outcomes (consequences), both positive and negative.[3] For example, many recycling program managers are now reporting concerns with their success in encouraging recycling. Although volumes of materials are being recycled that might otherwise have been put in landfills, managers believe they have significantly increased the use of recyclable materials. Anecdotal comments such as these confirm their fears: "I don't worry about printing extra copies anymore because I'm using recycled paper and I'll put any copies not used in the recycling bin" and "I don't worry about buying small bottles of water to carry around because I can recycle them." As a result, environmentalists in some communities are now beginning to direct more of their efforts to the other legs of their "three-legged stool": "Reduce use" and "Reuse."

Process Measures

Several additional measures of social marketing efforts include *process measures*. Further insight regarding outcomes can be gained through review and analysis of campaign activities, those under the social market's control. Typical process measures that might be relevant and important to evaluation efforts include the following:

- Changes in policy and infrastructure

- Reach and frequency

- Media coverage

- Total impressions

- Dissemination of materials

- Participation and contributions from outside sources

- Assessment of implementation of campaign programs

1. Changes in Policy and Infrastructure

A legitimate campaign goal may focus on causing an important change in *policies* or *infrastructures* that will encourage and/or support behavior change. In the interest of oral health for children, for example, efforts have paid off in some communities from persuading grocery stores to remove candy and gum from check-out lanes.

2. Reach and Frequency

Planners often place media buys to achieve a specific desired goal relative to reach and frequency (e.g., 50% of high school teens will hear the "Zero Tolerance" radio ads five times over the 3-month campaign period). Measures include estimating the *number of people who might be exposed to a campaign element, as well as the number of times they were exposed* (e.g., the number of motorists and the number of times they drove on the section of the road where a demonstration pile of litter had been left for a week's publicity effort).

3. Media Coverage

Measures of media and public relations efforts (earned media) may include reporting on numbers of *column inches* in newspapers and magazines, *minutes on television and radio* news and special programs, and *people in the audience* attending a planned speaker's event. Efforts are often made to determine and report what this coverage would have cost if it had been paid for.

4. Total Impressions/Cost per Impression

This measurement combines information from several categories, such as reach and frequency, media exposure, and material dissemination. Typically, these numbers are combined to create an estimate of the total number of people in the target market who were exposed to campaign elements. Taking this to the next level, *to achieve a cost per impression, total campaign costs associated with this exposure can then be divided by the estimated number of people exposed to the campaign.* For example, consider a statewide campaign that targets mothers through messages to increase children's fruit and vegetable consumption; the campaign may have collected exposure information from media buys (e.g., parent magazines) and any additional efforts (e.g., messages on grocery bags). Let's assume they were able to estimate that 100,000 mothers were exposed to these campaign efforts and that the associated costs were $10,000. Their cost per impression would be $10. These statistics then can be used over time to compare the cost-efficiency of varying strategies. Suppose, for example, that in a subsequent campaign, efforts reached 200,000 mothers after funds were redirected to sending messages home from child care and preschools, thus reducing the cost per impression to $5.

5. Dissemination of Materials

Where significant or relevant, evaluation reports might include numbers of program materials distributed (e.g., brochures, flyers, key chains, bookmarks, booklets, and coupons).

6. Participation and Contributions From Outside Sources

Levels of participation and contributions from outside sources are significant and worthy of mention in evaluation reports. These may include numbers of and hours spent by volunteers, partners, and coalition members participating in the campaign, as well as amounts of cash and in-kind contributions received from foundations, media, and businesses.

7. Assessment of Implementation of Campaign Programs

Thorough social marketing plans include detailed action plans used for implementing tactics and activities. An audit of major activities planned and implemented (or not) may shed light on campaign outcomes. An assessment can include asking ourselves: Did we do everything we planned to do? Did we complete activities on time? Were expenditures more (or less) than anticipated and why?

Many of us expect campaign goals to be achieved even though we did not implement all planned activities or spend originally allocated funds in planned time frames.

HOW WILL IT BE MEASURED?

Our second step in developing an evaluation and monitoring plan is to identify methodologies and techniques that will be used to actually measure indicators established in our first step. Chapter 4 outlined typical methodologies available to the social marketer, a few of which are most typical for evaluation and monitoring measures. In general, audience surveys will be the primary technique used in measuring outcomes, given the focus on the actual impact on our target audience in terms of behavior, knowledge, and beliefs. On the other hand, records, contact reports, and project progress reports will be the primary sources of data for measuring processes.

Quantitative Techniques

When reliable data are key to evaluation (e.g., percentage increase in levels of physical activity), *quantitative studies* are often called for and are most commonly conducted using telephone surveys, mailed questionnaires, or in-person interviews. These may be proprietary or shared-cost studies, in which several organizations have questions for similar populations. They may even rely on established surveys such as the Behavioral Risk Factor Surveillance System (BRFSS), presented in Chapter 7.

Qualitative Techniques

When evaluation requirements are less stringent or more subjective in nature, *qualitative techniques* may be more appropriate, such as focus groups, informal interviews, and capturing anecdotal comments. Focus groups might be appropriate for exploring with child care providers which components of the immunization tracking kits were most and least useful and why. This information might then refocus efforts for the next kit reprint. Informal interviews might be used to understand why potential consumers walked away from the low-flow toilet display, even after reading accompanying materials and hearing testimonials from volunteers. Anecdotal comments regarding a television campaign might be captured on phone calls to a sexual-assault resource line.

Observation Research

In some cases, *observation research* is the most appropriate technique and can be used for evaluating behavior (e.g., wearing a life vest, washing hands before returning to work, or topping off gas tanks) or assessing skill levels (e.g., sorting garbage and placing it in proper containers or observing a WIC client finding his or her way around a farmers' market for the first time).

Control Groups

In combination with quantitative and qualitative instruments, ideal evaluation methodologies often use *control groups,* further ensuring that results can be closely tied to campaign and program efforts. A drug and alcohol prevention campaign might be implemented in high schools in one community but not in another similar community. Extra precautions can even be taken to ensure the similarity of the control groups by conducting surveys prior to the selection of the groups and then factoring in any important differences. Results on reported drug use in the control group of high schools are then compared with those in the other (similar) communities.

Records and Databases

Keeping records and using databases will be most appropriate for several indicators, particularly those measuring responses to campaign elements and dissemination of campaign materials. This may involve keeping accurate track of numbers of calls (e.g., to a Tobacco Quit Line), numbers of requests (e.g., for child care references), numbers of visits (e.g., to a teen clinic), numbers of people served (e.g., at car seat inspections), or numbers of items collected (e.g., needles exchanged). This effort may also involve working with suppliers and partners to provide similar information from their records and databases, such as numbers of coupons redeemed (e.g., for trigger locks), tangible objects sold (e.g., compost tumblers featured in the campaign), or requests received (e.g., organ donation applications processed).

WHEN WILL IT BE MEASURED?

Earlier, we distinguished between evaluation and monitoring, referring to final assessments of efforts as *evaluation* and ongoing measurements as *monitoring.* Timing, then, for measurement efforts is likely to happen as follows:

1. *Prior* to campaign launch, sometimes referred to as precampaign or baseline measures
2. *During* campaign implementation, thought of as tracking or ongoing measures, one time only or over a period of years
3. *Postcampaign* activities, referring to measurements taking place when all campaign elements are completed

Baseline measures are often critical when campaigns have specific goals for change and future campaign efforts and funders will rely on these measures for campaign assessment. These are then compared with postcampaign results, providing a *pre- and postevaluation* measure. Monitoring efforts during campaigns are often conducted to provide input for changes "midstream" and to track changes over time. Postcampaign (final) assessments are the most typical points in time for evaluation, especially when resources and tight time frames prohibit additional efforts. A few programs will use all points in time for evaluation, most common when significant key constituent groups or funders will require solid evidence of campaign outcomes.

ADDITIONAL CONSIDERATIONS AND CONCERNS

Clarify How the Information Will Be Used and Who Will Be Using It

Before finalizing the plan for evaluation and monitoring, discussions should take place regarding how the information will be used, who will be using it, and for what purpose. (This should be reminiscent of Andreasen's "backward approach" to research mentioned in Chapter 4, in which we develop our plan with answers to these questions in mind.)

1. Clarify with key stakeholders how the information will be used and for what purposes. Is it so that we can do a better job the next time? Is it to fulfill grant expectations? Is it to help secure funding in future years? Other reasons?
2. Prepare audiences for the idea that many factors will be considered when interpreting results. Whether goals are met or not, a review of contributing factors will include assessments of decisions and implementations related to each element of the plan, including the following:

> *Selection of target markets* (Were they the right ones?)
> *Goals* (Were they realistic?)
> *Product platforms* (Was the behavior clear and doable?)
> *Pricing* (Did perceived benefits outweigh perceived costs?)
> *Place* (Was access convenient?)
> *Promotional messages* (Were they on target?)

Promotional channels (Was it the right mix?)

Implementation activities (Did we do what we said we would do?)

3. Gain consensus (ahead of time) among key stakeholders on key elements of evaluation techniques, reporting format, audiences, and timing.

Consider Additional Advice From Experts

Weinreich gives several warnings and identifies numerous challenges social marketers may face in planning, conducting, and reporting on evaluations, including those in the following list:[4]

- Unrealistic expectations for campaign impact
- Limited resources (funds, staff time, or expertise)
- Reliance on a single method, potentially skewing results
- Using the wrong model for evaluation
- Asking the wrong questions
- Technical problems, making results invalid
- Resistance from program staff or participants, who may feel threatened by results
- Waiting until the program is over to start evaluation, making baseline measures impossible
- Failure to use evaluation results by "putting them on the shelf"

In 1999, the Centers for Disease Control and Prevention developed and published a framework for program evaluation in public health settings. This framework is composed of six steps, seen as starting points for tailoring an evaluation to a particular public health effort at a particular time. The steps are described as follows:

1. *Engage stakeholders,* those persons having an investment in what will be learned from an evaluation and what will be done with the knowledge.

2. *Describe the program,* the need it addresses, expected effects, planned activities, resource requirements, stage of development, context (setting and environmental influences with which the program operates), and logic model (sequence of events for bringing about change).

3. *Focus the evaluation design* on its purpose, users, uses, questions, methods, and agreements (roles and responsibilities among those who will execute the evaluation plan).

4. *Gather credible evidence,* information that will convey a well-rounded picture of the program and will be perceived by stakeholders as credible and relevant for answering their questions.

5. *Justify conclusions* by linking conclusions to the evidence gathered and judging against agreed-upon values or standards set by the stakeholders.

6. *Ensure use and share lessons learned* through deliberate efforts to ensure that the evaluation processes and study findings are used and distributed appropriately.

The second element of the framework is a set of 30 standards for assessing the quality of evaluation activities, organized into groups reflecting the evaluation's use, feasibility, propriety, and accuracy.[5]

CHAPTER SUMMARY

1. Key components of an evaluation and monitoring plan include answers to the following questions: What will be measured? How will it be measured? When will it be measured? How will results be used?

2. Key factors to be measured include *outcomes* (results) and *processes* (activities).

3. Potential indicators for *outcome measures* include changes in behavior, behavior intent, knowledge, and beliefs; campaign awareness; responses to campaign elements; and customer satisfaction.

4. Potential indicators for *process measures* include changes in policy and infrastructure, reach and frequency, media coverage, total impressions (on our target audiences), dissemination of materials, participation and contributions from outside sources, and assessment of program and campaign implementation.

5. Options for measuring these factors include *quantitative* techniques, such as telephone, mail, and in-person surveys; *qualitative techniques* using focus groups, informal interviews, and anecdotal comments; *observation research; control groups* in which results are controlled for one or more variables; and *records and databases,* both internal and external. In general, outcome measures will use target audience surveys, and process measures will rely more on records and databases.

6. Choices will be made relative to the timing of evaluations, considering opportunities to measure *prior* to campaign launch, *during* campaign implementation, and *postcampaign.*

7. Other considerations while developing this plan include gaining consensus on how results will be used and by whom and preparing key stakeholders for how results will be interpreted.

KEY TERMS AND CONCEPTS

Outcome measures
Process measures
Evaluation

Monitoring
Baseline measures
"Pre" and "post" measures

ISSUES FOR DISCUSSION

1. In the research highlight at the end of this chapter, it is reported that behavior changes were not maintained at the 6-month follow-up level. What factors would you consider in evaluating this result, and what recommendations would you make for future campaigns?

2. For a social marketing campaign promoting blood donation, identify and describe at least two potential outcome and four potential process measures.

3. For this same hypothetical campaign for blood donation, what are potential baseline, monitoring, and "post" measures?

RESEARCH HIGHLIGHT: EVALUATION PLANNING FOR TEAM NUTRITION PROGRAM

The Impact of Multiple Channel Delivery of Nutrition Messages on Student Knowledge, Motivation, and Behavior (Part II): Results From the Team Nutrition Pilot Study

R. Craig Lefebvre, Carol Olander, and Elyse Levine
Innovations in Social Marketing Conference,
Montreal, Canada, 1999

Results

Only three of the school districts identified any formal nutrition education in their curricula prior to the pilot. All four of the districts participating in the pilot outcome evaluation were successful in completing most of the required activities. On average, students received between 12 and 33 hours of classroom curricula and had the opportunity to participate in 4 to 10 school and community activities during each phase.

Team Nutrition Raised Students' Skill-Based Knowledge

The theoretical model underlying the Team Nutrition initiative suggests that changes in knowledge and motivation are necessary precursors to any changes in voluntary behaviors. From this standpoint, measuring changes in students' knowledge and motivation that may be attributable to their involvement in Team Nutrition was a necessary first step in evaluating the effectiveness of the initiative. If we observed significant changes in knowledge and motivation, then we would be more likely, though not assured, to detect behavior changes as well.

For the pilot evaluation, regression analyses were used to estimate the effects of participation in Team Nutrition on nutrition-related knowledge, skills, and motivation. The following table [14.1] shows that at the end of both phases, Team Nutrition had a significant positive impact on two of the three skill-based knowledge measures. This positive impact was maintained at the 6-month follow-up.

Team Nutrition Sparked Motivation to Eat Healthier

Students who participated in Team Nutrition likewise showed positive and statistically significant changes in their motivation to make healthy food choices when compared with students from comparison schools. These changes were seen for all three measures of motivation in Phase I, Phase II, and at follow-up. [See Table 14.2.] Although there is some variation in the regression coefficients across phases, none of these differences were significant.

Team Nutrition Encouraged Students to Eat Healthier

Finally, and perhaps most importantly, Team Nutrition students showed healthful changes in their self-reported and observed nutrition behaviors. At posttest, students in Team Nutrition were significantly more likely than students in the comparison schools to give more healthy responses when asked about their usual food choices, food choices made in the last 2 weeks, and the variety of foods they reported eating "yesterday." [See Table 14.3.] However, these differences were not maintained at the 6-month follow-up.

Cafeteria observations indicated modest but statistically significant increases in the variety of foods consumed and the amount of grains consumed when they participated in Team Nutrition. [See Table 14.4.] In most districts, consumption of vegetables, low-fat milk, and the overall diversity of tasted items also increased, although the participants' behavior often was not significantly different from the comparison group.

Multiple Channels Strengthened Team Nutrition Effects

Multivariate modeling was utilized to attempt to explain what factors influenced the students' self-reported changes in behaviors. Students' nutrition behavior was found to be significantly related to having high nutrition knowledge and motivation at baseline, being female, having a high household income, having a greater number of positive role models, and having a parent who attempted to influence their nutrition behavior.

Three different multivariate models of Team Nutrition impact on nutrition behavior were examined: a "uniform treatment" model that treated the Team Nutrition initiative as a single intervention, a "discrete components" model that looked at the effectiveness of each Team Nutrition intervention component, and a "level of exposure" model that treated

TABLE 14.1 Overall Team Nutrition Impact on Number of Correct Answers to Nutrition Skill Questions (Regression Coefficients)

Students' Ability to:	Immediate Impact by Phase		Impact at 6-Month Follow-Up
	Phase I	Phase II	Phase I
Identify healthier choice	0.31**	0.33**	0.16*
Apply food guide pyramid knowledge	0.68**	0.83**	0.49**
Apply balanced diet concept	0.02	0.09	0.10

NOTE: Regression coefficients reflect the Team Nutrition-related increase in the number of correct answers in comparison with the scores received in the pretest.
*$p < 0.05$; **$p < 0.01$.

TABLE 14.2 Overall Team Nutrition Impact on Nutrition Motivation (Regression Coefficients)

Students' Motivation	Immediate Impact by Phase		Impact at 6-Month Follow-Up
	Phase I	Phase II	Phase I
General attitudes	0.48**	0.50**	0.49**
Perceived consequences of more fruits, vegetables, and grains	0.28**	0.41**	0.53**
Cognitive rules for healthy choices	0.71**	0.64**	0.50**

NOTE: Regression coefficients reflect the Team Nutrition-related increase in the number of answers that indicate positive nutrition motivation, in comparison with the scores received in the pretest.
**$p < 0.01$.

TABLE 14.3 Overall Team Nutrition Impact on Self-Reported Nutrition Behavior (Regression Coefficients)

Students' Behavior	Immediate Impact by Phase		Impact at 6-Month Follow-Up
	Phase I	Phase II	Phase I
Usual food choices	0.53**	0.96**	0.11
Choices in last 2 weeks	0.43**	0.53**	0.17
Variety of food choices yesterday	0.38**	0.34**	0.07

NOTE: Regression coefficients reflect the Team Nutrition-related increase in the number of answers that indicate healthy eating behavior, in comparison with the scores received in the pretest.
**$p < 0.01$.

TABLE 14.4 Summary Effect Size Statistics for Team Nutrition Implementations

Food Group	Measure	Mean Effect Size[a]	Homogeneity Across Districts and Phases[b]
Grains	Number selected	0.13*	No
	Number tasted	0.20*	Yes
	Amount consumed	0.13*	Yes
Fruits	Number selected	−0.01	No
	Number tasted	0.18*	No
	Amount consumed	0.01	No
Vegetables	Number selected	0.04	No
	Number tasted	0.03	No
	Amount consumed	0.09	No
% Fat, Milk	% Fat, milk selected	0.01	Yes
	% Fat, milk tasted	0.04	Yes
Diversity	Group/day, tasted	0.22*	Yes
	Item/day, tasted	0.22*	Yes

a. Effect size was calculated by district and phase by dividing each raw unit impact estimate by the corresponding statistical index of student variability. Thus, mean effect size depends on both raw unit impact estimates and between-student variability. In cases when raw effect size is large relative to the variability index, effect size can be substantially larger than the raw unit impact estimate from which it was calculated. The mean effect size can exceed any raw unit impact estimate.

b. For this test of the hypothesis of no mean effect, difference across districts and phases, "No" means the hypothesis was rejected, so that effect means are not homogeneous; "Yes" means that this hypothesis was not rejected, so that effect means are homogeneous.

*$p < 0.05$.

the initiative as an accumulation of students' exposure to Team Nutrition messages through a variety of channels. The elements included in the analyses were: student exposure to a Team Nutrition public service announcement, receipt of the Team Nutrition curriculum, participation in cafeteria events, participation in community events, parent participation in nutrition events at school, and parent participation in nutrition events at home. All three models supported this general overall finding:

Team Nutrition had a small but statistically significant positive impact on students' eating behavior even after adjusting for other predictive factors.

Analysis of the three models demonstrated that the "level of exposure" was the strongest model and was also theoretically plausible within the SLT and social marketing frameworks. As shown in Table 14.5, the mean scores of students' self-reported nutrition behavior increased directly with the number of channels through which they reported participating

TABLE 14.5 Level of Exposure Model: Mean Scores for Students' Self-Reported Nutrition Behavior, by Number of Channels of Participation

Number of Channels of Participation	Usual Food Choices		Choices in Last 2 Weeks		Variety of Food Choices Yesterday	
	Phase I	Phase II	Phase I	Phase II	Phase I	Phase II
0	4.3	4.0	4.4	3.9	3.1	3.0
1	4.5	4.5	4.8	4.7	3.3	3.3
2	4.7	4.6	5.3	5.3	3.4	3.0
3	4.8	4.7	5.5	5.5	3.5	3.3
4	5.4	5.5	5.4	5.6	3.7	3.7
5	5.6	5.9	5.6	6.4	4.0	3.9
6	5.1	6.6	5.9	6.7	4.3	3.8

in the Team Nutrition initiative (all *p*-values for each nutrition behavior = 0.0001). This suggests that future Team Nutrition initiatives, as well as other nutrition education efforts, focus more clearly on maximizing the exposure of their target audiences to multiple channels of communication.

Conclusions

The results demonstrated that Team Nutrition did lead to modest but significant changes in self-reported nutrition knowledge, motivation, and behavior. Especially when examining behavior change, this pilot evaluation utilized several different sources of data, including student self-reports, parental reports (not shown), and observed behavior in the school cafeteria. Each methodology has its strengths and limitations, and each method shed a different perspective on whether students involved in the Team Nutrition initiative changed their behavior. Yet, all three methods converged in demonstrating some behavior change.

At the 6-month follow-up, changes were maintained for knowledge and motivation, but not for behavior. This finding underscores that nutrition education needs to be a sustained process over time if it is to result in long-term behavioral change—though this notion itself requires further empirical study.

It was found that exposure to multiple Team Nutrition components, rather than a particular one, was most predictive of behavior change. This finding is the first empirical evidence we are aware of that supports the social marketing maxim of utilizing multiple distribution channels in message delivery. Indeed, the degree of self-reported behavior change was directly related to the number of channels students reported being exposed to during implementation. This finding has potentially significant implications for the development and design of social marketing programs for other audiences and content.

The self-reported changes in nutrition knowledge, motivation, and behavior among students in Team Nutrition were comparable, and in some instances better, than what one would expect from the available research in this area (cf., Contento et al., 1995; Domel et al., 1994; Perry et al.,1990). While it is not possible to definitively attribute these findings to any one aspect of Team Nutrition, as noted above, the multiple channel strategy of Team Nutrition may be the explanation.

The Team Nutrition intervention also incorporated new strategies and tactics that future research efforts will need to examine to enhance their relative effectiveness. These included linkages with food and nutrition resources in the community to develop and implement nutrition education activities in the schools and at community sites, as well as active media outreach to promote child nutrition generally and Team Nutrition activities occurring in the schools. Finally, the use of existing district staff to coordinate and manage the Team Nutrition effort offers a special degree of support and impetus for nutrition education activities in our schools.

References

Bandura, A. (1986). *Social Foundations of Thought and Action: A Social Cognitive Theory.* Englewood Cliffs, NJ: Prentice Hall.

Contento, I., Balch, G. I., Bronner, Y. L., Lytle, L. A., Maloney, S. K., White, S. L., Olson, C. M., & Swadener, S. S. (1995). The effectiveness of nutrition education and implications for nutrition education policy, programs, and research: A review of research. *Journal of Nutrition Education, 27*(6), 277-422.

Domel, S. B., Baranowski, T., Davis, H., Leonard, S. B., Riley, P., & Baranowski, J. (1994). Fruit and vegetable food frequencies by fourth and fifth grade students: Validity and reliability. *Journal of the American College of Nutrition, 13*(1), 33-39.

Lefebvre, R. C., & Flora, J. A. (1988). Social marketing and public health intervention. *Health Education Quarterly, 15,* 299-315.

Perry, C. L., Stone, E. G., Parcel, G. S., Ellison, R. C., Nader, P. R., Webber, L. S., & Luepker, R. V. (1990). School-based cardiovascular health promotion: The Child and Adolescent Trial for Cardiovascular Health (CATCH).*Journal of School Health, 60*(8), 406-413.

Notes

1. Kotler, P. (1999). *Kotler on Marketing: How to Create, Win, and Dominate Markets* (p. 185). New York: Free Press
2. Andreasen, A. R. (1995). *Marketing Social Change: Changing Behavior to Promote Health, Social Development, and the Environment* (p. 127). San Francisco: Jossey-Bass.
3. Kotler, P., & Roberto, E. L. (1989). *Social Marketing: Strategies for Changing Public Behavior* (pp. 354-355) New York: Free Press.
4. Weinreich, N. K. (1999). *Hands-On Social Marketing: A Step-by-Step Guide* (pp. 206-208). Thousand Oaks, CA: Sage.
5. Framework for Program Evaluation in Public Health (September 17, 1999). Centers for Disease Control and Prevention. Retrieved from CDC Web site 4/2/2001 from http://www.cdc.gov/epo/mmwr/preview/mmwrhtml/rr4811a1.htm

KEY CHAPTER QUESTIONS

1. How are social marketing budgets determined?

2. Where can social marketers turn for funding their plans?

3. What can be done to persuade potential funders?

CHAPTER 15

Establishing Budgets and Finding Funding Sources

Alone we can do so little; together we can do so much.

—Helen Keller

MARKETING HIGHLIGHT: SUICIDE PREVENTION

This case is an example of program funding secured, in part, by persuasive cost/benefit analysis, and resources that were leveraged through community partnerships and volunteers.

Youth Suicide Prevention: A Community-Based Approach

Susan H. Eastgard, M.S.W.

President, American Association of Suicidology

Background

For many people, suicide is a difficult subject to think about. It is burdened with judgment, shame, and misinformation. Some view it as wrong and sinful; some see it as a selfish act. Others can't imagine anyone feeling so depressed that death would be a relief from the pain of living. But for many youth, suicide is seen as the only way out. In 1998, in the United States, 4,459 young people (aged 5-24) killed themselves: an average of one suicide every 2 hours![1]

In addition to the young people who complete suicide each year, a quarter of all high school youth report having seriously considered suicide, and 1 out of 10 reports having attempted suicide in the previous year. Boys are at higher risk of completing suicide, whereas girls are more likely to engage in nonfatal suicidal behaviors. Gay, lesbian, bisexual, and transgender youth are at higher risk of suicide, along with academic "high achievers," homeless youth, and youth struggling with depression, alcohol and other drug use, and/or school problems.

Target Audience Profile

Most suicidal youth don't really want to die—they just want their pain to end. The key to prevention is recognizing the warning signs and knowing what to do to help. There are several signs to watch for, including the following:

- ▶ A depressed or "down" mood

- ▶ Previous suicidal behavior

- ▶ Increased alcohol and substance use

- ▶ Loss of interest in once-pleasurable activities

- ▶ Isolation

- ▶ Feeling hopeless

- ▶ Sleep and eating changes

- ▶ Talking about suicide or making a plan

- ▶ A preoccupation with death

Three other key risk factors increase the likelihood of suicide attempts by young people:

▶ Readily accessible firearms (the number one way in which youth complete suicide)

▶ Impulsiveness and taking unnecessary risks

▶ Lack of connection to family and friends (no one to talk to)

Young people contemplate suicide for many reasons, which can generally be clustered into four categories:

▶ *Individual* (e.g., increased feelings of depression, hopelessness, and anxiety, increased use of drugs and alcohol, concerns or questions about one's sexual orientation)

▶ *School* (e.g., failing grades, suspension, academic pressures)

▶ *Home* (e.g., family conflicts/fights, death/divorce, abuse)

▶ *Relationship* (e.g., breakup with a girlfriend or boyfriend, pregnancy)

Objectives

There are three simple and helpful ways to intervene with a suicidal youth:

1. *Show you care*—It is important to communicate to at-risk youth that you care about them; talk about your feelings, and ask about theirs. Listen carefully to their worries, problems, and concerns. Avoid giving advice, changing the subject, or dismissing their feelings.

2. *Ask the question*—don't hesitate to raise the subject of suicide. Be direct in a caring, non-confrontational way. Calmly, and without judgment, ask whether he or she is thinking about suicide.

3. *Get help*—don't leave the youth alone. Suggest calling a crisis line together or offer to go with him or her to get help. Reassure the youth that you are willing to help.

Strategies

Across the United States, educators are joining together with religious leaders, community advocates, and professionals from mental health, substance abuse, juvenile justice, and medical services to implement programs that raise awareness about the issue of youth suicide and teach assessment and intervention skills. We have historically prioritized suicide prevention education for the mental health professional, school counselor, or psychologist, but in reality, a coach, math teacher, pediatrician, church group leader, or neighbor may be the person to whom the youth initially confides feelings of despair and hopelessness. Parents also need to be educated to recognize the signs of depression and suicide in children and adolescents and to understand the need for appropriate diagnosis and treatment. And finally, students need to be taught how to identify whether their friends are at-risk of suicide. Teaching youth about suicide does not increase suicidal behaviors but instead, provides the knowledge and skills to intervene and refer for help.

Funding

While the costs for treating suicidal youth are astronomically high (an estimated $945,000,000[2] was spent on medical costs for hospitalized youth suicide attempters in the United States in 1996 alone!) money for prevention programs remains limited. (It should be said that the costs to treat suicide attempters, though dramatic, fail to reflect the "costs" in terms of human anguish suffered by families, friends, schools, and communities.) Budgets will vary depending on the size of the target audience, the intervention strategies, and the planned outcomes.

Some programs are funded through state dollars and administered through state departments of health and/or mental health. Other programs secure funding through private foundations/corporations (e.g., Ronald McDonald House Charities and United Way). Funding is occasionally available through grants from the federal government. One of the goals of the Surgeon General's recently released *National Strategy for Suicide Prevention* is to develop broad-based support for suicide prevention through public-private partnerships.

Evaluation

Every suicide prevention program needs to include evaluation activities that help to determine the efficacy of the services. Given the complexity of the issue (and the cost of doing research) it may be impossible to determine whether a program is responsible for a decrease or increase in mortality and morbidity rates, but a program evaluation can answer questions related to changes in attitudes, skills, and knowledge. For example, evaluation might focus on one of the following:

▶ Does training increase the likelihood that a teacher can accurately assess and intervene with suicidal youth?

▶ Are there more referrals to the school counselor as a result of a curriculum focused on enhancing help-seeking behaviors?

▶ Do parents who have attended an educational presentation feel more comfortable asking young people directly about suicide?

▶ Can more youth identify the warning signs for suicide after the introduction of a curriculum than before?

In summary, suicide is a public health problem that we can do something about. Prevention programs can reduce the barriers to accessing crisis resources; they can confront the myths that discourage talking about suicide; they can empower youth and adults to intervene with those who are despairing; and they can make a difference in the staggering statistics of youth suicide. States, community groups, and individuals must be creative when identifying the financial resources to implement programs, but without increased public awareness and training, more young people will die.

NOTE: Susan Eastgard is also Director of the Youth Suicide Prevention Program in Washington State.

CHAPTER OVERVIEW

Step seven, the budgeting process, is "where the rubber hits the road." We are now ready to identify price tags for possible strategies and plans. Our planning model is spiral in nature, and we may find that total costs for preliminary strategies exceed our current or projected budget. We may need to consider other options.

Our outline of the budgeting and funding process includes several steps:

1. Determine costs associated with implementing strategies identified in Step 5 (Product, Price, Place, and Promotion Strategies) and Step 6 (Evaluation Measures).
2. Review current funding and, if needed, identify potential additional resources.
3. If appropriate, pursue additional sources for funding.
4. If indicated, adjust goals and strategies to align with actual budgets.

These discussions address common budgeting and funding questions and challenges for the social marketer:

*   What are my options if the costs for the campaign I've just planned exceed currently available funds?

*   Where do I look for potential additional funding and resources?

*   How do I appeal to funders for additional funds?

DETERMINING BUDGETS

In the commercial as well as nonprofit and public sectors, several approaches are often cited as possibilities to consider for establishing marketing budgets.[3] The following three have the most relevance for social marketing:

The *affordable method*. Budgets are based on what the organization has available in the yearly budget or on what has been spent in prior years. For example, a county health department's budget for teen pregnancy prevention might be determined by state funds allocated every 2 years for the issue, and a local blood bank's marketing budget might be established each year as a part of the organizational budgeting process.

The *competitive-parity method*. In the social marketing situation, budgets are set or considered on the basis of what others have spent for similar efforts. For example, a litter campaign budget might be established on the basis of a review of media expenses from other states that have been successful at reducing litter using mass media campaigns.

The *objective-and-task method*. Budgets are established by (1) reviewing specific objectives, (2) identifying the tasks that must be performed to achieve these objectives, and (3) estimating the costs associated with performing these tasks. The total is the preliminary budget.[4] For example, the budget for a utility's marketing effort for recycling might be based on estimated costs, including: *staffing* a new telephone service center for questions on what can be recycled; *plaques* for recognizing multifamily unit dwellings with outstanding efforts; *stickers* on containers recognizing homeowner participation; and *promotional strategies* including television ads, radio spots, statement stuffers, and flyers. These total costs are then considered in light of any projections in increased revenues and decreased costs for the utility.

The most logical of these approaches, and one consistent with our planning process, is the objective-and-task method. Desired objectives and goals were established in Step 3. Strategies to achieve these objectives and goals were identified and delineated in Step 5. Research efforts for evaluation and tracking were established in Step 6. At this point in the planning process, these tasks will be reviewed, and those with cost implications will be included in the preliminary budget. The aim is to develop a *preliminary total* for costs associated with implementing the proposed plan. In the final section of this chapter, we discuss options to consider when this preliminary budget exceeds currently available funds.

It should be noted that in a case in which preliminary budget totals actually meet currently available funds or are approved as presented, the budgeting process is not yet complete. It is still important to conduct a final review of budget items to ensure (a) their significance to campaign objectives, (b) that proposed costs are competitive, and (c) that proposed activities are cost-effective.

Costs for implementing the marketing plan may be associated with any number of tasks identified in the marketing mix (product, price, place, and promotion), as well as in evaluation and tracking efforts. More detailed descriptions of typical costs follow. A brief case is included to further illustrate the nature of tasks with budget implications. In this example, a hospital has developed a draft marketing plan to decrease the number of employees commuting to work in single-occupant vehicles. The campaign *objective* is to influence employees to use public transportation, car pools, vanpools, or walk or bike to work, with a *goal* to decrease the number of single-occupant vehicles on campus by 10% (100 vehicles) over a 12-month period.

Product-related costs are most often associated with developing and producing any accompanying tangible objects and developing and/or enhancing associated services needed to support the behavior change. The organization should identify all major cost implications for the marketer's recommendations.

Example: Product-related costs considerations for the hospital may include the need to lease additional vans from the county's transit system, install new bike racks, and construct several additional showers for employee use if marketing goals are met. Incremental service charges might include costs for temporary personnel to provide rideshare-matching or to build and maintain a special on-line software program for ridesharing.

Price-related costs most often include those associated with any incentives, recognition programs, and rewards. In some cases, it includes revenue associated with tangible objects and services.

Example: Price implications in this case may be for incentives including cash incentives for carpooling, reduced rates for parking spots close to the building, costs for occasional free taxi rides home when staff need to stay late, and providing free bus passes.

Place-related costs are related to providing new or enhanced access or delivery channels, such as telephone centers, online purchasing, extended hours, and new or improved locations. There may also be costs related to distribution of any tangible objects associated with the program.

Example: In our example, there may be costs for developing additional parking spots for car pools close to the main entrance of the hospital or for staffing a booth outside the cafeteria for distributing incentives and actual rideshare sign-up.

Promotion-related costs are those associated with costs for developing, producing, and disseminating communications.

Example: Promotional-related costs in this case might include costs for developing and producing fact sheets on benefits, posters, special brochures, and transportation fairs.

Evaluation-related costs include estimated costs for any planned measurement and tracking surveys.

Example: In this case, there might be costs for conducting a baseline and follow-up survey that measures employee awareness of financial incentives and rideshare-matching programs.

FINDING FUNDING SOURCES

Major sources for additional funding outside the organization include foundations, associations, corporations, advertising agencies, media coalitions, and governmental agencies. This section briefly describes each of these, and the next discusses how to appeal to these funding sources.

Foundation Grants and Contributions

There are more than 50,000 active independent corporate, community, and grant-making foundations operating in the United States, with missions to contribute to many of the same social issues and causes addressed by social marketing efforts.[5] Kotler and Andreasen identify four major relevant groups: *family foundations,* in which funds are derived from members of a single family (e.g., Bill and Melinda Gates Foundation); *general foundations,* usually run by a professional staff awarding grants in many different fields of interest (e.g., the Ford Foundation); *corporate foundations,* whose assets are derived primarily from the contributions of a for-profit business (e.g., Bank of America Foundation); and *community foundations,* set up to receive and manage contributions from a variety of sources in a local community, making grants for charitable purposes in a specific community or region.[6]

Example: The "I Am Your Child Foundation"(IAYC) received a $1 million gift from the Bill and Melinda Gates Foundation in November 2000 to support a *national public awareness and engagement campaign to make early childhood development a top priority in the United States.* Working with renowned early-childhood-development leaders, key policymakers, and media partners, IAYC provides parents, teachers, health professionals, and other caregivers with information, technical assistance, and support; their goal is to ensure that every child gets a healthy start in life and enters school ready to learn. With this support, IAYC will expand its national program of dissemination and will form alliances with several states to make research-based information available to new parents on a voluntary basis. The state campaigns will have opportunities to use IAYC's educational video series and accompanying print materials as a centerpiece.[7]

Relative to behavior change, a similar campaign in Washington State was launched in July of 2000 and included a brochure for parents on *Ten Simple Ways to Encourage a Child's Ability to Learn.* Upbeat and easy to understand, the brochure offers practical advice on how to help a young child feel safe, secure, and confident so that he or she is able to embrace learning with enthusiasm. (See Figure 15.1.)

Corporate Partnerships and Contributions

Although contributions are a minor activity for corporations in comparison with foundations, they represent an important opportunity for social marketing efforts. Corporate giving with the most relevance for social marketers falls into one of

Ten Simple Ways
to Encourage a Child's
Ability to Learn

Brought to you by the Washington State Governor's Commission on Early Learning, I Am Your Child,
Washington Early Learning Foundation, and Children's Hospital and Regional Medical Center.

Figure 15.1. Brochure Adopted From I Am Your Child (IAYC) for Washington State's Campaign

three major categories: *cause-related marketing, in-kind contributions,* and *cash contributions.*

Cause-Related Marketing (CRM) is an increasingly popular strategy with a "win-win-win" proposition. In the typical scenario, a percentage of sales of a company's product is devoted to a nonprofit organization (e.g., at one time, a percentage of sales of Evian bottled water was contributed to the World Wildlife Fund). The strategy is based on the premise that buyers care about the civic virtue and caring nature of companies. When market offerings are similar, buyers have been shown to patronize the firms with the better civic reputations. Carefully chosen and developed programs help a *company* achieve strategic marketing objectives (e.g., sell more product or penetrate new markets) and demonstrate social responsibility, with an aim of moving beyond rational and emotional branding to "spiritual" branding. CRM raises funds and increases exposure for a *social issue or cause* and gives consumers an opportunity to be involved in improving the quality of life.[8] Well-known partnerships include programs such as American Express and Charge Against Hunger, Avon and Breast Cancer, and Nike and The Reuse A Shoe program illustrated in Figure 15.2. Local programs promoting community issues, such as the brewery illustrated in Figure 15.3, are also increasingly common. National surveys indicate that the majority of consumers would be influenced to buy, or even switch and pay more for brands, when the product supports a cause, especially when product features and quality are equal. However, if the promotion rings hollow, customers may be cynical; if the charitable contribution doesn't amount to much or the promotion doesn't run long enough, customers may be skeptical; if the company chooses a cause of less interest to their customers, it will gain little; and if the company chooses a cause and other causes feel miffed, it may lose out.

In-kind contributions can include providing services (e.g., producing a video), allowing use of equipment (e.g., printers), offering supplies (e.g., paper), or contributing tangible resources, such as staff time for consulting, visibility for materials, and distribution of tangible objects at retail locations. Providing space for messages and materials is a valuable contribution for most social marketing efforts, as seen in the example in Figure 15.4, in which a nutritional message is a placed in a prominent location on a snack food box.

Cash contributions from corporations (as opposed to their foundations) are awarded for a variety of purposes, including sponsorship mentions in communications, potential for building traffic at retail or Internet sites, and opportunities for visibility with key constituent groups.

Example: Child Care Resources is a nonprofit organization in Washington State providing information and referral assistance to families seeking child care,

Figure 15.2. A Win-Win-Win for Kids, Customers Who Care, and NIKE

Figure 15.3. One Strategy to Distinguish a Brand

training and assistance for child care providers, and consulting and advocacy for quality child care. In the mid-1990s, SAFECO, an insurance company based in Seattle, provided a generous grant to Child Care Resources to strengthen the ability of child care providers to promote and track immunizations of children in their care. Formative research with child care providers provided input for developing training and a kit of materials that included immunization tracking forms, posters, flyers, stickers, door hangers, and brochures for parents, with refrigerator magnets and immunization schedules. (See Figure 15.5.) In partnership with numerous local and state health agencies, Child Care Resources developed and disseminated more than 3,000 kits to child care providers in the first year of the grant. An evaluation survey among approximately 300 of the providers indicated that 94% felt the materials helped them encourage parents to keep their children's immunizations up-to-date. The grant was extended for a second year, and trainings and kit distribution were taken statewide under the direction of the Washington State Child Care Resource and Referral Network.

Advertising and Media Partnerships

Advertising agencies often provide pro bono services to support social causes with contributions, ranging from consulting on media buying and creative strategies to actually developing and producing advertising campaigns. Several factors motivate their choices, including opportunities to contribute to issues in the community, give their junior staff more experience, have more freedom to "call the shots" in developing creative strategies, and make new and important business contacts.[9]

The Ad Council, formed in 1942 as the War Ad Council to support efforts related to World War II, has played a significant role in producing, distributing, promoting, and evaluating public service communication programs. Familiar campaigns include Smokey Bear's "Only You Can Prevent Forest Fires," "Friends Don't Let Friends Drive Drunk," and McGruff the Crime Dog's "Take a Bite Out of Crime." After the tragic events in the United States on September 11th, 2001, the council developed a variety of campaigns; one features First Lady Laura Bush encouraging parents to talk to kids. Each year, the council

The Food Guide Pyramid helps you put sound nutritional guidelines to work. Use it as a guide for the quantity and type of foods to eat each day.

3 Melba Toasts or 5 Melba Snacks are a deliciously crunchy way to fulfill ONE serving from the Bread, Cereal, Rice & Pasta Group.

Keep in a cool, dry place.

©1997 OLD LONDON® is a registered trademark of Old London Foods, Inc.

Figure 15.4. Incorporating the Food Pyramid on Commercial Packaging

Figure 15.5. Door Hanger Used at Child Care Centers to Remind Parents to Check Immunization Status

supports approximately 40 campaigns to enhance health, safety, community involvement, strengthening families, and protecting the environment, chosen from several hundred requests from nonprofit organizations and public sector agencies. Factors used for selection include criteria that the campaign is noncommercial, nondenominational, and nonpolitical in nature. It also needs to be perceived as an important issue and one that is national in scope. When a proposal is selected, the council then organizes hundreds of professional volunteers from top advertising agencies, corporations, and the media to contribute to the campaign.[10]

Television and radio stations are often approached to provide free or discounted ("two for one") airtime for campaigns with good causes. Even more valuable, they may also be interested in having their sales force find corporate sponsors for campaigns, who then pay for media placement. In this win-win-win situation, the social marketing campaign gets increased frequency and guaranteed placement of ads on programs that appeal to their target audience; the local corporations get to "do good" and "look good" in the community; and the television or radio stations get paid, versus public service advertising.

Example: King County Sexual Assault Resource Center is a nonprofit organization that provides a variety of services to victims of sexual assault, including a 24-hour resource and information line. Their challenge, experienced by other similar agencies as well, is to influence rape victims to call, with national studies indicating that more than half of rape victims never tell anyone. An agency donor and supporter persuaded a local advertising agency, FCB Worldwide, to develop print ads (pro bono) to encourage victims to call, using the tag line "Most people don't know what to say. We do." They were also able to work with a major television station in the area with a similar demographic audience to develop a high-quality television spot. The television station then promoted sponsorship packages to several major corporations in the community, ensuring a guaranteed broadcast schedule.[11]

Coalitions and Other Partnerships

Many social marketing campaigns have been successful, at least in part, due to the resources and assistance gained from participating in coalitions and other similar partnerships. Coalition members may be able to pool resources to implement larger-scale campaigns. Networks of individual coalition members can provide invaluable distribution channels for campaign programs and materials (e.g., the local department of license offices airs a traffic safety video in the lobby, where a captive audience awaits their numbers to be called).

Example: In the late 1990s, the Academy for Educational Development (AED), with funding and a cooperative agreement with the Environmental Protection Agency Office of Mobile Sources, undertook a challenge to get America's youth involved in the reduction of vehicle miles traveled (VMT). The premise was that by reducing VMT, kids nationwide could do something proactive to help improve air quality in their communities. Thus, "Let Kids Lead" was created. Three sites across the nation—Boston, Kansas City, and Tampa—were pilot sites for the program. Each had the goal of creating a replicable and sustainable program for involving youth and their families in reducing VMT. In addition to the students, partners in these communities included local governmental agencies, coalitions, councils, commissions, school district administrators, teachers, professional associations, corporations, and concerned citizens. Student activities ranged from conducting surveys, developing catalogues, organizing marches, and making presentations at public meetings to sustainable and ongoing programs, including forming clubs and participating in curriculum development and adaptation. In terms of concrete results, in Boston, the kids got buses rerouted; in Tampa, the American Lung Association fostered clubs for kids working on pollu-

Figure 15.6. Theme Used to Encourage Youth Involvement in Community Issues

tion; and in Kansas City, kids mapped new routes for bikes and walking trails. Going forward, training and program materials have been developed by AED to support other communities nationwide to "let the kids lead."[12] (See Figure 15.6.)

Government Grants and Appropriations

Federal, state, and local government agencies are common sources of funds and grants for social marketing efforts. Potential sources, especially for nonprofit organizations, include state and local departments of health, human services, transportation, ecology, traffic safety, natural resources, fish and wildlife, parks and recreation, and public utilities.

Example: Efforts to secure $500,000 in state funds for a youth suicide prevention program in Washington State were supported by presentation of cost/benefit statistics. It is estimated that the state of Washington spent $22,000,000 in costs for completed youth suicides and medically treated suicide attempts by youth in 1996. These costs include emergency transport, medical, hospital, rehabilitation, pharmaceuticals, and related treatment costs, as well as funeral/coroner expenses for fatalities and administrative costs for processing medical payments to providers. These costs do not include mental health care, police, fire, and victim services. Nor do they include work losses by family and friends who care for depressed and suicidal children.

APPEALING TO FUNDERS

In general, the same principles we have outlined for influencing target audiences are applicable for influencing potential funders. They could be viewed, simply, as another type of target audience. A customer orientation is called for:

1. We begin by identifying and prioritizing segments (potential funders) who represent the greatest opportunities for funding our program. Several criteria may guide this prioritization, with a special focus on organizations with which we have existing contacts and relationships, common areas of focus and concern, and similar target audiences, publics, or constituent groups.
2. We formulate clear, specific potential requests.
3. We spend time deepening our understanding of funders' wants, needs, and perspectives. What are potential benefits and concerns with our proposal? Who is the competition, and what advantages and disadvantages do we have?
4. On the basis of this information, we refine and finalize our specific request. Our preliminary inquiries may reveal, for example, that a large request (risking the "door in your face") may in fact make it more likely that we receive funding for a smaller one.
5. We develop a strategy using all elements of the marketing mix, a proposal that (a) articulates clear value for the funder (what's in it for them) and benefits to the cause (target audiences), (b) addresses concerns and barriers, (c) ensures a smooth and responsible administrative process, and (d) provides assurance of measurable outcomes.

Several tips from the "pros" are useful guidelines when developing and presenting proposals:

- Establish common areas of focus and interest.

- Demonstrate that you've done your homework. Share the formative research that has guided the decision-making process and any pretesting that ensures that the strategy is on target.

- Make the campaign as real as possible, sharing the detailed plan and bringing to life all elements of the marketing mix.

- Emphasize the desired outcomes and how they will be measured and reported. Relate these to planned budgets, summarizing expected and measurable returns on their investments (e.g., the number of high school students who will attend mock drunk-driving demonstrations made possible by the sponsor).

- If applicable, offer options for participation and contribution, ranging from cash contributions to in-kind services to considerations for any CRM opportunities.

- Carefully follow any published guidelines for submitting requests and applications.

- Nonprofit organizations should be prepared to share their "Sources and Uses of Funds Statement." Funders will be interested in knowing how much of donated funds are used for administration and overhead, versus direct project funding

It is helpful to know that corporations evaluating an opportunity for a CRM effort are likely to consider the following questions:

1. Is there a natural bond between the cause and the company?
2. Is it an issue that our target markets care about?
3. Is there an opportunity for staff to be involved?
4. Can we own or at least dominate the position of corporate partner?
5. Can we stick with the program for at least 2 to 3 years?
6. Is there synergy with our current distribution channels?
7. Does it provide enhanced media opportunities?
8. Can we develop an optimal donation model that provides sales incentives at an economically feasible per-unit contribution?
9. Will we be able to absolutely measure our return on investment?

IMPLICATIONS TO THE DRAFT PLAN

What happens if funding levels are still inadequate to implement the desired plan? In this familiar scenario, planners will consider the following options to make ends meet:

Develop Campaign Phases: Spread costs out over a longer period of time, allowing for more time to raise funds or to use future budget allocations. Options for phasing could include targeting only one or a few target markets the first year; launching the campaign in fewer geographic markets; focusing on only one or a few communication objectives (e.g., using the first year for awareness-building or preparing the way for subsequent years of behavior change messages); or implementing some strategies the first year and others in subsequent years (e.g., waiting until the second year to build the demonstration garden using recyclable materials).

Strategically Reduce Costs: Options might include *eliminating strategies and tactics* with questionable potential impact; *choosing less expensive options* for non-critical executional strategies (e.g., using black and white instead of four colors for brochures or lower-grade paper); and where feasible, *bringing some of the tasks in-house* (e.g., the development and dissemination of news releases and organizing special events).

Adjust Goals: Perhaps the most important consideration is the potential need to return to Step 3 and adjust our goals. Clearly, in situations where we have chosen to spread campaign costs over a longer period of time, goals will need to be changed to reflect new time frames. In other situations where time frames cannot be adjusted and additional funding sources have been explored, we may need to eliminate one or more key strategies (e.g., television may not be an option, even though it was identified as key to reach and frequency objectives). In this scenario, we will then need to adjust the goal (e.g., reach 50% of the target audience instead of 75% that television was anticipated to support). Planners are encouraged to return to their managers, colleagues, and team members with frank discussions for the need to adjust preliminary goals so that "promises" are honest and realistic.

CHAPTER SUMMARY

1. Preliminary budgets are determined by using the *objective-and-task method*, in which budgets are established by (1) reviewing specific objectives, (2) identifying the tasks that must be performed to achieve these objectives, and (3) estimating the costs associated with performing these tasks. The sum of these costs is the preliminary budget.[13]

2. In cases in which proposed budgets are funded, it is still important to review budget items to ensure that they are critical to campaign success, as well as being competitive and cost-effective solutions.

3. Desired objectives and goals were established in Step 3. Strategies to achieve these objectives and goals were identified and delineated in Step 5. Research efforts for evaluation and tracking were established in Step 6. At this point in the planning process, these tasks will be reviewed, and those with cost implications will be included in the preliminary budget.

4. When preliminary budgets exceed current funding, several major sources for additional funds include foundations, associations, corporations, advertising agencies, media coalitions, and governmental agencies.

5. In general, the same principles we have outlined for influencing target audiences are applicable for influencing potential funders. They could be viewed, simply, as another type of target audience and call for a customer orientation.

6. If proposed budgets still exceed funding sources even after exploring additional funding sources, the social marketer should consider developing campaign phases, strategically reducing costs, and/or adjusting campaign goals established in Step 3.

KEY TERMS AND CONCEPTS

Cause-related marketing (CRM)
In-kind contributions
Cash contributions
Coalitions
Government grants and
   appropriations

Objective-and-task
  method
Advertising and media
  partnerships
Campaign phases
Price tags

Affordable method
Competitive-parity method
Promotion-related costs
Foundation grants and
    contributions

Product-related costs
Price-related costs
Place-related costs
Corporate partnerships
    and contributions

ISSUES FOR DISCUSSION

1. Assume that you are a state senator serving on a legislative committee reviewing a request for $500,000 for a 2-year statewide youth suicide prevention program. The request and presentation has included information on current suicide rates and planned strategies (uses of the funds). What questions do you have for the program manager?

2. Assume that your preliminary budget determined using the objective-and-task method for a nutrition education campaign totals $75,000 for the next calendar year. Your administration responds that $25,000 is the maximum amount that is currently available. What are four different options available to you? Describe each one.

3. For a campaign to reduce binge drinking among 18- to 24-year-olds in your state, what are four potential funding sources you might explore for a 3-year campaign plan?

RESEARCH HIGHLIGHT: BASELINE AND TRACKING SURVEY FOR DROWNING PREVENTION

This research highlight features a case in which baseline, tracking, and post-campaign surveys were used to measure the impact of campaign efforts. It is also an appropriate case for this chapter, featuring partnerships, coalitions, and corporate sponsors.

Stay on Top of It Drowning Prevention Campaign: An Evaluation of a Three-Year Effort

Elizabeth Bennett, MPH, CHES

Background and Situation

In 1992, drowning was the second leading cause of injury death for children under 15 years of age in the United States. From 1990 through 1994, there were 5,344 drownings among children in the United States in this age group.[14]

In King County and Washington State, swimming pools were the leading sites of drowning among children less than 5 years old. Natural bodies of water (lakes, rivers, and ponds) were the second most common location and bathtubs the third most common. For older children, natural bodies of water were the most common sites for drowning. Swimming, wading, inner tubing, and playing on docks or on lake and river edges were the leading activities that preceded drowning.[15]

A countywide campaign to increase life vest use was developed to address drowning in a variety of sites among children and teens.

As a means of identifying current behaviors relative to drowning prevention and to measure effectiveness of the program, a research evaluation plan was incorporated into the campaign. Evaluation would determine campaign awareness, change in life vest use and ownership, and predictors of life vest use.

Target Audience and Objectives

The drowning prevention campaign, called "Stay on Top of It," was established by Children's Hospital and Regional Medical Center in March 1992 and designed to run through three summers in Seattle and King County, Washington.[16] The primary target was children up to 9 years old and second, up to 14 years old. Messages and tactics depended on the child's age, water site, and activity. For example, life vest use in boats was recommended for all children, use in pools was targeted toward younger children.

The primary objective was to increase life vest use among 1- to 14-year-old children on boats, docks, at beaches, and swimming pools.

Strategies

Structure Campaign and Use Successful Models

A social marketing framework provided the structure for the selection of target groups, implementation planning and tracking, use of multimedia channels, and evaluation.[17] (See Table 15.1.) Program elements were also guided by survey results, drowning prevention literature, and the Seattle bicycle helmet campaign.[18] The bike helmet campaign demonstrated effectiveness of a comprehensive approach that incorporated media, publicity, public education, a coalition, and a discount coupon. These elements were replicated in the Stay on Top of It campaign. The bulk of the campaign was implemented from April to August each year.

TABLE 15.1 Drowning Prevention Campaign Elements, King County, Washington, 1992-1994

Media and Publicity	1992	1993	1994
Press conference	X	X	
Television news and public service	X	X	X
Newspaper news and public service	X	X	X
Radio news and public service	X	X	X
Bus advertisement	X	X	
Banners at water activity sites	X	X	X
Advertisements on grocery bags	X	X	
Hotline number to order materials	X	X	X
Printed Education Materials			
Parent booklet and fact sheets	X	X	X
Activity booklet for children		X	X
Ten sports hero trading cards		X	X
Hospital publications	X	X	X
Day camp activity booklet			X
Tip sheet for boaters			X
Targeted mailings	X	X	X
Promotions/Special Events			
Staffed booths at events	X	X	X
Display tank of dolls in vests	X	X	X
Interactive board with vests		X	X
Rubber raft with life vests	X	X	X
Plastic take-home bags		X	X
Stickers	X	X	X
Ice cream coupons for vest use			X
Raffles	X	X	X
April Pool's Day sponsorship	X	X	X
Life Vest Programs			
Loan programs	X	X	X
Discount coupons	X	X	X
Retail displays	X	X	X
Bulk buy for public pools			X

Funding and Partnerships

The following relationships were developed to leverage a limited budget: coalition support and involvement, community partnerships to develop and disseminate materials, sponsor relationships and grants to fund specific program components, and ad agency pro bono support to develop the slogan, messages, and public service components. Many of the campaign elements were disseminated through organizations and care providers who had direct contact with families, creating a pyramid effect in terms of outreach. For example, pediatricians provided information at well-child visits, and pools had life vests to borrow during family swim times.

Sponsorships

Mustang Survival, a life vest manufacturer, initially made a 3-year commitment that included financial support, free life jackets, a discount coupon, bulk buy program, and in-kind printing. Financial support was used to develop a parent's guide, children's activity booklet, and an interactive display. Their support of the program continues 10 years later. From their perspective, this is due to clear and mutually beneficial objectives, a cohesive plan, ongoing communication and feedback, strong project leadership, and a results orientation. Campaign staff worked closely with the Seattle King County Drowning Prevention Coalition to work toward shared goals and objectives. This resulted in both traditional and unlikely partners and supporters. For example, a local spa company actively promoted the life vest coupons and education materials, and pool programs promoted boating safety. Local pools sponsored "April Pool's Day" annually to draw attention to water safety and life vest use.

Funding and Staffing

A variety of mechanisms were employed to fund and staff the campaign. For example, King County

Emergency Medical Services and Trauma Care Council provided several grants to start and expand the life vest loan program at lifeguard supervised beaches and pools. Parks personnel provided the administrative oversight and built the display frames for the loaner life vests.

Advertising and Research

Local advertising firms donated creative time for slogan development, television, radio, TV, and other media and publicity. A number of other advertising and communications professionals donated time for development of specific elements. A children's radio station provided a special rate to develop a comprehensive program that included ads and options for children to call in and receive information. A research firm conducted the baseline telephone survey at no cost to the campaign. The decision was made not to seek a specific media sponsor but to leverage existing relationships to assure that public service announcements and news appeared on all stations.

Volunteers

U.S. Power Squadrons and U.S. Coast Guard Auxiliary provided volunteers for special events. They had water safety expertise and were also interested in community outreach. One particularly successful relationship was with a Coast Guard Auxiliarist who was also a water safety clown. Boat ramp operators distributed ice cream coupons to children observed wearing their life vests.

Education Materials

Seattle's Child parenting newsletter shared the cost to develop a guide for parents and an activity booklet for children. Members of the Seattle King County Drowning Prevention Coalition reviewed and approved materials and disseminated them.

A local food-processing company sponsored the development of 10 trading cards with water safety messages in English and Spanish, and Bartell Drugs provided in-kind printing of five different fact sheets, even though they didn't sell life vests themselves.

Tracking and Evaluation

To determine whether parental knowledge, attitudes, and reported use and ownership of life vests by children changed as a result of exposure to the campaign, four telephone surveys were conducted. There was a *baseline (precampaign)* survey in March 1992, two *tracking* surveys in September 1992 and 1993, and a *postcampaign* survey that combined tracking and behavior change in September 1994. The baseline survey assessed behaviors, attitudes, and potential strategies. The tracking surveys measured awareness, and the postcampaign survey assessed awareness, behaviors, attitudes, and factors associated with life vest use. Survey results were also a measure of campaign effectiveness in motivating behavior changes.

Results

The campaign was recalled by 50% of families surveyed. From before to after the campaign, reported life vest use by children on docks, beaches, or at pools increased from 20% to 29% ($p < 0.01$) and life vest ownership for children increased from 69% to 75% ($p < 0.06$). Among parents aware of the campaign, reported child life vest use increased from 20% to 34% ($p < 0.01$), and ownership increased from 69% to 80% ($p < 0.01$). Among families unaware of the campaign, neither life vest use nor ownership changed significantly. Children were more often reported to wear life vests if a parent knew of the campaign, was confident fitting the vest, was younger than 40 years, felt the child could not swim well, and owned a life vest for the child. Based on 1990 United States census data, an estimated 13,000 families increased their life vest use, at an estimated campaign cost of $7 per family.[19]

Conclusions

This communitywide drowning prevention campaign resulted in a significant, although modest, increase in reported life vest use and ownership among children. (See Table 15.2.)

TABLE 15.2 Comparison of Life Vest Use by Children Aged 1 to 14 Years Before and After Drowning Prevention Campaign, Kings County, Washington, 1992-1994

	Life Vest Use by Child on Docks, at Beaches, or Pools More Than Half the Time					Own a Life Vest for Child			
	No. Families Interviewed	No. (%)	% Change	95% CI	p Value	No. (%)	% Change	95% CI	
Precampaign	332	65 (20)				230 (69)			
Postcampaign									
Aware of campaign	240	81 (34)	+14%	+7% to +22%	0.001	191 (80)	+11%	+3% to 17%	0.006
Unaware of campaign	240	57 (24)	+4%	-3% to +11%	0.2	170 (71)	+2%	-6% to +9%	0.7

Notes

1. *Final Vital Statistics Report, 1998.* National Center for Health Statistics, Department of Health and Human Services, Hyattsville, MD.

2. Cox, K., & Miller, T. (1999). The Children's Safety Network Economics & Insurance Resource Center, The Pacific Institute for Research and Evaluation (PIRE).

3. Kotler, P., & Armstrong, G. (2001). *Principles of Marketing* (pp. 528-529). Upper Saddle River, NJ: Prentice Hall.

4. Kotler & Armstrong, *Principles of Marketing,* p. 529.

5. Foundation Center. Retrieved 6/8/2001 from their Web site, topic "Researching Philanthropy," Foundation Center Stats at http://fdncenter.org/fc_stats/index.html www.fdncenter.org

6. Kotler, P., & Andreasen, A. (1991). *Strategic Marketing for Nonprofit Organizations* (p. 285). Englewood Cliffs, NJ: Prentice Hall.

7. Source: Press Room—Bill & Melinda Gates Foundation (2000). "I Am Your Child Foundation Receives $1 Million Grant From the Bill and Melinda Gates Foundation." Retrieved 6/8/01 from http://www.gatesfoundation.org/pressroom/release.asp?PRindex-325.

8. Pringle, H., & Thompson, M. (1999). *Brand Spirit: How Cause Related Marketing Builds Brands.* New York: John Wiley; Earle, R. (2000). *The Art of Cause Marketing.* Lincolnwood, IL: NTC Business Books.

9. Kotler, P., & Andreasen, A. (1991). *Strategic Marketing for Nonprofit Organizations* (p. 319). Englewood Cliffs, NJ: Prentice Hall.

10. Ad Council. (2001). Retrieved from Web site 10/10/01 at www.adcouncil.org and www.adcouncil.org/body_about.html

11. Stone, M. E. (2001, Second Quarter). Guest Columnist. *Media Inc.,* 30-31.

12. Smith, W., & Benstein, R. (1999). *Let Kids Lead.* Washington, DC: Academy for Education Development.

13. Kotler & Armstrong, *Principles of Marketing,* p. 529.

14. Baker, S. P., Fingerhut, L. A., Higgins, L., et al. (1996). *Injury to Children and Teenagers State by State Mortality Fact.* Baltimore, MD: Johns Hopkins University Injury Prevention Center.

15. Quan, L., Gore, E. F., Wentz, K., et al. (1989). "Ten-Year Study of Pediatric Drownings and Near Drownings in King County," *Pediatrics, 83,* 1035-1040.

16. Bennett, E., Cummings, P., Quan, L., & Lewis, F. M. (1999). "Evaluation of a Drowning Prevention Campaign in King County Washington." *Injury Prevention, 5,* 109-113.

17. Kotler & Andreasen, *Strategic Marketing for Nonprofit Organizations.*

18. Bergman, A. B., Rivara, F. P., Richards, D. D., et al. (1990). "The Seattle Children's Bicycle Helmet Campaign." *Am J Dis Child* 144(727), 31.

19. This highlight is an edited version of Bennett, E., Cummings, P., Quan, L., & Lewis, F. M. (1999). "Evaluation of a Drowning Prevention Campaign in King County Washington." *Injury Prevention, 5,* 109-113.

KEY CHAPTER QUESTIONS

1. What are benefits and key components of an implementation plan?

2. What frameworks can be used to organize a plan in phases?

3. How can we support behavior change over the long term?

CHAPTER 16

Completing an Implementation Plan and Sustaining Behavior

If the success or failure of this planet and of human beings depended on how I am and what I do, how would I be? What would I do?

—R. Buckminster Fuller

MARKETING HIGHLIGHT: WATER QUALITY

This case highlights a strategy that uses principles of prompting, reminding, "just in time" messaging, and community involvement to change and sustain responsible behaviors.

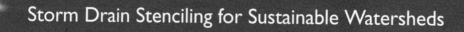

Storm Drain Stenciling for Sustainable Watersheds

Rhonda Hunter
Founder, Earthwater™ Stencils, Ltd.

Background

The Problem

According to 1999 and 2000 Roper-Starch national surveys, many people still believe that industry is the greatest source of water pollution. But it's not just industry that pollutes! It's all of us! According to the U.S. Environmental Protection Agency (EPA), more than 60% of our water pollution comes from urban and agricultural storm water runoff. This polluted runoff includes oil and vehicle fluids, animal fecal wastes, litter, sediments, chemical pesticides and fertilizers, and so on. Suburban storm water runoff often carries even higher pesticide loads than rural agricultural runoff. The way we manage (or fail to manage) our wastes does not sustain the water quality of our rivers, bays, lakes, or underground aquifers.

Situation

Many people unknowingly believe that storm drains connect to sewer treatment systems. Careless dumping of used oil, antifreeze, and household or garden chemicals down storm drains has become a common pollution problem. But even more prevalent is inadvertent polluted runoff. Overfertilized lawns or gardens laced with pesticides and herbicides leach these chemicals into the water. Then, rainfall or irrigation take the water to the gutter and down the storm drain to a river or lake. Paved surfaces collect oil and antifreeze leaked from cars, car wash suds from the driveway, sediments from construction sites, pet waste left on the sidewalk, litter from the street . . . and all this flows down the storm drain untreated, directly to the nearest beach, stream, or underground aquifer. Basically, what goes down the storm drain or on the ground ends up in the water, potentially affecting aquatic or marine habitats and human health.

Who Is Earthwater?

Earthwater's mission is to foster public awareness of, involvement in, and support for storm water pollution prevention. Earthwater accomplishes this through community-based storm drain stenciling and related local programs for sustainable watersheds.

Earthwater works with governments, teachers, and businesses across the country to engage citizens of all ages in localized watershed education programs to prevent storm water pollution. The premise is that people want clean water, and when they understand their own local watershed, they are more likely to protect it.

Target Audience

Storm drain stenciling is promoted to three target audiences: local governments, volunteer organizations, and community residents.

Program Coordinators and Volunteers

Local governments or state and federal environmental agencies are contacted to coordinate with volunteers. Volunteer organizations stencil the storm drains and distribute local community pollution prevention information.

Community Residents and Businesses

The primary audiences are community neighbors, householders, vehicle owners, students, small business owners, and others. They are told where their storm water really goes, and they are given specific steps and locations for managing their wastes and preventing pollution.

Objective

The stenciling program focus is public understanding and stewardship of residents' own watershed through storm water pollution prevention. The stencil on the street tells people what *not* to do and *why* ("Dump No Waste—Drains to Lake"). The rest of the program gives them simple, convenient options of what they *can* do and *how* to protect local water quality. Commonly provided information tells where to recycle used oil from their cars and where to take household hazardous wastes (leftover cleaners, paints, garden poisons, and chemicals). Reminders are posted to pick up pet wastes, compost garden trimmings, wash cars on the lawn, and divert roof downspouts into the garden. (See Figures 16.1-16.4.)

Figure 16.1. Dump No Waste, Drains to Bay

Figure 16.2. Dump No Waste, Drains to River

Figure 16.3. Dump No Waste, Drains to Lake

Figure 16.4. Dump No Waste, Drains to Stream

Strategies

The first step is to coordinate with local public works offices for permission and resources, such as maps and traffic safety vests. They choose messages to specify local destination of the storm water (lake, bay, river, etc.). They often customize the stencil to include the name of the local stream or lake for a better "sense of place" and neighborhood stewardship ("Drains to Oak Creek").

Program coordinators build partnerships among local groups:

- ▶ Classroom teachers looking for service learning projects and community action.

- ▶ Eagle Scouts, Girl Scouts, 4-H, Church youth groups.

- ▶ Local fishing clubs.

- ▶ Local lakes associations or neighborhood associations.

- ▶ Big Brothers and Big Sisters in the Midwest use stenciling as a community project with their kids.

- ▶ Friends of the River organizations and watershed councils.

- ▶ Sponsors also include a local business to provide materials for stenciling (paint, etc.). This informs even more community members and helps the business consider their own commitment to and impact on local water quality.

Evaluation: Indicators That Stenciling Works

Studies in Wisconsin, Oregon, and Washington have shown that stenciling works to raise awareness of pollution and storm water runoff destinations. More than 75% of people who had seen the stenciled drains knew where their water went, compared with about a third of those who had not seen a stenciled drain. People who have seen stenciled drains appear to be willing to change some behaviors once they understand where the drains go.

Local Success Stories

Pollution Prevented by Storm Drain Stencils

Volunteers at Jackson Bottom Wetland Preserve in Hillsboro, Oregon, found excessive litter entering the marsh from a storm drain culvert. Within days after the students had stenciled the neighborhood storm drains, debris and litter coming out of the wetland culvert dropped to near nothing.

Wisconsin Stenciling Survey

The University of Wisconsin and Wisconsin Department of Natural Resources conducted a 1998 survey to check the results of their statewide stenciling program.

Stenciling activities seem to increase awareness of one particular storm water fact: Storm drains discharge to nearby waterways. For example, 71% of the people who said they had seen the stenciled message knew that storm drain pipes lead directly to the nearest water body, compared with 40% of those who had not seen them.

Stenciling Raised Oregon Neighborhood Awareness

A 1997 Portland, Oregon, study shows that after 3 years of storm drain stenciling, 73% of streamside residents knew that their storm drain led to a local creek or river, compared with 53% before stenciling. Upland residents' awareness grew to 62%, nearly doubling from the previous 35% who knew where their storm drains led.

Figure 16.5. Businesses Stencil to Remind Employees of Watershed Protection

Figure 16.6. Local Stream Team Stencils Neighborhood Drains

*Maine Students Stencil
After Monitoring Storm Drains*

Mt. Desert High School students tested water from storm drains leading to their local bay. They found oil, trash, fecal bacteria, and chlorine. Applying the knowledge gained from science class, the high school students reasoned that if they could reduce pollution, it might help reopen their local shellfish beds, which had recently been closed to harvest. Using GIS maps, the students identified a grid of storm drains leading to the offending pipes. Then, they organized a storm drain stenciling project with the image of a fish and the message "Dump No Waste—Drains to Bay." (See Figures 16.5 and 16.6.)

*Environmental Protection
Agency Recommendations*

EPA recommends storm drain stenciling in the new Phase II Storm Water Rule. EPA's inventory found urban runoff discharges from storm sewers to be a major source of water quality impairment nationwide. The new EPA Clean Water Act Phase II storm water nonpoint rule for urban areas requires public education and involvement for even smaller cities than before. In guidance under this rule, EPA recommends storm drain stenciling for public education, involvement, and illicit discharge prevention.

NOTE: Earthwater can be found at http://www.earthwaterstencils.com; Rhonda Hunter is the founder of Earthwater™ Stencils, Ltd., and she began storm drain stenciling in Washington State in 1987.

CHAPTER OVERVIEW

Not even the most carefully formulated social marketing plan can succeed in reaching objectives and goals if it is not effectively implemented.[1] And to go beyond this initial success, contributing to long-lasting social change will require even more from us, efforts McKenzie-Mohr and Smith refer to as "fostering sustainable behavior."[2]

For some, the implementation plan *is* the marketing plan, one that will reflect all prior steps and is considered our final major step in the planning process (Step 8). This chapter outlines considerations and templates for developing these plans.

We also present advice from veterans and experts in the field on how to sustain desired behaviors over time.

IMPLEMENTATION PLANS

Key Elements and Benefits

Kotler and Armstrong describe *marketing implementation* as "the process that turns marketing strategies and plans into marketing actions in order to accomplish strategic marketing objectives."[3] They further summarize that many managers think that *doing things right* (implementation) is just as important as *doing the right things* (strategy). In this model, both are viewed as critical to success.

Key components to a comprehensive implementation plan include addressing the classic action-planning elements of what will be done, by whom, when, and for how much:

- *What will we do?* Key activities necessary to execute strategies identified in the marketing mix (Step 5) and the evaluation plan (Step 6) are captured in this document. Many were reviewed and then confirmed in the budgeting process activity (Step 7) and will be incorporated in this section.

- *Who will be responsible?* For each of these major efforts, key individuals and/or organizations are identified for program implementation. In social marketing programs, typical key players include *staff* (e.g., program coordinators), *partners* (e.g., coalition members or other agencies), *sponsors* (e.g., a retail business or the media), *suppliers* (e.g., manufacturers), *vendors* (e.g., an advertising agency), *consultants* (e.g., for evaluation efforts), and other internal and external publics, such as *volunteers, citizens,* and *lawmakers.*

- *When will it be done?* Time frames are included for each major activity, most commonly noting expected start and finish dates.

TABLE 16.1 Sample Implementation Plan Format

WHAT	WHO	WHEN	HOW MUCH

- *How much it will cost?* Expenses identified in the budgeting process are then paired with associated activities.

This implementation plan functions as a concise working document used to share and track planned efforts. It provides a mechanism to ensure that we do what we said we would, on time, and within budgets. It provides the map that charts our course, enabling timely feedback when we have wavered or need to take corrective actions. It is not the evaluation plan. It incorporates evaluation activities, ensuring that they are implemented.

Formats

Most commonly, these plans represent a minimum of 1-year activities and, ideally, 2 or 3 years. In terms of format, several options are common, ranging from simple plans included in executive summaries of the marketing plan to complex plans developed using software programs.

Table 16.1 presents a simple outline of a plan format incorporating suggested implementation plan elements. For campaigns that span multiple years, a plan could be developed for each phase. Table 16.2 illustrates a potential format for summarizing major campaign activities at a glance. In reality, many additional activities would be identified in each phase.

Phasing and Potential Organizing Frameworks

Implementation plans can be organized using one or more of many potential frameworks chosen to create the most relevant and meaningful campaign phases and/or associated time frames. As mentioned in discussions on budgeting, the reali-

TABLE 16.2 Summary Calendar

	1Q 02	2Q 02	3Q 02	4Q 02	1Q 03	2Q 03	3Q 03	4Q 03	1Q 04	2Q 04	3Q 04	4Q 04
Phase 1	▓	▓										
		▓	▓									
			▓									
			▓	▓								
Phase 2			▓	▓	▓							
			▓	▓	▓	▓						
					▓	▓						
					▓	▓						
Phase 3							▓	▓	▓	▓	▓	▓
							▓	▓				
											▓	▓

ties of funding often necessitate spreading campaign efforts over a period of time. Natural options include creating phases that are organized (driven) by some element of the marketing plan: *target markets, geographic areas, campaign objectives, campaign goals, stages of change, products, pricing, distribution channels, promotional messages, media channels, funding,* or some *external environmental factor.* The following are examples and situations in which a particular framework might be most appropriate.

Phases Organized by Target Market

In a differentiated strategy in which several market segments are targets for the campaign, each phase could concentrate on implementing strategies for a distinct segment. This might be most meaningful when strategies differ for each market, as they would for a drowning prevention campaign. A potential phasing might proceed as follows:

Phase 1: *Parents of toddlers*
Phase 2: *Parents of children in elementary school*
Phase 3: *Teenagers*

Phases Organized by Geographic Area

Phasing by geographic area has several advantages. It may align with funding availability and offer the ability to pilot the campaign, measure outcomes, and then make important refinements prior to subsequent implementation. A scenario for a campaign promoting moderate physical activity might look like this:

Phase 1:   *Launch in one major city in state*
Phase 2:   *Add three additional counties*
Phase 3:   *Go statewide*

Phases Organized by Objective

In a situation in which a campaign, for example, the litter prevention case, has identified important objectives related to knowledge and beliefs as well as behavior, campaign phases are organized and sequenced to support each objective. A variety of factors may contribute to choosing this framework, including allowing more time to gain support of partners (e.g., law enforcement), secure sponsors (e.g., fast-food restaurants), and establish important infrastructures (e.g., broad distribution channels for litterbags and incorporating questions on fines for litter in drivers' education tests). As mentioned earlier in this case, phases for this campaign included the following:

Phase 1:   *Creating awareness of laws and fines*
Phase 2:   *Altering beliefs that "no one's watching" or cares*
Phase 3:   *Changing littering behavior*

Phases Organized by Goal

Campaigns may have established specific benchmarks for reaching interim goals, in which case activities and resources would then be organized to support desired outcomes. In a case on water conservation, for example, efforts might be planned and monitored to achieve specific benchmarks for reduction of residential and business water consumption:

Phase 1:   *1% reduction in water consumption from baseline*
Phase 2:   *5% reduction in water consumption from baseline*
Phase 3:   *10% reduction in water consumption from baseline*

Phases Organized by Stage of Change

In keeping with objectives of moving audiences through stages of change, it may make most sense to phase a campaign effort by first targeting those "most ready for action" and then using this momentum to move on to other markets. In the case of food waste composting, for example, efforts might be made to set up demonstration households in neighborhoods with eager volunteers who can then be supported and promoted to spread the word to neighbors. In this case, phases might appear as follows:

Phase 1: *Promote to households with consistent participation in all curbside recycling (maintenance segment)*

Phase 2: *Promote to households participating only in paper and glass curbside recycling (in action segment)*

Phase 3: *Promote to households that had responded to and inquired about information in past but are not regular curbside recyclers (contemplator segment)*

Phases Organized by Service and Tangible Object Introductions or Enhancements

When new or improved services and tangible objects have been identified for a program plan, it may be necessary and strategic to introduce these over a period of time. A Women and Infant Children Program (WIC) clinic, for example, might phase the introduction of service enhancements by starting with those perceived to have the most potential impact on increased use of farmers' markets and then move on to those providing added value:

Phase 1: *Counselor training and support materials*

Phase 2: *Market tours and transportation vouchers*

Phase 3: *Clinic classes on freezing and canning*

Phases Organized by Pricing Strategies

A program may plan a pricing strategy in which significant price incentives are used early in the campaign as a way to create attention and stimulate action. In subsequent phases, efforts may rely on other elements of the marketing mix, such as improved distribution channels or targeted promotions. In the case of a utility promoting energy-efficient appliances, pricing strategies might change over time as follows:

Phase 1: *Rebates for turning in old appliances*
Phase 2: *Discount coupons for energy-efficient appliances*
Phase 3: *Pricing similar to competing appliances and increased emphasis on contribution to the environment*

Phases Organized by Distribution Channels

A campaign relying heavily on convenience of access might begin with implementing distribution channels that are quickest, easiest, or least expensive to develop and then move on to more significant endeavors over time. In the case of blood donations, for example, goals might be aligned with the ability of an effort in a new community to begin with strategies that can be implemented in the short term, moving on to those requiring more lead time:

Phase 1: *Bloodmobiles to major worksites*
Phase 2: *Small-scale operations on college campuses*
Phase 3: *Community blood bank center opens*

Phases Organized by Messages

When multiple campaign messages are needed to support a broad social marketing program (e.g., natural gardening), behavior change may be facilitated by introducing messages one at a time. This can help our target adopter spread costs for change over a period of time, as well as feel less overwhelmed (increased self-efficacy). A phased message scenario might include the following:

Phase 1: *Natural fertilizers and pesticides are effective*
Phase 2: *Native plants are beautiful*
Phase 3: *Mowing your grass high and letting clippings lie adds natural fertilizer and retains moisture*

Phases Organized by Media Channels

With the onset of major threats such as the spread of AIDS or mad cow disease, program planners may need to first reach broad audiences in a short period of time. Once this phase is complete, efforts may shift to more targeted audiences through more targeted media channels.

Phase 1: *Mass communication channels: TV, radio, print*
Phase 2: *Selective channels: posters, flyers, brochures*
Phase 3: *Personal selling: presentations and counseling*

Phases Organized by Funding and Grant Requirements

Availability of funds (e.g., annual budgets) or agreed-upon deliverables (e.g., outcome measures) often dictate timing of activities. Resource allocation for a tobacco prevention campaign, for example, may have the bulk of its dollars allocated in the second year. This may point to selecting activities for Year 1 with relatively few out-of-pocket expenses, such as program planning and creative development. Grants and funders also often specify points in time for deliverables such as final reports. In these cases, activities might be grouped according to the following:

Phase 1: *Planning and creative development*
Phase 2: *Launch*
Phase 3: *Evaluation and reporting*

Phases Organized by External Factors

Activities might be organized and timed according to a future external but related event, such as the passing of a new law (e.g., banning talking on handheld cell phones while driving) or an anticipated breakthrough in technology (e.g., hands-free, voice-activated cellular phones). Working backward from the expected time frame for these events might look like this:

Phase 1: *Advocating with lawmakers, sharing incidence data and surveys*
Phase 2: *Establishing partnerships with suppliers and distribution channels*
Phase 3: *Implementing mass communications regarding new laws, distributing discount coupons, and publishing locations of retail outlets for purchase of improved cell phone models*

Phases Organized by a Variety of Factors

In reality, it may be important to use a combination of phasing techniques. For example, campaign target markets may vary by geographic areas (e.g., farmers are more important target markets for water conservation in rural than in urban communities). As a result, different communities may have different target market phasing to their campaigns. As most practitioners will attest, campaigns will need to be meaningful to their specific communities or they will not receive the necessary support for implementation.

Phase 1: *Rural communities target farmers and urban communities target large corporations for water conservation.*

Phase 2: *Rural communities target businesses, and urban communities target public sector agencies.*

Phase 3: *Rural communities and urban communities target residential users.*

SUSTAINABILITY

At this point in the planning process, most strategies and tactics have been identified and scheduled to support desired behavior change objectives and goals. It is a worthwhile exercise, however, to give last-minute considerations to any additional tactics to include in the plan that will support our target audience in sustaining their behavior over the long term.

In keeping with our stages of change theory and model, we are specifically interested in ensuring the following:

- That those in the action stage don't return to contemplation

- That those in the maintenance stage don't return to irregular actions

- That those in the termination stage remain there

Typical strategies include the use of reminders, recognition, and existing infrastructures. Tactics and mechanisms include signage, stickers, mailings, friends and family, electronic reminders, labels on packaging, and taking advantage of existing infrastructures (e.g., habits). Examples illustrating each of these are presented in Table 16.3. We may have thought about these and incorporated them when we developed tangible objects to promote (e.g., Breathalyzers), services to offer (e.g., annual home safety checks), pricing strategies (e.g., recognition programs for carpoolers), place strategies (e.g., fruits and vegetables visible on the shelf), or promotions (e.g., reminder calls from the blood center).

Guidelines From McKenzie-Mohr and Smith

In their book *Fostering Sustainable Behavior,* McKenzie-Mohr and Smith offer insights, guidelines, tools, and checklists for the social marketer to consider for supporting continued behavior change. Major strategies they discuss include the use of *prompts, commitments, and norms.*[4]

TABLE 16.3 Sustaining Behavior

Issue	*Using Reminders, Recognition, and Existing Infrastructures to Sustain Behavior*
Tobacco cessation	Electronic alerts during vulnerable times in the day that signal "Come on, you can do it."[5]
Binge drinking	Small posters in bar restroom stalls showing someone bending over "the porcelain god"
Physical activity	Having a walking buddy
Unintended pregnancies	Keeping a condom in a small case on a key chain
Fat intake	Detailed data on food labels indicating fat grams and percent of calories
Fruits and vegetable	Placing fruits and vegetables in glass bowls at eye level in refrigerators
Water intake	Stickers at water coolers saying, "Have you had your 8 cups today?"
Breastfeeding	Pediatricians encouraging a nursing mom to continue breastfeeding at the 6-month checkup
Breast cancer	Shower nozzle hanger reminding about monthly self breast exams
Folic acid	Keeping vitamin pills by the toothbrush as an established habit
Immunizations	Mailings recognizing and reminding when a child's immunization is due (see Figure 16.7)
Diabetes	Using a beeper as a reminder for blood glucose monitoring
Car seats	Keeping a car seat in all cars used frequently by a child
Drinking and driving	Making breathalyzers available in bars
Booster seats	Air fresheners for cars with reminders about booster seats (see Figure 16.8)
Drowning	Providing life vests for toddlers at public beaches
Fire alarm	Placing reminder stickers in planning calendars for checking batteries on smoke alarms
Waste reduction	Label on a bathroom towel dispenser suggesting to "Take only what you need"
Electricity	Electric utility bill messages congratulating homeowners for decreased consumption
Commute trip reduction	Recognition pins on company name tags signifying "I'm not an SOV"
Litter	Messages on fast-food bags reminding patrons to dispose of litter properly
Water conservation	Tent cards on tables at restaurants explaining that they don't automatically serve water
Food waste composting	Stickers on recycle containers recognizing a homeowner who also composts food waste
Reducing use	Messages at coffee stands suggesting that "the regulars" bring their own cups
Air pollution	Stickers inside car doors reminding car owners when it is time to get their tires inflated
Organ donation	Lawyers asking their clients who are organ donors if they have talked to their families about their wishes

The Photo-Mag Plus™ will hold your favorite photo in daily view, plus serve as a note holder. ASI 68480. Bend and crease magnet along pre-cut line. Pull gently to separate.

Happy First Birthday!

FROM CHILD PROFILE

Figure 16.7. Refrigerator Magnet, Mailed to Child on First Birthday to Remind About Upcoming Immunications

Kids 4-8 Need Booster Seats

Figure 16.8. Air Freshener for Car

TABLE 16.4 Guidelines From McKenzie-Mohr and Smith

Use prompts as reminders:

- Make the prompt noticeable
- The prompt should be self-explanatory, explaining simply what the person is to do
- The prompt should be presented as close in time and space as possible to the targeted behavior
- Use the prompts to encourage people to engage in positive behaviors rather than to avoid harmful actions

Use commitments to increase participation:

- Get it in writing
- Make them public
- Use existing points of contact
- Combine with other behavior change techniques

Use social norms to your advantage:

- Communicate what are accepted behaviors
- Stress any very high participation rates
- Make the norm visible

SOURCE: From Doug McKenzie-Mohr and William Smith, *Fostering Sustainable Behavior: An Introduction to Community-Based Social Marketing*, pp. 46-81, © 1999. Reprinted by permission of New Society Publishers.

According to McKenzie-Mohr and Smith,

> [Prompts are] visual or auditory aids which remind us to carry out an activity that we might otherwise forget. The purpose of a prompt is not to change attitudes or increased motivation, but simply to remind us to engage in an action that we are already predisposed to do.[6]

Several prompts were among those listed in Table 16.3, including signs, stickers, labels, mailings, and individuals. Their recommended guidelines for incorporating prompts include those listed in Table 16.4.

Gaining commitments from target adopters has been proven surprisingly effective. "Individuals who agreed to a small initial request were far more likely to agree to a subsequent larger request."[7] Examples include a backyard wildlife sanctuary program in which the homeowner signs the application promising to follow the natural gardening guidelines, or a client at a WIC clinic who signs a receipt for farmers' market coupons stating that she is interested in using these in the next 3 months. Evidently, McKenzie-Mohr and Smith report, "When individuals agree to a small request, it often alters the way they perceive themselves."[8]

The concept of the social norms approach discussed in Chapter 8 is also cited by McKenzie-Mohr and Smith as a powerful tool for sustaining behavior. "Clearly, perceived norms can have a substantial impact upon behavior."[9] Where applicable, this approach should be considered when developing marketing plans, because it is likely to sustain behavior over a longer term. Examples of how this approach might be used successfully include issues such as binge drinking and tobacco use among teens: The desired behavior is more the norm, and yet the target audience thinks just the opposite.

CHAPTER SUMMARY

1. Developing an implementation plan is Step 8, the final step in this marketing planning model. It turns strategies into actions and is critical to *doing things right,* even if we've planned *the right things.*

2. Implementation plans function as a concise working document that can be used to share and track planned efforts. It provides a mechanism to ensure that we do what we said we would do, on time, and within budgets.

3. Key components of an implementation plan include the following:

   - What will we do?
   - Who will be responsible?
   - When will it be done?
   - How much will it cost?

4. Formats for plans vary from simple plans incorporated in the executive summary of the marketing plan to complex plans using software programs. The ideal plan identifies activities over a period of 2 to 3 years.

5. Plans are often presented in phases, usually broken down into months or years. Several frameworks can be used to determine and organize phases, including *target markets, geographic areas, campaign objectives, campaign goals, stages of change, products, pricing, distribution channels, promotional messages, media channels, funding,* or some *external environmental factor.*

6. In Chapter 3, we challenged social marketers to consider measures that would take their plan "beyond success" by not only changing behaviors but also *sustaining* these changes into the future. Typical strategies include the use of reminders, recognition, and existing infrastructures. Tactics and mechanisms include signage, stickers, mailings, electronic reminders, labels on packaging, and taking advantage of existing infrastructures.

KEY TERMS AND CONCEPTS

Doing things right
Doing the right things
What
Who
When
How much
Phasing frameworks
Phasing by target market
Phasing by geographic area
Phasing by objective
Phasing by goal
Phasing by stage of change

Phasing by product strategy
Phasing by pricing strategy
Phasing by distribution channels
Phasing by messages
Phasing by media
Phasing by funding/grant
   requirements
Phasing by external factors
Sustaining behavior
Prompts
Commitments
Norms

ISSUES FOR DISCUSSION

1. In the marketing highlight on storm drain stenciling, why is this an example of sustaining behavior?

2. For a campaign to increase the number of registered voters participating in national elections, what are four potential phasing strategies for a 4-year campaign? Describe each one.

3. For a campaign to increase student attendance at football and basketball games on campus, what is a potential activity you might explore to ensure that those in action don't return to contemplation? That those in the maintenance stage don't return to irregular actions?

Notes

1. Kotler, P., & Roberto, E. L. (1989). *Social Marketing: Strategies for Changing Public Behavior.* New York: Free Press.
2. McKenzie-Mohr, D., & Smith, W. (1999). *Fostering Sustainable Behavior: An Introduction to Community-Based Social Marketing* (pp. 46-81). Gabriola Island, British Columbia, Canada: New Society.
3. Kotler, P., & Armstrong, G. (2001). *Principles of Marketing* (p. 71). Upper Saddle River, NJ: Prentice Hall.
4. McKenzie-Mohr & Smith, *Fostering Sustainable Behavior,* pp. 46-81.
5. Source: MyAlert.com. As described in INSIDE 1 to 1, an online newsletter, Spring 2001.
6. McKenzie-Mohr & Smith, *Fostering Sustainable Behavior,* p. 61.
7. Ibid., p. 47.
8. Ibid., p. 48.
9. Ibid., p. 76.

1. What ethical dilemmas do social marketers face? When?

2. What guidelines can be used for making ethical decisions?

CHAPTER 17
Making
Ethical Decisions

*My belief is that no human being or society composed of
human beings ever will come to much unless their conduct
is governed and guided by the love of some ethical ideal.*

—Thomas Huxley

MARKETING HIGHLIGHT: ANIMAL RIGHTS

Several questions are useful to consider as you read the following marketing highlight, featuring the organization People for the Ethical Treatment of Animals (PETA). Is there anything wrong with going as far as they do to achieve their results? Do you think they would get even more support from the businesses they target if they worked together, as partners in the issue? Are the tactics too shocking, especially for children? Or does the end justify their means?

People for the Ethical Treatment of Animals (PETA): Using Marketing Principles and Techniques to Influence Their Public's Behavior

Background and Focus

People for the Ethical Treatment of Animals (PETA) has more than 700,000 members and is the largest animal rights organization in the world. Their focus is on four areas in which they believe the largest numbers of animals suffer: on factory farms, in laboratories, in the fur trade, and in the entertainment industry. They work through public education, cruelty investigations, research, animal rescue, legislation, special events, celebrity involvement, and direct action.

Target Audience and Objectives

In the past year, efforts targeting the fast-food industry have been featured in the news, aimed first at McDonald's and then, at Burger King.

Specific requests (desired behaviors) that PETA has of Burger King were posted in spring of 2001 on their Web site (MurderKing.com):

- ▶ Require slaughterhouses to fully stun all animals before they're killed.

- ▶ Make sure that every slaughterhouse is subject to unannounced audits by a qualified animal-handling expert.

- ▶ Require suppliers to humanely kill any animals who arrive at the slaughterhouse unable to walk, with broken limbs, or in severe pain.

- ▶ Stop buying eggs from suppliers that withhold food and water to increase egg production.

- ▶ Buy chickens raised truly free-roaming only.

- ▶ Buy chicken flesh and eggs only from suppliers that don't debeak chickens.

- ▶ Institute humane guidelines for catching chickens.

- ▶ Require suppliers to stop breeding broiler chickens for weight.

- ▶ Phase out buying from farms that confine sows to stalls.

Strategies and Tactics

In a January 2001 article in *Sales & Marketing Management,* the group's strategies and tactics were described as "forceful, persistent, pointed, and attention-getting." Five "marketing mantras" and associated activities were identified:[1]

Start with the top. Begin with the most visible and highly respected company in the industry. This will capture the attention of other companies and may prompt them to follow suit in order to avoid similar damages to their image and sales.

Don't give up. According to some analysts, PETA's endurance record (e.g., battling a Las Vegas animal trainer and entertainer for more than 15 years) has developed brand awareness and a "formidable presence."[2] According to this article, "In the group's 20-year existence activists have never walked away from a marketing campaign."[3]

Tell anyone and everyone. PETA's Web site (www. Peta.org) and online links are key to fundraising and their real time and mass communications, providing the ability to reach tens of thousands of supporters "with the click of one button."[4] Members and visitors to their sites stay informed on national efforts, as well as local demonstrations and letter writing campaigns. They can view videotapes graphically depicting alleged animal abuse and preview upcoming events. In addition to the Internet, the organization relies on direct mail efforts, speaking engagements, special events, demonstrations, lobbying, and corporate presentations.

Use a famous face. It seems that PETA has no shortage of celebrity supporters and is not shy about using the public's fascination with stars to grab the public's attention and capitalize on the positive feelings associated with these faces. For example, efforts to stop animal testing for developing grooming products were bolstered when ex-Beatle Paul McCartney returned his razor to Gillette. More recently, Alec Baldwin and Richard Pryor sent a joint letter to the 1,618 owners of all 10,366 Burger King franchises on PETA's behalf. According to PETA's June 2001 news release, their letter states, "Last October, PETA asked Burger King to follow McDonald's lead. Regrettably, while Burger King has issued several statements, it has made no improvements whatsoever in the appalling living and dying conditions for the animals it uses."[5] Demonstrations against Burger King took place throughout March in more than a dozen countries, hundreds of cities, and every U.S. state and will continue until animal care improvements are established and enforced.

Shock them. In the summer of 2000, adults and children alike were shocked when they visited one of the 400 McDonald's in 23 countries where PETA volunteers handed out McCruelty Unhappy Meals. The boxes contained a plastic butchered pig, a cow amid blood-stained hay, a "Son of Ron" waiving an ax, and photos of a skinned cow's head hung from a butcher's hook, alongside the phrase, "Want fries with that?" (See Figure 17.1.) Similar tactics were planned for Burger King's order counters, with PETA volunteers urging lunchtime crowds to take their business elsewhere until the fast-food giant took minimal steps to ensure that its suppliers do not skin and dismember conscious animals, starve hens for up to 2 weeks to force them to produce more eggs, or cut off the beaks of baby chicks with a hot blade. Apparently, PETA is not bothered by those who are offended or upset—not bothered, because they say it works.

Figure 17.1. Campaign Materials Used to Target McDonald's

Figure 17.2. PETA Reports That Burger King Agreed to Requests

In the fall of 2000, PETA suspended its 11-month campaign against McDonald's after the fast-food chain announced that it would conduct unannounced audits of it slaughterhouses, stop purchasing from suppliers that fail the audits, increase the amount of living space for laying hens on factory farms, stop chopping the beaks off laying hens, and prohibit force-molting (starving chickens to force them to produce more eggs).[6]

And on June 23, 2001, PETA announced[7] that they were halting protests against Burger King, which had complied with demands for improved animal welfare.[8] (See Figure 17.2.)

CHAPTER OVERVIEW

Conscientious social marketers will face ethical dilemmas throughout the planning and implementation process. In each of the eight planning steps covered in this text, ethical questions and concerns will be raised, if not by the social marketers, then by their constituent groups.

In our first chapter, we defined social marketing as *the use of marketing principles and techniques to influence a target audience to voluntarily accept, reject, modify, or abandon a behavior for the benefit of individuals, groups, or society as a whole.* We have outlined sound steps to accomplish this. This chapter's discussion focuses on guiding those who use this tool to use it in an ethical manner.

Thinking back to the opening case for this chapter, we see that PETA's strategies are reminiscent of principles and techniques discussed throughout this book. According to information presented in the marketing highlight, they appeared to have an unwavering focus for their efforts (more humane treatment of animals); defined target markets (leaders in the fast-food industry, among others); specific desired behaviors (changes in policies and practices); an understanding of their target audience's perceived benefits and potential costs (threatened customer loyalty); and strategies that capture attention and, apparently, change behavior. But some feel they go too far, crossing ethical borders of respect and professionalism, and believe that their shock tactics and aggressive maneuvers will alienate their publics, not to mention the industries they target.

This chapter briefly discusses ethical considerations that social marketers will face in their decision making. We present more questions than answers, with an intention to increase awareness of "ethical moments" and the chances that our decisions will be based on a social conscience that leads us to "higher ground."

ETHICAL CONSIDERATIONS: AT EVERY DECISION POINT

Though ethical considerations are varied and apply to each of the steps in our planning process model, several themes are common: issues concerning *social equity, competing priorities, full disclosure, responsible stewardship, conflicts of interest,* and whether the *end justifies (any) means.* We have taken this opportunity to integrate a final revisit of the steps in the planning process.

1. *Choosing a Program Focus.* Social issues can be positively affected using several different approaches. What happens to those not selected? What if the focus that was selected undermines alternative approaches? For example, a program to reduce teen pregnancies may have selected a focus for the plan of increased access to condoms. Distribution channels may include schools, teen clinics, even popular concerts, dance clubs, and sports events. Some may argue this now sends a signal to teens that sexual activity is somehow condoned. Others will lobby for an equal amount of effort to be directed toward abstinence messages and programs, threatening planned resource allocation levels.

2. *Selecting Target Audiences.* In campaigns in which a majority of resources have been allocated to one or a few market segments, how does the planner address concerns with social inequity? Or what about reverse situations in which resources are allocated equally, when in fact only one or a few market segments have the greatest need? For example, a state water conservation effort may send messages to all residents in the state to voluntarily reduce water usage by a goal of 10% over the next 6 months. Take shorter showers. Flush one less time. But what if water levels and resources are actually adequate in half the state? Should residents on one side of the mountain (where it rains "all the time") be asked to make these sacrifices as well? What is fair?

3. *Setting Objectives and Goals.* What if trends indicate that a behavior objective we are supporting (e.g., recycling) is in conflict with other desired behaviors (e.g., reducing use); or what if our research reveals that the goals that our funders or sponsors would like to support are not realistic or attainable for our target audiences? For example, a community clinic may know they are to encourage and support pregnant women to quit smoking, completely. But what if research has shown that cutting down to 9 cigarettes a day would have significant benefits for those not able to quit? Can they consider their efforts a success if they persuade pregnant women in their clinic to decrease from 24 cigarettes a day to 9? Do they suggest a more attainable objective for this segment instead of just sending a "Quit" message?

4. *Researching Audience Knowledge, Beliefs, and Behaviors.* At Step 4 in the planning process, we explore existing knowledge levels, beliefs, and behaviors of our target audience relative to objectives and goals established in Step 3. Ethical issues range from deceiving respondents regarding purposes of research (e.g., not telling them the survey will be used for focus group screening versus research purposes) to creating concerns with confidentiality and trust (e.g., persuading a respondent to share personal experiences of domestic violence). As Kelman observed,

> Deception violates the respect to which all fellow humans are entitled and the trust that is basic to all interpersonal relationships. Such violations are doubly disturbing since they contribute, in this age of mass society, to the already powerful tendencies to manufacture realities and manipulate populations. Furthermore, by undermining the basis of trust in the relationship between investigator and subject, deception makes it increasingly difficult for social scientists to carry out their work in the future.[9]

What if funders have awarded the grant with a particular goal level in mind and this research indicates that the goal is either unattainable or too easy? For example, a grant for increasing blood donations in a community may have been awarded on the basis of a commitment to increasing donations from current donors by 25%; and then, a representative survey of past donors indicates that more than 40% plan to give blood during the established time frame. Is the goal revised or merely exceeded?

5. *Product: Designing the Market Offering.* In the social marketing model, the product platform was described to include a core product (benefit of the behavior), an actual product (desired behavior), and in some cases, an augmented product (tangible object or service). Ethical considerations

will arise with each level. In the case of promoting moderate physical activity, for example, how are expected health benefits explained and qualified? How far do you go in describing which activities count as moderate physical activity and which ones don't? What criteria are used to determine the list of local exercise facilities that will be mentioned in communications?

6. *Price: Managing Costs.* Ethical considerations related to pricing strategies include issues of social equity (e.g., fixed versus sliding scale fees); potential exploitation (e.g., offering monetary incentives to drug-addicted women for voluntary sterilization); and full disclosure of all costs (e.g., requirements to toss food composters daily in order to receive stated benefits). In the case of promoting farmers' markets to Women and Infant Children Program (WIC) clients, each of these issues might apply. Should clients receive additional coupons if they use all of their first set, making it necessary to give some clients only half a pack? What do we do about the fact that many items at the market are less than the $2 coupon denomination, and yet change cannot be given? Are we consistent about telling our clients that they will probably need to pay $3 for parking while at the market?

7. *Place: Making Access Convenient.* Issues of equity and conflicting priorities are common when planning access strategies. How do working mothers get their children to the free immunization clinic if it is only open on weekday mornings? How do drug addicts get clean needles if they don't have transportation to the exchange site? Do critics of the ecstasy-testing volunteers at dance clubs have legitimate and higher-priority concerns that this will increase use of the drug? What about those who argue that restricting access (e.g., alcohol to teens) leads to more serious consequences (e.g., driving home drunk)?

8. *Promotion: Creating Messages.* Many of the ethical issues regarding communications seem straightforward. Information should be accurate and not misleading. Language and graphics should be clear and appropriate for audiences exposed to communications. Gray areas are hard to avoid, however, and what and whose criteria should be used to decide whether something is appropriate? In the case of the sexual assault campaign, is the tag line in the radio spot, "If you force her to have sex you're screwed," too risky, even though it tested well with the target audience? Should someone blow the whistle on a local television station that promotes the television sitcom *Friends* on an outdoor billboard featuring photos of the three slender stars and the headline "Cute Anorexic Chicks?"

9. *Promotion: Choosing Communication Channels.* As outlined in Chapter 13, options for media channels are numerous, and several selection criteria were identified, including audience profile and campaign resources. Ethical considerations will also be a factor. Does the end justify the means in a case in which anti-abortionists block the entrance to clinics and threaten the lives of doctors? Or what about a case in which activists threaten (but do not physically harm) a woman wearing a fur coat? Does this meet the "no harm" guideline? And consider the ethical issues in the following example. In January 2000, the CBS program *60 Minutes* focused on a controversial approach (adoption events, such as picnics) to secure adoptions for hard-to-place children. In these settings, prospective parents come to a well-promoted event and have a chance to meet the children and learn more about their special interests and personalities. Two of the children who were interviewed by the program's reporter shared that they had gone home and cried after the events in which they were not picked. They went on to report, however, that they were eventually adopted at a subsequent event and felt that "you just have to hang in there." In this case, does the end justify the means? Or was there an alternative media channel (e.g., videotaped interviews) that would do less harm and accomplish similar results?

10. *Developing an Evaluation Plan.* As with all research and tracking efforts, issues of concern will include ensuring the use of sound and appropriate methodologies and techniques, respectful treatment of respondents, accurate and fair interpretation and reporting of results, and full disclosure of study limitations. For example, an evaluation study that plans to use a purchased list of households with children to measure change in booster usage will need to disclose that findings may be biased toward factors used to compile the list (e.g., purchasing patterns or registration lists). Or a study that included only 50 respondents will need to report associated error ranges and perhaps only present findings in terms of qualitative versus quantitative indicators.

11. *Determining Budgets and Finding Funding Sources.* Ethical considerations regarding budgets and funding are probably familiar and include issues of responsible fiscal management, reporting, and soliciting of funds. Consider, though, the following additional dilemmas that could face a social marketer. What if a major tobacco company wanted to provide funding for television spots for youth tobacco prevention but didn't require the company's name to be placed in ads? What if a major lumber and paper manufacturer wanted to provide funding for a campaign promoting recyclable materials and did want the name of the company associated with

the campaign? What if a fast-food chain wanted to be listed as a sponsor of magazine ads featuring "The Food Guide Pyramid"? Is it okay to accept pro bono work from an advertising agency for a counter-alcohol campaign if the parent company has clients in the alcohol industry?

12. *Completing an Implementation Plan.* In the process of creating an implementation plan, many of the same familiar ethical issues arise, such as full disclosure (e.g., assumed responsibilities), realistic projections (e.g., time frames), and thoughtful analysis (e.g., planned expenditures). Several options for phasing campaigns were presented in Chapter 16. Ethical considerations may be raised, especially when campaigns are phased according to target market segments or geographic areas. This would mean, then, that certain markets might benefit before others or that some may receive fewer campaign resources.

AMERICAN MARKETING ASSOCIATION CODE OF ETHICS

The American Marketing Association has developed a member code of ethics, published on their Web site (www.MarketingPower.com) and presented in Box 17.1. Many of the principles apply to social marketing environments, with themes similar to those noted above: *Do no harm, Be fair, Provide full disclosure, Be good stewards, Own the problem, Be responsible,* and *Tell the truth.*

BOX 17.1

Code of Ethics
American Marketing Association

Members of the American Marketing Association are committed to ethical professional conduct. They have joined together in subscribing to this Code of Ethics embracing the following topics:

Responsibilities of the Marketer

Marketers must accept responsibility for the consequences of their activities and make every effort to ensure that their decisions, recommendations and actions function to identify, serve and satisfy all relevant publics: customers, organizations and society.

Marketers' Professional Conduct must be guided by:

1. The basic rule of professional ethics: not knowingly to do harm;
2. The adherence to all applicable laws and regulations;
3. The accurate representation of their education, training and experience; and
4. The active support, practice and promotion of this Code of Ethics.

(Continued)

BOX 17.1 (Continued)

Honesty and Fairness

Marketers shall uphold and advance the integrity, honor and dignity of the marketing profession by:

1. Being honest in serving consumers, clients, employees, suppliers, distributors, and the public;
2. Not knowingly participating in conflict of interest without prior notice to all parties involved; and
3. Establishing equitable fee schedules including the payment or receipt of usual, customary and/or legal compensation for marketing exchanges.

Rights and Duties of Parties in the Marketing Exchange Process

Participants in the marketing exchange process should be able to expect that

1. Products and services offered are safe and fit for their intended uses;
2. Communications about offered products and services are not deceptive;
3. All parties intend to discharge their obligations, financial and otherwise, in good faith; and
4. Appropriate internal methods exist for equitable adjustment and/or redress of grievances concerning purchases.

It is understood that the above would include, but is not limited to, the following responsibilities of the marketer:

In the area of product development and management:

- disclosure of all substantial risks associated with product or service usage;
- identification of any product component substitution that might materially change the product or impact on the buyer's purchase decision;
- identification of extra cost-added features.

In the area of promotions:

- avoidance of false and misleading advertising;
- rejection of high-pressure manipulations, or misleading sales tactics;
- avoidance of sales promotions that use deception or manipulation.

In the area of distribution:

- not manipulating the availability of a product for the purpose of exploitation;
- not using coercion in the marketing channel;
- not exerting undue influence over the reseller's choice to handle a product.

In the area of pricing:

- not engaging in price fixing;
- not practicing predatory pricing;
- disclosing the full price associated with any purchase.

(Continued)

BOX 17.1 (Continued)

In the area of marketing research:

- prohibiting selling or fundraising under the guise of conducting research;
- maintaining research integrity by avoiding misrepresentation and omission of pertinent research data;
- treating outside clients and suppliers fairly.

Organizational Relationships

Marketers should be aware of how their behavior may influence or impact the behavior of others in organizational relationships. They should not demand, encourage or apply coercion to obtain unethical behavior in their relationships with others, such as employees, suppliers, or customers.

1. Apply confidentiality and anonymity in professional relationships with regard to privileged information;
2. Meet their obligations and responsibilities in contracts and mutual agreements in a timely manner;
3. Avoid taking the work of others, in whole, or in part, and representing this work as their own or directly benefiting from it without compensation or consent of the originator or owner; and
4. Avoid manipulation to take advantage of situations to maximize personal welfare in a way that unfairly deprives or damages the organization of others.

Code of Ethics for Marketing on the Internet

Preamble

The Internet, including on-line computer communications, has become increasingly important to marketers' activities, as they provide exchanges and access to markets worldwide. The ability to interact with stakeholders has created new marketing opportunities and risks that are not currently specifically addressed in the American Marketing Association Code of Ethics. The American Marketing Association Code of Ethics for Internet marketing provides additional guidance and direction for ethical responsibility in this dynamic area of marketing. The American Marketing Association is committed to ethical professional conduct and has adopted these principles for using the Internet, including on-line marketing activities utilizing network computers.

General Responsibilities

Internet marketers must assess the risks and take responsibility for the consequences of their activities. Internet marketers' professional conduct must be guided by:

1. Support of professional ethics to avoid harm by protecting the rights of privacy, ownership and access.
2. Adherence to all applicable laws and regulations with no use of Internet marketing that would be illegal, if conducted by mail, telephone, fax or other media.
3. Awareness of changes in regulations related to Internet marketing.
4. Effective communication to organizational members on risks and policies related to Internet marketing, when appropriate.
5. Organizational commitment to ethical Internet practices communicated to employees, customers and relevant stakeholders.

(Continued)

BOX 17.1 (Continued)

Privacy

Information collected from customers should be confidential and used only for expressed purposes. All data, especially confidential customer data, should be safeguarded against unauthorized access. The expressed wishes of others should be respected with regard to the receipt of unsolicited e-mail messages.

Ownership

Information obtained from the Internet sources should be properly authorized and documented. Information ownership should be safeguarded and respected. Marketers should respect the integrity and ownership of computer and network systems.

Access

Marketers should treat access to accounts, passwords, and other information as confidential, and only examine or disclose content when authorized by a responsible party. The integrity of others' information systems should be respected with regard to placement of information, advertising or messages.

Any AMA member found to be in violation of any provision of this Code of Ethics may have his or her Association membership suspended or revoked.

American Marketing Association

SOURCE: American Marketing Association. (June 2001). Reprinted with permission. Retrieved from their Web site at www.MarketingPower.com

---

CHAPTER SUMMARY

1. Social marketers will face ethical considerations at every step in the planning process. The key is to be conscientious at these moments.

2. Recurring themes include issues of *social equity, competing priorities, full disclosure, responsible stewardship, conflicts of interest,* and whether the *end justifies (any) means.*

3. Ethics professionals suggest we follow classic guidelines, including the following: *Do no harm, Be fair, Provide full disclosure, Be good stewards, Own the problem, Be responsible,* and *Tell the truth.*

KEY TERMS AND CONCEPTS

Social equity   Responsible stewardship
Competing priorities   Conflict of interest
Full disclosure   End justifying the means

ISSUES FOR DISCUSSION

1. Relative to PETA activities described in our opening case, do you see any ethical problems? What additional or alternative strategies would you recommend they consider to achieve stated outcomes?

2. Ethical guidelines emphasize that we do no harm. Give an example of an organization or a campaign that, in your opinion, is practicing social marketing principles but is violating this ethical guideline.

3. How do you answer the question "What is fair?" in the example in which citizens statewide are being asked to conserve water, even though water shortages are only significant in parts of the state?

4. Give an example of a social marketing campaign that, from your perspective, seems to be following ethical guidelines?

Notes

1. Cummings, B., & Irwin, J. (2001, January). "Shock Treatment: Why PETA's Radical Marketing Tactics Work." *Sales & Marketing Management,* 64-70.
2. Ibid., p. 69.
3. Ibid.
4. Ibid.
5. PETA Media Center. (2001). Retrieved 6/4/2001 from http://www.peta.com/news/0601/0601MiamiBK.html
6. Ibid.
7. PETA. (2001). Retrieved 10/1/01 from http://www.murderking.com/release.html
8. Case Source: Cummings, B. (2001, January). *Sales and Marketing Management,* and Peta's Web site information retrieved 6/24/2001 at www.Peta.org; Betsy Cummings is Executive Editor of *Sales and Marketing:* bcummings@salesandmarketing.com
9. Kelman, H. C. (1992). "The Rights of the Subject in Social Research: An Analysis in Terms of Relative Power and Legitimacy." *American Psychologist, 27,* 999.

Appendix

Social Marketing Planning Worksheet

STEP I
CONDUCT A SITUATION ANALYSIS

1.1   What is the social *issue* this campaign is addressing (i.e., unintended pregnancies, threatened salmon species)?

1.2   What is the campaign *focus* (i.e., teen abstinence, residential gardening practices)?

1.3   What is the campaign *purpose*, the intended impact (benefit) (i.e., reduced teen pregnancies, protection of salmon habitats)?

1.4   What internal *strengths* will your plan maximize (e.g., resources, expertise, management support, internal publics)?

1.5   What internal *weaknesses* will your plan minimize (e.g., resources, expertise, management support, internal publics)?

1.6   What external *opportunities* will your plan take advantage of (e.g., external publics and cultural, technological, demographic, natural, economic, and political/legal forces)?

1.7   What external *threats* will you plan and prepare for (e.g., external publics and cultural, technological, demographic, natural, economic, and political/legal forces)?

1.8   What findings from *prior and similar efforts* are noteworthy?

REFER TO CHAPTER 5 FOR DETAILED DESCRIPTIONS OF PROCESS.

Social Marketing Planning Worksheet

STEP 2
SELECT TARGET AUDIENCES

2.1   Describe target audiences for your program/campaign in terms of size, problem incidence and severity, and relevant variables, including demographics, psychographics, geographics, behaviors, and/or stages of change.

2.2   Which of these are your primary targets?

2.3   Which are secondary?

REFER TO CHAPTER 6 FOR DETAILED DESCRIPTIONS OF PROCESS.

Social Marketing Planning Worksheet

STEP 3
SET OBJECTIVES AND GOALS

OBJECTIVES:

3.1   <u>Behavior objective:</u>

What, very specifically, do you want to influence your target audience to *do* as a result of this campaign or project?

3.2   <u>Knowledge objective:</u>

Is there anything you need them to *know,* in order to act?

3.3   <u>Belief objective:</u>

Is there anything you need them to *believe,* in order to act?

GOALS:

3.4   What quantifiable, measurable goals are you setting? Ideally, this is stated in terms of behavior change. Other potential measures include goals for campaign awareness, recall and/or response, and changes in knowledge, belief, or behavior intent levels.

REFER TO CHAPTER 7 FOR DETAILED DESCRIPTIONS OF PROCESS.

Social Marketing Planning Worksheet

STEP 4
ANALYZE TARGET AUDIENCES AND THE COMPETITION

RELATIVE TO YOUR OBJECTIVE (DESIRED BEHAVIOR) AND YOUR TARGET AUDIENCE:

4.1   What is their *current behavior*?

4.2   What do they currently *know*?

4.3   What do they currently *believe*?

4.4   What *benefits* do they perceive?

4.5   What *costs* do they perceive?

4.6   What *barriers* do they perceive?

COMPETITION:

4.7   What are the major competing *alternative behaviors*?

4.8   What *benefits* does your audience associate with these behaviors?

4.9   What *costs* does your audience associate with these behaviors?

REFER TO CHAPTER 8 FOR DETAILED DESCRIPTIONS OF PROCESS.

Social Marketing Planning Worksheet

STEP 5
DEVELOP MARKETING STRATEGIES

PRODUCT: DESIGN THE MARKET OFFERING

5.1.1   What is the *core* product, benefits of the desired behavior?

5.1.2   What is the *actual* product, the desired behavior?

5.1.3   Relative to the *augmented* product (tangible objects and services)

    5.1.3.1   Are there any *new tangible objects* that will be included in program and campaign efforts?

    5.1.3.2   Are there any *improvements* that need to be made to existing tangible objects?

    5.1.3.3   Are there any *new services* that will be included in program and campaign efforts?

    5.1.3.4   Are there any *improvements* that need to be made to existing services?

REFER TO CHAPTER 9 FOR DETAILED DESCRIPTIONS OF PROCESS.

Social Marketing Planning Worksheet

STEP 5
DEVELOP MARKETING STRATEGIES
(Continued)

PRICE: MANAGE COSTS OF BEHAVIOR CHANGE

IDENTIFY EXIT COSTS:

5.2.1   What *monetary* costs will target audiences associate with abandoning their current behavior?

5.2.2   What *nonmonetary* costs will target audiences associate with abandoning their current behavior?

IDENTIFY ENTRY COSTS:

5.2.3   What *monetary* costs will target audiences associate with adopting the new (desired) behavior?

5.2.4   What *nonmonetary* costs will target audiences associate with adopting the new (desired) behavior?

ESTABLISH PRICING STRATEGIES:

5.2.5   What prices will be set for tangible objects and services associated with the campaign?

5.2.6   Will there be any monetary incentives?

5.2.7   Will there be any nonmonetary incentives?

REFER TO CHAPTER 10 FOR DETAILED DESCRIPTIONS OF PROCESS.

Social Marketing Planning Worksheet

STEP 5
DEVELOP MARKETING STRATEGIES
(Continued)

PLACE: MAKE ACCESS CONVENIENT

5.3.1   *Where* will you encourage and support your target audience to *perform the desired behavior* and *when*?

5.3.2   *Where* and *when* will the target market acquire any related tangible objects?

5.3.3   *Where* and *when* will the target market acquire any associated services?

5.3.4   Are there any enhancements that would increase the appeal of the location?

REFER TO CHAPTER 11 FOR DETAILED DESCRIPTIONS OF PROCESS.

Social Marketing Planning Worksheet

STEP 5
DEVELOP MARKETING STRATEGIES
(Continued)

PROMOTION: CREATE MESSAGES

5.4.1   What key messages do you want your campaign to communicate to target audiences?

5.4.2   What are your specific communication objectives?

    5.4.2.1   What do you want your target audience to know?

    5.4.2.2   What do you want your target audience to believe?

    5.4.2.3   What specific actions do you want your target audience to take as a result of this campaign?

5.4.3   What benefits will you promise?

5.4.4   What will be said or featured to support this promise?

5.4.5   What communication style and tone will be used?

5.4.6   What are important copy, graphics, and format recommendations, considerations, requirements, and/or restrictions?

REFER TO CHAPTER 12 FOR DETAILED DESCRIPTIONS OF PROCESS.

Social Marketing Planning Worksheet

STEP 5
DEVELOP MARKETING STRATEGIES
(Continued)

PROMOTION: CHOOSE COMMUNICATION CHANNELS

5.4.7   What media types will be used?

5.4.8   What media vehicles will be used?

REFER TO CHAPTER 13 FOR DETAILED DESCRIPTIONS OF PROCESS.

Social Marketing Planning Worksheet

STEP 6
DEVELOP A PLAN FOR EVALUATION AND MONITORING

6.1   What goals from Step 3 will be measured?

6.2   What techniques and methodologies will be used to conduct these measures?

6.3   When will these measurements be taken?

6.4   How will measurements be reported and to whom?

REFER TO CHAPTER 14 FOR DETAILED DESCRIPTIONS OF PROCESS.

Social Marketing Planning Worksheet

STEP 7
DETERMINE BUDGETS AND FIND FUNDING SOURCES

7.1   What costs will be associated with product-related strategies?

7.2   What costs will be associated with price-related strategies?

7.3   What costs will be associated with place-related strategies?

7.4   What costs will be associated with promotion-related strategies?

7.5   What costs will be associated with evaluation-related strategies?

7.6   If costs exceed currently available funds, what potential additional funding sources can be explored?

7.7   What strategies will you use to appeal to these potential funders?

REFER TO CHAPTER 15 FOR DETAILED DESCRIPTIONS OF PROCESS.

Social Marketing Planning Worksheet

STEP 8
COMPLETE AN IMPLEMENTATION PLAN

8.1   Will there be phases to the campaign? How will they be organized (i.e., by market, objectives, activities)?

8.2   For each phase, what will be done, who will be responsible, when will it be done, and for how much?

REFER TO CHAPTER 16 FOR DETAILED DESCRIPTIONS OF PROCESS.

Credits

CHAPTER 1 Figure 1.1. Reprinted with permission of Washington State Substance Abuse Coalition; Figure 1.2. Reprinted with permission of RockTheVote.org; Figure 1.4. © March of Dimes Birth Defects Foundation, 2000. Reprinted with permission; Figure 1.5. Reprinted with permission from Children's Hospital & Regional Medical Center, Seattle, Washington. Photograph by Mike Urban; Figure 1.6. Provided by National Archives and Record Administration; Figure 1.7. Reprinted with permission of Merck & Co., Inc.; Figure 1.8. Reprinted with permission of Advantage Interlock, Inc.; Figure 1.9. Reprinted with permission of Puget Sound Energy; Figure 1.10. Reprinted with permission of Washington Traffic Safety Commission. Photo by Mark Freye.

CHAPTER 2 Figure 2.1. Reproduced from the National Heart, Lung and Blood Institute Publication titled *Protect Your Heart: Prevent High Blood Pressure;* Figures 2.2.-2.5. Salmon Friendly Gardening program materials were developed by Seattle Public Utilities. Reprinted with permission.

CHAPTER 3 Figures 3.1-3.3. Reprinted with permission of Crispin, Porter & Bogusky, from The Truth Campaign; Figure 3.4. Reprinted with permission of Puget Sound Blood Center; Figure 3.5. This photo courtesy of the Produce for Better Health Foundation; Figure 3.6. Reprinted with permission of Children's Hospital & Regional Medical Center, Seattle, Washington; Figure 3.7. Reprinted with permission of Carol Bryant; Figure 3.8. Reprinted with permission of Seattle Public Utilities; Figure 3.9. Reprinted with permission of North Carolina Department of Transportation (2001). The North Carolina Governor's Highway Safety Program.

CHAPTER 4 Figure 4.1. Reprinted with permission of Carol Bryant.

CHAPTER 6 Figure 6.1. Reprinted with permission of Washington Department of Health; Figure 6.2. Reprinted with permission of Washington Department of Health; Figure 6.3. "The Spiral of Change" from Changing for Good by James O.

Prochaska and John C. Norcross and Carlo C. DiClemente. Copyright © 1994 by James O. Prochaska, John C. Norcross and Carlo C. Diclemente. Reprinted by permission of HarperCollins Publishers Inc.; Figure 6.4. Reprinted with permission of SRI Consulting Business Intelligence.

CHAPTER 7 Figures 7.1-7.3. Reprinted with permission of Seattle Public Utilities; Figure 7.4. Reprinted with permission of the AAA Foundation for Traffic Safety; Figure 7.5. Reprinted with permission of Indiana Organ Procurement Org. Inc.; Figure 7.6. © March of Dimes Birth Defects Foundation, 1999. Reprinted with permission.

CHAPTER 8 Figures 8.1-8.2. Linkenbach & D'Atri, 1998. Reprinted with permission; Figure 8.3. Linkenbach & Associates, 2000. Reprinted with permission; Figures 8.4-8.5. Reprinted with permission of Centers for Disease Control and Prevention, Atlanta, Georgia.

CHAPTER 9 Figure 9.1. Reprinted with permission of Carol Bryant; Figure 9.3. Reprinted with permission of CDC'S Media Campaign Resource Center; Figure 9.4. Reprinted with permission of Tumbleweed Sales; Figure 9.5. From Newsweek, 10/2/00 © 2000 Newsweek, Inc. All rights reserved. Reprinted by permission. Photograph © Nicole Rosenthal; Figure 9.6. Reprinted with permission of Pilgrim Plastics, Brockton, MA; Figure 9.7. Reprinted with permission of Puget Sound Blood Center. Photo by Craig Harrold; Figure 9.8. Reprinted with permission of Mitchell High School, a Students Against Drunk Driving (SADD) sponsored event; Figure 9.9. Reprinted with permission of PhotoDisc™ Images © 2000 PhotoDisc, Inc.; Figure 9.10. Reprinted with permission of Puget Sound Energy; Figure 9.11a. © 1998-2001 Texas Department of Transportation; Figure 9.11b. Used with permission by Pennsylvania Resources Council (PRC) Environmental Living Center, 3603 Providence Road, Newtown Square, PA 19073; Figure 9.11c. Reprinted with permission from New South Wales Environment Protection Authority.

CHAPTER 10 Figure 10.1. Reprinted with permission from Washington State Department of Ecology; Figures 10.4. & 10.5. Reprinted with permission of Harborview Injury Prevention and Research Center; Figure 10.6. Source: Puget Sound Energy. Reprinted with permission; Figure 10.7. Source: Washington Department of Fish and Wildlife; Figures 10.8-10.10. Copyright © 2001 by Washington State office of Superintendent of Public Instruction.

CHAPTER 11 Figures 11.1-11.3. Reprinted with permission of Tacoma-Pierce County Health Department, Snohomish Health District, and Public Health Seattle and King County; Figure 11.4. Reprinted with permission from Washington Dental Service Foundation. *Making Dental Care for Children More Accessible,* The

SmileMobile was developed by Washington State Dental Services (WDS), the Washington State Dental Association (WSDA), and Washington Dental Service Foundation (WDSF); Figure 11.6. Reprinted with permission of King County Metro's Rideshare Operations.

CHAPTER 12 Figures 12.1-12.2. Copyright © 1998 Washington State Office of Crime Victims Advocacy. Funding: CDC Preventive Health and Health Services Block Grant. Original poster concept created by the Wisconsin Coalition Against Sexual Assault; Figure 12.3. Picture appears courtesy of Keep America Beautiful, Inc.; Figure 12.4. Image courtesy of Keep America Beautiful and the Ad Council; Figure 12.5. Image courtesy of www.adbusters.org; Figure 12.7. Copyright © 2001 by Washington State office of Superintendent of Public Instruction; Figures 12.8 a & 12.9a. Source: Washington Department of Health; Figure 12.8b. Photo by Pete Stone. Reprinted with permission of Arnold Worldwide; Figure 12.9 b. Copyright © 2001 by Washington State office of Superintendent of Public Instruction; Figure 12.9c. Reprinted with permission of Washington Traffic Safety Commission; Figure 12.9d. Reprinted with permission of Children's Hospital and Regional Medical Center, Seattle, Washington; Figure 12.9f. Courtesy of Marin County Sheriff's Department, Office of Emergency Services; Figure 12.10. Guy Seese, Art Director. Advertising Agency: Messner, Vetere, Berger, McNamee, Schmetterer/Euro RSCG.

CHAPTER 13 Figure 13.1. Reprinted with permission of The Swiss AIDS Foundation and the Federal Office for Public Health; Figures 13.2-13.3. Reprinted with permission of Popular Services International; Figure 13.4. Reprinted with permission of Partnership for a Drug-Free America; Figure 13.5. Reprinted with permission of Friends of Animals, Inc., Advertising Agency, Mad Dogs and Englishmen. Chris Callis (Photographer), Prisca Ekkens and Vivienne Wan (Creatives), Helen Phin (Planner), Cheryl Garber (Account Executive), Paddy Morahan (Project Manager); Figure 13.6. Courtesy of the U.S. Department of Transportation and the Ad Council; Figure 13.7. Water Quality Consortium's 1996 campaign. Reprinted with permission of Washington State Department of Ecology. Partners were WA State Dept. of Ecology, King County, and the cities of Bellevue, Seattle, and Tacoma; Figure 13.8. Mercer Island Reporter, March 14, 2001. Copyright (2001), Horvitz Newspapers, Inc. Reprinted with permission; Figure 13.9. Copyright © Steven Ellison/Corbis Outline. Reprinted with permission of Corbis Outline; Figure 13.10. James Schnepf/People Weekly. Copyright © 2000. Reprinted with permission; Figure 13.11. Reprinted with permission of Seattle Public Utilities; Figure 13.13. Reprinted with permission of Hazelden Foundation; Figure 13.14. Reprinted with permission of King County Water and Land Resources Division; Figure 13.18. Copyright © 2001 by Washington State Office of Superintendent of Public Instruction; Figure 13.19. Reprinted with special permission of North American Syndicate; Figure 13.21. Materials provided by Washington Traffic Safety Commission; Figure 13.24.

Photo by Richard Lee. Reprinted with permission of Detroit Free Press. Text from Newsweek 3/13/00 © 2000 Newsweek, Inc. All rights reserved. Reprinted by permission; Figure 13.25 Copyright © 2001 U.S. News & World Report, L.P. Reprinted with permission. Photograph © Michael Maslan. Reprinted with permission of Corbis Images; Figures 13.26-13.32 reprinted with permission of Martin McCarthy, Jr.

CHAPTER 15   Figure 15.1. Brought to you by the Washington State Governor's Commission on Early Learning, Washington Early Learning Foundation, I Am Your Child, and Children's Hospital and Regional Medical Center. Photo © Rosanne Olson rosanneolson.com; Figure 15.2. Reprinted with permission courtesy of NIKE, Inc.; Figure 15.3. Reprinted with permission of Fish Brewing Company; Figure 15.4. Reprinted with permission of Old London Foods, Inc.; Figure 15.5. Materials developed by Child Care Resources and SAFECO Insurance; Figure 15.6. Reprinted with permission of Academy for Educational Development (AED) Washington, DC.

CHAPTER 16   Figures 16.1-16.6. Reprinted with permission of Earthwater Stencils; Figure 16.8. Refrigerator magnet developed by CHILD Profile of Washington State.

CHAPTER 17   Figures 17.1-17.2. Reprinted with permission of PETA.org.

Name Index

Andreasen, A., 9, 79, 81, 124, 126, 170, 302, 352
Armstrong, G., 202-203, 243, 277, 311-312
Ashley, N., 105-107

Bloom, P., 9
Britt, J., 238-242
Broder, M., 74-76
Brown, K. M., 86-88
Brown, S. S., 208
Bryant, C. A., 9, 86-88, 190-194

Chakravorty, B., 202
Chiles, L., 48
Coughlan, A. T., 252
Covey, S. R., 161

DiClemente, C., 9, 121-123
Doner, L., 9, 264, 266, 273, 312

Eastgard, S. H., 346-348
Eisenberg, L., 208

Fishbein, M., 172, 173
Fitzgerald, K., 260-263
Flora, J., 9
Forthofer, M. S., 86-88
Fox, K., 223
Fuller, R. B., 371

Garzia, D., 288-291

Gibbs, N., 137
Gladwell, M., 254-256
Glantz, S., 93

Hicks, J. J., 48-50
Hochbaum, G., 170
Hunter, R., 372-375
Huxley, T., 391

Isaacs, S. L., 47

Junge, T., 255

Kegels, S., 170
Keller, H., 112-115, 345
Kelman, H. C., 396
Kerr, N. A., 182-185
Kotler, P., 8, 9, 171, 202-203, 243, 252, 268, 277, 304, 305, 323, 352

Lautenberg, F. R., 92
Lefebvre, R. C., 9, 324-326, 337-342
Levine, E., 324-326, 337-342
Lewin, K., 170
Lindenberger, J. H., 86-88, 190-194
Linkenbach, J., 162-166, 173

Maas, J. M., 259
McCarthy, M., Jr., 316-319, 376
McKenzie-Mohr, D., 176, 274, 376, 383, 386-387

Mintz, J., 9

Newton-Ward, M., 208-211
Norcross, J., 9, 121-123
Novelli, W., 9
Nowak, G. J., 79

Olander, C., 324-326, 337-342

Perez, J., 91, 93
Popcorn, F., 73
Prochaska, J., 9, 121-123

Reeves, R., 264
Revson, C., 196
Roberto, E. L., 9, 171, 202-203, 252, 268, 304, 305, 352
Rogers, E. M., 171
Roman, K., 259
Rosenstock, I., 170

Sacco, P., 213
Schroeder, S. A., 47
Shoemaker, F. F., 171
Shute, N., 189
Siegel, M., 9, 264, 266, 273, 312
Siska, M. J., 79
Smith, B., 203
Smith, W., 176, 274, 376, 383, 386-387
Stern, L. W., 252

Valente, T., 255

Wanamaker, J., 287
Warfield, M., 214-216
Wilk, Eric, 74-76
Williams, C. A., 137

Zaltman, G., 8, 9

Subject Index

Academy for Educational Development (AED), 359

Access strategies, 59, 244-251. *See also* Place

Achievers, 133

Action-oriented consumers, 133

Action-planning, 376

Actual product, 196

    decisions about, 199

Action stage, 122, 273

Actualizers, 133

Ad Council, 357

Adoption costs, 217, 219-220

Adoption program, 398

Advertising, 141, 241, 292, 304

    funding sources, 357-358, 367

    See also Media channels

Affordable budgeting method, 349

Aided awareness, 329

AIDS, 255-256, 288-291

Alcohol use, 162-166, 173

Alliances, 100

America's Blood Centers, 74-76

American Legacy Foundation (ALF), 92

American Marketing Association Code of Ethics, 399-402

Animal rights, 392-394

Anti-litter campaign, 214-216, 269

Anti-tobacco campaigns, 48-50, 63, 91, 92-94, 267, 279

Appeal indicators, 328

Assets model, 105

Audience. *See* Target audience

Audience participation, 61

Augmented product, 196

    decisions about, 200

Awareness:

    creation, 215

    goals, 153

    indicators, 329

    surveys, 263

Backyard Wildlife Sanctuary Recognition Programs, 227-229

Barbara Ann Karmanos Cancer Institute, 247-248

Barrier perceptions, 168, 171, 176

Baseline measures, 334

Behavior change:

    alternative strategies, 17-19

    behavior objectives, 138, 142, 143-146, 199

    defining social marketing, 5

    indicators, 328

    measures, 338

    potential, 95

    sustaining behavior, 383-387

    stages of change model, 121-123

Behavior variables, 120

Behavioral Risk Factor Surveillance System (BRFSS), 113, 150-151, 157-158, 332

Belief change indicators, 328

Belief goals, 153

Belief objectives, 139, 142, 146-148

Believers, 134

Beneficiaries, 8

Benefit perceptions, 167-168, 171, 173, 175, 199

Benefit-to-benefit superiority, 176, 178

Benefit-to-cost superiority, 178

Benefits to promise, 265

"Big Idea," 277

Bike helmet coupons, 222-223

Bill and Melinda Gates Foundation, 352

Billboard advertisement, 241, 304

Blood donation, 74-76, 120

Blood pressure education, 30-33

Booster seats, 225-226

Branding, 50, 196, 202-203

Breast cancer, 86-89, 247-248

Breastfeeding promotion, 57-59

Budgeting, 348-349

allocation for media and outreach, 63
allocation for research, 64
approaches, 349-351
campaign phasing, 362, 382
ethical issues, 398
litter prevention campaign, 216
managing with inadequate funds, 362
media strategies and, 307
planning worksheet, 415
strategic planning phase, 39
typical costs, 350-351
See also Funding
Burger King, 392-394

Campaign focus, 94, 95-97
Campaign goals, 7, 142
alternatives for goal setting, 153-154
budget constraints and, 362
draft, 143, 154
ethical decision making, 396
ideal goals, 148
hypertension prevention case, 31-32
nature of, 148-153
outcome measures and, 327
phasing by, 379
planning worksheet, 407
revising after understanding target audiences,
179-180
role in campaign evaluation, 154-155
setting, 38, 39
Campaign objectives, 7, 97, 142
behavior objectives, 138, 142, 143-146
belief objectives, 139, 142, 146-148
draft, 143, 154
ethical decision making, 396
hypertension prevention case, 31-32
knowledge objectives, 139, 142, 146-148
litter prevention campaign, 215
phasing by, 379
planning worksheet, 407
revising after understanding target audiences, 179-
180
role in campaign evaluation, 154-155
setting, 38, 39
suicide prevention program, 347
water conservation campaign case, 138-142
water pollution prevention program, 373
Campaign phasing, 303-304
budgeting and funding, 382

by a variety of factors, 382-383
by distribution channels, 381
by external factors, 382
by funding and grant requirements, 382
by geographic area, 379
by goal, 379
by media channels, 381
by message, 381
by objective, 379
by pricing strategies, 380
by service and tangible object, 380
by stage of change, 380
by target market, 378
implementation plans, 377-383
Campaign process goals, 154
Campaign purpose, 94, 97
Campaign timing, 303
Cancer mortality statistics, 4
Car pooling, 250-251
Cash contributions, 354
Casual observation, 82
Cause-related marketing (CRM), 354
Celebrity sponsors, 393
Centers for Disease Control and Prevention (CDC),
156-158, 170, 182, 335-336
Child Care Resources, 356
Child safety seats, 225-226
Clinical trials, 315-319
Coalitions, 359
College health campaigns, 173
College student drinking, 162-166
Commercial (traditional) marketing, 10-11, 21-22
product levels, 195-198
segmentation variables, 117-121
social marketing principles and techniques and, 7
See also specific models, techniques
Commitment, 67, 174, 383, 386
Communication channels. *See* Media channels
Communication objectives, creative brief section, 265
Communications "in the event of," 310-311
Communications "just in time," 308-310
Community involvement, 16
Community services, 200
Competing priorities, 395, 403
Competition, 10, 174-179
defined, 174
examples, 175
place considerations, 250-251
planning worksheet, 408

tactics for creating competitive advantages, 175-179

understanding, 32, 38, 56. *See also* Target audience, understanding

See also Target audience

Competitive advantage, tactics for creating, 175-179

Competitive-based pricing, 229

Competitive-parity budgeting method, 349

Competitive superiority, 176

Concentrated marketing, 129

Confidentiality, 396

Conflicts of interest, 399-400, 395

Contemplation stage, 121, 147, 273

Contraceptive use attitudes, 208-211

Control groups, 82, 315-319, 333

Controlled observations, 82

Convenient access, 59, 244-251. *See also* Place

Convenient response mechanisms, 62

Core product, 195-196

decisions about, 198-199

Corporate partnerships and contributions, 352-357

Cost per impression, 331

Cost perceptions, 167-168, 171, 173, 176, 198-199

Costs, 217-220. *See also* Price and pricing

cost-based pricing, 229

cost-to-benefit superiority, 178

cost-to-cost superiority, 179

decreasing, 222-226

management strategies and tactics, 220-222

marketing plan implementation, 350-351

Counseling services, 200

Countermessages, 174

Coupons, 223, 239, 242

Creative brief, 264-267

Crisis communications, 292

Cues to action, 171

Cultural forces, 102

Current alliances and partners, 100

Customer orientation, 7, 11

Customer satisfaction levels, 329

DARE, 107-108

Databases, 333

Deception, 396

Defenselessness, 127

DeLaunay Phillips Communications, 52

Demarketing, 229

Demographic variables, 102, 119

Dental care, 244-245

Diabetes health promotion, 200

Differentiated marketing, 129

Diffusion planning, 171-172

Displays, 299

Distribution channels, 243, 251-253

phasing by, 381

"Doing the right things," 376

"Doing things right," 376

Domestic violence campaign, 120

Door-to-door surveys, 87

Drowning prevention, 56, 364-368

Drug abuse. *See* Substance abuse prevention

Drug testing, 249

Earthwater, 372-375

Easy access, 59

Eating disorder education, 65-66

Economic strategies, 17

Economic forces, 102

Ecstasy pill testing, 249

Educational strategies, 19

Education-related services, 200

Effective campaigns, elements of successful campaigns. *See* Successful marketing campaign elements

Effective communication, 274

Effectiveness evaluation. *See* Evaluation

Effectiveness scores, 128

Efficiency scores, 128

Effort costs, 219, 223

Emotional elements, 268

"End justifying the means," 395, 398

Endangered Species Act, 138

Endorsements, 199, 224, 270

Energy conservation, 227

Entertainment, popular education, 302

Entry costs, 217

Environics Research Group, 283

Environmental pollution statistics, 4

Environmental protection, 16

Backyard Wildlife Sanctuary Recognition Programs, 227-229

"Let Kids Lead," 359

Salmon friendly gardening, 36-42

storm water pollution prevention, 372-375

Ethical decision-making, 391-403

American Marketing Association Code of Ethics, 399-402

animal rights campaign, 392-394

target audience selection, 395

Evaluating segments, 124-128
Evaluation, 323-324
  baseline measures, 334
  CDC framework, 335-336
  drowning prevention program, 368
  ethical issues, 398
  gun safety campaign, 242
  hypertension education case, 33
  information use issues, 334-335
  litter prevention campaign, 216
  measurement methodologies and techniques, 332-333
  nutrition education case, 324-326
  outcome measures, 327-329
  physical activity promotion case, 115
  pitfalls and guidelines, 335
  planning, 39
  planning worksheet, 414
  pre- and post-evaluation measures, 334, 368
  process measures, 329-332
  related costs, 351
  research, 79
  role of objectives and goals, 154
  successful campaign elements, 65
  suicide prevention case, 348
  timing, 333-334
  water conservation case, 142
  water pollution prevention program, 373-374
  See also Research
Events, 310-311
Exchange theory, 11, 217
Execution strategy, 264, 266-272
Execution styles, 270-272
Exit costs, 217
Experiencers, 133-134
Exposure measures, 331
External factors, 95, 97, 102
  phasing by, 382
External publics, 102

Face-to-face meeting, 305
Face-to-face selling, 302
Fantasy execution style, 270
Fear-based messages, 268
Feedback, 11. See Evaluation
Firearms safety, 238-242
"5 A Day for Better Health," 55
Florida Cares for Women Program, 86-89
Focus groups, 82, 86, 113, 280, 332

Folic acid, 170
Format, 271, 272
Formative research, 79, 260
Foundation grants and contributions, 352
Frequency, 305-306, 330
Fulfilleds, 133
Full disclosure, 397, 398
Funding, 99, 348-349
  appeals to funders, 360-361
  coalitions and other partnerships, 359
  corporate partnerships and contributions, 352-357
  ethical issues, 398
  evaluating potential for, 97
  government grants and appropriations, 360
  media and advertising partnerships, 357-359
  phasing by, 382
  planning, 39
  planning worksheet, 415
  sources, 351-360
  suicide prevention program, 347-348
  youth drowning prevention program, 367-368
  See also Budgeting

General responsiveness, 127
Geographic area, phasing by, 379
Geographic variables, 131
GO GIRLS!, 65-66
Goals, social marketing campaign. See Campaign goals
Government grants and appropriations, 360
Governmental agencies and organizations, 12
Grants and contributions, 352, 360. See Funding
Group meetings, 82
Gun safety campaign, 238-242

Harm reduction, 249
Health Belief Model (HBM), 170-171
Health Canada, 283
Health promotion, 15. See specific programs, topics
Healthstyles Segmentation System, 124, 125
Healthy People 2010, 33, 151-152
Humorous messages, 268
Hypertension education, 30-33

Implementation plan, 43, 376-383
  ethical issues, 399
  formats, 377

phasing, 377-383
planning worksheet, 416
In-kind contributions, 354
Incentives, monetary, 226-227
Incremental costs, 127
Influence, 5
Informal interviews, 231
Infrastructure change goals, 330
Infrastructure integration, 67
Injury prevention, 15-16
Innovation diffusion model, 171-172
Integrated marketing communications, 308
Intent to change goals, 154
Intercept interviews, 82
Internal factors, 95, 97, 99-100
Internal publics, 100
Internal records and tracking, 82
Internet, 302
Issue priority, 100
It's About Time for Kids, 105-107

Joe Camel, 270
Just in time communications, 308

KAPB model, 82, 170
Key message, 265
Knowledge, Attitude, Practice, and Beliefs (KAPB)
    model, 82, 170
Knowledge change measures, 328, 338
Knowledge goals, 153
Knowledge objectives, 139, 142, 146-148

Legacy, 67
Legal strategies, 18
"Let Kids Lead," 359
Life vests, 56
Lifestyle execution style, 270
Literature search and review, 82, 87
Litter prevention, 199, 214-216, 269
Lobbying, 292
Loving Support Program, 58
Leveraging prior efforts, 52-53

Macroenvironment, 102
Mail surveys, 82
Maintenance stage, 122

Makers, 134
Mammograms at the Mall, 247-248
Management support, 100
Mapping environment, 94-104
Market demand, 95-96
Market research, 7
Market segmentation, 7, 10, 116-117
    criteria for evaluating, 124-128
    Healthstyles Segmentation System, 124, 125
    ideal strategies, 124
    social marketing models, 121-124
    traditional variables, 117-121
    VALS Segmentation, 132-134
    See also Target audience
Market supply, 96-97
Marketing implementation, 376
Marketing mix, 7
    strategic planning, 38, 41
    target market responsiveness to, 127
    See also Place; Price and pricing; Product;
        Promotion
Marketing planning process. See Strategic planning
Marketing research, 11. See Research
Markets of greatest opportunities, 129-130
Markets ready for action, 53-54
Mass media, 292, 304. See also Advertising; Media
    channels
McDonald's, 392-394
Measures of success, 51
Media channel, 42, 243, 287-320
    advantages/limitations of media types, 306
    AIDS prevention cases, 288-291
    alternative media, 313
    appropriate resource allocation, 63
    budget issues, 307
    campaign timing and phasing, 303-304
    choosing specific media vehicles, 303
    ethical issues, 398
    factors influencing media strategies, 304
    hypertension prevention cases, 33
    integrated approach, 308
    just in time communications, 308-310
    matching media and target market, 307
    media categories, 292-303
    objectives and goals, 304-305
    openings section of creative brief, 266
    phasing by, 381
    planning worksheet, 413
    principles guiding decision making, 307-313
    public service announcements (PSAs), 312

publicity, 311-312
radio advertisement, 241, 261-262, 289, 304, 358
reach and frequency, 305-306
sexual assault prevention program, 261-263
Media coverage measures, 330
Media habits, 307
Media partnerships, 357-359
Media reach, 63
Media types, 292-303
Message creation, 42, 259-285
"Big Idea," 277
creative brief, 264-267
ethical issues, 397
execution strategy, 264, 266-272
message strategy, 264
pitfalls, 279
planning worksheet, 412
pretesting, 274-281
principles and theories, 273-274
sexual assault prevention case, 260-263
stages of change, 273
types of execution styles, 270-272
Messages, phasing by, 381
Microenvironment, 95
Monetary costs, 217, 218-219
decreasing, 222-223
Monetary incentives, 226-227
Monitoring, 326, 333-334
Behavioral Risk Factor Surveillance System
(BRFSS), 113, 150-151, 157-158, 332
drowning prevention baseline and tracking survey,
364-368
information use issues, 334-335
measurement methodologies and techniques, 332-
333
planning, 39
planning worksheet, 414
research, 79
successful campaign elements, 65
Montana Model of Social Norms Marketing, 163
Mood or image execution style, 270
Moral elements, 269
Mortality and morbidity statistics, 4
MOST of Us Campaign, 162-166
Motivation change measurement, 338
Motivational and attention-getting messages, 60
Musical execution style, 270

National Cancer Institute (NCI), 55

National High Blood Pressure Education Program
(NHBPEP), 30-33
Natural forces, 102
Needle exchange programs, 254-256
News coverage, 311-312
Niche marketing, 129
Nike, 354, 355
Nonmonetary benefits, 227-229
Nonmonetary costs, 219-220
decreasing, 223-224
Nonprofit organizations, associations, and foundations,
12-13, 153
Nonverbal elements, 269
Norms, 67, 383, 386
North Carolina seat belt use program, 60-61
Nutrition education, 55, 324-326
breastfeeding promotion, 57-59
Personal Energy Plan (PEP), 182-185

Objective-and-task budgeting method, 349
Objectives, communication, 265
Objectives, social marketing campaign, 7. See Campaign
objectives
Observation research, 333
Online access, 246
One-level channel, 252
One-on-one presentations, 302
One-sided messages, 268
Online surveys, 82
Openings, 266, 304
Opportunities and threats, 95, 103
Opportunity communications, 310-311
Organizational capabilities, 128
Organizational match, 97
Outcome measures, 327-329
Outreach, appropriate resource allocation, 63. See also
Reach

Packaging decisions, 203
Partnerships, 100, 216
corporate, 352-357
funding sources, 352-359
media and advertising, 357-359
Past efforts, 95
People for the Ethical Treatment of Animals (PETA),
392-394
Perceived barriers, 168, 171, 176

Perceived costs and benefits, 32, 56, 167-168, 171, 173, 175, 176, 198-199, 217
    teen sexual abstinence campaign, 231-234
Perceived seriousness, 171
Perceived susceptibility, 171
Personal Energy Plan (PEP), 182-185
Personal interviews, 82, 280, 332
Personal media, 305
Personal selling, 302
Personal services, 200
Personality symbol, 270
Persuasive communication, 264
Pet adoption, 246
Phasing. *See* Campaign phasing
Phillip Morris, 93
Physical activity promotion, 64-65, 112-115
    Personal Energy Plan (PEP), 182-185
Physical discomfort costs, 220, 223
Place, 7, 41, 237-256
    access strategies, 244-251
    appealing locations, 247-249
    being at point of decision making, 249-250
    convenience versus competing behaviors, 250-251
    defining, 243
    distribution channel management guidelines, 251-253
    ethical issues, 397
    gun safety campaign, 238-242
    hypertension prevention case, 33
    media channel and, 243
    objective, 243
    planning worksheet, 411
    proximity, 244-246
    related costs, 351
Planning process, 29-45. *See* Strategic planning; *specific elements*
Policy change goals, 330
Political/legal forces, 102
Pollution prevention, 372-375
Popular education, 302
Positioning statement, 203
Pre- and post-evaluation measures, 334, 368
Precontemplation stage, 121, 147, 273
Pregnancy health promotion, 170
Preparation stage, 122, 273
Pretesting, 79, 274-281
Prevention Marketing Initiative (PMI), 289-290
Price and pricing, 7, 41, 213-235, 264
    adoption costs, 217, 219-220
    breastfeeding promotion case, 58

cost management strategies and tactics, 220-222
decreasing costs relative to competition, 225-226
decreasing monetary costs, 222-223
decreasing nonmonetary costs, 223-224
defining, 217
ethical issues, 397
exchange theory, 217
hypertension prevention case, 32
litter prevention case, 214-216
monetary costs, 217, 218-219, 222-223
nonmonetary costs, 219-220, 223-224
monetary incentives, 226-227
nonmonetary benefits, 227-229
objectives, 229
phasing by pricing strategies, 380
planning worksheet, 410
price-setting considerations, 229
related costs, 351
tangible objects and services, 229
types of costs, 217-220
water conservation case, 139
Price tags, 348
Primary research, 79, 82
Principle-oriented consumers, 132
Printed materials, 297-298
Problem incidence, 126
Problem severity, 127
Process evaluation, 325
Process measures, 329-332
Produce for Better Health Foundation, 55
Product, 7, 10, 41, 189-211
    access issues. *See* Place
    branding and packaging decisions, 202-203
    decisions for each level, 198-203
    defining, 195
    ethical issues, 396-397
    need for substitute, 201-202
    planning worksheet, 409
    product platform design, 194-195
    related costs, 350
    three levels of, 195-198
    water conservation case, 139
Product positioning, 175, 176, 203-205, 266
Program evaluation. *See* Evaluation
Program funding. *See* Funding
Promotion, 7, 42, 264, 281
    creating messages, 259-285. *See* Message creation
    ethical issues, 397-398
    media channel selection, 287-320. *See* Media channels

planning worksheet, 412-413
Promotion-related costs, 351
Prompts, 67, 383, 386
Proven awareness, 329
Psychographic segmentation system, 132
Psychographic variables, 120
Psychological costs, 219-220, 223
Psychological rewards, 224
Public relations, 140, 292, 304
    measures, 330
Public service announcements (PSAs), 312
Publicity, 311-312
Purpose, 94

Quantitative and qualitative research, 81, 85-88, 162, 332.
    See also Research

Radio advertisement, 241, 261-262, 289, 304, 358
Randomized clinical trials, 315-319
Rape prevention, 52-53, 260-263
Rational elements, 268
Reach, 305, 330
    indicators, 328
Reachability, 127
Records, 333
Red flags, 279
Repeat donor segment, 53-54
Research, 11, 73-89
    applicable to each research step, 77
    appropriate resource allocation, 64
    blood donation case, 74-76
    campaign phase and, 79, 80
    characterized by technique, 81, 82
    decisions and questions addressed by, 78
    exercise promotion case, 113
    nutrition education, 337-342
    primary and secondary, 79-82
    steps in project design, 81, 84
    strategic planning process and, 44
    teen sexual abstinence campaign, 231-234
    types of, 77-81
    understanding target audiences, 169
    See also Evaluation
Research highlights:
    breast cancer screening, 86-89
    CDC's surveillance system, 156-158
    contraceptive use attitudes, 208-211

drowning prevention baseline and tracking survey,
    364-368
    interviews for teen sexual abstinence, 231-234
    It's About Time for Kids, 105-107
    needle exchange programs, 254-256
    Personal Energy Plan, 182-185
    SIDS prevention, 283-285
    skin cancer prevention, 315-319
    VALS segmentation, 132-134
Resources, 99, 133. *See also* Funding
Response goals, 153
Responsible stewardship, 395
"Reuse A Shoe" program, 354
Rewards, 67
Rideshare programs, 250-251

SAFECO, 356
Safety seats, 225-226
Safety statistics, 4
Salmon friendly gardening, 36-42
Sample size and source selection, 83
School-based programs, 107-108
School nutrition program, 324-326, 337-342
Scientific evidence execution style, 270
Seals of approval, 224
Seat belt use promotion, 60-61
Secondary data, 156
Secondary research, 79-82
Segment prioritization, 129
Segment size, 126
Selective media, 289-290, 305
Self-efficacy, 173, 202
Self-esteem, 120
September 11th terrorist attack, 15
Service delivery, 99
Service quality improvement strategy, 190
Services, 200
    monetary costs, 218
    phasing by, 380
    See also Tangible objects or services
Sexual abstinence campaign, 231-234
Sexual assault prevention, 52-53, 260-263, 397
Sexually transmitted infection (STI) prevention, 208-211,
    288-291
Shridhar, Preeti, 138-142
Signage, 299, 304
Single, doable behaviors, 54-55
Situation analysis, 116, 146

planning worksheet, 405
See also Social marketing environment, analyzing
Skin cancer prevention, 315-319
Skin Sense, 316-319
Slice of life execution style, 270
Slogans, 272
SmileMobile, 244-245
Smith, William, 29
Smoking cessation campaign, 200
Social cognitive theory (SCT), 172-173, 324
Social equity, 397
Social issues, 14-17, 94
Social learning theory, 172-173
Social marketing, 5-9
    beneficiary of, 8
    campaign goals and objectives. *See* Campaign goals; Campaign objectives
    campaign focus, 94, 95-97
    campaign purpose, 94, 97
    definition, 5
    difference from commercial sector marketing, 10-11, 21-22
    elements of successful campaigns. *See* Successful marketing campaign elements
    evaluating outcomes. *See* Evaluation
    history of, 8-9
    planning process. *See* Strategic planning
    planning worksheet, 405-416
    practitioners of, 12-14
    pricing. *See* Price and pricing
    product. *See* Product
    relation to other approaches, 19
    social issues, 14-17
    traditional commercial marketing and, 7
Social marketing environment, analyzing, 94-108
    choosing campaign focus, 94-97
    external forces (macroenvironment), 102
    identifying campaign purpose, 94, 97
    internal factors (microenvironment), 99-100
    SWOT analysis, 95, 97
Social norms, 67, 162-166, 173, 176, 387
South African AIDS prevention campaign, 290-291
Special events, 292
Special promotional items, 298
Spiral of change, 123
Spiral planning process, 43
Sponsors, 199, 216, 367, 393
    organizational match, 97
    See also Funding
Stages of change model, 121-123, 273

phasing by, 380
Status-oriented consumers, 133
Storm water pollution prevention, 372-375
Strategic planning, 29-45
    eight steps in, 34-43
    goals. *See* Campaign goals
    hypertension education case, 30-33
    implementation plan, 43, 376-383
    objectives. *See* Campaign objectives
    outline, 35
    phases. *See* Campaign phasing
    situational analysis. *See* Situational analysis
    spiral, 43
    research and, 77, 79
    use of marketing research, 44
    worksheet, 405-416
Strengths and weaknesses, 95, 100-101
Strivers, 134
Strugglers, 134
Substance abuse prevention, 107-108
    harm reduction, 249
    needle exchange programs, 254-256
    specific targets, 152
    social norms approach, 162-166
Substitute product, 201-202
Successful marketing campaign elements
    allocation for media and outreach, 63
    appropriate media, 61
    audience participation, 61
    convenient access, 59
    convenient response mechanisms, 62
    indicators of, 51
    leaving a legacy, 67
    leveraging prior efforts, 52-53
    markets ready for action, 53-54
    motivational and attention-getting messages, 60
    promoting single, doable behaviors, 54-55
    resource allocation for media and outreach, 63
    situational analysis, 52
    sustained behavior change, 67
    tangible objects or services, 55-56
    tobacco campaign case, 48-50
    tracking results and making adjustments, 65
    understanding perceived benefits and costs, 56
Sudden Infant Death Syndrome (SIDS) prevention, 283-285
Suicide prevention, 346-348, 360
Surveys, 83
    telephone, 82, 87, 242, 283-285, 289-290, 305, 326, 332

See also Research
Sustainable behavior, 67, 383-387
Sustainable watersheds, 372-375
Swiss AIDS Foundation, 288-289
SWOT analysis, 95, 97

Tag lines, 272
Tangible objects or services, 55-56, 196, 200-201
    monetary costs, 218
    special promotional items, 298
    phasing by, 380
Target audience, 7
    animal rights campaign, 392
    benefits of, 117
    choosing an approach, 129-130
    creative brief section, 265
    criteria for evaluating segments, 124-128
    difference between social marketing and
        commercial marketing, 10
    drowning prevention campaign, 365
    ethical decision making, 395
    gun safety campaign, 238-239
    how markets are selected, 128-129
    hypertension prevention campaign case, 31-32
    ideal segmentation strategies, 124
    litter prevention case, 215
    market size, 304
    markets of greatest opportunities, 129-130
    phasing by, 378
    physical activity promotion case, 112-115
    planning worksheet, 406
    revising, 179-180
    segmentation, 116-117
    selecting, 37-38
    sexual assault prevention program, 260
    social audience models, 121-124
    steps involved in, 116-117
    suicide prevention program, 346-347
    total impressions/cost per impression measure,
        331
    traditional variables used to segment markets,
        117-121
    understanding, 38, 40
    VALS Segmentation, 132-134
    water conservation case, 139
    water pollution prevention, 373
Target audience, understanding, 161-174
    competition behaviors. *See* Competition
    drinking and driving campaign case, 162-166

    ethical decision making, 396
    models, 169-174
    perceived costs/benefits of behaviors, 167-168
    planning worksheet, 408
    revising goals, objectives, and target markets, 179-
        180
Target market, 7. *See* Target audience
Tattoos, 313
Team Nutrition, 324-326, 337-342
Technical expertise execution style, 270
Technological forces, 102
Technological strategies, 17
Teen sexual abstinence campaign, 231-234
Teens Stopping AIDS, 289
Telephone surveys, 82, 86, 242, 283-285, 289-290, 305,
    326, 332
Television advertising, 358
Termination stage, 122
Testimonial, 270
Texas anti-tobacco campaign, 63
Texas WIC, 190-194
Theater/exposure testing, 82
Threats and opportunities, 95, 103
Three-level channel, 252
Time costs, 219, 223
Time lines, 216
Tobacco prevention campaign, 48-50, 63, 91, 267, 279
    industry response, 92-94
Tone, 49, 271
Total impressions, 331
Traditional marketing. *See* Commercial (traditional)
    marketing
"Truth" anti-tobacco campaign, 48-50, 91
Two-level channel, 252
Two-sided messages, 268

Unaided awareness, 329
Undifferentiated marketing, 128-129
Unintended outcomes, 329
Unpaid advertising, 292
USDA School Meals Initiative for Healthy Children,
    324-326

VALS Segmentation, 132-134
Value-based pricing, 229
Voluntary behavior change, 5
Volunteers, 62, 367, 373

Water conservation, 59, 138-142
Water quality, 372-375
Weaknesses and strengths, 95, 100-101
Web sites, 246
Woman, Infants & Children (WIC) program, 190-194, 224, 397
    National Breastfeeding Promotion Project, 57-59
Word choice, 271, 272

Youth involvement, 49
Youth Tobacco Prevention Creative Brief, 267, 270

Zero-level channel, 252

About the Authors

Philip Kotler is the S. C. Johnson & Son Distinguished Professor of International Marketing at the J. L. Kellogg Graduate School of Management, Northwestern University, Evanston, Illinois. Kellogg was voted the "Best Business School" for 6 years in *Business Week*'s survey of United States business schools. It is also rated as the "Best Business School for the Teaching of Marketing." Professor Kotler has significantly contributed to Kellogg's success through his many years of research and teaching there.

He received his master's degree at the University of Chicago and his Ph.D. degree at MIT, both in economics. He did postdoctoral work in mathematics at Harvard University and in behavioral science at the University of Chicago.

Professor Kotler is the author of *Marketing Management: Analysis, Planning, Implementation and Control*, the most widely used marketing book in graduate business schools worldwide; *Principles of Marketing; Marketing Models; Strategic Marketing for Non-Profit Organizations; The New Competition; High Visibility; Social Marketing; Marketing Places; Marketing for Congregations; Marketing for Hospitality and Tourism; The Marketing of Nations*, and *Kotler on Marketing*. He has published over 100 articles in leading journals, several of which have received best-article awards.

Professor Kotler was the first recipient of the American Marketing Association's (AMA) "Distinguished Marketing Educator Award" (1985). The European Association of Marketing Consultants and Sales Trainers awarded Kotler their prize for "Marketing Excellence." He was chosen as the "Leader in Marketing Thought" by the Academic Members of the AMA in a 1975 survey. He also received the 1978 "Paul Converse Award" of the AMA, honoring his original contribution to marketing. In 1995, the Sales and Marketing Executives International (SMEI) named him "Marketer of the Year."

Professor Kotler has consulted for such companies as IBM, General Electric, AT&T, Honeywell, Bank of America, Merck, and others in the areas of marketing strategy and planning, marketing organization, and international marketing.

He has been Chairman of the College of Marketing of the Institute of Management Sciences, Director of the American Marketing Association, Trustee of the Marketing Science Institute, Director of the MAC Group, former member of the Yankelovich Advisory Board, and member of the Copernicus Advisory Board. He is a member of the Board of Governors of the School of the Art Institute of Chicago and a member of the Advisory Board of the Drucker Foundation. He has received honorary doctoral degrees from Stockholm University, University of Zurich, Athens University of Economics and Business, DePaul University, the Cracow School of Business and Economics, Groupe H.E.C. in Paris, the University of Economics and Business Administration in Vienna, the Catholic University of Santo Domingo, and the Budapest School of Economic Science and Public Administration.

He has traveled extensively throughout Europe, Asia, and South America, advising and lecturing to many companies and organizations. This experience expands the scope and depth of his programs, enhancing them with an accurate global perspective.

Ned Roberto is the Coca-Cola Foundation Professor in International Marketing at the Asian Institute of Management in Metro Manila, Philippines. His teaching and research areas of interest include basic marketing, marketing research, social marketing, social marketing research, and consumer behavior. He has also taught at Northwestern University's Kellogg Graduate School of Management Chicago Campus and at the Euro-Asia Centre of INSEAD Macau and Singapore programs.

Professor Roberto is currently the chairman and president of Roberto & Associates, Inc., a marketing research and consulting agency, and sits on the board of directors of several corporations. He is on the Editorial Board of the *International Journal of Research in Marketing*. He was the 1985 president of the Marketing and Opinion Research Society of the Philippines (MORES) and the recipient of the Philippine Marketing Association AGORA Award for Achievement in Marketing Education in 1983.

Professor Roberto has authored seven books: two marketing research textbooks, *Applied Marketing Research* and *User-Friendly Marketing Research;* two social marketing books, *Strategic Decision Making in a Social Program* and *Social Marketing: Strategies for Changing Public Behavior* (co-authored with Philip Kotler); a market segmentation book, *Strategic Market Segmentation* and *A Guide to the Socio-Economic Classification of Filipino Consumers;* and a local governance book, *Making Local Governance Work.* In 1975, he wrote the first social marketing book, *Strategic Decision Making in a Social Program,* published by Lexington Books of Massachusetts (USA). He has also published several articles on marketing and social marketing in international journals and has contributed chapters in major books of readings in the field of marketing.

Before joining the Institute, Professor Roberto was executive vice president of Consumer Pulse Inc., the ASEAN's largest survey research organization; vice president of Media Pulse, Inc.; and executive director of the International Council for the Management of Population Programmes (ICOMP).

He has done extensive consultancy work regionwide for national and transnational corporations and multilateral agencies. In the Philippines, he has been consultant for marketing planning, product management, and marketing research to practically all the leading multinational corporations in the consumer goods, pharmaceutical, household products, beverage, cosmetics, processed food, banking, advertising, and airline industries. He has consulted overseas for several major multinational corporations in Australia, Hong Kong, Indonesia, Japan, Malaysia, Singapore, Thailand, and Taiwan. He has also been involved in social marketing planning and research, consulting for such international organizations as the World Bank, the UN Fund for Population Activities, the International Labour Organization, the UN Development Programme, the Asian Development Bank, the Ford Foundation, the International Development Research Centre, the Population Council, and the UN Economic Commission for Asia and the Far East.

Professor Roberto received his doctor of philosophy in Marketing and a master's degree in Business Administration from the Kellogg Management School of Northwestern University (1973).

Nancy Lee has more than 20 years of professional marketing experience, with special expertise in social marketing, marketing research, and marketing communications. She received her master's degree in business at the University of Puget Sound and her bachelor of science in education at the University of Illinois. She is an adjunct faculty member at the University of Puget Sound and Seattle University, and a guest lecturer at the University of Washington.

Ms. Lee has held numerous corporate marketing positions, including Vice President and Director of Marketing for Washington State's second largest bank, Director of Marketing for the region's Children's Hospital and Medical Center, and positions in other local banks as Marketing Research Manager and Advertising Manager.

As President of Social Marketing Services, Inc., Ms. Lee has consulted with more than 100 non-profit organizations and has participated in the development of more than 50 social marketing campaign strategies for public sector agencies. Clients in the public sector include Washington State Department of Health, Office of Crime

Victims Advocacy, County Health and Transportation Departments, Department of Ecology, Department of Fisheries and Wildlife, Washington Traffic Safety Commission, and the City of Seattle and Office of Superintendent of Public Instruction. Campaigns developed for these clients targeted issues listed below:

- *Health:* teen pregnancy prevention, nutrition education, diabetes prevention, adult physical activity, tobacco control, arthritis diagnosis and treatment, immunizations, dental hygiene, senior wellness, and eating disorder awareness

- *Safety:* drowning prevention, underage drinking and driving, youth suicide prevention, binge drinking, and safe gun storage

- *Environment:* natural gardening, preservation of fish and wildlife habitat, recycling, trip reduction, water quality, and water and power conservation

Ms. Lee has taught introduction to marketing and social marketing in business and public administration programs in the Seattle area. She has conducted social marketing workshops for more than 200 public sector employees involved in developing public behavior change campaigns in the areas of health, safety, and the environment. She has been a keynote speaker on social marketing at conferences for family planning, nutrition, recycling, teen pregnancy prevention, and tobacco control.

Ms. Lee is active in the American Marketing Association, having served as president of the state's largest chapter and a board member for more than 15 years. She has been a guest columnist for MARKETING, the state's professional marketing magazine, and Washington CEO. She received the local American Marketing Association's "Marketing Plan for the Year" award in 1980, was voted "Best Marketing Professional" in Seattle by MARKETING Magazine in 1987, and was the recipient of Impact Player of the Year for Rainier Bank in 1988.